MARRIAGE AND FAMILY RELATIONS

HARPER'S SOCIAL SCIENCE SERIES

F. Stuart Chapin, Editor

MARRIAGE AND FAMILY RELATIONS

AN INTERDISCIPLINARY APPROACH

Lawrence S. Bee

PROFESSOR OF HOME ECONOMICS, SOCIOLOGY, AND ANTHROPOLOGY
UNIVERSITY OF KANSAS

HARPER & BROTHERS, PUBLISHERS, NEW YORK

To the memory of my Mother,
and my Father
and
Hazel, Bob and Ann

MARRIAGE AND FAMILY RELATIONS
An Interdisciplinary Approach

Printed in the United States of America

D-I
Library of Congress catalog card number: 58-11584

CONTENTS

PREFACE

THE MEANING of *successful marriage* in a democratic society must necessarily vary according to differences in the way couples look at man and the meaning of life. Consequently, this writer believes that the good marriage will be more like an epic poem or a piano concerto for two, rather than anything that could be described in terms of behavior traits, statistical factors, or cultural norms.[1] Such a marriage achieves its own idiom, its own power, and its own artistry. In its fuller attainment it may be as different from another good marriage as a Chopin polonaise is different from a Bach chorale.

However differently the good marriage may be conceived by different couples in our culture, it seems evident to this writer that self-other understanding, interpersonal competence in the art of human relations, and some kind of self-transcendant outlook are indispensable to maximal growth and productivity as individuals and as a pair. Consequently Part I, "What We Bring to Marriage," is devoted to the development of a theory of "basic personality." Here an attempt has been made to show how a

[1] Gardiner Murphy, describing the impact of Freud on psychology wrote of Freud's epic view as "a way of looking at man, in which artistic congruity and power are even more important than internal consistency or detailed conformity to fact . . ." Address to the Division of Clinical Psychology, American Psychological Association Meeting, August 30, 1956.

number of selected aspects of personality pattern into predictible "kinds of people." These aspects of personality provide the bases for compatibility or incompatibility in marriage. It is posited that physique, temperament, intelligence, and emotional and ideological maturity are aspects of personality that provide deeper needs, expectations, orientations, and modes of reaction to others; and, that these facets of the self develop into a congress, dynamic "basic personality" as a result of inheritance and of experience. Hypothetical "types" of basic personality are postulated, described, and illustrated from biographical literature.

Following this cross-sectional treatment of the individual, the *development* of personality is described in a number of contrasting cultures. This is to show the tremendously important relationship between the way different families rear their children and the different patterns of personality that emerge. The life cycle of the individual, especially his psychosexual development, is traced in this social and cultural context.

The final part of the first section is concerned with patterns of emotional and ideological maturity and immaturity, sex as an expression of basic personality, and the meaning of love.

The theory of *basic personality* developed in the first section is used to analyse and discuss the content of the subsequent sections of the book. The intent of the writer in Part I is to give the reader a better understanding of the more basic facets of personality that different kinds of people carry into courtship and marriage, and consequently, more insight into the deep and unique aspects of the reader's own personality. It is assumed that the greater the awareness and understanding of the self, the better one will understand and appreciate the prospective partner. Such understanding will minimize the intrusion of idealization and other distorting elements into the relationship and leave the couple free to interact on a higher level of reality.

Part II is devoted to the courtship process—"normal" and neurotic bases of attraction, selection, testing of the relationship, and summation or preparation for marriage. Included here is the scientific research and clinical experience found in the "prediction and forecast" studies.

Part III takes up the marriage relationship and patterns of family interaction. The first part of this section will be devoted to the way different couples feel, think, and act toward one another and why. Problems of growing together, cutting some of the ties with the past, of moving forward to the achievement of a particular style of living, the social psychology of pregnancy, confronting and working through crises, divorce, and other problems confronted in marriage will be treated.

Part IV consists of sociopsychological portraits of three contrasting families, chosen to illustrate how different couples work toward their own fulfillment and that of their children, each family in its own inimitable way. These three cases Chapter 16 have been selected not as examples of ideal families, but of families experiencing the highlights and shadows of life in their very real struggle toward self-other transcendance.

In Part V, the disorganization and reconstruction of patterns of marriage are discussed. The final chapter describes the phenomenal development of interest and activities in a "family life movement" that has emerged during the past 25 years, as a new creative force in Western Civilization.

This book is designed to serve two primary purposes: (1) It brings together in a common context—the family—materials and orientations from the liberal arts and the professional fields of sociology, psychology, anthropology, physiology, literature, education, home economics, psychiatry, and social work. The writer feels that the time has come when relevant materials from these fields should be brought together in larger contexts. This is part of the aim of a broader liberal arts (general) education. (2) It brings together materials from the field of marriage and family relations that will be personally relevant to the reader. This is a more immediately practical function, aimed at helping the reader acquire basic facts and orientations that will help him better understand the development of his own personality and the social and cultural circumstances that have molded his patterns of reaction to others, and to help him better to anticipate his future relations with others, primarily in his marriage and family relations, or their substitutes.

The content of this book does not stop at the descriptive level. It seeks to make meaningful and useful the facts and orientations that have emerged as the products of research, clinical experience, academic theory, and ideological assertion. The writer has attempted to indicate and distinguish fact from supported theory, and theory from some men's fancy.[2] Empirical truth is one; ideologies are many. The reader is urged to attempt to distinguish the two constantly; even more, to attempt to interpret a given set of facts according to the different views held by various groups. This might be an exercise in gaining and maintaining open-mindedness, a step toward fuller understanding. There is probably no other field in which there is a greater temptation to form opinions before acquiring adequate knowledge and thus run the risk of stagnating in preconceived bias, prejudice, malice, and neurotic anxiety.

This book has been written primarily for the young adult. He or she will do well to distinguish between a set of attitudes —intellectual open-mindedness in the search for truth—and a stable set of personal habits. To attempt to understand the position of another is not the same as doing what he does.

The ambitious aim of the writer in presenting these materials is to assist those who believe that whatever measure of effective

[2] The overtones of social theory contained in this book might be regarded as characteristic of that described by Blumer: "There are . . . legitimate and important kinds of social theory. . . . One of them seeks to develop a meaningful interpretation of the social world or of some significant part of it. Its aim is not to form scientific propositions but to outline and define life situations so that people may have a clearer understanding of their world, its possibilities of development, and the directions along which it may move. In every society, particularly in a changing society, there is a need for meaningful clarification of basic social values, social institutions, modes of living and social relations. This need cannot be met by empirical science, even though some help may be gained from analysis made by empirical science. Its effective fulfillment requires a sensitivity to new dispositions and an appreciation of new lines along which social life may take shape. Most social theory of the past and a great deal in the present is wittingly or unwittingly of this interpretative type. This type of social theory is important and stands in its own right." Herbert Blumer, "What Is Wrong With Social Theory?" *American Sociological Review,* XIX (February, 1954), 5.

family living has been attained can be improved; that man does have the ability to determine the success or failure of this fundamental area of his life—his family. The underlying assumption is positive in two senses. First, the book is based primarily on scientific and clinical evidence, and second, an individual's future is subject to partial control by the individual himself and not dependent upon chance.

A word is in order for those who believe that the subject of marriage and family living should be treated only from a "positive point of view." The reality of marriage penetrates the individual's innermost feelings and habits, which are a mixture of both creative and destructive elements. When only the "best" in the self and the spouse is considered, the "worst" is left to play capricious and insidious pranks. In the study of maladjustment, immaturity, and to a limited extent, pathology, feelings of anxiety and depression may be aroused in the reader. This is part of the pain of knowing. At the same time, the writer has attempted to accentuate the creative processes and goals of "successful" family living. Part of the larger task of working with young adults is to assist them in the process of "creative disillusion," that is, the process of tearing down barriers of idealization and self-deception that prevent growth, so that the individual may reach a higher level of development.

The writer has attempted to hold recommendations and advice to a minimum. There are few, if any, specific rules that people "ought" to adhere to under all circumstances. In a democratic society the wholesome marriage and family will take diverse forms, meeting the unique needs of divergent families. The attempt has been to present materials that will help persons acquire facts and principles that will assist them in *developing their own standards and levels of conduct*. The "expert" may have a better suggestion for meeting a specific situation but if the one seeking accepts the counsel without understanding he is left without the ability to define his own problems and to formulate his own solutions. The aim of these materials is to further understanding and growth; not to suggest what people ought to do.

The larger point of view prevailing throughout this book is

much like that designated by one of the pioneers in this field, Joseph K. Folsom, as preventive social psychiatry—the application of social psychology to normal human growth and adjustment.

I want to express my deepest gratitude to a number of colleagues for their encouragement and assistance in the writing of the manuscript. Leonard S. Cottrell first introduced me to the marriage and family relations field. Many of his views entered into the writing, without special reference. Robert and Ise Sternfeld, Bert and Hermia Kaplan, Erich M. and Bea Wright, James L. and Mary Wortham read different sections of the manuscript related to their professional interests and gave invaluable critical comments and suggestions in a context of encouragement. Walter Stokes read a preliminary expository brief of the manuscript, commenting at length. W. Whitney and Alice Smith were most gracious in giving much of their time to reading the entire manuscript. Their help and encouragement was deeply felt.

Finally, words can only most inadequately express my heartfelt gratitude to my wife, whose continuous affirmation and support, assistance in research, case writing, and (never least) typing the many versions made the manuscript possible. Hazel, "Thanks."

LAWRENCE S. BEE

August 5, 1958
Lawrence, Kansas

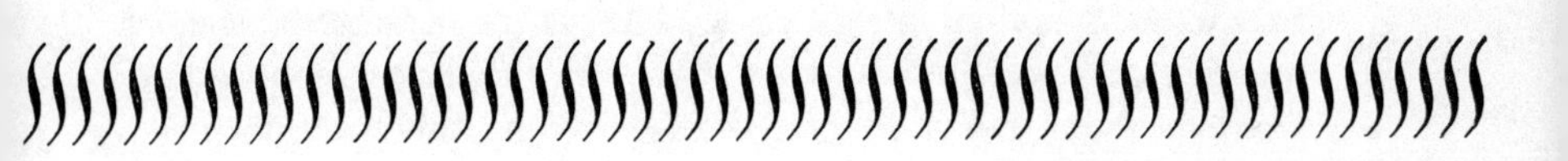

INTRODUCTION

Chapter 1

THE IMPACT OF SOCIAL CHANGE ON AMERICAN COURTSHIP, MARRIAGE, AND FAMILY LIVING

THERE ARE a great many American marriages that have gained a relatively full measure of deep understanding, companionship, mutual erotic fulfillment, and a sense of mutual care. There are others that are incomplete in some basic respect, but are still regarded by the couples themselves as successful. There are still others that are seriously disturbed by incompatibility in many aspects of marriage.

Attempts to estimate the number of marriages of varying degrees of deeper frustration and failure are impossible. The evidence of marital failure often comes out in forms that disguise the fact from the couple themselves. Psychosomatic symptoms, compulsive drinking and gambling, occupational frustrations, espousing radical political, economic, and religious movements, and even war itself, are often the results of lack of satisfaction of emotional needs in marriage.[1] To this toll of incomplete or broken marriages must be added the divorces that are recorded in our courts, and the separations that do not become a matter of record.[2]

It can only be concluded that far too many couples fail to achieve a modicum of satisfaction and happiness in one of the most fundamental areas of living—their marriage.

NEED FOR PREVENTIVE SOCIAL PSYCHIATRY

There is today great need for preventive social psychiatry, i.e., the application of liberal arts and sciences to emotional education and reëducation. This need is always greater during an era of rapid social change. The past generation has witnessed drastic and widespread change symbolized by the difference between the Model T Ford and atomic engines.

From a political, economic, religious, or personal point of view the orientations and habits of Americans have undergone marked alteration during the last 40 years. We have witnessed political revolution in virtually every civilized country of the world with the armed overthrow of many major governments—Russia, Germany, Italy, Spain, China, Japan, and many South American countries. The shift of governments in France and Great Britain toward socialism is a sharp

[1] T. W. Adorno, Else Frenkel-Brunswik, Daniel J. Levinson, and R. Nevitt Sanford, *The Authoritarian Personality,* New York, Harper, 1950; Karen Horney, *The Neurotic Personality of Our Time,* New York, Norton, 1937; Erich Fromm, *Man For Himself,* New York, Rinehart, 1947; Mabel A. Elliot and Francis E. Merrill, *Social Disorganization,* New York, Harper, 1941.

[2] Ray E. Baber, *Marriage and the Family,* 2nd ed., New York, Mcgraw-Hill, 1953, pp. 472–473.

Some changes:
18 yr. girl - grandma.
changes are symbolic.
- shift from institutionalism to personalism
(early) (now)

departure from tradition. In the United States the growth of the labor movement and collective social services has been tantamount to revolutionary, in the political sense of the term.

If it were not for the fact that America's youth participated in two world wars during this period, we might fail to sense the significance of recent world revolution. But we have witnessed the widespread social changes that followed these events and the rise of mass expression of emotional bitterness.

American communities and American families have experienced both direct and indirect consequences of these world events. Among the direct consequences are family dislocation occasioned by the two wars, the inflation of the 1920's, the depression of the 1930's, and now the threat of World War III is too evident to comment on at length. It is the indirect effect of the changes incident to these events that needs to be reflected upon more fully.

Changing Roles in the Family

The most significant change affecting courtship and marriage in this country is the shift from a rural to an urban way of life.[3] Less than 100 years ago there were only 30 million persons living in the United States. The early part of the twentieth century witnessed the rapid rise of cities. World War I called millions of American youths into military service and war production. Many never returned to the farms. Mass production methods, developed during the War and continued following the War, markedly increased the mechanization of rural communities. New opportunity for employment in urban industry helped complete the con-

[3] Joseph K. Folsom, *The Family and Democratic Society*, New York, Wiley, 1943, pp. 150–151.

centration of population and the rise of the industrial city.[4]

It is the youth who migrate. In the great exodus from the farms young men and women were cut free from the patriarchal family ties and the social sanctions, controls, and expectations of the rural community and church.[5] Many areas of life that had been sponsored by the church became secular matters. In addition, there was the drastic change in tempo and complexity of living. Speed and anonymity contributed to greater expediency in living.

This vast and rapid change in our national life, occasioned by the emergence of cheap, fast transportation, new techniques for the preservation of food, and other basic inventions, brought about concomitant changes in American courtship, marriage, and family living patterns. Some of the most far reaching changes were those in the social and psychological roles of the individual in relation to the family.

The traditional role of the man in the rural family was that of the "patriarch."[6] He was a sober, hard working man who felt it not only his duty but, to his profit to have a big family. He worked with growing things, was versatile, and enjoyed the deep satisfaction of viewing the products of his home enterprise as things he had produced. His work was at home without the interference and temptation of commercial recreation and the presence of eligible members of the opposite sex associated with his day's work. The level of living he could provide was rarely subject to comparisons which might prove damaging to his prestige or self-esteem. He was not expected to be romantic or provide companionship in the

[4] Ruth Shonle Cavan, *The American Family*, New York, Crowell, 1953, chap. 2, 3.

[5] Erich Fromm, *Escape From Freedom*, New York, Rinehart, 1939.

[6] David Riesman, *The Lonely Crowd*, Garden City, Doubleday Anchor, 1953, pp. 19 ff. See also Cavan, *op. cit.*, p. 42.

home. His experience and superior skill gave him a position of unquestioned authority in the eyes of his wife and children where the farm enterprise was concerned. His role in the church gave him authority concerning matters of conduct. Science and education were not present to threaten his ideological domain.

Today in contrast, the role of the man in millions of American homes is not primarily that of protector and provider but that of companion to his wife and children. The traditional qualities of the man are still presumed and, in addition, he is expected to fulfill many of the standards set by *Esquire* and *Vogue,* that is, he is expected to be reasonably handsome, romantic, educated, and urbane. More often his work is routine rather than creative. He is in competition not with himself but with many others with specialized training who stand in close occupational proximity. What he can provide must be more elaborate and expensive than his level of living of yesteryear. There is the everpresent reminder of higher standards portrayed by all the art and persuasion of modern advertising. His opinion no longer carries the weight of authority it did formerly because his wife is as well educated and oriented as he is. It is no longer his male prerogative to present himself as unquestionably right. He must reconcile and mediate his opinion with his wife's. The psychological double standard is waning. In the area of his sex life he is counseled in indirection and consideration of his wife's interests and expectations. Sex is no longer his prerogative and her duty, but a difficult attainment in mutuality.

The role of woman has likewise undergone marked change with the rise of urban living.[7] In the agricultural home

[7] Cf. Margaret Mead's introduction to A. M. Krich (ed.), *Women,* New York, Dell, 1953, pp. 9–24.

her central role was that of mother and "handmaiden" to her husband. Close to the Victorian portrait of a woman, she was modest, frugal, hard working, and emotionally restrained. Her self-fulfillment was in bearing and rearing a "fine" large family. There were no radio, television, movie, Sunday supplement, and magazine reminders of the great romance that might have been, the all electric kitchen, or the leisure of today's middle-class women. Companionship was a luxury seldom dreamed of. Her husband was granted momentary lapses with the little brown jug, but not she. She was not the disciplinarian in her home, but the peace maker. Sex, for her, was God-given for the sole purpose of reproduction. To conceive of it as a sensitive medium of communication and pleasure between herself and her husband would be looked upon as not only frivolous and indecent, but shockingly immoral. Pleasure in recreation was not to be sought as an end, but to be enjoyed as an overtone of some productive activity. Personal grooming was considered a delicate compromise with the devil.

Today the model middle-class woman regards her central role as that of a homemaker and companion to her husband and children.[8] Her husband expects her to be free enough from enervating work to keep herself attractive and romantically inclined. She has full partnership in the family firm but often finds herself in the role of vice-president in charge. She may take employment outside the home, but more often her activities consist of the social, civic, and educational. She is often the disciplinarian. She regards the communication-pleasure function of sex as decent and desirable. She wants

[8] Sidonie M. Gruenberg and Hilda Sidney Krech, *The Many Lives of Modern Woman,* New York, Doubleday, 1952.

as many children as she can rear commensurate with her projected standards and personal freedom.

The change in the surface roles and expectations of men and women has taken place largely during the past two generations, much of it during the past 25 years. Such broad and deep shifts in the social and psychosexual patterns of living cannot be thoroughgoing within such a short period of time. There remains, then, the residue of the old standing in contrast to and at variance with the new.[9]

The Atomistic Family

The result of this vast change in our national life has been the emergence of the atomistic family, that is, one no longer held together by the authority of parents, economic necessity, and educational and protective obligations which were the bases of "strength" in the paternalistic family.[10] Such an atomistic family leads a rooming house existence. Its members have few bonds of deep understanding, common interest, and mutual care and satisfaction. Where this atomizing process has become more complete, family members are "free" from the last vestiges of authority and responsibility.[11] They are neither coerced nor protected. They are left psychologically abandoned because they do not feel emotionally close and related to persons outside themselves. They lack the resources to direct their own lives on a productive level. This is the basis for much of the neurotic personality of our time

[9] Ernest W. Burgess and Harvey J. Locke, *The Family*, New York, American Book Co., 1945, chap. 16.

[10] Carle C. Zimmerman, *Family and Civilization*, New York, Harper, 1947, chaps. 20, 22, 29.

[11] See Fromm, *Escape From Freedom, op. cit.*

because the individual has not gained, through experience, new bases of stability, companionship, and productive self-expression.[12]

World War II served to complete the break from our early rural mode of living and to displace still other urban dwellers. The old and the young from farms and cities left home to enter military service or war production plants. Separation from loved ones and established friendships disrupts habits of intimacy, security, and emotional acceptance. Unfulfilled gaps are left in the deeper areas of the personality.[13]

Results of Recent Family Dislocation and Change

As a nation in its early maturity we have been so busy building an empire that excessive extroversion has kept us from mature examination of ourselves and the direction of our striving. We are now confronted with the task of re-evaluating and reformulating our goals of living and of developing the capacity for deeper "inner" experience and more meaningful social experience. The protection of parents, teachers, and ministers with ready-made formulas for living, given with the not-to-be-questioned authority of their station, is now passed for millions of Americans.[14] This is evidenced in the current controversies regarding the rearing of children, educational theory, political and economic assumptions, standards of personal conduct, and religious thought. The

[12] See Horney, *op. cit.;* Erich Fromm, "Individual and Social Origins of Neurosis," *American Sociological Review,* IX (1944), 380, reprinted in Clyde Kluckhohn and Henry Murray (eds.), *Personality in Nature, Society, and Culture,* New York, Knopf, 1948.

[13] Reuben Hill, *Families Under Stress,* New York, Harper, 1949, chap. 4.

[14] See Riesman, *op. cit.* This entire book deals with the change in the "American character" from "tradition directed" to personal autonomy.

masses who in the past tended to believe what they were taught without understanding, are now demanding the right to question, to test in their own experience, and to participate in determining new policies regarding their own welfare.[15]

For many the complexity and frustration of the immediate past have stimulated greater effort with resultant growth, productivity, and happiness. They have found themselves. Many others have not. They have taken neurotic flights into different modes of anxious and compulsive living and have "escaped" into excessive emotional striving: excessive *sociability*, seeking assurance in affection, intimacy, and social approval; excessive *aggression* against people, ideas, and things; excessive *withdrawal* into communion with themselves, the occult, the abstract.[16]

These neurotic modes of reaction to excessive personal and social stress are accompanied by reduced creative productivity, feelings of ill-being, sickness due to sustained emotional pressure (psychosomatic illness), dissipating activities, and overdrawn ritual—*the bases of much of the marriage and family instability of today.*

OUTLOOK FOR THE FUTURE OF THE AMERICAN FAMILY

There are those who believe that the disorganization of the family is symptomatic of the decay in Western civilization, the Judeo-Christian democratic era.[17] Others, without

[15] Erich Fromm, *Man For Himself*, New York, Rinehart, 1947, chap. 6.
[16] Karen Horney, *Our Inner Conflicts*, New York, Norton, 1945.
[17] "Sorokin takes up the family as a part of his general analysis of the changes in western culture and gives us very specific statements as to the future of this system. He states very definitely that the culture which has dominated western society for the past five centuries is breaking down. The present difficulty is not 'local' or 'superficial,' but is one of the 'deepest crises of its life.' For the family he holds: 'The family as a

denying the seriousness and painfulness of the present situation, believe that it is not a death rattle, but the pain of birth, severing ourselves from outmoded and restrictive tradition to permit greater freedom and opportunity for creative self-expression, more meaningful relationships with others and accompanying regard for the common good.[18]

Freedom today is for many an empty and meaningless freedom from authority without the inner motivation and controls that enable people to become their better selves. Lack of morale and morality stands as a form of pointless rebellion against authority, now nonexistent for them except in the mental images of their own consciences.[19]

The family of the past has descended from the peak of paternalism into the shadow of disorganization. The task ahead is to bend every liberalizing force and institution to assist people better to know themselves and their unique opportunities, and to assist them with the program, skills, and goals that will enable them to build marriages of lasting companionship.

---

sacred union of husband and wife, of parents and children, will continue to disintegrate. Divorces and separations will increase until any profound difference between socially sanctioned marriages and illicit sex-relationship disappears. Children will be separated earlier and earlier from parents. The main socio-cultural functions of the family will further decrease until the family becomes a mere incidental cohabitation of male and female while the home will become a mere overnight parking place mainly for sex relationship.'

In other words, Sorokin predicts a further and further breakdown of the family until the relations between husband and wife and between parents and children will become incidental and chaotic. Neither Westermarck nor Sorokin set any foreseeable limit to this gradual breakdown of the family relation and the attendant dispersal of social values." Zimmerman, *op. cit.,* pp. 795–796. See also "The Future of Family and Civilization," pp. 784 ff.

[18] See Fromm, *Man For Himself, op. cit.,* chap. 5.

[19] See Fromm, *Escape From Freedom, op. cit.,* chap. 4.

There is widespread need for understanding the fact that a great many marriages fail and that the contemporary crisis in America is providing the circumstances that confuse, frustrate, and blind many who would, under other circumstances, choose a mate more wisely and plan the kind of courtship that would provide a foundation for a lasting, creative marriage. Failure to understand this fact will leave young people free from the serious, adult responsibility of marrying well. The blind idealization of marriage, untried self-confidence, youthful "wholesome sincerity," and an indoctrinated "faith" in the outcome of their own marriages, are not enough.[20] There must be more: understanding of human nature and of the particular personal needs of one's self and one's spouse, the self-affirmation that permits one to love another as the self, having attained some valid norms of conduct within a larger framework of humanitarian ethics, and a mature faith in both human reason and creative emotion. The challenge to American youth is to know themselves, to build a foundation for confidence in themselves, to be themselves, and to build a marriage for themselves.

[20] "It seems to me that a critic who is not keenly aware of all the defects of a lovely thing . . . is but a crude critic. . . . I feel contempt for 'love' that is blind; to me there is no love without clear vision. . . ." Havelock Ellis, *My Life,* Boston, Houghton Mifflin, 1939, p. 226.

Child is person
is considered
understand
authority
in
home
parental
action

Childhood - re-def. -
center of gravity returns to parent. → permitted to learn at first hand.
"permissiveness"
change from authoritarian

Adolescence - mobility (car)
exercise psyco-sexual freedom

Grad. from H.S - attainment of adulthood
older teenagers cut from family
parents influence less
tradition & influence going out.

Effects & Consequences on families different. p. 9

Experience spontaneous expression of knowledge.

FAMILY DISLOCATION

" + "

"TOO RAPID CHANGE"

Break - Change - Freedom

Tradition

Part One

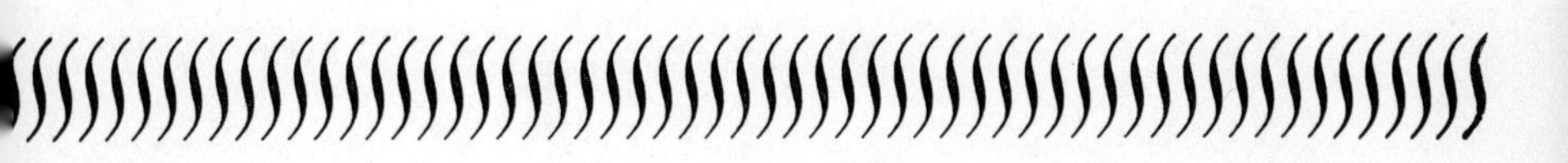

WHAT WE BRING TO MARRIAGE

Mon. Feb. 15.

Chapter 2

BASIC PERSONALITY

ONE OF the deepest, most absorbing, and continuing interests of people is to come to know themselves, and in courtship to know their prospective mates. While on a date young people spend endless hours in expressing, questioning, comparing their personal reactions to everything that crosses the threshold of their consciousness. Whether aware of it or not, the quest is for deeper social and psychological understanding of one's self and one's potential marriage partner. The greater the maturity, the more consciously and systematically is the pursuit undertaken.

One of the questions most frequently asked by college students in the marriage course is this: "What are the really important personality characteristics that provide the deeper bases for compatibility or incompatibility in marriage, how does personality pattern itself, are there discernible modes or 'types' of personality, and, is there any way of coming to know just what one's potential is and the possible directions of growth and development?"

failure to know one's self & consequently another

We may not have conclusive answers to that extended question, but we can say that research and clinical practice have given us some valuable information. As to the first part of the question, it has been found that the personality characteristics among the most important in the intimate companionship of marriage are temperament; level and direction of intelligence, talents, and interests; emotional and ideological maturity; ideological assumptions; patterns of sexual expectation and response; concept of love and its expression; and constitutional make-up. To the second part of the question the answer is a qualified "yes." Personality does take discernible modes or patterns with inherent and predictable "potentials." There is considerable evidence that a person of a given temperament tends to prefer certain interests, activities, values, and mode of expressing his thoughts and emotions, that are consistent with one another and to a considerable extent predictable. However, we can speak of "types" of human personality only in very abstract and theoretical terms. Human personality is too complex and people are too strikingly different in so many ways to justify placing them in neat categories or pigeonholes. However, we do achieve "shapes of our own," as a blend of colors achieves its own "hue," which may be like another, but never the same as another. Wayne Dennis stated it meaningfully in metaphor:

> We must not infer that the fitting of man into social patterns is strictly analogous to the pouring of wax into a mold. "The metaphorical wax, neurological, glandular, and otherwise, which comprises the human individual" has tendencies towards a *shape of its own.* The work of the agents of a society in shaping new organisms in the direction of *pre-existing patterns* is more comparable to that of a skillful gardener who starts with a natural setting which he can never completely alter or control. But, with the prearranged form in mind, he can limit this growth, encourage

that, destroy some weeds entirely for at least a season, accelerate a flowering, shape by pruning, train vines to grow in directions they would not have followed if only natural forces had had their way.[1]

From the different disciplines in the behavioral sciences and from clinical experience this writer has developed a theory of personality that has proved useful in helping to understand one's deeper self, and thus one's partner. It will be referred to throughout the book as *basic personality,* Dennis' "shape of its own," the deeper, dynamic self that each of us brings to marriage.[2] By studying and applying the

[1] Wayne Dennis, quoted in Clyde Kluckhohn and Henry A. Murray (eds.), *Personality in Nature, Society, and Culture,* New York, Knopf, 1948, pp. 107.

[2] The frame of reference developed here to describe basic personality has emerged primarily from the writings listed below. *Basic personality* as used here differs from Kardiner's use of the concept in that Kardiner denotes a pattern of psychosexual development appropriate to a given culture pattern. The present writer assumes that and more. Sheldon's emphasis is on temperament. Fromm seems to presume temperament differences while focusing on character, that is, patterns of emotional and ideological maturity and immaturity. Horney writes in terms of modes of neurotic behavior. Morris focuses on "paths of life," or patterns of values. White and Berne include most of the foregoing components of personality, including with Sheldon, a recognition of the importance of physiological factors (morphology) in personality. The present writer differs from White and Berne more in emphasis than in substance. He has utilized orientations from many sources but primarily from the foregoing which he has attempted to bring together in his conception of basic personality. The writings of Murray and Rorschach have had an important but indirect influence on the theoretical formulations developed in this chapter, but even more in the subsequent chapters. William H. Sheldon and S. S. Stevens, *The Varieties of Temperament,* New York, Harper, 1942; Karen Horney, *The Neurotic Personality of Our Time,* New York, Norton, 1937; Karen Horney, *Our Inner Conflicts,* New York, Norton, 1945; Erich Fromm, *Escape From Freedom,* New York, Rinehart, 1939; Erich Fromm, *Man For Himself,* New York, Rinehart, 1947; Abram Kardiner, *The Individual and His Society,* New York, Columbia University Press, 1939; Charles Morris, "Individual Differences and Cultural Patterns," in Kluckhohn and Murray, *op. cit.;* Robert W. White, *The Abnormal Personality,* New York, Ronald, 1948; Eric Berne, *The Mind in Action,* New York, Simon and Schuster, 1947; H. Rorschach, *Psychodiagnostics,* New York, Grune and Straton, 1942.

following theory of personality, it is believed that the quest for more articulate self-understanding and understanding of one's potential partner can be furthered. However, the student should bear in mind that any theory of personality, especially one as comprehensive as this one, is in its formative stages of development and cannot be presumed to have been validated by empirical research. It will undoubtedly be changed, supplemented, and corrected, and some aspects of it may possibly be proved invalid. Such is true of any theory.

THE COMPONENTS OF BASIC PERSONALITY

Basic personality might be thought of as being made up of three components analogous to the three primary colors. Just as we do not find spectrum red, yellow, or blue in nature without some blending, so the three basic personality components are always found in varying "amounts" in any given human being. Before we consider the complexity of any one person, let us look at each of the components separately as if it existed in pure form without the other two.

Component A: The Socially Engaging-Affirming

TEMPERAMENT[3]

A person high in component A of basic personality is marked by an easy flow of emotion. He is sociable, warm,

[3] The word *temperament* as used here will be in accordance with its customary meanings as outlined by MacKinnon, but it will also include additional meanings stemming from the research of Sheldon. It will include: "(1) characteristic emotional experience (strength, depth, and speed of emotional arousal, changes of mood, etc.); (2) assumed physiological bases for such experience (glandular differences for example); and (3) kinetic characteristics (energy and control of motor responses, expressive movements, etc.)." (White, *op. cit.*, p. 149.) In addition, differences in

amiable, and drawn *toward* people. He tends to be somewhat passive and compliant in his reactions to others. Unless he has considerable emotional maturity, the center of social gravity tends to remain in other persons rather than in himself and thus he may suffer some lack of personal autonomy. He is even-tempered and tends toward a sanguine outlook on life. The tempo of his reactions is slow, but not necessarily inferior in quality.

When under social and emotional stress the person high in the A-component tends to be thrown back onto a more primitive level of reaction; he becomes more of his "basic" self—*he moves toward people.*[4] He becomes dependent on others and reaches out excessively for recognition, affirmation, and

---

mode of reaction to social relationships will be included such as (1) social companionability, (2) social assertiveness, or (3) social shyness and withdrawal. (Sheldon, *op. cit.*)

The student may be interested in how one psychoanalytic psychiatrist has employed ideas modified from Sheldon in writing about the development of the normal personality. See Berne, *op. cit.*

Temperament is related to the way one expresses a given mood, but not to mood level. That persons differ in the feelings of elation and happiness or unhappiness and depression is a fact not necessarily related to temperament but to another dimension of personality that concerns emotional maturity and stability. (Sheldon, *op. cit.*) This distinction in the use of temperament stands in contrast to that of Terman who used it as practically synonymous with mood level. (Lewis M. Terman, *Psychological Factors in Marital Happiness,* New York, McGraw-Hill, 1938.) There is also evidence that persons of different temperament do not necessarily differ in *amount* of intelligence and talents. However, the *manner* in which persons express their abilities seems to be related to differences in temperament. (Sheldon, *op. cit.*) The neurotic expression of the three components will be taken up later.

[4] Modes of reaction under stress have been treated by Karen Horney in *Our Inner Conflicts.* The relationship between Sheldon's description of the reaction of persons of varying temperament components and Horney's postulation of three basic modes of reaction to psychological stress has already been noted in the text and will be further related here. "Horney's three trends correspond rather closely to the social traits associated with Sheldon's three components of temperament; moving toward people with viscerotonia, moving against people with somatotonia, moving away from people with cerebrotonia." See White, *op. cit.*, p. 225.

intimate response from others. If he develops more severe emotional instability he tends toward extreme swings of mood. Hospital experience indicates that he remains relatively close to reality and responds well to psychiatric treatment.

DIRECTION OF INTERESTS AND ABILITIES

The reader should bear in mind that research to date indicates that temperament has nothing to do with the level of interests and talents (whether high or low), but only with the direction that interests and abilities take.

The person high in the A-component and low in the B- and C-components of basic personality tends to be earthy, literal, and colorful in his interests. He would prefer a technicolor movie to a book, a landscape or portrait to an abstract painting, rhythm and harmony to "technique." He tends to be high in human interests and seeks to work with people more in a ministering than in an administrative role. Aesthetic interest is relatively high when talent is present, as is appreciation for polite ceremony. Intellectually the socially engaging-affirming person seeks to synthesize, to bring out likenesses rather than differences.

PATTERN OF VALUES OR "PATH OF LIFE"

The "path of life" generally chosen by the person high in component A has been characterized as closely resembling the Christian as described by Charles Morris:

> This way of life makes central the sympathetic concern for other persons. Affection should be the main thing in life, affection that is free from all traces of the imposition of oneself upon others or of using others for one's own purposes. Greed in possessions, emphasis on sexual passion, the search for power over persons

and things, excessive emphasis upon intellect, and undue concern for oneself are to be avoided. For these things hinder the sympathetic love among persons which alone gives significance to life. If we are aggressive, we block our receptivity to the personal forces upon which we are dependent for genuine personal growth. One should accordingly purify oneself, restrain one's self-assertiveness, and become receptive, appreciative, and helpful with respect to other persons.[5]

Ideologically a person high in component A is drawn toward liberal values that emphasize equality and fraternity among people, rather than authoritarianism or social self-containment and withdrawal.

CONSTITUTION (MORPHOLOGY)

There is some empirical evidence that persons high in component A and low in B and C, tend to have a body shape and structure of the following characteristics. They are rotund or "pneumatic" like Santa Claus, with slanting shoulders, a heavy "ham" contour to the upper arm, and the upper thigh between the legs closed and overlapping. The gait is smooth, rhythmic, and slow. When relaxed there is a general slumping of the body into the contour of the chair. The body is relatively insensitive to changes in temperature, loud or shrill noises, changes in diet, etc. Toxins like tobacco and alcohol are assimilated with high tolerance. The sex organs tend to be relatively small, as are the body extremities such as hands, feet, nose, and ears. The pituitary, thyroid, and gonadal functions are relatively "low," and the sex drive or "hunger

[5] Professor Charles Morris, a philosopher who is widely known for his rigorous contributions to semantics, has related somatotype to certain patterns of living. He raises the question of what kinds of persons with their varying constitutional endowments will invent, accept, or reject certain patterns of living and has some evidence as indicated by his statistical studies. See Morris, *op. cit.*, pp. 131–143.

level" tends to be low. These persons are often physically strong but low in endurance.[6]

Component B: The Socially Assertive-Ascendant

TEMPERAMENT

A person high in component B with little of A and C tends to be active, socially expressive, assertive, forward, and ascendant. He is characteristically demonstrative, often enjoying astounding others, but he is not necessarily self-centered. The latter is more a function of emotional maturity or immaturity than of temperament. He enjoys the competitive, tending to pit himself against people or obstacles, but is not necessarily antagonistic in this competition. He expects people to respond to him in a like manner and enjoys this reaction. His basic "strategy" in life which may be conscious or quite unconscious, is that of *moving against people.*[7]

Under stress this temperament pattern becomes accentuated and he becomes impulsive, direct, restless, overly competitive, compulsive, and overaggressive. When social and personal pressures in his life become too great and his mental health is markedly impaired, he launches into attacks against his presumed adversaries. He projects blame onto others, failing to take into account his own limitations. He becomes presumptous and overestimates his own abilities while attacking others. He moves against people with hostility.

[6] Sheldon, *op. cit.;* George Draper, C. W. Dupertuis, and J. L. Caughey, Jr., *Human Constitution in Clinical Medicine,* New York, Hoeber, 1944, chap. 6; William H. Sheldon, assisted by C. W. Dupertuis and E. McDermott, *Atlas of Man,* New York, Harper, 1954.

[7] Horney, *Our Inner Conflicts, op. cit.,* chap. 4.

This writer has noted in clinical experience that persons high in component B and low in A and C are characteristically somewhat lacking in sense of humor—the ability to place themselves in the psychological position of another and look at their own weaknesses, limitations, and incongruities with detachment and amusement. Without presuming a lack of native empathic and introspective ability, it is possible that this person has competed so favorably as a child in his "specialty" activities, that he has not learned to take the role of the person on the side lines, thus failing to develop more fully the ideational component of his personality. He resembles William James' description of the "tough minded" as contrasted with the "tender minded."

DIRECTION OF INTERESTS AND ABILITIES

The socially assertive person is the builder rather than the designer, the performer rather than the composer. He is the "salesman-administrator," pitting himself against obstacles. He is attracted toward the professions—law, medicine, engineering, industrial and labor management—rather than toward the liberal arts and sciences. The aesthetic, poetic, and philosophic are less inviting.

PATTERN OF VALUES OR "PATH OF LIFE"

The path of life that tends to be chosen by the person high in component B has been characterized as follows:

> A person should not hold on to himself, withdraw from people, keep aloof and self-centered. Rather merge oneself with a social group, enjoy cooperation and companionship, join with others in a resolute activity for the realization of common goals. Persons are social and persons are active; life should merge energetic group activity and co-operative group enjoyment. Meditation,

restraint, concern for one's self-sufficiency, abstract intellectuality, solitude, stress on one's possessions all cut the roots which bind persons together. One should live outwardly with gusto, enjoying the good things of life, working with others to secure the things which make possible a pleasant and energetic social life. Those who oppose this ideal are not to be dealt with too tenderly. Life can't be too fastidious.[8]

CONSTITUTION

A person high in component B and low in A and C tends to have physiological characteristics as follows. Their bone and muscle structure are heavy and well developed. The body is angular, with square shoulders, thick neck, narrow hips, muscular legs. Their facial features are angular with a "square" appearance. They appear older than they are. The gait when walking is springy with the weight on the ball of the foot. There is a need for physical activity which they engage in with marked endurance and without fatigue. These persons have a high pain threshold, actually enjoying activities that are physically shocking or painful to others. The sex drive is vigorous and these persons tend to be direct, self-assertive, and somewhat aggressive in sex expression.

Component C: The Socially Shy–Withdrawing

TEMPERAMENT

Persons high in component C and low in A and B, tend to be very shy, quiet, nondemonstrative, reflective, and sensitive to people about them. They tend to be self-conscious in the presence of people, especially when they are expected to respond or to express a personal view. They have a sense of feeling "vulgar" when expressing something that is

[8] Morris, *op. cit.,* p. 142.

personal to them. Mentally, they are quick to react, but their speech tends to be uncoördinated and inaudible; their thoughts tend to get ahead of their ability to express themselves verbally. Their basic "strategy" in life is to *move away from people.*

When under stress the socially shy person retreats from the presence of people and becomes excessively withdrawn into books, poetry, theology, abstract music and art, fantasy, etc. If the pressure becomes too great and mental illness develops, the person high in component C withdraws and becomes separated from reality, living in a special dream world of his own making. In his private world he expresses his thoughts and feelings in symbolic and abstract form. He is characteristically noncommunicative, expressing himself in abstract pantomime that seems to have no continuity or logic, but does have psychological meaning to him.

DIRECTION OF INTERESTS AND ABILITIES

Persons high in component C tend toward creative and abstract interests rather than overt activity or administrative or social roles. However, of all three theoretical types, research has shown that these people are the most practical in dealing with day-by-day affairs. They disdain the colorful and excess of any kind whether it be food, drink, physical activity, or personal and social demonstrativeness. They enjoy the symbolic rather than the literal representation of meaning, art, music, poetry. The tendency is to "hide" the import of what they may be representing as if they were hiding themselves. They are the dreamers and architects, not the builders. Considerable solitude is important as are a few close friends rather than many casual acquaintances. They are the theologians, not the preachers; the music critics, not the concert performers; the researchers, not the classroom teachers; the diagnosticians, not the surgeons. They have little interest in the application of knowledge or activities aimed at the "uplift" of man. There is probably nothing as painful and deafening to their psychological ears as a room full of chattering people. In their intellectual interests they tend to analyze rather than synthesize; they are given to seeking out dissimilarity and divergence. In social interaction this often makes them appear overly critical and unfriendly, even though this is not necessarily their intention. Actually they may be hiding their self-consciousness with a psychological smoke screen of diversion; they may be caught up in an "objective" analysis; or, they may be attacking what they feel is the stupidity of overgeneralization. Finally, they tend to be "untidy" whether it is in the unsystematic organization of their research notes, a cluttered desk, or an ill-fitted suit, because these are "details" of living which are unimportant to them.

PATTERN OF VALUES OR "PATH OF LIFE"

The path of life generally chosen by the person high in the C-component has been characterized as follows:

> The individual should for the most part "go it alone," assuring himself of privacy in living quarters, having much time to himself, attempting to control his own life. One should stress self-sufficiency, reflection and meditation, knowledge of himself. The direction of interest should be away from intimate associations with social groups, and away from the physical manipulation of objects or attempts at control of the physical environment. One should aim to simplify one's external life, to moderate those desires whose satisfaction is dependent upon physical and social forces outside of oneself, and to concentrate attention upon the refinement, clarification, and self-direction of one's self. Not

much can be done or is to be gained by "living outwardly." One must avoid dependence upon persons or things; the center of life should be found within oneself.[9]

CONSTITUTION

A person high in component C and low in A and B, tends to have physiological characteristics as follows. They are of slight bone and muscle structure. Their skin, hair, and facial features are fine rather than coarse. They tend to look younger than they are. The torso appears long and thin, with a minimum of visceral (internal organs) development. The arms and legs also appear long and thin with minimal muscular development. The gait when walking appears uncoördinated and awkward. The sense of direction and of kinesthetic feeling seem impaired to the self and to others. When seated they tend to slouch in the chair and sit in a humped position or in a somewhat tense posture. They suffer an almost continuous feeling of fatigue. Their reaction to environmental changes such as in light, sound, food, and temperature are deep and often painful. They have a low threshold of pain. They dislike heat, cold, and water. They are very sensitive to toxins such as tobacco and alcohol, which are almost poisons to their systems. They resist, physiologically, succumbing to anesthetics or the influence of alcohol. They might be characterized as a 17-jewel watch in a cellophane case. However, they have the longest life expectancy of the three "types" postulated. Their sex feelings are intense but their drive tends to be low, due probably to their feeling of enervation, and they respond deeply, symbolically, and somewhat possessively toward their sex partners.

[9] *Ibid.*, p. 141.

ARE THERE BASIC PERSONALITY TYPES?

On some levels of discourse there may be value in thinking in terms of "types" of human personality, if one is quite conscious of the fact that this is deliberate oversimplification. It is something like talking about "men and fish." It may make quite a difference in a given situation to know whether one is talking about a sucker or a shark. In another situation it may suffice to place men in one category and fish in another.

It may be a necessary part of intellectual development for the less trained student of human personality to think at first in terms of a few oversimplified theoretical types of basic personality, as has been done in the foregoing development of personality theory—"red," "yellow," or "blue"—all or none. But in reality we soon observe that very few if any persons can be found who have *all* of the characteristics of one type and *none* of the others.

The next step in refining our thinking is to combine the three according to whether a person is relatively high or low in each of the components. This would lead to the following theoretical types: ABC, ABc, Abc, AbC, aBC, aBc, abC, abc.

The last step in the refinement of one's thinking that would get away entirely from theoretical types and put every one analyzed on an "individual differences" basis, would be to make a continuum of each of the three components. Assuming a seven-point (or hundred-point) scale of each component, a given individual might be rated as A1, B4, and C3. There would be, consequently, no limit to the refinements of each continuum.

As one gains skill in the analysis of human personality he moves from "typological" thinking to an "individual differences" point of view. He thinks of an "A type," or "oral type," or "paranoid type," or "tender minded type," only as the grossest, most predominant, or most apparent characteristic, then moves on to qualify his conception by adding whatever other characteristics obtain.[10]

To the question of whether there are types of persons according to basic personality, the answer would seem to be, "Yes, as oversimplified theoretical constructs," and, "No, in reality." The more valid and productive way of thinking about given persons to understand their deeper needs, expectations, and modes of reaction, is to think of personality as a *pattern* of given "amounts" of A-, B-, and C-components. It is important to bear in mind that when two theoretically different components are found in one person, they affect one another and a modified characteristic emerges. For example, a person high in A and C but low in component B will be sensitively and self-consciously sociable (AC), but neither wholeheartedly outgoing (A) or sensitively retiring (C). This is further illustrated in the cases that follow and throughout the book.

CASES ILLUSTRATING PATTERNS OF BASIC PERSONALITY

The following biographical excerpts have been selected because they illustrate rather clearly different basic personality patterns. Furthermore, they are examples of how different basic personality components combine into the total basic personality of a given person.

[10] The question as to whether new components emerge when varying amounts of A, B, and C combine, is a challenging one that empirical research has shed little light upon. Clinical insights into the complexity of "emergent" patterns probably are more valid at the present time though more difficult to communicate than are the most advanced statistical, factor analysis approaches yet developed.

Ernie Pyle

Let us consider first the life of Ernie Pyle, the late, widely reported correspondent who lost his life at the close of World War II. Ernie Pyle's basic personality seems to have been made up of a strong, preponderant C-component, with considerable A and little overt B. The following excerpts have been taken from the book, *Ernie Pyle,* by Lee Miller:

With the American troops in Africa, George Biddle gives a description of Ernie as follows: "This morning I did a drawing in red sanguine of Ernie Pyle. I only put into it, I am afraid, a small part of his rare personality. He seems Yankee to the core, though hailing from Indiana farm stock. Ascetic, gentle, whimsical, shy. Frugal in his habits. Like so many Americans, his expression is fundamentally sad, yet full of tenderness. Of course a stubborn, thin lipped individualist, and probably hard as granite under his timid manner. I like to think of him as he sits on the beach toward sundown, a white and slender Gandhi, swathed in towels and wrappers, for he hates the cold as much as he fears the sun. He does not swim and dislikes bathing. So he spends his week's holiday as follows: he sleeps three hours each day; reads for three hours; then being at his wit's end what to do, he sits down and writes a column. He puts his whole life into his column: his shy love of human beings, his tenderness, and his hard, salty, Indiana farmer humor."

Don Whitehead of the A.P. reminisced later on: "Ernie was all man, but that made you want to take care of him, to lend him a hand whenever possible. I suppose we sensed that war was a heavier burden on him than on most of us because he was more sensitive to cold and hunger and pain and the shock of seeing men killed and wounded. Generally it was in Ernie's room where we gathered to drink and talk. Usually he would be huddled in his bedding roll with only his head sticking out, looking like a pixie in that knit cap. He suffered some terrible fits of depression in Italy."

Mrs. Roosevelt praised his book *Here Is Your War* in her column, and Ernie sent a thank you note, which brought an invitation to tea. He explained to the First Lady's secretary, that the only coat he possessed was an old gray one with both elbows out, and she said to think nothing of it. Nevertheless he was nervous, and he paced Lafayette Park for twenty minutes before the appointed hour.

In England he was in bed with one of his many heavy colds and he wrote his wife, Jerry: "I seem to be suffering more than ever from timidity and an inferiority complex. It's just a horror for me to go out and talk to people. I feel like I'm conspicuous and ignorant and have reached forty years old with so little knowledge I can't even hold a conversation with twenty year olds."

This was written to his employer concerning his three months leave of absence: "I'm a fine one to quibble when all you're doing is to be the finest employer a human ever had. But I do have to quibble over my salary during this three month leave. . . . This leave of absence is to try to rejuvenate Jerry, one of the most important things in the world to me. It is also to build myself back up again, as you say, so I can swing hard when I start again. And to do either one, I've got to be absolutely free while doing it. I've got to know the time is *my* time and that I *own* the time because I've paid for it in absence of salary. If my salary goes on, I can't but consider it *your* time, and every loafed minute will be under strain, and I will be fretting and restless about getting back to work. . . ."

While still in France Ernie wrote his secretary: "I have a feeling I've used up all the chances a man is endowed with, and when I have to tempt Fate further, I get the horrors inside. If I ever was brave, I ain't any more. Much of the time I'm quite depressed, and hang on only by the feeling that it can't be too long now. Writing is difficult these days—I seem bored with the war and impatient with the end. Wouldn't it be cute of me now that I've got all the papers in the world and the prizes and the front cover of Time, just to quit and go into seclusion!"[11]

Babe Didrikson Zaharias

Babe Didrikson's basic personality is an example of a person with a very strong component B, with considerable A and little C.

At their first sight of Mildred Didrikson Zaharias on the golf course, spectators often react like sideshow gawkers; they are first filled with awe, then with doubt, then with wonder. Obviously, they feel, no woman should be able to hit a golf ball so far (her longest drive 315 yards).

But in 20 years of competition, this 5 ft. 6 in. phenomenon with grey-green eyes, slightly bowed legs and squared shoulders has accomplished feats which for sheer diversity have seldom been equaled by any athlete, male or female. She broke two world records at the 1932 Olympics, was twice selected All-American basketball forward, has pitched for the St. Louis Cardinals (in an exhibition game), and has toured the country giving billiard exhibitions. Anything that requires muscular co-ordination is her meat. She has excelled at tennis, swimming, diving, bowling, shot-putting, lacrosse, fencing and polo. She can type 86 words a minute and has been heard to say of her husband, George Zaharias, a 300-lb. ex-wrestler: "Yep, I threw him last night with a flying mare."

Babe stalks the fairway with a conscious sense of theater. She flips king-size cigarettes into the air and catches them nonchalantly in her mouth, then lights her match with her fingernail. Her hawkish, sun-toughened face is frozen for the most part in a thin-lipped mask, but she knows when to let go a wisecrack. When one of her tremendous drives sails out of bounds, she turns to the crowd and explains, "I hit it straight but it went crooked."

[11] Lee G. Miller, *The Story of Ernie Pyle,* New York, Viking, 1950. (Italics mine.)

If she sinks a long put, she is apt to fall to her knees and praise Allah; when she misses a short one she may exclaim, "I feel like nuts and bolts rattling together." On a hot day, she once gathered a circle of women around her on the golf course while she shed her petticoat; another time she startled the gallery with a highland fling. She once insisted on being paid her tournament money in one-dollar bills ("It makes me feel richer"). She operates like a woman whose life is a constant campaign to astound people.

Babe takes her housewifely chores as seriously as her golf. She designed the modern, push-button kitchen which, like the dining room, is painted a violent yellow. "Kinda loud," Babe admits, offhandedly, "but you get used to it."

The only door inside the house is to the bedroom where George sleeps in a double bed and Babe in a single bed. She hates doors: "They clutter up the place."

She disdained lipstick, plastered her hair back, talked out of the side of her mouth with a thick Texas drawl and riveted reporters with such remarks as: "Are you the guy who took pictures of my feet in Jersey?"

When she decided to concentrate on golf, she tightened up her game by driving as many as 1,000 golf balls a day and playing until her hands were so sore they had to be taped. She developed an aggressive, dramatic style, hitting down sharply and crisply on her iron shots like a man and averaging 240 yards off the tee.

One day in 1938, George Zaharias, who had met Babe a year before when they were both playing in a golf tournament, looked into her eyes and said, "We get married on Friday or we're through." They got married on Friday.

Babe tried to stop bragging and boasting. She made George give up wrestling. She began giving herself home permanents ("I just follow the directions on the box"). With housewifely zest, she pitched into making curtains and raising flowers. But even in the garden there was competition. "I know I can't make my flowers grow any faster," she said, "but I want them to be the prettiest and the healthiest." In line with her determination to be a "grown-up married woman and not a 14-year-old javelin thrower," she concentrated on golf, hoping that some of its gentler graces would rub off on her. Some did.

As the best player and biggest draw in women's golf, Babe stopped wearing a chip on her shoulder. Instead of greeting all the rivals with, "Yep, I'm gonna beat you," she began encouraging the younger girls on the circuit and established a working friendship with the older ones. When George is not traveling the circuit with her, she often rooms with Patty Berg, who has been her chief adversary for years.

Her mind seems almost as wiry as her body. "There isn't a crossword puzzle I can't finish in half an hour," Babe admits modestly. She likes to play gin rummy but is too good at it to get many opponents. The once lonely, homely tomboy is now a social success; she is an extremely graceful ballroom dancer and the life of almost any party, doing imitations of herself as a child singing "I Get the Blues When It Rains," or hauling out a harmonica and rocking into a hill-billy air. Babe once banked $3,500 for taking her harmonica on the stage for seven days. She quit because she felt cooped up and "had to get out and see the sky again."[12]

Franklin D. Roosevelt

There is considerable evidence from the writings about our late President, that he was a person whose basic personality was preponderantly made up of component B. However, he was strong in A with very little C. It is interesting to note that his wife and many of his closest advisors were persons high in component C.

I once heard it said that Roosevelt's most effective quality was receptivity. But also he transmitted. He was like a kind of universal joint, or rather a switchboard, a transformer. The whole energy of the country, the whole power of one hundred and

[12] *Time,* February 2, 1953, pp. 41 ff. Courtesy TIME; copyright Time Inc. 1953.

forty million people, flowed into him and through him; he not only felt this power, but he utilized it, he retransmitted it.

The President was inveterately personal, and people were inveterately personal about him. His radiant, energetic smile—even with the touch of glucose in it, even when it seemed contrived—stirred people with confidence and hope.

His mind had defects; nobody would deny this. He had little taste for philosophical abstraction; he was "a broker of ideas rather than an architect of systems," as Harold Laski once pointed out. He got stimulus from conversation, not from meditation.

Finally in this general field of the mind, there is a consideration above the mind—Roosevelt's sixth sense, his supernal sensitiveness to hunches, his delight in proceeding not by the book but by the spirit, and his wariness. Like a horse in quicksand, he had a highly developed sense of self-preservation and instinct for solid soil. No matter what he put his foot in, he could get it out.

He was an extremely superior and confident person; then came the attack of infantile paralysis which caused an almost complete temporary disintegration of personality. Nothing of his character or career can be understood without reference to his illness.

To make up for the fact that he was paralyzed he developed the tremendous drive, exuberance, and radiating energy that carried him into the White House.

The single clue that is the best common denominator to all multifarious paradoxes of his character is his love for action. He resolved most confusions by the simple process of doing something, *acting*.[13]

VALIDITY OF THE BASIC PERSONALITY THEORY

The question is often asked, "Isn't the theory of basic personality too 'neat' and does one really find a high correlation between temperament, interests, choice of values, mode of

[13] John Gunther, *Roosevelt in Retrospect,* New York, Harper, 1950. (Italics mine.)

neurotic reaction, and constitutional make-up?" First, let it be said that the theory is very controversial academically, probably as controversial as psychoanalysis was at the turn of the century and is today in some quarters. And, while this is not the place to try to settle a matter that will take years of coöperative research to resolve, it should be clearly stated that this and any other such comprehensive theory of personality is in a theoretical stage of formulation.

For the student of personality any final conclusions regarding the present theory might be held in critical abeyance seeking new evidence. However, the person who is trying to understand his own deeper nature—not only what one is as determined by social and psychological influences and pressures acting on original nature, but, trying to understand and predict what his *potential* development might be—must act on the basis of "what we *now* think we know and can apply." He cannot wait for more final answers to emerge from research.

Since the first Harvard studies positing the temperament aspects of the basic personality theory were published 16 years ago, this writer has attempted to test the theory in clinical practice. He has found it immensely useful in the diagnosis and prediction of behavior, especially in cases which deviate from expected "norms." At the same time it must be recognized that any such total view of anything so complex as human personality, especially as presented in the present cursory form, is at best the statement of an extended hypothesis. This theory, even granting considerable validity, will be refined and supplemented, aspects of it will undoubtedly be changed according to new evidence, and at best it will be a growing, emerging idea.

Often in clinical practice one sees a person whose social

and emotional roles are quite incongruous with what one would expect on the basis of the theory of basic personality. It must be recognized that talented people especially are capable of learning quite a diversity of roles, much as an accomplished actor. And while any role that a person plays is "real," the question is, is this role compatible with the deeper nature of the person, the "shape of its own," or the "prearranged form?" In other words, does the basic personality that one brings to marriage have its own deeper, compatible needs, expectations, directions, and limitations? Or can one become almost "anything" and adjust to "almost anyone?" Granting the latter up to a point, it seems that there are many things for which one is fit and many for which one is not fit. To know one's self more fully and to marry another most compatible with one's own "shape" or "form" would seem to be most conducive to the reduction of unnecessary and destructive interpersonal pressures, and to the facilitation of greatest self-transcendence and unity between two people.

PATTERNS OF "INCONGRUOUS" BASIC PERSONALITY

There are persons who give evidence of having a pattern of temperament that is inconsistent, according to our theory, with an expected pattern of values, interests, or physique. Are they necessarily exceptions to the theory? They seem not to be. This writer has met people like this in his clinical practice. They seem to fall into two categories: (1) the pseudopersonality—those who have been brought up in a home where parental expectations forced social roles upon them that were different from and incompatible with their basic personalities; (2) the immature—those who have developed one component of basic personality while leaving another(s) latent and undeveloped. This occurs when the expectations of others reward one mode of self-expression and leave the others unrewarded or punished.

One of the writer's clients was a young woman just out of military service. Her body was large and barrel shaped. At first she was very quiet and noncommunicative and appeared to be quite strong in the C-component of basic personality. As the story unfolded she said that her "forceful" mother had always doted on her daughter becoming an English teacher. However, the daughter rejected and resented the idea and her defense and aggression toward her mother took the form of "running away," the apparent reason for her joining the Service. In service she continued to aggress against military authority by going AWOL and remaining outwardly surly with contained belligerence in the form of a silent grouch. When her occupational objective had finally been decided she had chosen and agreed upon becoming a geologist. "I can get out, hike, and do things I have always wanted to do," she said, "without people getting in my way."

This young woman is an illustration of what one might call "pseudo introversion." While some of component C was present, she was primarily B and A. Her contained hostility role had been learned. She could not hurt or cope with her strong mother or the Army, so she adopted the "false" role in order to maintain whatever sense of personal integrity she could unconsciously salvage.

Not infrequently people with some talent learn social and emotional roles unlike their "own" that give expression to one or the other expected (by environment) basic personality components. It is something like a Hollywood actor assuming a repertory of character parts in succession, each appropriate to the "expectations" of a given script. At the same time the actor is not all of these characters. He is himself. However, he does play with conviction and integrity the role of the "other." It is the writer's contention that this process goes on quite unconsciously, to some degree, in the everyday lives of many people. They do not give full expression to their own unique basic personality needs, but act like puppets on strings (the expectations and demands of others). To use Riesman's term, they are "other-directed."[14]

When a person quite unconsciously denies his own deeper needs and builds incongruous social roles on the surface, he tends to lack personality integration. He experiences conflict within himself, conflict between what he tries to be and what his deeper nature portended him to be. We see about us people who are accountants, chafing because they are not social workers; or salesmen who inwardly cringe at the doorbell, who dream of the day when they can retire to the solitude of their gardens.

One of the developmental tasks of young adults is to come to know their own basic personality to lessen the risk of courting and marrying a person whose basic personality may develop into something quite different from what it was at the time of marriage. This is one of the real risks especially of early marriage. Many young people assume social roles appropriate to the expectations of their friends, relatives, and community values, to find when they get away from home that their deeper potentials have not come to fruition and expression. They have not been themselves. This is a risk accompanying social and emotional immaturity and will be discussed in Chapter 5.

[14] David Riesman, *The Lonely Crowd,* Garden City, Doubleday Anchor, 1953.

COMPATIBILITY OF BASIC PERSONALITY IN MARRIAGE

Of all the scientific research that has been carried on to understand compatibility in marriage, virtually none has been devoted to the study of *patterns of involvement* according to basic personality.[15] Studies have shown that homogamy of many social characteristics in marriage is positively related to "success" and "adjustment," i.e., that persons of the same social class, educational level, religion, etc., tend to select one another and score higher on the marital adjustment scales. However, recent research indicates that with regard to some psychological characteristics, "the tendency for an individual to select a spouse unlike himself in total emotional make-up far exceeds the tendency for him to select a person like himself in that respect."[16] However, we know little about how such a tendency is related to compatibility.

[15] Research to date has dealt largely with the analysis of personality traits and their correlation with marital happiness scores. This kind of atomistic analysis has its limited value but should not be regarded as a substitute for a more basic kind of personality theory that deals with the patterning of traits into larger, dynamic configurations.

Another limitation of the current literature dealing with compatibility in marriage is a lack of common definition of terms. This has led to confusion in the meaning of referents, and has obscured important areas of research that might have been undertaken by grouping important, independent personality variables together. As cases in point, one might look at the research of Johnson and of Terman. See *The Johnson Temperament Analysis Profile,* published by California Test Bureau, 1941, in which temperament traits are listed as nervous-composed, active-quiet, self-mastery-impulsive, etc. Terman found that the "unhappy temperament" is related to unhappiness in marriage, but he used the term as being practically synonymous with emotional maturity or immaturity, e.g., such traits as nagging, not affectionate, selfish, inconsiderate, etc. See L. M. Terman, *Psychological Factors in Marital Adjustment,* New York, McGraw-Hill, 1938, pp. 85–86.

[16] Robert F. Winch, "The Theory of Complementary Needs in Mate Selection: Final Results on the Test of General Hypothesis," *American Sociological Review,* XX (October, 1955), 552–555; Thomas Ktsanes, "Mate Selection on the Basis of Personality Type; a Study Utilizing an Empirical Typology of Personality," *American Sociological Review,* XX (October, 1955), 547–551.

Before presenting a "complementary-compensatory" theory of attraction according to basic personality, we shall consider in greater detail some aspects of personality that constitute deeper bases of compatibility or of incompatibility in courtship and marriage, namely, how the psychosexual aspects of personality develop.

Chapter 3

THE PSYCHOSEXUAL DEVELOPMENT OF PERSONALITY

IF A person would understand himself and his prospective spouse more fully, it is not enough to know the pattern of one's basic personality but also *how it developed.* To know how a thing is put together is to add depth to our understanding of it. That is why some very discerning people will spend years on a psychoanalyst's couch going back over their infancy and childhood, piecing together the formative influences and experiences that molded their personalities. Furthermore, one of the best ways of determining one's *potential* growth and direction of development is to understand how one *has* grown and developed. Some persons have had the most propitious kind of developmental experience, coming out of homes that reflect a relatively mature level of culture. Their personalities reflect this maturity and attendant stability. Others have been damaged, some so severely that their development has been rigidly fixated at a premature level. The purpose of this chapter is to show the influence of early social and emotional experience on the personality that one brings to marriage; to illustrate the striking differences in the way children are reared in different cultures and the kinds of people they turn out to be; and to point up the developmental experiences that are necessary for all children, irrespective of basic personality, so they can achieve maximal social and emotional maturity—one of the most indispensable aspects of a good marriage.

Students of human relations, including persons in the healing arts such as psychiatry, hold that the early physical, social, and emotional development of a child strongly affects his future personality. For many it is the mold into which the personality is cast, changing little thereafter. This does not mean that patterns learned during childhood cannot be changed. We know that they can. But many persons change little after this early formative period due to the constancy of their environment, lack of awareness of what they might become, lack of interest in change, and, not least, lack of educational and clinical assistance in effecting change.

CROSS-CULTURAL STUDIES

Primitive societies provide radically contrasting patterns of culture with their resultant common or modal personality patterns. In one culture the child is treated with consideration and understanding of many of his needs as among the Hopi Indians. The result is seen in the typical Hopi child who is intellectually and emotionally mature compared with other children living in the Southwest. In another culture such as the Marquesans, the child is treated with rejection and cruelty. The resultant modal personality as reconstructed from their early culture, was a cruel head-hunter. Let us look at different cultures including one segment of our American society in order to gain a more meaningful sense of the relationship between a pattern of child rearing and the kind of personality that results. Sketches from three primitive and one modern culture will help show the relationship between the "average" child's care and training and the related common personality characteristics resulting.[1]

The Alorese

The Alorese live on a small island in the Netherlands East Indies just south of the equator. This mountain-dwelling group is Oceania Negroid racially and Papuan culturally. They are poor and primitive. Central in their culture is a great deal of interest in financial transactions, trading, sharp practices, and the use of wealth to control others. In their religion there are some guardian spirits and good beings, but the Alorese are preoccupied with illness, death, life after death, spirits, and insanity. Warfare is practically nonexistent. Skills and physical strength are not honored, and their pursuit is regarded as a failure to compete for wealth.

THE FORMATIVE PERIOD

About ten days after the birth of the child the mother returns to the fields to work. The infant's breast feeding is

[1] The following sketches of child rearing in primitive societies were taken from the writings of Linton, Kardiner, and their colleagues at Columbia University. See Abram Kardiner, *The Individual and his Society,* New York, Columbia University Press, 1939; Abram Kardiner, *The Psychological Frontiers of Society,* New York, Columbia University Press, 1945. See also Stuart A. Queen and John B. Adams, *The Family in*

interrupted and premasticated food or gruel is given the infant by different people, irregularly and undependably. There is some fondling of the infant—rocking, joggling, mock-biting, more by young men than women because the women are too busy working. The young baby half sits and cries in a shawl that is slung over the guardian's shoulder. The shawl is abandoned when the child is about 3 years old. Weaning may take place early. The mother pushes the child away or slaps it and she may deliberately stimulate jealousy by taking another child to nurse.

Toilet training among the Alorese is gradual, with no evidence of overattention or concern about bowel and bladder control. Bathing is very painful because of the prevalence of skin sores and often provokes long and violent temper tantrums.

The sex activities of the child are confined to masturbation which is induced by the parents to quiet him (her). The child continues to masturbate freely and publicly. The child observes parental coitus and sex conversation is not restrained.

There is no permissive, encouraging, or deliberate training of the child. He learns by restrictive commands, shame, and ridicule. At the same time the child is not taught many avoidances. Frightening the child and threatening to cut off his ears or hands is common, but not for sexual misdeeds. Punishment is very inconsistent and the child maybe punished at one time and consoled at another for the same deed. Promises of reward for good behavior are not kept. Thus, children are most confused about what elders expect of them. When the mother deserts her child as she does daily

Various Cultures, New York, Lippincott, 1952; Clyde Kluckhohn and Henry A. Murray (eds.), *Personality in Nature, Society, and Culture,* New York, Knopf, 1948.

to work in the field, he beats his head on the ground in a temper tantrum. Quarreling between parents involving the child often results in the child's being taken by some unfamiliar person. The child's residence is unstable as the family is constantly moving from house to house in the village, and from village to village.

The adolescent period is one of continued rejection, inconsistency of treatment, free but clandestine sex activity, teasing, ridicule, threats of being sold into slavery, and fear resulting from gossip about the supernatural—malevolent spirits and witchcraft poisoning. Children may be struck with the knuckles, have their ears pulled or their mouths twisted by an eligible list of disciplining relatives. The adolescent has no feeling of being an actual participant in the community. The boy is not regarded as an adult until he becomes a father.

RESULTING MODAL PERSONALITY

What kind of a personality is characteristic of the foregoing kind of social and psychological experience in the culture of the Alorese? The attentive parental care ends two weeks after the birth of the child, resulting in the deep frustration of the child's basic needs for consistent, satisfying, and secure physical and emotional care. There is no one person to whom the child can grow close, learn to anticipate, and with whom he can associate the pleasure of relieving his tensions. Masturbation distracts the child in the wrong direction, seeking satisfactions in himself rather than becoming related to others. Aggravated by uncleanliness and itching sores, the child's feeling of rejection, first by his mother then by sibs and others leaves him deeply frustrated and emotionally insecure.

The child's speech contains many imprecations in which he invokes the evil of a protector. He is shy, reticent, and easily provoked into a tantrum in which he shows pathological loss of control of his aggression. The fear of these rages and what he might do results in repression (unconscious) that takes the following pattern: suppression (the conscious withholding) of some of these rages, the feeling that it "does no good to have a tantrum," which lays the foundation for a fear of any self-assertion or aggression; lowered self-esteem; inability to become interested in things outside the self; inability to sustain effort, and tendencies to aspire to little, to give up easily, to be hostile toward opposite sex, and to collapse in the face of danger.

Having learned no patterns of satisfaction, reward, and control, the child avoids his own retaliatory-destructive impulses with a rigid "front" of *passivity* and escape in seeking prestige, self-esteem, money, marital infidelity, and security through religious ritual. Money is not saved, but is used to control the activities of others. It is common to steal or to take by force anything that is denied. Tiring of the spouse in marriage is common, resulting in a very high divorce rate. Preoccupation with sharp financial transactions and ceremonial self-saving religion are important in day-by-day activities. These are the social and emotional diversions of the Alorese. Creative pursuits have remained at a low level of interest, prestige, and productivity.

The sex life of the adults gives evidence of mutual hostility which results in the woman's inability to abandon herself to a sexual relationship. Thus, she has a strong desire for a vigorous male while ridiculing men for their impotency. Infidelity and divorce are usually initiated by the man who is constantly in search of the "ministering and good mother" of his denied and unfulfilled childhood. The foregoing sex pattern results in exaggerating the value of potency and the value of social status and wealth comes to mean symbolically, the acquiring of the good mother and of being equal to and opposing the despotic father.

The sense of reality and conscience of the person both suffer faulty development and remain very weak. When one gets few rewards for obedience, punishment cannot evoke inner control. Religious and community prohibitions are not effective. The sense of shame and impending punishment are fears of external threat, not internalized controls.

The Marquesans

The Marquesans are a Polynesian people who live about 10° south of the equator on a chain of rugged volcanic islands in the South Pacific. They have little tillable soil and are subjected to devastating droughts with widespread, periodic starvation. Their anxieties center about food and are reflected in their personal habits, orientations, and institutions. The Marquesans have a peculiar and inexplicable sex ratio: several males to each female resulting in the plural marriage of several men to each woman. Women are vain about their bodies and personal adornment.

THE FORMATIVE PERIOD

When the infant is born it is bathed in one of the cold streams that flow down the volcanic mountains. He is not nursed, for the mother believes that nursing will distort the beauty of her breasts. The infant is laid on a mat of cocoanut fronds while the mother pours a thick gruel of chewed shrimp and cocoanut milk on its mouth. She wipes the child's gasping mouth with her forearm. To quiet the child his mother either lets him cry it out or masturbates him. The child's needs are of little concern to her. Her needs come first.

The child's care is taken over by his aunts and uncles who are responsible for his care, education, and protection from neighboring cannibals. The child is allowed unlimited freedom to play, wander within the tribal village, and engage in sex play. There is little sex differentiation between boys and girls. Virtually no discipline or responsibility is exacted from children. It is their obligation to assist in a blood feud and little else. The male child outranks his father from birth. He may order his father out of the house and leave him sitting on the tribal platform until the child can be persuaded to call off the taboo. The life of the child is carefree.

Unconscious aggressive tendencies are generated in a culture in which the child is frustrated in his basic physical and emotional needs and these tendencies are aggravated by anxieties concerning food shortages, women, and malevolent religion. For example, there is much concern about female ogresses with big pop-eyes and long, lashing tongues, and about a section of the spirit world where it is dark and dank, with a prevalent shortage of food. Both of these represent projections of childhood and adult anxieties.

The Marquesans live so close together and struggle so hard to live that outward aggression must be held to a minimum in order to survive. Consequently much pathological aggression of which they are capable is practically never expressed. It remains covered by strict adherence to quietening religious rituals and other compulsive acts. Much evidence of covert aggression is seen in their folklore which contains strongly oral fantasies of eating their parents, grandparents, and even the cooking utensils.

RESULTANT MODAL PERSONALITY

The typical adult Marquesan remains socially and psychologically undeveloped and childlike, notwithstanding the handsome physiques that they develop. The Marquesan adult has little sense of being a person with inner power to act on his own or to place himself in the position of another. He feels that his needs will be met and his actions controlled by someone else. He is controlled by fear and terror rather than understanding. He does not develop the capacity for sentiment or tenderness. Hostility characterizes relations between the sexes, and is expressed in sexual intercourse. Attitudes toward children are very hostile. Until recent years the Marquesans were head-hunters who would steal a child from a neighboring village and eat it, or bash in the heads of selected youths during religious ceremonies to satisfy the malevolent spirits. Cowards in war, they are not afraid of death but of the spirits. They eviscerate their dead relatives and cut off useful bones for tools and ornaments. Paradoxically, they are a socially graceful people, even the children. There is no vandalism or wanton mischief among them.

The Hopi Indians[2]

The Hopi live in the Southwest part of the United States, in a semiarid section of Arizona. They are poor but not squalid. Their tribal life is well organized on a coöperative basis. Their agriculture is highly developed as is their religious and aesthetic life. The objectives of the Hopi are to develop broad, rounded personalities devoted to the community

[2] See Wayne Dennis, *The Hopi Child,* New York, Appleton-Century, 1940.

good. Self-interests and accomplishments are strongly discouraged.

THE FORMATIVE PERIOD

The infant is close to its mother who cares for it with consideration of its needs. It is breast fed irregularly, given the breast when restless. It is weaned late, during the second year. During the early years the infant and child is indulged. Later when discipline is introduced, aunts and uncles minister to the child's needs, education, and discipline. The father remains a loving figure rather than a disciplinarian. The paternal uncle is the one who disciplines the child and the father remains close to the child, even closer than the mother. The child is permitted to express some hostility but patterns of aggression are mild, usually taking the form of tantrums or of hurting animals. There is little misbehavior. Thumb sucking and bed wetting are expected until the second year. A permissive rather than strict attitude towards sex is practiced.

Group goals and loyalties are encouraged and emphasis is placed on coöperating with and respect for the group. The acquiring of skills is also encouraged and the child is given responsibility relatively early because these skills and sense of responsibility will be of benefit to the group. Religious training is given an important place in the culture and the religion is ritualistic (a group activity) and aesthetic (individual pleasure in group activity). Self-assertion is strongly discouraged as are all antisocial activities such as stealing and fighting.

RESULTING MODAL PERSONALITY

It is the opinion of anthropologists, psychologists, and psychiatrists who have studied the Hopi that they have achieved a range and depth of emotion, intellect, and social behavior. Studies of Hopi intelligence show that their children do better on standardized tests than a standard group of white children living in the Southwest. The Hopi weigh meaningful detail in a context of broader meaning. They show diverse rather than stereotyped behavior. They maintain high levels of morality as judged by Western culture. Value is placed on personality rather than on material gain. Excellence is sought for its own sake rather than as a means of outdoing another. They seek beauty in the universal. Their group solidarity and self-reliance is evidenced in the fact that in 1952 they refused financial relief from the United States Government despite the drought they had experienced.

Plainville, U.S.A.[3]

Even within our American middle class, family patterns are diverse and very complex. But we have a qualified picture of the extension of our rural, agricultural culture base with urban additions and modifications. Few American communities have a distinctive culture. However, a fairly typical community has been selected for consideration here. Plainville is a small town between a "hillbilly" region and a richer farming area of the Midwest. The chief occupation is agriculture though a variety of other occupations are represented. The community appears backward but it has many contacts with other American communities and their patterns of culture.

THE FORMATIVE PERIOD

The role of the husband in the Plainville home is expressed in his feeling that he owes his wife a good living, and

[3] Kardiner, *The Psychological Frontiers of Society, op. cit.,* pp. 259 ff.

that he should be kind, true, and not meddle in household affairs. The wife's role is that of a helpmate, cook, efficient housekeeper, patient and faithful comforter to the children and her husband. She yields to her husband's demands and expectations and does not interest herself in the farm. The mother plays a more important part in teaching the children than does the father. Children in Plainville are expected to be moral, honest, willing to work, obedient, submissive to parental authority, and to love and respect their parents. The relation of the nuclear family to more distant relatives is warm but not close.

Children are born into an atmosphere of "everybody loves a baby." A boy child is desired as the first. An only child is pitied. Child care in the community differs. Some are raised "by the book," and others by the "old-fashioned rocking chair methods"—they are fed when hungry, sleep with their mother, nurse at night, are cuddled when they cry, weaned in the second year, discouraged in thumb sucking, and toilet trained when they can understand what is expected. Punishment during childhood is mild. Reasoning and a "spat" rather than harshness is the mode. Both mother and father may discipline or punish the child, but it is more often the mother. Shaming, teasing, scolding, and nagging are supplementary disciplinary methods used, as are privations, rewards, encouragement, and the adjunctive role of the schools and Sunday school. There is early sex differentiation in children's roles with clear-cut boys' and girls' activities. Girls are supposed to be pretty, passive, and submissive, while boys are expected to be dominant and aggressive, and to hold girls in contempt. They are expected to be self-reliant and rebel, while girls are regarded as "naturally" obedient and are taught modesty.

RESULTING MODAL PERSONALITY

Close early attention to the child's needs reduces the difficulty of adjusting and the capacity for creative inner experience is furthered. Later, social adjustment becomes more difficult because of unconscious ambivalence (affection and aggression) toward parents. The ambivalent feeling results when the early closeness of the child to the parents becomes fused with necessary obedience, sex denial, financial dependence, and conformity to the expectations of parents, teachers, and religious leaders. In effect the early spontaneous and creative interests of the child become hemmed in. The result is surface conformity with inner rebellion coming out in disguised forms such as prudery and striving for prestige, accomplishment, leadership, and material security. Restrictive and authoritarian discipline prevents the child from learning to evaluate his own experience and assume more expansive roles. Accepting authority rather than weighing evidence in a more self-contained manner becomes the common approach to problems. Noncreative, routine interests and activities prevent the development of productive work. Conscience becomes burdened and inflexible, constricting spontaneous self-expression and self-assertion.

Striving for high position of prestige, wealth, and social acceptability gives evidence of unconscious feelings of inferiority. Antisocial feeling is expressed in hostility between men and women, jealousy, envy, malign gossip, and condemnation of people who "live their own lives." Sexual expression becomes blocked, resulting in excessive pursuit, avoidance, or perverted experience. Intellectual and aesthetic interests are blocked. The creative impulse is channeled into mechanisms of compulsion, such as excessive obedience, cleanliness, and orderliness, disrespect for education (though paying lip service to it), and reasoning by authority rather than by evidence. Conflict between the person's inner needs and the meaningless surface strivings is evidenced in excessive organizational affiliation and activities. It is also seen in other forms of recreation like movies, radio and television programs in which star personalities such as Charlie McCarthy, Bob Hope, Jack Benny portray stinginess, unmanly looks, boys taking girls' roles, failure with women and disrespect for teachers, and other programs in which violence is portrayed.

The above may characterize, more or less, a modal middle-class person in our culture and many "successful" people who regard themselves as productive. There are those among us who have developed truly productive modes of living. However, it can serve a useful purpose to understand the restrictive substratum in our society that is a residual or more fully developed characteristic of much of our American culture. To fail to understand and to accept it, is to continue in patriotic idealization with resultant failure to take corrective steps in our personal and familial living and in needed educational and religious reformulation.

Implications of Cross-Cultural Studies

The foregoing and other studies of culture to be found in anthropological literature provide great "experiments" in the origins of personality. One profoundly important conclusion that can be drawn is this: the manner in which the family meets the child's physical, psychological, and social needs patterns the future shape of his basic personality and the modal social forms that it takes. It is these influences that mold temperament and set the level and direction of the intellectual, emotional, and ideological dimensions of his personality. It is these experiences that provide the general framework for his future choices and avoidances, the manner in which he will express his love and aggression, the people with whom he will identify himself and thus accept or reject, the values that he will espouse, and the ideological patterns with which he will identify himself.

Comparing the Alorese and the Marquesans, we can see the origins of hostility, pride, materialistic values, and thwarted productivity. These and other immature personality characteristics stem directly from the manner in which child is treated during his formative years.

It is important to recognize comparable patterns of parent-child relations in our own culture. It is not often that children experience such extreme treatment, but there are families who, to some degree, reject and abandon their children, treat them inconsistently and harshly, and let their own needs crowd out those of the child. The result can be much the same as among the Alorese or the Marquesans according to the severity of the treatment. By the same token there are families today who resemble those of Plainville. They give their children a good start then allow prudery, unreasonable restriction, and boredom to take over. The product can be anticipated—people of limited vision, stifled intellectual and aesthetic development, mediocrity, and self-centered and excessively sensuous goals.

These people court and marry. Their problem marriages go much deeper than the symptoms of incompatibility on the surface. If we are to develop more widespread capacity for creative marriage we shall have to realize that an essential part of this development will have to take place in the cradle and the nursery. Adults can gain a greater measure of maturity by taking stock of their formative years, accepting their backgrounds, and then setting upon a modified course.

SOCIAL AND EMOTIONAL NEEDS OF THE CHILD[4]

Children, irrespective of culture and basic personality, have certain needs that must be met if they are to survive and develop. The more adequately these needs are met, the greater measure of maturity their personalities will attain. Among the more important are the needs for: early physical stimulation, a feeling of closeness to parental figures, and satisfaction of sensuous requirements; a sense of achievement in the regulation and control of his body and its functions; continuing affection and security about the love of others; exploratory experience; a sense of control and safety in the handling of his emotions, especially his affection and aggression; a sense of the boundaries of permissible behavior; and a feeling of personal adequacy and self-respect. Let us turn now to a consideration of the circumstances necessary for the fulfillment of these needs.

[4] The theoretical position taken here is essentially eclectic, but strongly oriented in the psychoanalytic theory of psychosexual development. As J. L. McCary wrote recently, "Widely varied approaches to the problem of understanding personality have bombarded the literature during the past decade. Although few have withstood careful scrutiny and investigation, several have weathered criticism better than most . . ." Of those that "weathered," six chosen for presentation and critical discussion are by Leopold Bellak, Raymond B. Cattell, George S. Klein, David C. McClelland, Margaret Mead, and Nevitt Sanford and they appear in a recent publication, J. L. McCary (ed.), *Psychology of Personality: Six Modern Approaches,* New York, Logos, 1956. Each of the writers contributing to the symposium, included carefully selected, up-to-date bibliographies on each of the theories of personality presented. See also Charles Brenner, *An Elementary Textbook of Psychoanalysis,* Garden City, Doubleday Anchor, 1957. This comprises Dr. Brenner's course that he is currently giving to psychiatric residents at the Yale Medical School. It is devoted largely to the understanding of the development of personality and deals little with psychopathology.

The Oral Phase

First, the infant and child must be assured of full and satisfying physical experience. Prior to birth the pressure of the mother's body against the fetus provides a feeling of "closeness." The gentle movement of her body constitutes stimulation. Following birth the infant has a need for the continuing feeling of "being held," gentle movement, and a nursing experience in which the arms and legs can push rhythmically against the confining arms of the mother. Nursing thus becomes a *total* physical experience, not a segmental oral experience. Dr. Margaret Ribble found in her research that an infant who has this type of full physical experience takes more oxygen into the blood and learns faster than an infant whose physical needs remained frustrated and unsatisfied.[5]

The satisfaction of the infant's oral needs is primarily a sensuous experience, but also, it is the first social contact of the child. Increasingly he responds to his mother or mother figure as a person, tactually, visually, and verbally. In the manner in which she cares for her child she reflects her deeper attitudes toward him, her pleasure and affirmation of him, or her dissatisfaction and rejection. This is the first "definition" of himself he receives, reflected in the voice, movement, postures, gestures, and other characteristics of his mother. Increasingly their communication becomes less physical and more symbolic, with gestures and words taking the place of physical contact. The physical satisfaction with its overtones of love and affirmation may be thought of as the first cornerstone in the foundation of the child's personality.

[5] See Margaret A. Ribble, *The Rights of Infants,* New York, Columbia University Press, 1943, chap. 2.

The Anal Phase

The second phase of the child's psychosexual development centers around his toilet training experiences. The erogenous zone of the eliminative organs becomes the focus of attention. As was characteristic of the oral phase, there is the building up of tension, evacuation with a mild feeling of pleasure, and then relaxation. Again, it is to be noted that this is not a segmental physical function, but one that involves a total body reaction, including the internal organs (viscera). Gaining of bowel and bladder control, while not as physically close a relationship with another person as nursing, is nevertheless an extended sociopsychological relationship with a parent or parent figure. The infant seems to have an unconscious sense that the products of his body are extensions of himself. Again, the parent is in a crucial position of defining for the child his feelings and later his orientations toward his body and self. The parent who understands and loves her child will have patience and not find the experience unaesthetic. In her manner, tone of voice, etc., she will reflect an "appreciative" attitude toward the child's attempts to coöperate with her expectations. She will affirm him and not make negative references either to the eliminative process or its products. The child will take pride in meeting her expectations, with overtones of self-affirmation. When the child is ill or anxious and exceptions occur and the child soils or wets himself, these exceptions will not be accentuated or singled out as "bad," but will be regarded as normal reactions to stress. The parent who is not aware of the child's needs or one who is anxious, apprehensive, overly orderly, or is unhappy with her child will tend to react in two extreme ways: either become overly attentive, drawing excessive attention to and thus associating guilt and anxiety with toilet training, or find the whole process distasteful and unpleasant, imparting to the child feelings of uncleanliness, unworthiness, and a generalized feeling of negation toward his body and its functions.

The Phallic Phase

The third phase of the child's psychosexual development centers around his discovery of his body, differences between the sexes and the question of "where babies come from." This is an extended period beginning with the "discovery" of his hands and toes which he can manipulate. This discovery is primarily a process of feeling and manipulating the different parts of his body, including his genitals. Little boys are capable of achieving an erect penis and are given to some intermittent manual self-stimulation. Little girls, with their genitals largely hidden within the body, may rub their thighs together and experience a very mild, diffuse, erotic feeling. These are referred to as infantile masturbatory experiences.

Later the child will be interested in the anatomical differences between boys and girls and will seek to satisfy his curiosity by viewing, questioning, comparing with adults, and play in which more extended roles of "doctor" or "nurse" provide the opportunity for further discovery of himself and the opposite sex. The parent is again in an important position where her reactions to this extended chain of events can define the child's role in a way that will be warm and affirming, or will contain some degree of negation, "nastiness," or morbidity. If the parent has an orientation of sex affirmation rather than negation she will understand that this is an important stage of development the child is going through. She will permit the child to express his curiosity, gradually helping him understand that there are personal matters that people confine to the intimacy of the family. Increasingly the meaning of modesty can be communicated. The way the child comes to feel about his body reflects parental attitudes and will determine whether or not he will accept from within, the parental definition of many personal situations involving his intermittent but continued interest in sex throughout his entire formative period.

Men and women who have deeper doubts about their own masculinity or femininity, or persons who harbor orientations of sex negation and even morbidity, can do great and sometimes irreparable harm to the child's psychosexual maturation. The victims of faulty parental treatment may suffer only slightly impaired self-respect and sexual adequacy. Others are so overwhelmed that they remain sexually undeveloped or develop forms of perversion such as displaying themselves (exhibitionism), peeping at others (voyeurism), dressing in the clothes of the opposite sex (transvestism), vesting objects with special devotion (fetishism), and inability to respond sexually (frigidity, impotence).

The manner in which the psychosexual needs of the child are met is important though the details vary and may be quite unimportant. If the child can feel that the parent loves him unconditionally, the child will reflect this orientation toward himself. The conditions for his optimal growth will have been established. As Dr. Samuel Hartwell said in an informal classroom statement years ago, "If you let a child know that you know all about him and still love him while going through these early stages of sexual development, the emotional stability of his future will be assured and he will be strong enough to face anything that life can hand out." Parents might disapprove of a child's acts, impose sanctions, be firm in exacting discipline, and even restrain him. In this instance it is the child's conduct and not his ego or self that is involved. There is no threat of withdrawing love nor implied attack on his integrity.

Some parents, however, are conditional in the extension of their love. They say in effect, "If you do that mommy won't love you," then sulk, and act offended. Those are the wrong stops on the organ and the music can only be sour. Other parents in the name of love are indulgent, failing to understand the profound difference between *indulgence* and *permissiveness*. To act in a manner that allows a child to do anything he pleases, is to deprive the child of the kind of genuine affirmation he needs and to render him insecure. Children want parents to define the boundaries of acceptable behavior even though the parents may permit the child to go beyond these boundaries in testing the limits. To permit a child to learn by his mistakes and regrets, appropriate to his level of maturity, is not to condone what he does. There is abundant research evidence that parental discipline that is *firm but not harsh* has a high correlation with the kind of maturity requisite for successful marriage.

Affection, Aggression, and Possessiveness

It is in the context of the foregoing orientation that we can now best consider the child's need for assistance in regulating and controlling his expression of affection, aggression, and possessiveness. Affection and aggression are at first undifferentiated in the child. We have seen above how they become functionally separated. Very gradually and over a long period of time the child first learns to espouse with his mouth and to bite; to coöperate with his mother at the toilet and "give her a gift," products of his own body, or to aggress by soiling or withholding; display or look at the genitals of another or experience sexual arousal when angry. These infantile forms of affection and aggression are stages of development that the child normally goes through. How his parents meet the child's needs for increasing regulation and control appropriate to the situation is of crucial importance.

Usually we have little difficulty with the demonstration of "affection" as described above, with the possible exception of genital display or curiosity. However, the manner in which the child's aggressive needs are expressed and the parental reaction to them seem to run the gauntlet from uninhibited expression, "sick 'em kid, beat the hell out of him," to the complete smothering of any aggressive tendency under a wet blanket of "loveliness and light." Children will not learn how to handle their aggression unless they are permitted to act out their provocation and learn through successive developmental experiences how to regulate and control it from within. Parents are vulnerable to projecting onto their children their own emotional immaturity and thus err in encouraging the extremes of excessive timidity or hostility and of inconsistent and inappropriate expression of aggression. This will be taken up later in the discussion of emotional maturity.

An important segment of the child's emotional security is bound up with his feelings of "possession." When he receives something new and he especially likes it, he will keep it near him, guard it against possible dispossession, and take it to bed with him. Psychologically it becomes part of him. If he is secure and has been allowed to possess his toy *unconditionally* he will be able to share it, even give it up. If he is insecure, or has learned that what he has will have to be shared before he has felt secure in his possession, he will resent and resist any threatened sharing. The parent, by word and deed, is again in the important position of defining for the child what he may expect and do. Clinicians are dealing constantly with adults who went through this early experience unsuccessfully and are now insecure and unsure of anything that they "love," haunted by a generalized feeling of jealousy, covetousness, and dispossession.

One of the most convincing examples of how early dispossession can affect children can be seen in Balinese culture. The Balinese mother teases her child by pushing it from her breast and taking a neighbor's child to nurse. Her own child then goes into a tantrum which can be so severe that it may result in temporary unconsciousness. As adults the Balinese retain a substratum of emotional instability symbolized in a ritualistic dance in which they attack a "witch," a female figure with large artificial breasts. In the dance they become increasingly violent, aggress against the witch, turn their ceremonial knives against themselves, and then go into a trance. They are brought back to consciousness by an elaborate religious ritual administered by protective male figures.

From the foregoing we can see that the problem of childrens' possessiveness is not a simple, segmental "moral" problem. It is a profoundly complex human relationship expressed throughout all stages of psychosexual development, from the oral to the phallic. Whatever form of coercion a parent might employ to force a child to share or to give up anything—from the mother's breast to a toy—before he is emotionally ready, contributes to the deepest form of generalized insecurity. Moralizing only deepens the child's feelings of guilt. Vague threats of spiritual condemnation can be the most lethal in the arsenal of psychological weapons.

When the child expresses his first curiousity about differences between the male and female body or asks about the origin of babies he does not want detailed adult answers. He needs simple statements given with an attitude of warm approval but not sentimentality. While the mother is stirring up a cake or washing the dishes and the child asks, "Mommy, where did I come from?" the mother can make any one of a number of statements such as, "You grew inside your mommy." Such answers usually suffice for the time being. It must be recognized that genuine sex curiosity seeking more detail may be expressed by the child in this casual manner, with an offhand approach serving to disguise the extent of his interest. However, the sensitive parent will determine the extent of his query and respond appropriately to the child's needs at that particular time. Later, when more detailed questions are asked, the parent can give simple factual answers using a vocabulary that has already become familiar to the child in his bathing, dressing, and toilet activities in the home. Words used to describe the genitals and secondary sex characteristics will already have been used and thus not only be familiar to the child, but will not be emotionally loaded. Prearranged fireside chats in an atmosphere of tense, posed ease will be unnecessary. The child's orientation will grow imperceptibly as part of his general family experience.

Early Sex Education

Boys and girls appreciate a factual orientation with regard to their own bodies and to the opposite sex as well. Illustrated descriptions of the reproductive systems written for different age groups appear in attractive books and schoolroom charts. Such books can be presented to the child along with other favorite books, without special occasion or significance except possibly that of, "Here is something that you will especially enjoy." This writer feels that sentiment toward the "marvelous reproductive system" is appropriate and desirable, but not sentimentality. Children respect a parental attitude of quiet admiration and wonder at any natural process. Giddy self-embarrassment or posed, cloistered awe are quickly sensed and cheapen the parent-child relationship. These times when personal matters are being discussed can result in closer understanding and warmer feelings of confidence between parents and children than more ordinary occasions.

Accompanying discussion of the reproductive systems of males and females and the process of reproduction, boy-girl relations and other aspects of widening personal and social relations can be brought in. At this time elementary discussion of the bases of moral conduct and the reasons behind moral codes can be the subject of many quiet conversations. Moral fear and apprehension gained as part of a floating community orientation (discussions with other children or adults) can be gradually displaced with an understanding of the ethics of consideration and responsibility in one's personal life. The young adolescent will appreciate the parent's confidence expressed in the discussion of the amoral sex practices of some primitive cultures and segments of our own culture. It will give the child a feeling of appreciation for his own values.

Movies showing diagrams of the reproductive systems shown in the schools can provide the bases for discussion in the home. When these are films that have been prepared by reputable agencies, rather than some of the lurid commercials that have been shown, and are accompanied by the leadership of trained teachers, parents have strongly favored their use. There are some parents who object to reputable sex education on the ground that "those things were just not talked about in my day," or "such discussions will encourage young people to experiment." Those parents seem unwilling to accept the fact that most children get their basic "facts" from other children before entering the first grade in school. The question is not whether young children should receive sex education. They will receive it one way or another. Rather, the question is whether we should leave sex education to the 5- and 10-year-olds, or whether it should be undertaken by the home, the school, and the church. To take any other stand is to leave it to the barnyard and the gutter.

Definition of Sex Roles

One of the most important aspects of sex orientation is the emerging definition of the child's larger sex role, masculinity or femininity. It is desirable that boys should come to identify themselves with their masculine fathers, symbolized by the respect they reflect toward their own genitals. Likewise girls who identify themselves with their feminine mothers take on and accept their own femininity. In all cultures these generalized sex roles are among the most important determinants of personal and social relations, and provide the bases for feelings of social acceptance and well-being. Where boys develop girls' roles and vice versa, it is usually indicative of weak parent-child identifications, with insecure, rejecting, and unstable feelings on the part of the child toward his parents. When parents cannot invite, by weight of their own masculinity or femininity, the identification of the child of their own sex, the child should have other heroes in fiction and reality. This identification of the child with the parent cannot be commanded or indoctrinated. It must come as a product of emotional acceptance, companionship, and confidence. Parents who encourage the "cute" opposite sex identifications of their children's roles may be impairing desirable identifications. Children naturally identify themselves with the parent of the same sex after the period of early childhood if the parent does not drive the child into a counteridentification by faulty action. No such problem is involved in emotionally healthy families.

The foregoing is not meant to imply the strict segregation of masculine and feminine roles as overt activities, but more as attitudes of self-regard and a manner of acting. Actually, there is no strict line of male-female demarcation in human personality. All men have physiological, social, and psychological feminine components in their personalities. The strength of the opposite-sex component differs in different men. The same is true of women. They have masculine components in their personalities which vary with the individual. A hereditary factor is involved, probably of endocrine origin, but the developmental factor seems to be of greater significance in the majority of people, and seems to be related to differences in basic personality.

One of the tasks of maturing is to come to know and to accept one's own psychosexual makeup. From this clinician's point of view the problem of men with a rather large feminine component in their personalities is not the strength of the feminine but the relative weakness of the masculine. Some men have strength in both components. They are often persons of psychosexual "versatility." They have a broader range of reaction patterns than others as a result of being high in two or three of the components of basic personality. It has been said of the late President Franklin D. Roosevelt that the "maternal" in his personality was a quality of great personal and political significance. However, he was capable of behavior that would meet the criterion of the "most masculine" in our culture.

There has been much needless worry on the part of men of unquestionable masculinity about the feminine component. They cannot accept and turn to good use the feminine latent in their personalities. The same is true of many girls and women who, as children, have been chided for their tomboy activities. Many truly feminine women have painfully and needlessly denied the active, assertive B-component in their basic personalities.

There is much evidence that our culture is moving rapidly to a position of thinking about men and women not in terms of traditional masculinity-femininity, but in terms of individual differences in basic personality. In the past a lady was supposed to be a thinly veiled, delicate, deferent inhabitant of some out-of-reach tower. Men were supposed to be buckled in heavy armour and ready to charge at one another on fiery steeds. With two world wars in which women went into heavy production work, and the rapid movement toward urbanization, a vast change has taken place in a relatively short period of time. Today the football hero is pictured in his campus apartment cooking and changing the baby. Women with the temperament inclinations have taken their rightful place in factories, offices, and executive positions. The women in the Cabinet today occupy central "manpower" positions in government.

A healthy psychosexual attitude is not only a matter of early experience but one of adult orientation. Faulty and antiquated assumptions about this very important aspect of personality have been an unnecessary burden on many persons and their marriages, for they have prevented them from achieving greater self-realization and thus from developing greater range and depth of their potential human capacities.

ILLUSTRATIVE CASES

In the writer's experience two former students, both intelligent and talented, came from two dramatically different homes. The psychosexual development of Sue and Karl were different with different results in the social and emotional substrata of the two personalities.

Sue

Sue's family lived in a small city. Her father owned and operated a prosperous business. He was a quiet, mild-mannered man. Her mother was an active, energetic, and dominant woman. She participated outside the home extensively in community activities. Sue was followed by a brother three years younger. The family was not close in shared activities or emotional ties. Her parents had little in common. The only shared family activity was its weekly attendance at church which was regarded by all of them as more a duty than a pleasure.

One of Sue's earliest memories concerned her feeling of rejection by her mother who found no time to do "little" things with Sue. Her mother left Sue a great deal with a housekeeper who paid little attention to Sue except to prevent her from playing with the boys of the neighborhood. Sue felt rejected, lonesome, and "trapped." She reacted with aggression toward authority with resultant feelings of guilt often bordering on panic. The older people in Sue's life harped on her "keeping herself neat and clean like little girls ought to do."

Sue was punished harshly for disobeying her mother and the maid. She stole out to play with the boys. Her mother called her a "dirty, selfish, naughty girl." She felt that she had been "branded forever." Sue was high in native intelligence, but was failing in school. She dropped books, whispered, and was noncoöperative with the teacher (another woman). The teacher called her down and gave some of Sue's art work to another child. Sue retaliated by stealing over to an abandoned street and "going to the toilet there, where I imagined that a policeman saw me." She suffered feelings of guilt and generalized aggression toward any authority (mother, teacher, and the law).

With the onset of adolescence Sue resented, resisted, and unconsciously half denied the fact that she was a girl. Outward aggression subsided and she increasingly withdrew into her books and listening to phonograph records. She kept company with a sole girl friend and confidant, becoming more and more withdrawn from social reality. She did not understand her unresolved conflict and her unhappiness continued.

After graduation from high school, Sue entered college. Conflict, unhappiness, and social withdrawal continued. She received only passing grades, though she was capable of very superior work. Sue registered in several classes that gave her some understanding of her early feelings of rejection and her rebellion against authority in general and women in particular. Her understanding served to diminish her anxiety and hostility.

During a visit home from school, Sue's mother confided a "prolonged illness" her father had suffered that had stood in the way of her parents' marital happiness. Her mother regretted that she had spent so much time escaping from home and that she had failed to be a companion to Sue. With continued understanding of her early social and emotional development, Sue's aggression was gradually replaced by pity for her mother and then compassion. Her school work improved markedly. Her interest in boys which had not expressed itself before began to develop.

At the time of the last contact Sue was out of college, efficient in a job, and was looking forward to a productive future with self-confidence and a feeling of heightened morale.

Karl

Karl, at the time of relating his life story, was 16 years old and a sophomore honor student in college. His family was made up of his parents, both of whom were pursuing professions, and a younger brother. The family was emotionally very close and coöperative. They were troubled with problems, but united in meeting and solving their difficulties. Karl's maternal grandmother lived in the household and was accepted by all.

Karl's early health and life expectancy were very poor. Utmost care was exercised with him. His mother discontinued her work outside the home in order to assume Karl's full care despite the fact that they had a full-time maid. Consideration and understanding on the part of the mother was shown in his early care. Because of Karl's illness he had difficulty in not wetting the bed. When his mother noticed that he was worried about it, she placed an attractive picture of a gold fish above the bed so that he could blame the fish. (It is to be noted that there is danger in permitting or assisting a child to blame another for his own limitations, thereby avoiding personal responsibility for his own acts. This device should be used with caution and an awareness of its results.)

Karl was too ill to play outside his home. His mother selected books about rugged, adventuresome boys of Karl's age, with whom he could identify himself, avoiding roles of passivity and dependency. His mother spent much time telling him interesting stories. Karl's parents did not moralize directly, but provided toy soldiers who in play, were named, given courageous roles, assigned moral qualities, and encountered interesting fictional as well as historical situations. Karl's first interest in peoples of other lands, history, great epochs, was generated and sustained in this engaging play.

Karl's parents provided him with many toys. He was allowed possession and control over them. Later he was generous in sharing them. Understanding and regard for his emotional attachment to his toys was shown by his mother when she bought two identical stuffed rabbits so that when one was sent to the cleaner, it could be replaced by the other and Karl would not have to miss it even for an evening (he took it to bed with him).

When Karl was about five his parents introduced formal learning, lessons in French. They insisted kindly but firmly that he do his lessons each day, and well. No excuse was accepted for failure to do his work. Karl accepted duty with interest and initial wonder at his parents' firmness. His grandmother helped him with his work by motivating him with stories about French personalities and history and French songs.

Though Karl's father was in ill health, he participated increasingly in his companionship and rearing. His father treated him with adult regard in the company of friends and colleagues. Karl was proud of his father's attitude toward him in these "manful" situations.

When Karl entered school he went directly into the fourth grade where he remained at the head of his class. He loved school, his teachers, his elders, and even wanted to study on Saturdays. Karl was active in student affairs and was elected honorary captain of the football team because of his interest though he could not play. He developed a keen sense of humor, with spontaneous, outgoing interest in everything and everybody he contacted.

Karl expressed a deeply spiritual quality without evidence of fanaticism or intolerance. He placed less emphasis on the institutional aspects of religion, though he enjoyed the "beauty of the music and the ritual," but was given to long discussions of ethical relations among people. He enjoyed church attendance despite long services held in a large, unheated cathedral, where mass often lasted six hours.

The following quotation from his autobiography is characteristic of his outlook on life. "I am aware of many of my limitations, but I think that my good qualities include a love of and ability for study and play, and my ability to adjust myself to different persons and situations without undue stress. I have traveled extensively and like all places that I have been and all peoples I have come to know. I conclude with a statement of beliefs. I have a deep faith in the essential goodness of man, the church and its morals. I'm a democrat and an optimist."

When the writer last heard from Karl he was 19 years old. He had finished college and one year of graduate work, was fluent in five languages, and was serving in an Americal Intelligence Division somewhere in Central Europe in World War II.

Chapter 4

SEX AND PERSONALITY

SEXUAL FULFILLMENT is a universally pursued goal. In Western civilization and some other parts of the world the genital expression of sex has evolved from a form of primordal impregnation to a highly developed form of emotional, intellectual, aesthetic, and social experience—a relationship in which the simple biological function is vested with the deepest feelings and intellectual overtones. Sex is one of the deepest forms of self-other affirmation and has become especially important in contemporary living because of the impersonality and fragmentation of so much of our social life. So much of anyone's workaday life is carried on in urban anonymity, that sex has become one of the few forms of intimacy experienced by a great many persons.

As a culture we have striven to rid ourselves of the shackles of sex negation handed down by our Victorian forebears. Many couples have achieved an orientation of sex affirmation and the ability to abandon themselves to a deep psychophysical experience with overtones of continuing satisfaction and personal "renewal." Others have not, and have been damaged to some extent in their capacity for deeper, heterosexual, monogymous sex expression. The latter constitute a large enough group in our society to stand as a commentary on a great contemporary need, as we shall see in the light of recent research.

One of the stumbling blocks in achieving greater sexual maturity is not the lingering sex negation or that the subject is not socially acceptable. Many young people can discuss sex in mixed groups with a feeling of social discretion and appropriateness. The word *sex* is in good taste on radio and television. Public schools are offering sex education on all levels from the primary grades up. Rather, our problem lies in our bounded orientation that sex is a physical, segmental experience involving reproduction, while failing to understand the manifold nature of sex in human personality.

SEX AS A MEDIUM OF COMMUNICATION

The erogenous zones of the body may serve a variety of functions. We recognize as we have seen in the preceeding chapter, that one can employ the mouth, teeth, and lips to obtain, masticate, and convey food to the stomach—an eating function. Another oral function that has nothing whatever to do with eating is that of espousing with the lips, kissing, biting—a psychosexual function, with its overtones of interpersonal closeness or hostility. Still another is the verbal communication function of speech. It is of note that while these are oral functions their separate purposes could be carried out without involving the oral region. One could be fed intravenously, caress or strike with the hand, and communicate through writing. In one sense, none of these

obtaining
pursuit Bell
eating
kiss of affirmation or death

has anything to do with the mouth. *They are expressions of the total personality,* meeting survival, psychosexual, and social needs.[1]

Applying this orientation of the *separate* functions of the erogenous zones of the body to the genital zone, we can understand that elimination, reproduction, and psychosexual communication fulfill distinct and different needs involving the total person. These do not have to be met through the use of the genitals. Artificial insemination and Caesarean section delivery are well known. Other parts of the body can be sensitized and respond orgastically to sensuous stimulation, as in the case of masochism—sexual excitation while experiencing pain.

As man has evolved, his primitive survival needs which are satisfied through the functions of the erogenous zones of his body, have taken on increasingly separate and refined functions. Primitive devouring has little in common with a well-appointed dinner, with its emotional, intellectual, aesthetic, and social overtones. Primitive "herd mating" is indeed different from the complex "communication" that takes place between two sensitive and differentiated people in a sexual embrace.

The way is now clear for us to think of sex as a psychophysical relationship in which the deepest meaning of which man is capable is being communicated, even when the "other" is not present but carried in the imagination. "Meaning" is not used here in any articulate, verbal sense of the term, but as that which is conveyed through the senses. For example, one may *speak* of bereavement or of love, but the

[1] See the psychoanalytic literature dealing with the psychosexual development of personality. Charles Brenner, *Psychoanalysis,* Garden City, Doubleday Anchor, 1957, pp. 16–62; Margaret A. Ribble, *The Rights of Infants,* New York, Columbia University Press, pp. 83 ff.

Sex never begins & never ends in healthy people.
Sex goes into old age.

depth of the *experience* of mourning or of caressing a loved one transcends any verbal statement. Sex, then, is a medium through which anything that man is capable of experiencing is communicated to and vested in another, ranging from the most "positive" to the most "negative" emotions with their ideational overtones. "But what," one may ask, "just what is communicated?" This writer would have to answer, "It is comparable to, if not the same as, that which is communicated through any aesthetic medium or social experience." Let us look at some examples. What is the import of a polonaise? The writer or the performer is portraying the heights and depths of human striving, as in the case of Chopin—the nostalgia for his native Poland, identification with his fatherland, extolling of her virtues, remorse in leaving, faith in her destiny, hope for her preservation. Sibelius put his total personality into Finlandia, an esoteric identity with what his native Finland meant to him. One cannot view the sculpture of Thorwaldsen without sensing some of what he felt toward women, children, and religious figures; a Bach chorale gives evidence of his spiritual serenity. Havelock Ellis wrote about an experience he had. On one occasion when he had not been thinking about sex and had in no way been physically stimulated or aroused, he experienced a spontaneous sexual orgasm in response to a particularly meaningful thought that he had just read.

Just as the most noble feelings and thoughts may be expressed through sex, so may the most ignoble—forms of jealousy, hostility, exploitation, and even the taking of another's life. Rape-murder stands as a dramatic example of the sexual expression of hostility.

Let us look at some of the more common meanings that a sexual act can have—expressions of the self with deeper emotional, intellectual, aesthetic import. In addition to common meanings held, there may be other more esoteric meanings determined in part by differences in basic personality and sociocultural background. The sex act can be:

An expression of devotion, affirmation of the self-other, and tender care.

A coin to buy affection, protection, or something from another.

A way of reducing tension, serving as a pacifier.

An expression of the buoyant, the frivolous, or the ecstatic.

An expression of sympathy and pity.

A mode of pursuit, conquest, adventure.

A weapon to hurt, withhold from, make jealous, get even with, or defile another.

A way of seeking emotional self-assurance.

An expression of anxiety, compulsive fear, or need for punishment.

An expression of reckless bravado.

A substitute reliving of a previous experience.

An expression of bereavement.

Ad infinitum, the expression of any *feeling with its attendant meaning* that a person is capable of expressing.

SEX ORIENTATIONS AND PRACTICES IN AMERICA

Premarital[2]

Following the relatively quiet latency period, with the onset of adolescence there is a renewed interest in sex and

[2] The composite picture of sex orientations and practices in the United States is made up of research conclusions drawn from many sources, but primarily the following: Ernest W. Burgess and Paul Wallin, *Engagement and Marriage,* New York, Lippincott, 1953; Alfred C. Kinsey, Wardell B. Pomeroy, and Clyde E. Martin, *Sexual Behavior in the Human Male,*

sexual activity. If the boy has not continued his early masturbation he may begin again coincident with the onset of nocturnal emissions. Less supervised boys will tend to practice some group forms of displaying their genitals or masturbate together in the group while making comparisons of their genitals. During the early part of this *gang* (group) stage, continued interest in sex is manifest in group discussions and more confidential discussions with a close friend or pal. A more serious interest in the opposite sex begins. Group dating is often begun at this time when boys and girls will have parties and go out together in groups of two or more couples.

By the age of 16 the average boy in our society will have established a frequency of sex outlet that will tend to prevail for the next several decades in his life. The average middle-class boy will continue to masturbate a given number of times a week or month. During this period of later adolescence he becomes increasingly expressive with each of a number of girls he dates, moving from lighter to heavier forms of physical intimacy. Some confine their expression of affection to kissing and hugging. Others go on from necking to heavy petting. Still others go further and experience mutual orgasm by some means of close physical or digital stimulation. About one-half to two-thirds of our middle-class men have premarital intercourse, depending on the segment

---

Philadelphia, Saunders, 1948; Alfred C. Kinsey, Wardell B. Pomeroy, and Clyde E. Martin, *Sexual Behavior in the Human Female,* Philadelphia, Saunders, 1953. Two excellent evaluations of the Kinsey reports are: Donald Porter Geddes and Enid Curie (eds.), *About the Kinsey Report, Observations by 11 experts on "Sexual Behavior in the Human Male,"* New York, Signet, 1948; Karl M. Bowman, M.D., Spurgeon English, M.D., Manfred S. Guttmacher, M.D., Alfred C. Kinsey, Sc.D., Karl Menninger, M.D., and Norman Reider, M.D., Robert W. Laidlaw, M.D., Moderator, "Psychiatric Implications of Surveys on Sexual Behavior," *The Psychoanalytic Review,* XLIII, No. 4 (October, 1956).

of our culture from which they come. Of those who do, the majority have sexual intercourse with their future spouse only, usually during the engagement period. The promiscuous person is relatively infrequent, as is the homosexual.

Males of our lower-income groups differ markedly from middle-income males in sexual expectation and practice. The implications of these differences for courtship and marriage are of great importance as will be seen in Chapter 9. In general, lower-education-income boys are less protected in their early experimentation with sex. They go through a briefer period of masturbation. A large proportion enter into sexual intercourse at an earlier age than middle-class boys. They tend to regard protracted sexual preliminaries (petting) as being "off color," somewhat perverse. They are more immediate and direct in their advances. A very high proportion of lower-class men report having had premarital intercourse. Kinsey found some "100 percent communities" in which every adult male interviewed in those communities reported that he had had premarital sex relations.

In striking contrast to these different orientations and practices of boys, girls of different social classes do not show the same differences in development and expression of their genital sexuality. The average girl becomes awakened later. She may masturbate more or less frequently, but in the average instance does not. When left sexually unawakened and unstimulated she tends to have feelings of arousal that lead to masturbation about once every three weeks, usually just before, or less frequently just after menstruation. She may and most frequently does enjoy physical closeness as in dancing or necking but remains relatively unawakened. Her sexuality is much less genital, thus less direct and much more diffuse, with the other erogenous zones of her body maintaining lower-level, diffuse sensitivity as compared with the boy. However, this is only before sexual awakening. Just about half of our middle-class girls remain virginal. The other half have premarital intercourse but the majority have it only with their future spouse and usually during the engagement period. Promiscuity among American middle-class women is indeed much lower than many women themselves think, and strikingly less in fact than many men would have one believe, judging by the number of scalps they wear around their psychological belts displayed during their frequent bull sessions.

Differences in the sex orientations and practices of women as compared with men seem to be due to nature and to nurture. In the first place the areas of her body other than the genitals seem to be more sensitive than those of the male, resulting in a greater diffusion of sensitivity. Secondly, her genitals are largely hidden and thus are not as subject to direct stimulation as are his which are nearly entirely outside the body and thus subject to direct as well as localized stimulation. Recent gynecological research indicates that much of the woman's potential physical sensitivity lies in the musculature surrounding the vagina rather than as previously assumed in the clitoris or in the linings of the vagina. Research indicates that these vaginal muscles do not become activated as a natural process of maturation, but as a matter of education, that is, through the proper kind of stimulation. And last, but by no means least, a woman's responsiveness and sex practices seem to be affected not only by the general cloistering in her formative experience, but also by her religious background.

These profound differences in the sexuality of men and women need to be more widely understood, not only as guides to premarital behavior, but for their import in marriage. This will be taken up in the chapters on courtship.

It is interesting to note that one of the most important determining factors in the sex orientation and behavior of both men and women is religious background. However, the differences in what people do are greater within any one of our major religions than it is between the major religious groups. For example, considering the Protestants, Catholics, and Jews, it is found that sexual activity of Orthodox Jews is slightly less than that of either of the two other orthodox and religiously active groups. However, the differences among the three faiths were small and of little statistical significance. Of the religiously inactive, however, the Jewish were most active sexually, with the Catholics and Protestants following in that order. Thus activity or inactivity and degree of orthodoxy in one's religion seems to be one of the decisive factors in the sexual activity of persons, not whether one is a Protestant, Catholic, or Jew.

The foregoing is not intended to be a treatment of the relation between religion and sex expression. It is cited in order to illustrate the profound influence of sociocultural experience on what is so often regarded as a strictly biological phenomenon.

Sex in Marriage

Up to this point we have discussed only some of the premarital aspects of sexual development and expression. Let us continue on into marriage, leaving other aspects of the problem until later.

Upon entry into marriage virtually all males are capable of intromission and orgasm, whereas most females take some time to become sexually awakened and achieve orgasm. For some it is a matter of weeks or months, for others—between 25 and 40 percent of American women—responsiveness ranges from mild to moderate to complete nonresponsiveness. About three-fourths of American women experience orgasm during coitus. This rather marked difference between men and women in orgasm capacity seems to be partly due to the stricter rearing of women and partly due to the greater complexity of their entire genital system. The woman needs the right kind of stimulation to respond, which is much less the case with the man, but which depends a great deal on him.

After marriage the marked differences in typical frequencies of outlet between men and women changes, and she moves up to his premarital frequency of several outlets per week. This transition for her is usually made without difficulty. However, the typical male desires intercourse more frequently than the woman during the earlier years of marriage. This pattern continues with some, but not great diminution of frequency of outlet for many years. The average woman comes into her fullest sex maturity about 10 to 13 years later than the average male.

It is an interesting fact that American men experience a gradual diminution of their sex drive as the years go on, but many women do not. A significant proportion of women actually experience greater desire after menopause. We do not know precisely why, since her endocrine system undergoes so much greater change with the ending of her fertility, but part of the answer seems to lie in two facts: her gradual change of orientation with sexual experience from negation to affirmation, and less fear of pregnancy. Perhaps such other factors as the relative abandon and leisure with the children reared, greater financial security, etc., enter in.

A great many couples continue to express themselves sexually far into old age. Young people are often surprised to learn that many old people are nearly as active as they were during their middle years. This is a fact that should make all of us more sensitive to the loss of one's mate and the loneliness of old age, which is in part a sexual loss not to be underestimated in the lives of elderly people.

There is abundant evidence that the loss of sexual capacity, whether earlier or later in life, is due much more to one's attitude than to physiological changes. For many people sex is never lost. For others its loss is welcomed, and this attitude probably has played an important part in causing it to pass.

One conclusion that seems warranted from the recent research is that men and women are not as different in their sexual responsiveness or the speed of their arousal, as has been commonly believed. Now, and note the qualification carefully, *when a man and a woman have developed their fuller sexual capacities,* the length of time it takes to be aroused and to achieve orgasm is about the same in women as in men, that is, women are not necessarily slower to respond or less ardent. There is some evidence that they may respond more deeply, since many women experience several orgasms during a single coital engagement and about 3 percent actually swoon, momentarily losing consciousness.

The reason why so many people assume that there are such striking differences between men and women in the time it takes to become aroused and in orgasm adequacy, is probably immaturity and/or ignorance. It seems that less mature men tend to be faster and less responsive women slower to respond, and thus, because of their personal experience which is widespread in our culture, they have generalized about many others for whom this does not obtain. It must be said that it is not entirely a matter of maturity, but also of health and freedom from emotional pressures which have a direct bearing on sexual responsiveness.

Though men and women are not necessarily different in the speed of their responsiveness, the time that it takes to reach orgasm, and orgasm adequacy, there is evidence that they are different in their respective interest in and capacity for psychological stimulation. In the first place women are able to go for longer periods without coitus than men. Men are stimulated and, in our society, bombarded by a wide range of direct stimuli that seem to have relatively little effect on women. Furthermore, men seem to be aroused by thinking about sex to a much greater degree than women are.

In Kinsey's study of differences between male and female responsiveness to psychological stimulation, he found that of 33 types of directly erotic psychological stimulation, all were directly stimulating to men, but only 2 of the 33 were directly stimulating to women. Here are some examples: Is a woman as stimulated seeing a man in the nude as he is seeing her in the nude? The answer is no. Pornographic stories, nude drawings, seeing the genitals of the opposite sex, hearing erotic stories, etc., have little direct influence on arousing women erotically. The 2 exceptions out of the 33 studied, were the viewing of motion pictures and the reading of "literary materials" in which love is portrayed, and sex is an indirect and romantic part of a broader social and psychological relationship.

Kinsey concluded that women were less subject to psychological stimulation than men, but this conclusion is not necessarily warranted by the evidence he found. Rather, women may be as responsive, but in a different way. Putting it a little differently, men are stimulated more by sex as sex, in the genital sense of the term and women are stimulated more by personal affirmation, romance, and love.

It is very important to understand this difference. How much more could men and women appreciate one another if they knew that their capacities for sexual responsiveness are not unequal, but that the pathways to arousal as well as its meaning may be quite different. Such understanding could lead to greater consideration and care, with overtones of deeper and more meaningful relationships.

Let us consider briefly extramarital relations. Widows and widowers appear to have sex relations in a pattern and frequency more like that of married than unmarried persons, with widowers having more outlets than widows. This does not necessarily mean that they are more ardent. It may mean that it is easier for a man to take the initiative and that there is more opportunity for him than for a widow.

With married men, there seems to be quite a difference between the male of a grade-school education and the college-level male. The grade-school male is, as described earlier, quite promiscuous in his premarital behavior. Marriage cuts down but does not eliminate other women. Then, there is a gradual decrease of extramarital intercourse until around the age of 40, when intercourse with anyone but the spouse is almost completely eliminated.

In contrast, the college-level male is more likely to be virginal when married and to eliminate other contacts outside marriage for a number of years. At about 35 or 40 extramarital intercourse begins for those who enter into it and from then on there is a smaller proportion of total outlets with the wife. By the age of 55 the average college-level male has 62 percent of his total sex outlet with his wife, while the grade-school male is likely to have almost 100 percent.

So much then for what different groups of American men and women appear to be doing, as judged by our most recent and reputable research. We have tried to remain descriptive up to this point, to turn on the light before the heat. However, this writer does not believe that we can leave these considerations on a descriptive level and we must move on to an valuative level. We are committed to try to make some kind of sense out of these findings and move on in search of a solution to the problems where they exist.

IN QUEST OF MEANING[3]

Interpretation of the foregoing results of current research must be undertaken with thoughtful consideration and studied caution. There is no longer any question about whether or not young adults will have access to the current sex literature. That is already an accomplished fact. Digests of these materials are available in several editions at most drug stores or newsstands. Virtually every reputable magazine in the country has carried articles on the sex life of the American male and female. The problem now is to assist young adults (and some older ones!) in their interpretation of the meaning these studies hold as well as other studies now being reported.

[3] See Geddes and Curie, *op. cit.;* Morris Fishbein and Ruby Jo Reeves Kennedy (eds.), *Modern Marriage and Family Living,* New York, Oxford University Press, 1957; Lester A. Kirkendall and Curtis E. Avery, "Ethics and Interpersonal Relationships," issued by the E. C. Brown Trust, Portland, Oregon (mimeographed); Abram Kardiner, *Sex and Morality,* New York, Bobbs-Merrill, 1954; *Faith, Sex, and Love,* National Student Council of the YMCA and YWCA, 1954.

First, one must distinguish between three concepts: the *norm,* the *normal,* and the *ideal.* The *norm* is an average characterizing the "typical" in a given class or group. It is statistically derived and describes what *is* without reference to whether it is good, bad, or indifferent. The *normal* is an expression of a practical ideal which assumes the absence of the pathological. The *ideal* is a theoretical standard of "perfection," which in many instances is a goal to be pursued without expecting to attain it.

Now if we assume, as a great many professional people working in the field of marriage and the family do, that recent studies of sex behavior made by reputable researchers are approximately true (valid), then we may take the norms that they present as describing what different classes of American men and women do. But whether or not these norms of behavior are normal, that is, represent practical ideals, is an entirely different question. This writer and many of his colleagues believe that our sex norms are far from normal. There is no question that they are not ideal. There is too much unnecessary frigidity and impotency, homosexuality, intersex hostility, and other evidence of general psychosexual immaturity, to mention only a few of the more apparent sexual aberrations on the American scene.

To state the case a little differently, there has been a tragic loss of creative energy in our culture due to our inability to utilize more fully our sexual capacities. An essentially negative attitude toward sex has served to reduce to medocrity the talents and motivation of many people. It has resulted in an overwhelming amount of emotional stress that comes out in the disguised forms of physical illness. Some persons are only slightly affected with what amount to psychological head colds. Others are more seriously disabled in their work with symptoms of diminished energy, impaired motivation, restless striving, and the need for excessive emotional stimulation such as excessive drinking, gambling, and so on.

Our culture is confronted with the problem of recognizing and developing ways of utilizing the creative role that sex can play in human personality. We shall have to recognize that the role of sex in human personality is vastly more complex than in the subhuman primates, that it has evolved into a complex pattern of love-making with profound overtones of meaning and significance. The mating of two human beings is no more like the mating of lower animals than a well-appointed dinner is like the gorging of one animal on the other. As a culture we have developed our need for food into a highly aesthetic and social experience. At the same time we have left sex with its tremendous potentialities, at best undeveloped as an art. At worst, it still remains vulgar or even morbid. Lawrence Frank writes:

> We Western people, in our endeavor to bring some order and give some meaning to our lives, have not been very effective in utilizing this potentiality of human sexuality as productively as it might be utilized for human living. Some of our very high aspirations have been blocked and defeated by our inability to present to children and youth a conception of the role and place of sex that is compatible with these aspirations. The aspirations toward stable marriage, toward recognition of the worth of individual personality, or respect for the dignity of man and also of women and of children, have often been frustrated by these ancient beliefs about sex as nasty, low, and evil. They exist in our traditions and are being taught to our children and youth. We've all been exposed to them. Some of us have suffered from them in our childhood. I submit that we are all more or less confused and perplexed and often acutely disturbed over the question of the meanings and significance of human sexuality and how to use it productively. This is a question which gives all of us great concern. It is a question which will be answered

only if we have the courage and wisdom to critically reevaluate some of the traditional and outmoded patterns, rules, and regulations which interfere with the constructive utilization of sex as an expression of personal and social wishes.[4]

A host of professional people—clinicians, theologians, scholars, social workers, and others—have been interested in the questions: What are the sexual norms of different segments of our culture? What is normal? What is ideal sexual behavior? There seems to be a great deal more agreement among these various students of sexual ethics on what the norms are and what is ideal, than on the question of normal orientations and behavior. And, while these crucial questions are far from settled in the thinking of a great many conscientious people, it seems that one conclusion is warrented. *Normal sex behavior is being thought of more in terms of consideration, care, and responsibility in one's sexual expression than in terms of specific acts of behavior that all people ought to adhere to.* As a culture we seem to be moving toward the position that there are great differences in the individual needs of different persons who are living under strikingly different social and cultural circumstances. Consequently, since sex is an expression of the total personality, people will express themselves differently according to mode of expression, frequency, kind of partner, and circumstance. This is not to assume sexual anarchy and irresponsibility any more than to assume sexual authoritarianism with its expected conformity to a single standard; but, sexual democracy in which individuals and couples feel free to discover that which will enhance their whole mode of living. In this democracy, the sexual athlete and the sexual monastic would not seek to impose their views upon each other.

[4] Lawrence K. Frank, "Sex as an Expression of Personal and Social Values," *Pastoral Psychology,* February, 1953. See also Lester A. Kirkendall, *Sex Education as Human Relations,* New York, Inor, 1950.

From this writer's view, professional people in the marriage field seem to know more about sexual immaturity and abnormality than they know about different patterns of behavior that meet our "workable ideals." The recent past has witnessed the filtering down of the subject of sex from the cloisters and clinics to the living rooms of a vastly increasing number of people. The great debate is very much in session and in the open for millions of Americans as well as the people of traditionally conservative countries like England. Our clinical knowledge of "what won't work" has helped define and clarify many problems concerning sexual practices. Present and future research will undoubtedly contribute to our knowledge of what sex orientations and practices are related to the most healthful and productive personality.

During the "great debate" about sex, some young adults may be inclined to assume that the wisdom of the past has now been abrogated, that the "lid is off." They will assume roles of self-appointed pioneers. Some will end up as driftwood on the moral beachhead. Some may survive to point up new paths to a fuller life. Some may push the frontiers to the limits of experimental space and, discovering nothing better, return to the homestead of traditional Western sexual ideology. It seems apparent that many of their elders cannot or would not stop those who refuse to accept our present mores. However, every young person can be challenged to ask himself just where he stands and to consider more seriously than many are now doing just what course they intend to steer. This would tend to reduce the number of people who drift naïvely or aimlessly into their future sex life and would tend to reduce the number of persons who refuse to face up to these important issues because of anxiety and fear.

Chapter 5

EMOTIONAL MATURITY

THE QUEST for the meaning of emotional maturity has been implicit in the writings of theologians, philosophers, poets, practitioners of the healing arts, and a host of others since the beginning of Graeco-Judaic reflections on the meaning of life. And, whether it is Plato describing the philosopher king in the Republic, Anatole France chiding the immature citizens of Penguin Island, or a modern psychiatrist writing about *Love Against Hate,*[1] the quest for the meaning and articulation of maturity is quite evident.

It would be presumptuous to assume that we have now arrived at the fullest meaning of the concept *emotional maturity,* because any concept is limited by the social, psychological, and cultural circumstances out of which it grows. Succeeding generations may develop a concept of maturity as different from the present one as the present one is from

[1] Karl A. Menninger, *Love Against Hate,* New York, Harcourt Brace, 1942.

the Victorian. However, certain assumptions about the mature person have withstood the tests of time, scholarly pursuit, and clinical experience. Perhaps the foremost of these is the assertion that the mature person is capable of regarding the welfare of another as he regards his own. Variations of this idea are found in the great religious literatures of the world as well as in the contemporary writing of our psychiatrists.[2]

With modest caution, then, we can attempt to describe some of the facets of the emotionally mature personality, as they have been conceived in "ideal" (theoretical) form in sacred and secular literature, research in the behavioral sciences, and clinical experience.

In the realm of values we have no ultimate board of appeals, although some religious groups have set up absolute standards. Any writer's conception of the mature person must necessarily be distorted to some degree by his *own* intellectual provincialism and emotional immaturity. The concept of maturity expressed here is based largely, though not entirely, on a *clinical* point of view—theory and experience—with all of the fallacies inherent in any partial frame of reference.

CHARACTERISTICS OF EMOTIONAL MATURITY

The highest expression of emotional maturity is the *act* with its attendant feelings and orientations of regarding the welfare, dignity, inviolability, importance, and growth of the self and of others as the highest good. Another individual is vested with one's own feeling that life has purpose and that it

[2] See the Presidential Address of Robert G. Foster given before the National Council on Family Relations, East Lansing, Michigan, 1953 (mimeographed).

is fundamentally worthwhile.[3] This orientation might be regarded as the matrix from which the substantive characteristics of maturity emerge. These characteristics will be discussed separately later in this chapter.

Before going any further, we should be clear about the use of the phrases "emotional maturity" and "the emotionally mature person." They are theoretical constructs representing goals toward which persons may strive, rather than goals possible of attainment. As a preponderantly Christian culture we hold the Sermon on the Mount as an ethic we have been working toward for two thousand years. However, we do not presume to have attained it as a social reality. When referring to the maturity of a person we should speak of him as "more mature," i.e., having attained a greater measure of maturity than others with whom he might be compared without assuming that he has achieved "it." The belief that the purpose of life is to work toward the achievement of greater and greater maturity is compatible with the assumption that human personality is ever growing, changing, and emerging toward unknowable ends.

Range, Variation, and Flexibility of Emotional Expression

The mature person is capable of experiencing a range and variety of emotional expression. He can live the whole (normal) range of emotion from pathos to joy, anger to succor. He is emotionally expressive. Such a person has the ability to take the emotional roles of a "wide range" of others. This will be discussed later as an aspect of empathy.

[3] Erich Fromm, *Man For Himself*, New York, Rinehart, 1947, pp. 231–232; Harry Stack Sullivan, *Conceptions of Modern Psychiatry*, Washington, William Alanson White Psychiatric Foundation, 1947.

The immature tend to be *constricted* in emotional expression, or *labile*.[4] Constricted persons play their theme of life within a single octave of the scale, unable to feel the heights and depths of mood. They are caught in an emotional monotone. They are incapable of joy or sorrow. The labile person is so loose in his identifications that he tends to lose himself in others, to lose his own identity and individuation. Little of the self remains to reflect, regulate, and control. He tends toward the extremes of elation or depression in "sympathy" with another. Such a person may be emotionally explosive, lacking adequate control appropriate to the situation.

The mature are capable of expressing "negative" emotions. Truly provocative situations evoke anger. They can fight the "bad" with the fervor of the love they express toward the "good." However, the limits are bounded and controlled. Their reactions are appropriate to the situation. They are happy with those who are happy and do not enjoy the misfortunes of others. This is illustrated in the life of Christ. When Jesus was provoked at the money changers in the temple he went in, drove them out with a rope, and then proceeded to break up their tables. On occasion he could express righteous indignation without pulling his punches. It is quite likely that it was not their person but the principles underlying their operation that he resented.

Flexibility, stability, and balanced emotional reaction are achieved without undue stress. Some persons can express a range of emotion but shift with difficulty. They smoulder or remain excessively elated when it is unwarranted by the situation. We hear it said, "I know that I ought to get over it, but I just can't help feeling burned up." Other persons re-

[4] See the case of Ann in Bruno Bettleheim, *Love is Not Enough*, Glencoe, The Free Press, 1950, pp. 224 ff.

main in a state of cheerful idiocy. Still others shift in their feelings and are flexible, but the feelings are not appropriate.[5] They feel gay at another's misfortune or sad when others are happy. These are forms of immaturity.

The Creative Orientation

The creative orientation is evidenced in one who can view the subject of his interest as it is and *as it may become.* To reproduce reality is not enough. The creative person will add heretofore unrelated elements that lend a different perspective, emergent relationships, and new meaning. Let us take for example a photographer. He may want to get a panoramic view of the carnival in town. He could set up his camera and get a midday snapshot but this would not suffice so he sets up his camera in the evening. With the aid of colored film he can take a time exposure from an angle that will produce the elliptical line of the merry-go-round, ferris wheel, and whirling gondola in relation to one another. The result will be a photograph of pleasing line, color, light, and motion depicting the carnival atmosphere. It is not important that the photographer takes a picture. Just producing something is not the criterion for creativity. It is one's orientation.[6] The creative photographer can see the carnival in its noonday reality, but he can also sense its "becomingness," its potential.

Creative people tend to apply principles, not rules. They

[5] For a most illuminating discussion of the origins and symptoms of excessive emotional constriction and of lability see Leon J. Saul, "Physiological Effects of Emotional Tension," in J. McV. Hunt, *Personality and the Behavior Disorders,* Vol. I, New York, Ronald, 1945, pp. 269 ff. See also H. Rorschach, *Psychodiagnostics,* New York, Grune and Stratton, 1942. This includes an illuminating discussion of the criteria for evaluating emotional balance.

[6] Fromm, *op. cit.,* pp. 82 ff.

seek to discover new principles. Such a person is an artist at heart and a technician only in the use of his tools. He gets along with his work. He produces rather than procrastinates. He uses his time efficiently with a feeling of being pulled rather than driven by the task.

"Laziness" is often a compulsion against a job that "should" be done and can be expressed in the pursuit of a technical hobby or social service into which one escapes. Defensive modesty, "I don't want to be better (more competent) than others," is another disabling attitude. Such an orientation is not modesty at all, but a restrictive fear of self-assertion. Underlying such disabilities is often found an unconscious resentment of authority, some overbearing or exploiting person in one's formative experience.[7]

The quality of one's work is not as important as the emotional relationship of the person to the task, when the person is of limited talent. Creative activity can be on a level of simple gardening or more sophisticated plant breeding. Persistent shifting in interests tends toward instability.

Creative work is one of the most gratifying of all human experiences because it has a tendency to draw the individual into new experience outside the self. It is accompanied by the feeling of "getting along" with life, something like the feeling one has when the speedboat overcomes the inertia of the water by planing, with only the propellor shaft and a small section of the keel "holding back." It is one of the tragedies of modern living that so many men and women are bound to the routine of the assembly line. At best they are driven or pulled along like a heavily laden barge. Often such persons are so emotionally enervated by the boredom of their

[7] For a discussion of neurotic inhibition see Karen Horney, *The Neurotic Personality of Our Time,* New York, Rinehart, 1947, pp. 230–258.

work that they use their leisure time in emotionally excessive rather than creative activities. Their marriages suffer the obvious plight.

Responsibility

The mature person is willing to carry responsibility for the common good without sacrificing himself excessively except under dire circumstances. He maintains a healthy self-interest. He is able to make necessary self-sacrifices in the interest of others. However, he also balances his feeling of obligation to the common good with his own legitimate needs. He does not allow himself to become an emotionally bound martyr. People who permit themselves to be exploited by excessive organizational affiliation and responsibility often neglect their obligation to themselves and to their families. They cannot say no for they fear the displeasure of the group. In this instance the center of emotional gravity (responsibility) is in the group and not in the self.[8]

When responsibility is assumed some failure must be expected. The mature person accepts failure with a minimum of remorse rather than with undue feelings of self-recrimination.

The Structure of Goals

The mature person has achieved an orientation of "casting one's self free on the broad current of the sea of life."[9] This means that his life has direction, but is not bounded by goals

[8] See an elaboration of this idea in Fromm's discussion of the authoritarian conscience in *Man For Himself, op. cit.,* pp. 145 ff.

[9] This is a restatement of an idea expressed in an unpublished paper given by Carl R. Rogers at the Menninger Foundation in 1955.

that are too rigid or too specifically defined. He is free to leave the committed path for new experience or even redirected goals. There is a minimum of feeling that one "has something to live up to." His orientation is more one of traversing and discovering the forest than of following a charted path to the nearest safe village.

Time is taken with a minimum feeling of urgency. The early life of Carl Sandburg exemplifies the point.[10] During his youth Sandburg sold stereoscopic pictures for Underwood and Underwood of New York. When the smoke of a train beckoned, Sandburg would take off across the country. To him it was a way of meeting people in all walks of life, dipping into their thoughts, sharing their feelings, and writing about their reactions. He regarded it as a game in which he would stalk his prey, lose the trail, ponder his rejections, and set out anew. When his good friends in Galesburg asked him why he did not settle down and become a minister, lawyer, or something, he could not answer them for his logic and his yet undefined goals were not theirs. Sandburg's orientation may have been out of the same cloth as Jesus' when he said, in effect, "take ye not heed for the morrow."

The foregoing orientation stands in contrast to the prevalent American middle-class dictum of, "Succeed, young man. Make a name for yourself. Set your course straight and let nothing swerve you one way or another." Such a rigid orientation is worshiped by many as a highest good. Actually it is an unconscious fight against forces in one's formative experience that have stifled the spontaneous and creative in personality, forcing one into excessively competitive pursuits and mundane goals.

It is interesting that the goal of William James and Have-

[10] Karl W. Detzer, *Carl Sandburg,* New York, Harcourt Brace, 1941.

lock Ellis in taking out their medical degrees was not to practice medicine, but to learn more about life. Both completed their degrees but neither practiced, probably against the "best" advice of well-meaning relatives and friends.

Heterosexual Orientation

Maturity is evidenced in the capacity for deep feelings of secure and continuing intimacy with a person of the opposite sex. The high degree of adjustment and satisfaction may not be a full cup as described by the romanticist, but it is an adequate measure as felt by the couple. Security and continuity of the relationship is an overtone of mutuality and satisfaction rather than a pose or a result of resolution.

The mature person harbors an attitude of warm anticipation toward sex. It is neither overvalued nor devalued. Sex is neither "out of this world" nor is it *per se* vulgar, funny, or morbid. It can be a subject of normal interest or humor like any other experience. But when it is humorous it is the incongruous in human nature that is the point and not an unconscious attempt to gain easy intimacy with another through the recitation of dirty words in pointless stories. The difference is vast.

Sexual deviations are either absent or exert only a minimal and residual influence on the relationship between two mature people. Notably absent are narcissism, exhibitionism, perversions, promiscuity, frigidity, or impotence.[11] (For a fuller discussion see Chapters 3 and 4.) Extreme attitudes of prudishness or vulgarity are also absent.

Sex, to the mature, can be a profound experience like a

[11] For a discussion of patterns of sexual immaturity from a psychoanalytic point of view see Franz Alexander, *Fundamentals of Psychoanalysis,* New York, Norton, 1948, pp. 33–57.

polonaise, or it can be playfully coquettish and whimsical like a polka. It is neither weighty nor morbid.

One's sex orientation is a direct expression of one's general maturity or immaturity. The most valid and applicable evidence of a mature sexual orientation is the general behavior of a person toward the opposite sex.[12] They act warmly and affirmingly toward persons of the opposite sex. There is a notable absence of hostility, rivalry, invidious comparison, and stand-offish attitude of remaining psychologically incommunicado.

Immature sexuality can be cleverly hidden by the poses of talented people. However, in many little ways they betray themselves. It comes out in thinly clad hostility which is often passed off as clever repartee, "good humor," or in a myriad of other very special guises. It is not always easy to judge, for some psychosexually mature people are also given to quick repartee and genuine good humor, but they lack the glucose of the pose. Often only continued experience will reveal the true hand.

Integrity of the Individual

The mature person places the integrity and individuality of persons very high in any consideration. A nurturing attitude toward the other is expressed in extending one's self and the facilities of the institution (organization) to others. Self-development and self-fulfillment of the other person are regarded as important as one's own.[13] The uniqueness of the other is recognized and nurtured. There is a minimum of

[12] For a discussion of sex as an aspect of general personality see H. A. Overstreet, *The Mature Mind,* New York, Norton, 1949, pp. 58 ff.

[13] For a brief but thought provoking statement about "self-transcendence," see Nelson Foote, "Love," *Psychiatry: Journal for the Study of Interpersonal Process,* XVI, No. 3 (August, 1953), 250–251.

seeking to make him conform to one's own pattern. There is an orientation of granting the other the freedom to make his mistakes following the expression of his forthright opinion and to learn by experience, rather than "saving him from himself." The prevailing attitude is, "I am aware of many of what I presume to be your limitations and weaknesses, but I still like you for what you are rather than what I think that you ought to be." This is a genuine feeling rather than a presumptuous, condescending strategy.

The immature person tends to overvalue the welfare of the group, the organization, or the institution, or pursues excessively his own interests. He tends to sacrifice the individual to the "cause." He is presumptuous in imposing his pattern on others, either boorishly or disguised (usually unconsciously) with "I know best, and it is all for your own good." The foregoing does not imply the withholding of a forthright opinion or counsel, but suggests the withholding of sanction, coercion, pressure, and "do-gooding."

One of the premarital problems most frequently encountered by a counselor involves young couples, usually upper-division or graduate students in our universities, who want to marry but feel that they cannot. The typical story is something like this: "We are being graduated and plan to marry within the year. But we feel that one or more of our parents think that we ought to wait." When the counselor asks if the objection is based on financial or occupational insecurity at this time, the couple answers with an emphatic "No." "Mother thinks that Tom is nice enough, but she just doesn't want us to marry now," she remarks. The student usually shows marked anxiety with feelings of guilt. Not infrequently has parental disapproval been so emphatic and binding that one of the couple feels that the engagement ought to be terminated just to keep peace in the family.

Now, it is true that some parents correctly sense the immaturity or impending incompatibility of their children. Any attempt to reason with their children and their advice to wait largely fail. But such situations are relatively infrequent in this writer's experience. Often the children are overprotected by parents whose own marriages are unhappy. The parent is unable to give up the child who is "the only thing I have left."[14] Frequently such a parent is suffering some protracted illness that is used as a threat to hold the child in line. Fear of hurting the parent or even contributing to the parent's premature death is expressed. The student is caught in a gnawing ambivalence, a love and appreciation of the parent while feeling resentful and hostile toward the parent. The less mature the student the greater the conflict and the greater the conscious denial of the hostility toward the parent but the conflict grinds on in the deeper levels of the personality.

Such parents have been hurt themselves. It does no good to blame them. In their unhappiness they have grasped for a measure of self-fulfillment only to get a psychological strangle hold on their children. This does not take place suddenly. The children have been the unknowing victims of psychological smothering in the name of love for years. That is why they have such difficulty trying to cut the silver cord so that they may live their own lives. Their individuality and integrity have in effect been violated irrespective of the "good" intentions of the parent.

Reality Sense

One of the most difficult to describe, and yet important component of maturity is attaining a deeper and broader

[14] Edward A. Strecker, *Their Mother's Sons,* Philadelphia, Lippincott, 1946.

understanding of realities of life including the unpleasant aspects of living in an orientation of reality rather than fantasy. It is the ability to discern fact from opinion and assumption; what is from what one feels ought to be or is wished for. It is a valid sense of the empirical. The orientation is cosmopolitan and is just the opposite of ignorance and provincialism. As Robert W. White put it, ". . . it is a sense of the conditions imposed by reality."[15]

Take for example a child with a kitten. Ask the child what he holds and he may tell you, depending on the child's age and sex, that it is, "the biggest fiercest lion-cat in the world," or, pulling the blanket around it, "It is my baby." Later when the child has matured he may be dissecting the cat in the anatomy laboratory. The cat becomes much more "real" than the child's projected needs for security. It becomes a complex organism of nerves and muscles, and an example of creative life processes.

An undeveloped reality sense is seen in the adult primitive head-hunter with an emotional age comparable to that of a small child in Western culture. He may get a bone that a member of the tribe has been gnawing on, or anything else personal, such as a fingernail, and pronounce a curse upon his foe. If the cursed one does not meet the demands exacted he becomes ill and may even die of fear. Now, the curse is very real but not the assumptions behind it. Fear and superstition have prevented these people from developing a more mature reality sense.

One of the real stumbling blocks to the more sensible choice of a mate is the person's immature and fallacious assumptions about a great many important things involving

[15] Robert W. White, *The Abnormal Personality,* New York, Ronald, 1948, pp. 104–105.

religion, politics, customs, human nature, and even emotional maturity itself, *ad infinitum*. Some people just have not had enough experience to discern fact from assumption. It is something like making a promising young man of 16 president of his father's bank. The young man has achieved all of the intellectual "capacity" he will ever acquire. What he may not have learned is that some persons do not live by the promises they make. If he goes on idealistically assuming that all men do, he will soon be in bankruptcy. He has not had the requisite experience to mature his judgment, i.e., a sense of the real.

Another deterrent to knowing people and things as they are is the presence of fear and anxiety in the personality. People who fear to live life may find themselves in a social and psychological cloister. Take for example the sexually exploited mother who indoctrinates her daughter with the idea that all men are wolves and should be studiously kept at arm's length. Unless the daughter has other corrective experience her orientation regarding sex, men, and life itself will be distorted. Or, take the young man who has been brought up in the sheltered atmosphere of "loveliness and light" in the belief that the motivations of all men are all "good." He is allowed to "see no evil." He remains vulnerable to the authoritarian personality and culture, to say nothing of a "Korea." The abnormal need for safety has been sensed neither by his protective environment or himself. He would tend to avoid any real experience that would threaten his assumption that all men are good.

The person who knows life (reality) tends to be neither shocked nor disgusted at experience that would ordinarily evoke these reactions. Such is not to condone but to try to understand. He does not tend to think "judgmentally." He has achieved a more objective orientation, deeper understanding, and compassion.

Empathy

Empathy refers to the ability to feel "with" another, to place oneself in the position of another. It is "taking the role of the other" involving the capacity for identification.[16]

Identifying oneself with another involves the intellectual quality of understanding and the emotional quality of freedom from inhibiting defensive or aggressive tendencies toward the other. Putting it a little differently, it is the ability to share the "common meaning" of an experience.[17] It has been said that some people "have to have their legs broken before they can learn to walk, be blinded before they can see, or experience disaster before they can learn to feel." It seems that suffering is a requisite experience in the genesis of emphatic ability. Perhaps it is not suffering alone that is involved but the self-differentiation and strength gained in working through personal disaster to greater sensitivity, understanding, and mastery. It is probably not in spite of his suffering but because of it that Beethoven wrote his Moonlight Sonata after becoming deaf; Kierkegaard, his *Sickness Unto Death* during his despair following the breakup of his love affair; Goethe his *Faust* in search of Margurite, during his longing for his lost love. It might be fairly said that little has been accomplished by those who have not experienced some profound suffering.

A requisite amount of judgment or intelligence is involved

[16] George Herbert Mead, *Mind, Self and Society,* Chicago, University of Chicago Press, 1934, pp. 368–373.
[17] *Ibid.*

in empathy. One cannot expect the empathic potential or capacity from the feeble-minded that obtains in a person of sensitivity and differentiation which is the product of innate ability and meaningful social and emotional experience.

Frequently in marriage counsel one of a couple seems quite unable to sense or appreciate his spouse's need for understanding, personal affirmation, and sense of identity. She seeks in many little ways to gain his attention when he arrives home in the evening. She may ask him to help with the dinner, or the dishes, or the baby. It is not that she needs help in many instances but she is making a bid for attention in an indirect but unmistakable way.

When he lacks the requisite empathy, he does not understand what she really wants. He hears only her words. The result might be his capitulation to her request, or an argument over her domestic inefficiency, retirement to the sofa and television, or one of a variety of responses which, she feels, completely misses the point of her expectations. After nursing her psychological wounds she reacts according to her basic personality and moves in closer to "smother" him with affection, or to aggress against him, or to withdraw into her own brooding and doubting thoughts.

Most frequently in such a situation the wife complains of her husband's preoccupation with his work—too much of his time spent on medicine, engineering, or whatever he seems "to be married to." She wants to be more personal in their relationship and be the center of his interests and attention. She does not want to feel that she is displaced by any other interest. Not infrequently he takes his occupational preoccupation to the bridge party, imposing it upon everyone irrespective of their interests, and quite ignoring his wife and her bids for attention.

It often happens that such a woman suspects that he has other feminine interests at the office or the plant. Feeling that she cannot break through to attract his personal, undivided attention, she wonders if there is another woman. In counseling when such a man is confronted with her expectations and often her accusations, he seems utterly astounded. At first he appears perplexed, then somewhat angry or confused, depending upon his personality and the many different circumstances.

This type of empathic impasse is very common in marriage though it has many variations in the experience of different couples. However, the man in cases such as these is not always entirely at fault. Many men, especially those high in the B-component of aggressive and ascendant orientation, are given to interests in "things" rather than in individuals' deeper feelings and expectations. The wife's orientation may be socially affirming and her need for affirmation stands at variance with his basic personality. The result is a deep frustration of needs on both sides. She wants love, to be "appreciated," and a sense of personal identity. He wants her to understand how important his work is, not to "be so silly," and to be less personal and demanding. Such an example of frustration of orientation, expectation, and need might be multiplied many times in the different areas of any one given marriage.

Autonomy

The last of the components of emotional maturity to be discussed here is that of autonomy, a concept that has emerged recently to describe the ability of a person to be free to order and live his own life. It is to personal behavior what political freedom is to a citizen of a state. It means that one has command of his own ship. As captain he is not omnipotent. He does not command the sky and the water. He has however, gained his freedom from "inner imperatives" as well as the social forces outside himself. Such freedom is not to be understood as a reckless freedom from restraint and control, but a freedom to be one's better self.[18] For the present discussion we may consider two sources of sociopsychological servitude, or lack of autonomy: (1) those "instinctual" forces within oneself, the primitive needs postulated by the psychoanalysists—need for passivity, aggression, sexuality, etc. Included are those acquired habits which are the patterns attained by the development and extension of the primitive needs, such as excesses of any kind. (2) Those social, psychological, and cultural forces outside ourselves that seek to hold us in personal bondage. Examples might include overprotective or rejecting parents, authoritarian control of community organizations and institutions, etc., expressed through the social controls of taboos—"thou shalt not do this, that, and the other."

Minimal autonomy obtains, then, when one is bound by self-indulgence and deference to the expectations of the group—to be excessively self- or other-centered. Such a person may be submissive, passive, rebellious, hostile, rebellious-dominating, dominating, reserved, rigid, restricted, or anxiety ridden.[19] He is the galley slave, not the captain. He is a slave to himself and/or to his groups of affiliation. He is not autonomous.

[18] Erich Fromm, *Escape From Freedom,* New York, Rinehart, 1941.

[19] Howard R. Stanton and Eugene Litwak, "Toward the development of a short form test of interpersonal competence," *American Sociological Review,* XX, No. 6 (December, 1955), 668 ff.

EMOTIONAL MATURITY AND BASIC PERSONALITY

The foregoing characteristics of persons who have achieved a relatively high degree of emotional maturity seem to be unrelated to differences in basic personality as described in Chapter 2. However, emotionally immature or neurotic people have some common emotional characteristics. They are essentially self-centered. Not having achieved a satisfying measure of self-fulfillment—the meeting of basic needs for affection, security, achievement—the immature is egocentric. He cannot feel that he is essentially good and thus tends to act towards others with the same attitude that he holds toward himself.

Patterns of Emotional Immaturity Related to Basic Personality

Patterns of emotional immaturity tend to be expressed in larger social roles, expressed by Fromm as different "orientations," and by Horney as different "strategies."

THE RECEPTIVE ORIENTATION

Persons who are high in the A-component of basic personality (socially engaging-affirming) and low in the B-component (socially active-aggressive) and the C-component (socially shy-retiring) tend to follow a "receptive orientation."[20] They feel that the source of good things—knowledge, pleasure, love, etc.—is *outside* the self. Love means "being loved." These individuals tend to be promiscuous in the choice of a love object. They are attracted to anybody who gives love, recognition, response, and security. They are

[20] Fromm, *Man For Himself, op. cit.,* pp. 62 ff.; Karen Horney, *Our Inner Conflicts,* New York, Norton, 1945, pp. 48–96.

hurt most by criticism, rebuff, or the withdrawal of love. They would rather listen, receive ideas, and agree with people. In their religion they petition God as a magic helper to minister to their needs. Their feeling of loyalty and appreciation stems from their fear of being disapproved. They need many people to be loyal to and to insure them against the loss of approval. Because they are so preoccupied with seeking from others and pleasing them, their own critical faculties remain undeveloped. The ability to seek and to weigh evidence, and thus to come to independent conclusions is impaired. They mistrust their own opinions and tend to overrate others. Panic is often experienced at having to come to their own conclusions and to initiate action. Comfort is sought in sexual stimulation, food, drink, and sleep. Optimism and friendliness serve to quell the fear of offending others or of losing their favor. They participate in group activities, including the church, for the feeling of belonging, receiving help from the group, and being protected by a strong (omnipotent) helper.

THE MARKETING ORIENTATION

Persons who are high in component B of basic personality and low in A and C, tend to follow an "exploitative market orientation."[21] They too, as the A-component, feel that all good comes not from within but from outside themselves. What they get they must "take" by strategy, manipulation, or force. They are attracted to *things,* including a love object, because they belong to another or are attached to another. Stolen love is the sweetest. In intellectual pursuits others' ideas are taken and represented as their own. It is not that such persons necessarily lack talent, but that they are so busy

[21] *Ibid.*

borrowing from others that their own abilities are not developed. Theirs is an "oral-aggressive" characteristic, set jaws in envy and jealousy. Their membership in organizations, including the church, is for contact purposes—more people and situations to be drawn upon.

To one of the marketing orientation the value of persons, as well as their own self-regard, is determined by the feeling of "demand" by others. Thus people are vested with an "exchange" value, i.e., how they are regarded or sought out by others. The attitude toward people, including the self, is one of emotional detachment and impersonality. People are not loved or valued for their intrinsic qualities such as their capacity for love, integrity, individuality, but for appearance, popularity, and the ability to sell themselves. To be successful means to be in demand. Feelings of personal worth are based on popularity. Friendliness, ambition, aggressiveness, sensitivity to others, and the like, becomes skills utilized to influence people and win friends. Even clothing will be selected to meet the expectations of others and not to represent individuality. The different or "queer" will be avoided. Persons with individuality in their ideas and work are rejected. An individual is not loved or respected for what he is, but for his demand value.

The exploitative person's intellectual ability may consist of grasping things quickly but superficially rather than with depth or reason. Quantitative measurement is sought rather than deep understanding. Knowledge becomes a commodity. It must be practical and immediately applicable. Basic knowledge is regarded as academic, stuffy, and useless. Honesty and other virtues are not important. Of importance is what people "will bring" *as they appear*. Friendship is based on personality market value, not on common interests and loyalties. If a friend comes into popular disfavor he can be dumped on the market. Inconsistent and expedient behavior is quite consistent with the dominant orientation to get around the "customer's" objection and to sell oneself. He is like the chameleon—all things to all people. He is not guided by principles of conduct, but by a set of strategies. The center of gravity is not the self, but the public. He does not create, he markets; he is the go-between. The social graces, poise, flexibility, wit, capacity to shift from "one of the boys" to "sophistication," and the ability to defer or to challenge according to circumstance, are important strategic skills used not in the interest of truth or genuine good fellowship, but for personal gain.

THE HOARDING ORIENTATION

Persons high in component C of basic personality and low in A and B, have little confidence in anything they may get from outside themselves or through others.[22] Security lies in being cautious, withholding, saving. Giving of the self or of one's possessions, whether it be love, ideas, or material things, is accompanied by anxiety. These individuals surround themselves with a protective wall of "mine," fortified against giving out, and are bent on getting things within protective borders. Love and affection are not given but taken with the feeling of possessing the loved person or object. To possess means to control or to manipulate. Such persons look backward in their orientation rather than forward. They feel sure of their own ideas and opinions and tend to feel that they know the answers. Their thinking may be "shrewd" and agile, but sterile and nonproductive. The psychoanalysts have referred to this kind of person as an anal-erotic: taut

[22] *Ibid.*, pp. 65 ff.

faced, tight lipped, withdrawing, rather than seeking and inviting. Rigid, inflexible, unyielding, and tenacious, their basic need is security. Energy and mental effort are conserved. They feel spent rather than revitalized with the expansion of effort. The focus of attention and interest is more on death and expected misfortune, than on life, health, growth, and the assumption of reasonable risk with a chance of success.

COMBINATION MODES OF EMOTIONAL IMMATURITY

We must remember that the above modes of emotional immaturity are seldom seen in pure form. Most persons are blends of two or three of the orientations according to their basic personality make-up. The film, *Citizen Kane,* produced by Orson Welles, is illustrative of the life of a man whose basic personality was a combination of B- and C-components. His emotional immaturity correspondingly took the form of a *hoarding-exploitative orientation.* The story of his life opened when he was playing with his sled outside the weatherbeaten shack where he lived with his proud but poor parents. His wealthy uncle was to rear him and had come to get him. The boy left his sled, with a rosebud trademark on it, and the parents he loved. He was reared in wealth by his impersonal, rigid uncle. As a young adult he inherited his uncle's millions. He expressed a "sympathetic" interest in the laborers who worked in his plants, but he betrayed them in a showdown vote concerning their welfare. He married a passive woman whom he enjoyed "developing" and controlling. She did not have an operatic voice but he insisted that she study abroad. He built a large and ornate music hall for her debut in America. During an aria her voice broke. He retired with her in humiliation into the deep South. She loved people but he cut off all social contacts and insisted that she remain with him. For their "retirement" he bought up shiploads of European art treasures, including complete buildings that he brought to America and restored within the high walls of his southern mansion. He remained unloved and unlovable, holding onto the "treasures of the world" and his undeveloped Galatea as symbols of something deeply needed but never personally achieved—things of great meaning for others that he now vicariously tried to "take" from life. In the closing death scene he reached for a little glass ball containing a rosebud and artificial snow—the kind children shake and watch as the snow settles. But as he reached he hit the night stand with his sleeve. The glass ball, symbolic of his early love of his parents, rolled to the floor, on down the marble steps of his bedroom, out of his reach.

Like Citizen Kane there are some people who, deprived of love, security, and achievement, seek quite unconsciously in marriage to fulfill their deeper needs. But their early need for love is turned into a neurotic need to exploit and to possess. Citizen Kane exemplifies but one of many different patterns that emotional immaturity takes in persons of different basic personality.

IDEOLOGICAL MATURITY

Ideology will be used here to denote the outlook a person has toward different areas of human relations, ranging from very personal experience in one's family and such relationships as may obtain among friends, to educational, political, economic, and religious considerations.[23] One's ideological

[23] The concept "ideological maturity" is relatively new. It derives from a branch of academic endeavor that is a combination of anthropology, sociology of knowledge, and psychiatry. This interdisciplinary research to date has focused on such subjects as prejudice, anti-Semitism, the agitator,

outlook consists of patterns of attitudes and orientations that comprise one's assumptions about a given area of living and one's "life values." Thus, an individual may believe in progressive education and shun didactic teaching methods; believe in the labor movement and reject attempts to control labor organization; believe in scientific humanism and hold that it is not necessary to belong to a church in order to achieve the good life; believe in being permissive in the rearing of children rather than rapping them when they get out of line; and so on at great length. These assumptions (convictions) that people hold are often very important to them. The ideological outlooks of individuals may and frequently do provide the bases for close and lasting friendships or conflict.[24] Wars have been fought in an attempt to resolve differences in ideology.

The relationship between the ideological assumptions of a married couple and success in marriage is a branch of research that has remained undeveloped. Early studies of the authoritarian personality are suggestive for our studies, but they focused more on social and cultural dynamics than on the character structure of the individual or the relationship between two individuals.

The ideologically mature person is one who is interested in and aware of issues and problems of human relations, whether in the family, the community, or the culture. He has a sense of the radical, the liberal, the conservative. He has gained through experience and reflection, often at a price of inner doubt and turmoil, convictions on many basic issues.

---

and the authoritarian personality. The focus of attention in this endeavor is the *character structure* of persons. See Theodore W. Adorno *et al.*, *The Authoritarian Personality*, New York, Harper, 1950.

[24] Benjamin J. Keeley, "Value Convergence and Marital Relations," *Marriage and Family Living*, November, 1955, pp. 342–345.

He tends to be liberal rather than radical like the anarchist or authoritarian.

The ideologically immature tend to fall into two groups or some combination of the two: (1) the person who is simply unaware. Like a child he is not cognizant of the "great debate." Ideological issues just do not exist for him. He accepts the assumptions of his immediate environment without reflection or question. He is naïvely provincial. (2) The person who is "aware," but too emotionally distorted or disturbed to sense any other position than the one he has assumed. This person has been emotionally deprived or hurt. He adopts an outlook that meets his unconscious emotional and intellectual needs, not one based on a greater reality sense. Thus, the child who has been the victim of uninformed and harsh parents will be attracted to an extreme outlook and retire to the ivory tower of "loveliness and light" or of hate.

While working with youths in Central Europe during Hitler's rise to power this writer noted that young people who were reared in homes where companionship and consideration obtained tended to remain in the Boy Scouts. Others whose families were torn with strife and bitterness tended to drop out of scouting and join the Hitler youth movement. Their authoritarian family relationships seemed to carry over into their unconscious choice of an authoritarian outlook which offered them a socially acceptable outlet for the projection of hostility. Their outlook was a combination of limited experience, ignorance, and emotional disturbance.

In considering the relevance of this discussion of ideology for courtship and marriage, we should bear in mind that emotional and ideological immaturity are but two sides of a single coin. The level of emotional maturity that has been attained is closely related to the level of ideological maturity. Furthermore, the values assumed by persons affect marriage in at least two significant ways. First, authoritarian values are an expression of intellectual and emotional rigidity and hostility. Affiliation will tend to be with radical or with ultraconservative organizations and movements. A disposition toward prejudice rather than open-mindedness and tolerance will constitute a subterranean channel deep in the personality. Second, the authoritarian personality cannot be a companion to a spouse because of the basic assumption held by both sexes that men are superior to women. A dichotomous conception of the roles of the sexes makes true companionship impossible.

Basic Ideological Patterns

Recent clinical and statistical research has provided us with a picture of two basic ideological patterns: the liberal and the authoritarian.[25] The liberal person is cosmopolitan in his orientation. He views and evaluates a given situation by taking into consideration the viewpoints of persons of different orientations. He is liberal rather than conservative in his political and economic outlook. He resists the use of political or economic power to intimidate and coerce people. He believes that people should have an effective voice in determining the policies that affect their political and economic welfare. He is interested in and a support to "little people"

[25] Under "Types and Syndromes," Adorno discusses liberal and authoritarian syndromes (patterns of traits) that derived from their rigorous clinical and statistical studies of different types of liberal and authoritarian personalities. See Adorno *et al., op. cit.,* pp. 744 ff.

liberal & authoritarian

who are trying to gain a more self-expressive and secure station in life. He welcomes social change but resists destructive and irrational means of bringing it about.

The authoritarian person, on the other hand, is basically hierarchical. He thinks in terms of the status or station of people. He is paternalistic, power-influence oriented, exploitatively dependent on his sex partner and his God. He clings to anyone or anything that is strong and disdains the weak. He believes in dichotomies in the roles of men and women, values, and social relations, i.e., he makes neat divisions between the sexes, right and wrong behavior, and in-group and out-group identifications. He is conventional, rigid, unconsciously self-denying. He fears his own weakness and dependency and hides his fears by assuming roles of great strength and independence. His dependency is evidenced in his reaction to the opposite sex and the religious and social "demands" made on him. The center of gravity is not within himself, but lies in persons and institutions outside himself toward whom he remains ambivalent.

It can be readily seen that the authoritarian personality is incapable of living with a spouse on a companionship basis, and that his (her) relationship in the home and with the children will be emotionally austere, arbitrary, exploiting, conflicting, and unhappy. Two further implications seem quite apparent. First, achieving emotional and ideological maturity is a prime requisite for a creative marriage. Second, in choosing a mate this *dual* aspect of the prospective spouse's personality must be taken into consideration. It seems imperative that education for marriage and family living train young people to recognize the signs of emotional and ideological maturity or immaturity to help them gain a greater measure of maturity for themselves and to help them avoid selecting a mate of marked deficiency or difference in these respects.

It is very difficult to judge the amount of emotional-ideological maturity that one has gained. It is even more difficult to communicate to another how it may be evaluated. Some people appear to be mature in their conversation and actions when they champion "little" people, hurt people, and the underdog. However, in some cases their compassion and liberality is actually a near pathological identification of an injury to another with an injury to themselves. Theirs is not sentiment but sentimentality. They are incapable of genuine love. They aspire but have not yet attained. Their occasional unguarded outbursts of "righteous" hostility tip their hands.

One unfailing criterion of emotional-ideological maturity, if one is mature enough to judge another, is a person's genuine capacity for unconditional love—the ability to regard another as the self. Many persons of experience, intelligence, and talent have failed to recognize the difference between the genuine and the counterfeit. Almost anyone can recognize the grosser forms of immaturity just as they can recognize that a ten dollar bill printed on newspaper is not genuine. However, it takes considerable maturity to recognize maturity or immaturity in another. The best proof of the point is the number of persons of superior intellect and talent who have failed in their judgments.

Individuals like these are not necessarily doomed to marital purgatory. Some persons are willing and financially able to undergo prolonged psychotherapy with excellent results.[26] Others with the understanding help of the spouse, possible briefer psychotherapy, and supporting friends can come to

[26] See John Knight, *The Story of My Psychoanalysis,* New York, McGraw-Hill, 1951.

understand themselves, modify some personal characteristics, and accept their admittedly neurotic selves.[27] We can accept many of our own limitations in life without markedly impairing our happiness or our efficiency. There is no need for crippling morbidity about the matter, nor is there any necessity for feelings of self-recrimination and of being cheated by life. Calling oneself the bad name of "compulsive-obsessive neurotic" does no good, though it is often a weapon wielded by an equally neurotic spouse, who might double as an amateur psychologist. Furthermore, dreaming of the perfect marriage that might have been is equally unproductive. Often two persons who have become secure enough to face honestly their own reality, can work toward maturity and grow through one another. Like anything else worthwhile in life, a good marriage is not one that people fall into, but one that is created through understanding, work, and often a silent prayer!

TOWARD THE INTEGRATION OF PERSONALITY

People differ in their ability to integrate their inner needs with how they appear to others in their pursuit of greater interpersonal competence. The following orientations have been helpful to some in their pursuit of self-understanding and development.

Personality might be thought of as functioning on three levels.[28] The first level is an expression of the *public self*—the roles we assume in public. On the second level the *private*

[27] Karen Horney, *Self Analysis,* New York, Norton, 1942.
[28] H. S. Murray, *Explorations in Personality,* New York, Oxford University Press, 1938.

self is expressed—the roles we take in our thinking and in overt behavior which we express to a small group of intimate friends or confidants. The third level of thoughts and feelings are partly or wholly unconscious in the personalities of most people. This is the *primitive self*—the self that we glimpse in our dreams, fantasies, reactions under stress, humor, and slips of the tongue. The third-level personality might be thought of as a reservoir of primitive instincts or needs which are largely sensuous and aggressive.

The integrated person experiences harmony and consistency among the three levels of his personality—the public, private, and primitive selves. He recognizes and accepts his potential sensuousness and aggression. These deep needs are not denied but expressed in refined and socially constructive ways—love and achievement. His public self is an extension of his private self. He is privately what he appears to be publicly.

The person who, to some degree, lacks integration of personality tends to deny his deeper sensuous needs. Furthermore, the private self is at variance with the public self. He assumes one set of roles with their appropriate standards in his private life but acts according to the expectations of the public when in public. The difference among these variant roles is maintained by the necessity to please others. This person lives a psychological and moral double standard. The public self tends to be an expression of idealized behavior. The private self usually is a conscience-ridden, indulgent self.

Clinical experience indicates that the greater the variance among the three levels of the personality, the greater the person's emotional instability and mental ill health. In extreme cases where the third-level self (sensuous and aggressive needs) is denied and the public self is a perfectionist's pose, the personality tends to become dissociated. The case of Miss Beauchamp reported by Morton Prince is a classic example.[29] Miss Beauchamp was known to her family and friends as a sedate young woman who had attended finishing school, spoke French, and was always proper in her conduct. One night while serving as a nurse on the third floor of a hospital, lightning struck and she looked up from her work to see her boy friend standing illuminated outside the window. He had come up the fire escape to see her. The shock "changed" her into another personality whom the psychiatrist called Sally. Sally was a hard-talking, chain-smoking cut-up. She hated proper and sedate people. Sally discovered that she could touch herself with a lighted cigarette and be changed back into Miss Beauchamp. The psychiatrist discovered that Miss Beauchamp had four distinct and separate "selves." Sally and the other three were a combination of the second- and third-level selves developed on the fantasy level. It was his job to help integrate them into one person. This was accomplished by bringing the public self from its excessive idealism down to reality and by helping the guilt-laden private self attain more legitimate expression, satisfaction, refinement, and control.

Young adults tend to be quite "situational" in the expression of their different-level selves or their different social roles. They act in a manner appropriate to the expectations of others. As they mature they tend to be more consistent in their roles. Consequently, it is important that during court-

[29] Morton Prince, *The Dissociation of a Personality*, New York, Longmans, Green, 1905.

ship they know one another in a variety of situations other than orchids, subdued lights, and music. Only in a variety of situations will people express their *various* selves. You will never find out if he likes to shell peanuts in bed if you see him only on the dance floor. It might take a camping trip to bring out such idiosyncrasies.

A Psychoanalytic Point of View

There are a number of schools of psychoanalytic thought, but, generally speaking, they hold a common view of the problem of attaining a greater measure of personality integration.[30] Human personality might be thought of as made up of three elements. First, there is a reservoir of instinctual needs or drives, some of which are part of the inborn nature of man, and some of which are acquired through experience. They consist of the primitive sensuous needs for sexual satisfaction, aggression, etc. This element is called the *id*. But the id cannot express itself without regulation and control, as it does among the lower animals. Therefore, its expression is regulated through two other aspects of the personality called the *ego* and the *superego*. The ego is developed through experience and emerges as the rational part of the self, that is, it performs the cognitive function of recognizing the conditions imposed by reality. Thus, one may wish to seek sexual satisfaction promiscuously, or to express hostility by fighting with a neighbor, but reason dictates weighing the consequences and controlling impulses. The third aspect of personality according to the theory, the superego, is roughly the

[30] See Leopold Bellack, "Psychoanalytic Theory of Personality," in J. L. McCary, *Psychology of Personality*, New York, Logos, 1956, pp. 3–62; Charles Brenner, *Psychoanalysis*, Garden City, Doubleday Anchor, 1957.

same as conscience—the feelings that one has learned through the formative experience of internalizing the prohibitions of one's environment.

The young child expresses its needs for food, elimination, physical closeness to another, protesting, rebelling, etc., without awareness or regulation. Through experience he learns to express and to satisfy his sensuous needs by "taking in" the parental sanctions, rewards, and punishments. Feelings of pride or of guilt and mortification are at first quite unconscious. Increasingly, however, he acquires the ability to regulate his conduct through reason according to the conditions imposed by reality.

Some persons who remain quite immature express their more primitive needs with little regard to the consequences of their acts. They may have little sense of conscience or may have a weighty conscience, but they lack the requisite reasoned controls to enable them to function effectively in their social environment. When a person with strong sensuous drives has a weak conscience and reality sense, he acts boorishly without feelings of guilt or anxiety. If his conscience is strong, rigid, and irrational, he suffers deep feelings of guilt and anxiety, but continues to act boorishly. Thus, people differ greatly in: (1) the strength of their sensuous needs; (2) the strength, flexibility, and spontaneity of their "reasoning" or reality sense; (3) the strength and flexibility of their conscience. The person with the strong id and weak ego and superego might be thought of as a *sensuous* person. One with a weighty and rigid superego, with little ego, would be a *moralistic* person. One whose id needs are expressed with refinement and conscious flexible control and with feelings of the appropriateness of acts to the situation, might be regarded as a *rational* person—one whose id, ego, and superego are "integrated." The mature and integrated individual is regulated by a sense of the moral, and his needs are controlled by reason rather than by rigid "intellectuality," floating anxiety, or irrational fear.

Basic Personality and Personality Integration

People of different basic personality make-up tend to differ in their ability to achieve personality integration. Those whose personalities are made up preponderantly of *one* of the three components, A, B, or C, tend to achieve integration more easily than others. That is to say, a person who is preponderantly A in basic personality will tend to be an even-tempered, sociable person. The socially assertive person (B) will be active and expressive without too many qualms of self-consciousness. The socially withdrawing person (C) will be reflective and retiring without the intrusion of the sociable and the active. But a person who is high in all three components is driven in different directions by his divergent basic needs. And this is an important consideration, for people of divergent, versatile basic personality run the risk of marrying someone who meets only one of the other's component needs, and leaves the other two unfulfilled. People are especially vulnerable to this risk when they marry young, when the personality is still relatively undeveloped, and when experience has not yet developed other components of the personality.

Where integration of such divergent needs is achieved it is done primarily in one of two ways. A person either becomes rigid in giving expression to one component while largely denying the existence of the other two or learns to live more situationally, that is, plans a mode of life that gives expression to each component in turn. This writer has known teachers of versatile basic personality who have found expression of the A-component in personal counseling with students, expression of the B-component in lecturing, and expression of the C-component in reading, writing, and reflection. Many occupations seem to offer comparable opportunity for the fuller integration of personality.

THE QUEST FOR MATURITY

Emotional and ideological maturity is not inborn, but gained through experience, reflection, and the gradual change of one's way of life. For some it is a natural outgrowth of early relations with their families. For most people maturity is hard won. It is the product of painful introspection and retrospection followed by tearing down and rebuilding deep habits and attitudes. It is a product of learning to give up infantile self-indulgence for modes of conduct and satisfaction more compatible with adult reality, productivity, and responsibility.[31] It is a process of meaningful renunciation which is not to be confused with fearful avoidance, withholding, or ingratiation.

Physical inheritance of neural and endocrine stability and good health are aids in building emotional maturity. But they do not assure it if social and emotional developmental experiences are adverse. Some persons are handicapped by an inherited or acquired disposition toward undue sensitivity in provoking situations. However, this is true in fewer cases than commonly presumed.

[31] For a general discussion of attaining greater maturity see Henry A. Bowman, *Marriage for Moderns,* 3rd ed., New York, McGraw-Hill, 1954.

Two factors that tend to prevent maturity are adverse social and emotional experience, especially during the formative years and limited knowledge of the emotional patterns of others—the lack of opportunity to experience, to test the limits of experience, and to know life.[32] The first is a matter of having been hurt emotionally. The second is a matter of ignorance, provincialism, and ethnocentrism.

In order to reëducate ourselves emotionally or to assist in the growth of others, broad social experience is very helpful. Channels of communication and understanding must be developed and maintained. Meaningful relationships with others, the sharing of common interests and activities are the sustaining lines of communication. Sheltered protection of young adults should be minimal. There are always risks when they are cast into the rough seas of unexpurgated life experience, but reasonable risks must be taken. Living among people of different assumptions, values, and moral outlook and seeking friendships with others of different cultural background can promote growth. The study of biography, literature, and personal histories can give perspective to one's outlook and provide a challenge to think through one's values.

Professional consultants and educators can assist in the maturing process. They can provide tested knowledge to replace fallacious assumptions. They can provide both sympathetic and objective support, assist in the reduction of constrictive guilt and anxiety, help give vent to unconscious hostility and aggression, and assist the person in planning for his future reëducation. Unlike the doctor, however, the

[32] For a critical discussion of the social factors facilitating and impeding the gaining of personal "autonomy" and "competence" see David Riesman, *The Lonely Crowd*, Garden City, Doubleday Anchor, 1953, especially pp. 295 ff.

social-psychological consultant can effect no quick cure as in the case of surgery. In working toward emotional maturity the person must take a great amount of responsibility on himself and in the end succeed or fail by his own effort.

MATURITY AND MARITAL COMPATIBILITY

Mature persons of the same tastes and interests seek one another out in courtship and marriage. By the same token immature people are drawn toward one another.[33] Association with a similarly immature individual provides mutual affirmation of their false values. Such associations are not enduring unless growth takes place, for in their apparent strength lies their weakness. Each reminds the other of his own faulty personality. The presence of the mature person serves to give the immature or neurotic person a sense of insecurity, the former seeming to be an emotionally removed authority figure. There is often an unconscious fear of the personal, of becoming intimate. Since the values of the immature are primarily those of seeking security through material accumlation, status, and achievement, rather than through deeper communication and companionship, there is a basic incompatibility of values between the immature and the mature. The unconscious feeling of suspicious unfriendliness stems from the threat of the mature person to the false values sustained by the repressions of the immature. The mature is a threat to the compensatory ideas that the immature holds about himself.

[33] This conclusion has been stated by so many writers that no one can be credited with stating it first. For evidence to support the generalization see Lewis M. Terman, "Measuring and Predicting Marital Success," in Morris Fishbein and Ruby Jo Reeves Kennedy, *Modern Marriage and Family Living*, New York, Oxford University Press, 1957, pp. 232 ff.

A most important factor underlying successful marriage is a relatively good measure of emotional and ideological maturity. Young adults might do well not to expect too great a measure of maturity from one another lest they be disillusioned and disappointed. Certainly this is no ground for the perfectionist. A healthier attitude might consist of viewing the development of a fuller measure of maturity as a central purpose of marriage itself—two people growing together through one another.

Chapter 6

THE MEANING OF LOVE

The quest for the meaning of love is probably as old as any in the history of man. Yet, we seem to know so little about it. As Paul E. Johnson wrote recently in his book, *Christian Love,* "The most that we know about love is tragically meager; the least that we can do in so urgent a quest is to share what we can find with one another."[1] Theologians, poets, and a host of others have been writing about love through the ages. However, it is only recently that the social scientist and the clinician have been caught up in the pursuit, largely as a result of the impetus given them by psychoanalytically oriented clinicians. In their study of neuroses, the impediments to love, the quest shifted to the meaning of love itself. More recently students in the behavioral sciences have taken up the search. Together with renewed theological interest, there has emerged a new, interdisciplinary interest in the meaning of love.

[1] Paul E. Johnson, *Christian Love,* New York, Abington-Cokesbury Press, 1951.

One might assume that this recent movement would be welcomed by all students of human personality, but such is not the case. Recently, Dr. Nelson N. Foote, Director of the University of Chicago Family Study Center, published an article in the *Journal of Psychiatry* entitled "Love."[2] His paper provoked so many comments from his friends and professional acquaintances that he began to classify them, and found that they fell into four rough categories: cynical, joking, sentimental, and matter-of-fact. Cynicism, joking, and sentimentality are expressions of conflicting emotions—defensive attitudes of persons who have experienced some frustration and disappointment in love. Such ambivalence is to be expected in view of all the people who have been hurt by those who presumably loved them. Newspapers are full of emotional misdemeanors such as the fickle overthrow of another and major crimes of hacking the presumed loved one to pieces. Evidently, there is enough unfulfilled love in our society of competitive mating to evoke a great deal of cynicism, joking, sentimentality, and outright hostility.

Notwithstanding these limitations and impediments to understanding the meaning of love, there has emerged an orientation that has helped to distinguish mature love from immature and neurotic love which often provides the bases of attraction and emotional involvement leading to marriage. This orientation has emerged as a result of the study of the emotionally disturbed or impaired, those who strive to love or be loved without success, and the study of those who have gained a greater measure of deeper, creative relationships with others.

[2] Nelson N. Foote, "Love," *Psychiatry: Journal for the Study of Interpersonal Processes,* XVI, No. 3 (August, 1953), 245–251.

THE VARIETIES OF LOVE

Let us look at the way love manifests itself with different nuances of meaning and deeper import in a variety of situations.

There is the love of a mother for her baby. In the bathing, nursing, fondling, nibbling, and cooing, with his first smiles of response, there is the projection of her feelings of self-fulfillment, deep affection for her husband, and tenderness for her child. There are the wakeful hours nursing him through the inevitable illnesses, the lingering with him at the gate or the desk of his teacher on the first day of school. Later as he walks across the stage to receive his diploma there is the pride that swells in her as her thoughts race back over the years—years of joy deepened by blood, sweat, and tears. At the marriage, the final launching, a part of the self goes out, or, there is the choking grief experienced when the War Department writes of his loss and its regrets.

There is the love of a soldier for his flag, especially strong in one who has witnessed the loss of his buddies in defending it; or, the feeling of being caught up in the cause, expressed by Ernest Hemmingway's Robert Jordan in *For Whom the Bell Tolls,* a peace so pervasive that the loss of one's life is unimportant except that it be preserved in the interest of the common effort.

There is the serene love of life or of God described by those who have experienced conversion—the Tolstoys and the Schweitzers.

There is the love of a romantic crush, the crackling brilliant pitch bough lighted by the fire of youth, and the mellowing of this first love with the development of mutual interests and sympathies—the glow from the sustaining oak log.

There is the neurotic love of those whose positive emotions are entangled and expressed in pain—the love of hurting or of being hurt.

To discuss love from a behavioral point of view, we must consider the development of the total personality. In the past personality was regarded as biologically determined, rather than as a continuous process of recreation and development.[3] This concept of development is not found in the writing of the Greeks, the Scholastics, or the philosophers of the Enlightenment. As recently as the 1930's personality was conceived of largely in terms of biological inheritance.[4] Such bluestocking psychology assumes that one is "born of the manner."

Today, in sharp contrast, such thinkers as Fromm, Sullivan, Plant, Johnson, and others conceive of human personality—thus human love—in terms of an emerging, changing, growing social development. In this context Foote has defined love as ". . . that relationship between one and another which is most conducive to the optimal development of both."[5] Sullivan puts it a little differently: "When the satisfaction or the security of another person becomes as significant to one as is one's own satisfaction or security, then the state of love exists."[6] Fromm writes that the love of another is the extension of self-love, ". . . love is an activity and not a passion . . . the essence of love is to 'labor' for something and to make something grow."[7] As a corollary to this Fromm introduces another phrase, "to care," by which he means to

[3] *Ibid.*, p. 246.
[4] *Ibid.*, p. 246.
[5] *Ibid.*, p. 247.
[6] Harry Stack Sullivan, *Conceptions of Modern Psychiatry*, Washington, D.C., William Alanson White Psychiatric Foundation, 1947.
[7] Erich Fromm, *Man For Himself*, New York, Rinehart, 1947, pp. 129 ff.

care *about,* rather than to care *for.* In caring about another the sentiment of concern is present. One is emotionally "involved" and "committed."

Fromm goes on to say that a prime requisite for "caring about another" is *understanding* another; that blind care is like blind love and has little substance or endurance. Ellis put the same point a little differently when, after the death of his wife Edith, he wrote that he could not love a person of whose weaknesses and limitations he was not poignantly aware. Blind love would not be love at all, but a way of congratulating oneself in the affairs of the heart. Such self-deception would rank along with dependency upon another, neurotic clinging, possessive control, and narcissistic display as forms of immature and neurotic love.

These statements insist upon the fact that love is a matter of deep understanding and appreciation of another, that is, an intellectual matter in addition to whatever else it may be. Love as a form of *relatedness,* with its intellectual and aesthetic overtones, stands in contrast to a current notion of love as a euphemism for sex, or a "fixated attainment" of an emotion.

Such a notion does not minimize the meaning of sex, especially as one of the kindles of love and as a medium through which love may be expressed. It is noteworthy that the two greatest names in the psychology of sex, both medical doctors, writers, and profound students of human nature—Freud and Ellis—both wrote during their mature years in a similar vein. Ellis wrote of the "passion of love" transcending that of sex, while Freud wrote of ". . . the affectionate relations between parents and children, which were originally fully sexual, feelings of friendship, and the emotional ties in marriage which had their origin in sexual attraction."[8]

Neither Freud nor Ellis seeks to minimize the role of sex in the motivation and the expression of love. It should be recognized, however, that love and sex are not the same thing. Genital sex is the symbol and the medium of expression, not the substance. Hate can also be expressed through sex as in the case of rape-murder.

As we reflect on the great love relationships as portrayed in our secular literature, Shakespeare's *Romeo and Juliet* stands as a notable example of the difference between what the clerics and Greeks called *eros* and *agape,* or sex and love respectively.

The foregoing notion of love may appear drab to some people and may even evoke feelings of hostility, because they have never experienced the passion and paradoxically the serenity of love. When, by inference, sex is dissociated from love they seem to feel that they have been robbed of the emotional coin in their half-filled banks.

Study this

LOVE IN MARITAL COMPANIONSHIP

Rather than conceiving of love in the narrow sense of the "caress," it should be thought of in terms of the broader concept of the *companionship* of two people. Companionship is a complex relationship involving several orientations.

First, there is an *equalitarian regard* that each holds toward the other.[9] This does not mean that two people are

[8] Havelock Ellis, *My Life,* Boston, Houghton Mifflin, 1939, p. 629; Sigmund Freud, *Collected Papers,* ed. Ernst Jones, London, Hogarth, 1950, Vol. V, No. 37, p. 134.

[9] Lawrence S. Bee, *Marriage and Family Relations Outline,* Lawrence, University of Kansas Book Store, 1951.

equal in any dimension such as strength, intelligence, skill, height, or weight. There are the inevitable inequalities in every dimension.[10] However, in the many shared activities and interests there is a feeling toward the other as toward the self. There is no feeling of the superiority or inferiority of either person.

Second, though operating or interacting as a team, there is the *individuation* of each as a person. This is seen in two pianists playing a duet. While playing from a common music score, each is sensitively aware of the playing of the other. Each is playing a separate part but there is a sense of being attuned to one another. Each wants the other to be his unique self, "ultimately incommensurable with (the) other."[11]

A third aspect of love expressed through companionship, is *reciprocity*. Putting it axiomatically, the greater the reciprocity the greater the love. A mother can love her baby unconditionally and experience ineffable joy in its smile in return. However, such love does not approximate the *understanding* caress of her husband.

The fourth aspect of companionship involves the couple's orientation toward one another. In addition to the equality of regard is the awareness of the *bearing that each has on the other*—not only as they perform today, but as they move toward greater competence as individuals and as a team. They are critically appreciative of one another, objectively hopeful, neither patronizing nor condemnatory, sentimental or adulatory.[12] They expect from each other something better than ever before. In their sympathetic and informed understanding of one another, they do not exact unrealistic demands on

[10] Foote, *op. cit.*, p. 248.
[11] *Ibid.*
[12] *Ibid.*

one another that exceed their abilities, or try to be something that they are not.

Fifth, we have seen that love (companionship) is not only of the "heart" but of the "head," i.e., in addition to being *emotive* it is *cognitive*. The "critical dialectic" of love is contingent on the awareness of human nature in general, and the unique personality of the partner in particular, an important aspect of empathy.

Sixth, love is *unconditional*. In the early example of the mother caring for her baby she was extending her care for its needs because she enjoyed doing it. There was no thought of ultimate gain such as the honor, approval of family or friends, or any other good that such care for her baby might reflect. Furthermore, there was no feeling of duty, obligation, or self-sacrifice. She did not have to care for her baby. She wanted to. To the extent that there is any ulterior motive present in the extension of the self to the other, to that extent is love alloyed with what is presumed to be but is not love.

Thus, love is neither binding nor demanding. There is a sense of freedom in the relationship, freedom to be oneself, to come and to go. One does not feel bound by little restraints. There is no need for the employment of strategies. There is the underlying confidence that what one is and does will be understood by the other.

And last, but by no means least, is a motivational aspect of love, *the desire to perform at the limit of one's capabilities* and thus "continually transcend the limits of those capacities."[13] Stated in the metaphor of the piano duo, it is the desire to play today better than ever before, thus transcending one's own previous performance. After learning the standard

[13] *Ibid.*

repertory, the couple go on to the creation of their own compositions.[14]

The first precept of both the Judaic and Christian formulations of the good life—that of love—has meaning as "The Way" in which man transcends himself, i.e., the way in which the marriage transcends itself.

LOVE AND PERSONAL COMPETENCE

Returning to the orientation that love is intellectual as well as emotional and aesthetic, one's capacity to love might be thought of in terms of one's *skill* in the art of pursuing the *purpose* that the relationship holds.

Love that is aimed primarily at the adulation of the other is probably not love, but romance. Married love seems to have purpose beyond the immediate. Such purpose might be homemaking oriented with the rearing of the children—the growth and development of the family. It might be a mutual interest in horticulture—the breeding of new strains of blue delphinia; or it might be scientific research—the search for radium as in the case of the Curies. It can be anything, however simple or sophisticated. The relationship is not an *end in itself*, as in the case of romance, but oriented to a *purpose*. Tolstoy, in a letter to a cousin who was about to be married wrote:

I see that you are nearing the goal which you have set yourself and I feel like writing and telling you what I think about it. I think about it often both with joy and with fear. What I think is this: a marriage entered into for the sake of a more enjoyable life is doomed to failure. To make marriage itself—the union with the beloved—your only or your supreme aim is a great

[14] Bee, *op. cit.*

mistake. The reason for this is quite evident if you think about it. You make marriage your aim; you get married, what then? If your lives had no other purpose before you were married, it is difficult, if not impossible, for you to find one afterwards. It is indeed certain that if you had no common purpose before, then so far from drawing nearer to one another you will draw further apart. If two people who have the same aim meet on the way and say to one-another, "Let us go forward together," and go on hand in hand, then and only then will their marriage bring them happiness—but not if, being attracted to one another, they both turn away from their road.[15]

An aspect of purpose-oriented rather than pair-oriented love is the skill or sophistication with which it is pursued. Some couples enjoy their children in a family-centered marriage. However, they may have little orientation in the understanding of human nature, the development of human personality, the art of homemaking, etc. Others do. They participate in their childrens' development within a larger orientation of human relations. They are aware of the developmental tasks that their children might experience.

Common activities are fun but they may also have more extended purpose. Take the couple as they enjoy sitting on their patio in the evening watching the birds as they frequent the garden. They might distinguish the sparrows from the song birds, but their appreciation is on a level different from the couple who take a walk in the woods, equipped with binoculars and intent upon discovering and distinguishing the size, color, song, and flight patterns, characteristic of bird watchers. The first couple could not share their experience on the same vibratory and depth level of "appreciation" as those of greater competence.

[15] *The Tolstoy Home, Diaries of Tatiana Tolstoy,* trans. Alec Brown, New York, Columbia University Press, 1951, pp. 90–91.

In the metaphor of the couple seated at the piano of life, the first couple, romantically attracted to one another, are caught up in the exchange of ecstatic glances and sighs while playing Chopsticks in the key of G. Such a self-oriented relationship may provide the beginning of a one that could develop into love, but we must recognize the matter for what it is—sex. That may be all right as far as it goes, but it is not enough. If this couple develop their keyboard competence individually and together, they may someday achieve the capacity to enjoy the deeper and infinitely more profound satisfaction of interpreting together Beethoven, Bach, or Brubeck, moving on to their own unique compositions. The greater the personal and interpersonal competence, the greater the love.

That is why some marriages, perhaps many, fail. There is so little substance to their relationship. They become bored with one another, often blaming the other for romantic inadequacy which, at the bottom, is really incompetence in the art of living—lack of purpose and immature, mediocre skills.

In marriage counsel one sees many couples whose question is the same though its wording takes many different forms: "What has happened to our love and why do we have such an empty feeling toward one another?" Getting into the case one discovers with patent regularity that the marriage consists largely of the humdrum preparation of three meals a day and television or some other self-oriented pursuit in the evening. There are no vital common interests. Communication is superficial and drab. It is little wonder that their sex expression, a reflection of the general nature of their relationship, is also superficial, drab, and largely a matter of self-oriented relief.

Such a marital theme takes different forms among couples

of different social class, though the substance remains much the same. Couples may launch into social striving, together or separately, to avoid the ennui of sitting at home. Or, as is often the case with lower-income or "employed" couples, the wife's complaint is, "He just flops down on the sofa to watch television." Such absence of love is seen in a recent biographical sketch of the marriage of Joe and Marilyn (Monroe) DiMaggio. After returning from Japan where they were constantly on the move, occupied by the crowds who smashed doors and waded through fish ponds to see them, they were "at home." "Back home, the DiMaggios sat under their expensive thatch in Beverly Hills night after night with almost nothing to say to each other. They had fights, and on Oct. 4, 1954, nine months after the wedding, they announced that they would be divorced."[16]

LOVE AND SURRENDER

In the Judeo-Christian tradition the conception of love as a form of mystical "surrender" has provided the basis for a great deal of controversy evidenced in "the feminist movement," "the battle of the sexes," and more recently an international debate carried on in many magazines and drawing rooms about "European femininity vs. American femininity." The Old Testament abounds with male superiority and man's ascendant role over woman. In the New Testament St. Paul's statement has stood as one of the most controversial of all of his writings. For example, Bailey writes, "Nothing in St. Paul's teaching has been more misunderstood than his idea of subordination in marriage: Wives, be in subjection unto your own husbands, as unto the Lord. For the husband

[16] *Time,* May 14, 1956, p. 81.

is the head of the wife, as Christ also is the head of the church, being himself the saviour of the body. But as the church is subject to Christ, so let the wives also be to their husbands in everything (Eph. 5:22–4)."[17]

We know that in the majority of cultures, with some notable exceptions, the roles of the sexes have been defined in terms of the male's superordinate role of fighter, defender, provider, builder, family representative in the community, etc., while the female has played a role subordinate to his male "authority." Theological systems and religious organizations traditionally have underwritten this cultural fact.

In Chapter 1, we described the recent, dramatic, and widespread change in the roles of men and women from the paternalism of the beginning of the century to the almost chaotic lack of definition of roles in the lives of many couples today. In many middle-class marriages the traditional definition of sexual roles conflicts with the present psychosexual emancipation of women. As one young married woman expressed it in counsel, "I am caught in the conflict of wanting to be the active, dynamic, expressive, and even ascendant person I was as a girl in a very permissive family, yet I want to feel my husband's superiority and even dominance. Somehow I feel that I should be more Victorian and not challenge my husband in so many ways. . . ." And the husband may be just as confused as the wife. He may prefer a wife who is "sweet, deferent, and even long-suffering," but at the same time wish that she had the initiative and executive qualities of his secretary.

The controversy and confusion in the search for psychosexual identity and integrity in love relationships are de-

[17] Derrick Sherwin Bailey, *The Mystery of Love and Marriage,* New York, Harper, 1950, p. 129.

scribed in a great number of articles appearing in our newspapers and magazines. Representative of the different facets of this problem is an article written by J. Robert Moskin, staff writer for *Look* Magazine, entitled "The American Male. Why do WOMEN dominate him? Does he like petticoat rule, or has it been forced on him by the stronger sex?"[18] In the article Mr. Moskin quotes an imposing array of doctors, social scientists, writers, and statisticians, to develop the thesis set forth in the title. He holds that the American woman too often dominates her sons, goads her husband on to greater earning power, offers unfair competition in using her attractiveness in a business battle, "demasculinizes" her husband by exacting household duties, and with her leisure from enervating work makes sexual demands on him beyond his ability to meet her expectations, resulting in his: "Fatigue, passivity, anxiety, and impotency." Mr. Moskin concludes his article with the statement, "It is certain that, as women grow even more numerous and more dominant, we will have to invent new meanings and myths for maleness in America, because, as psychiatrist Dr. Irene Joselyn warns, 'we are drifting toward a social structure made up of he-women and she-men.' "

Whether the above caricature of young Mr. and Mrs. America is valid, and what proportion of our population this would characterize, are controversial questions. Certainly there are many men and women who would not fit the pattern. However, where there has been so much editorial smoke, there must be quite a blaze. And, whatever one wishes to call the dilemma of defining the psychosexual roles of men and women in love, it is a problem very much a part of contemporary American marriage. There is apparent need for wrestling with a new definition of who "surrenders" to whom and

[18] *Look,* February 4, 1958, pp. 77 ff.

under what circumstances. It is quite possible that, in a democratic society, we shall think more and more in terms of the individual differences in basic personality needs of each of the pair, rather than in terms of any culturally prescribed, more stereotyped "masculinity" or "femininity."

The word "surrender" carries such negative connotations of traditional male exploitation of women that perhaps it ought to be abandoned altogether. Or, maybe we should come to understand its meaning in another light and make more sense out of the presumed controversy.

Stating the case first negatively, to "surrender" should not connote servitude, subjection of the self in any menial sense of the term, or exploitation. Such a subordinate relationship is not implied if "submission" is to the relationship rather than to another individual. Playing in a symphony is a literal rather than a metaphorical example of submission in the sense of playing in concert with another(s). When individuals play in concert with one another, there is no status implied and certainly no invidious comparison. Whether they are males or females is of no consequence. It is a complementary relationship. And, perhaps, the word *complement* ought to supplant the word *surrender*.

There is little doubt that in reality there are some married men who want to dominate and exploit their wives, and some women who want just that or seem to be quite miserable when they are not mistreated. Such is evidenced in the philosophy of "keep 'em pregnant and barefoot."

To return to the positive rather than the immature or neurotic meaning of surrender, there remains another issue. When the connotation of status or of invidious comparison is eliminated, there remains a matter of social and psychological division of labor in the love relationship. The idea was made more articulate by a Japanese-American graduate student studying for the Buddhist ministry. He described the roles of his father and mother in their home:

> I feel that the roles of the sexes in the sacred Japanese family have been misunderstood by many Americans, even such sympathetic and observing people as James A. Michener and Ruth Benedict who have written well about Japanese culture and its people. At any rate, in our home there was the division of labor which in Japanese society served to cut down confusion and express the principle of economy which is so important to the Japanese.
>
> My father was the provider and the representative of the family in the community. Mother was the "mother" in the traditional Western sense of the term, but she was also the source of the moral and the spiritual atmosphere and the psychological administrator of the home. My father's feeling of self-regard in the home and his role in the community was in a very real sense created and granted by my mother. I am confident that she did not look up to him and him down on her; but, that they looked up to one another. Without experiencing this intimate oneness in the privacy of the Japanese family, you Americans could only misunderstand what you mistakenly presumed to be, as judged by the overt roles of Japanese men and women in public . . .

It is quite possible that in a democratic society there will be different psychosexual axes or patterns of ascendance or equalitarianism according to the unique basic personality needs of different couples. Furthermore, these patterns may and often do change with the development of the personalities of the two. Some ascendant women are attracted initially to a more submissive male to find years later that they have changed and need a man who will play more of the leadership-ascendant role. In marriage counsel this writer has found this to be more true than the opposite in which the initially passive woman becomes more ascendant. At any rate, these deeper, most often partially if not wholly unconscious needs are very important bases of the kind of love that is experienced by the couple, and the success or failure of the marriage.

LOVE AND IDENTIFICATION

In the sacred literature the word *henosis* or "one flesh" is an expression of the deep unity of two individuals. In this literal as well as symbolic unity the metaphysical oneness or mutual identification of one with the other achieves profound depth of meaning in some couples. As important and meaningful as the sex-linked experience may be, the sexual union *per se* is not as important to some persons as the implied deeper identification of one person with another. In marriage counsel it is a common experience to hear a woman say, "As much as it hurts to know that my husband is having an affair with another woman, I hope that it is me that he loves and not her." Whatever the reason for the differences in reaction, women more than men seem to link sexual intercourse with its symbolic import of deeper pair identity.

In the Christian literature "one flesh" is strongly identified with procreation, but not exclusively. As Bailey notes, more emphasis has recently been given to the unique relationship of pair identity.

> Nowhere in the New Testament is any prominence assigned to procreation, whereas the great Pauline conception of marriage as the analogue of Christ's union with His Church is indisputably unitive . . . Moreover, intercourse has no exclusive connexion with procreation, though that alone may be its biological end; it does not always result in conception, it can take place during pregnancy and menstruation, and is satisfactorily possible after a woman's childbearing days are over. And when the delicate and

complicated organization of human sexuality is considered it becomes difficult to explain it, or to explain it away, in terms of generation alone. It seems perfectly clear, as Brunner says (The Divine Imperative, p. 368), that ". . . the Christian ethic must stand for the independent meaning of the erotic and sex element within marriage as an expression of love, not merely as a means of procreation."[19]

The relationship between the capacity for identification with another and basic personality has received little attention from researchers. However, it has been this writer's experience that people high in the socially active-ascendant component tend to be less able to identify with others than those who are high in the socially affirming component or the shy "ideational" kind of person.

LOVE AND IDEALIZATION

Idealization is the tendency to "read into," to project onto the love object, ennobling thoughts, feelings, and sentiments. "You" becomes vested with "Thou." The best is accentuated while limitations and defects are minimized. One is disposed to feel that the cup is half full rather than half empty.

Idealization can take place on the high ground of objectivity or reality, but it can also be a way of distorting reality by projecting onto another qualities that do not exist. Such immature or neurotic projection often obtains in "love at first sight" when one does not know the other but nevertheless feels that the other must be "perfect."

Take the case of Betty. She was attractive, but the sister of a very popular older brother who tended to berate her and

[19] Bailey, *op. cit.*, pp. 106–107.

draw invidious comparisons between her and his older, more sophisticated girl friends. Betty developed quite profound feelings of personal and social inferiority. She tried to get his attention, do things for him, and win his approval. Meeting with rebuff she would retire to her room and bury herself in romantic magazines, dreaming of her Prince Charming who for certain, she knew, would come along some day. Boy friends her own age seemed to hold little attraction for her even though they did provide affirmation of her attractiveness.

While taking golf lessons at the Country Club she was strongly attracted to her professional golf instructor. He was attentive, socially graceful, and popular with a group of older girls at the Club. Unconsciously reënacting her former relationship with her brother, she idealized his every gesture. They were married and it seemed for a while that their relationship was perfect. Increasingly, however, she began to feel that he showed other women more attention than was professionally necessary. Minor sallies grew into suspicious accusations. During a party at which she had been drinking quite heavily she openly accused him of having an affair with one of the guests who was present. Subsequently they were divorced.

Betty suffered the old feelings of rejection, but returned to the fray by finding "most attractive" a young obstetrician who had just come into their community to practice medicine. They started dating and she was caught up in a new infatuation. Concentrating on his position in the community, his potential income, and the fact that other women sought him out, she could not see his irregular hours, canceling the dinner dance at the last moment, and his necessary attention to his women clients. She had idealized an aspect of his professional role without seeing the reality of his larger role. They were married. The same sequence of events that she experienced with her brother and her first husband followed.

Until Betty began to understand her neurotic need for a certain kind of man, one whom she could idealize on an impaired reality basis, she was incapable of loving herself or anybody else. She experienced only the semblance but not the substance of love. She was the victim of projection-idealization sustained by her ability to rationalize—to give plausible sounding and socially acceptable excuses for something that did not exist. With other personal assets Betty can grow up, possibly with professional help to break through her defenses and build a new orientation based on reality and not on the adolescent projection of her fantasies.

Returning to the more positive aspect of idealization, we can appreciate the role of expecting, looking for, and assuming the best in the other when it is based on reality. It can then serve to motivate and to elicit the best in the other. It is one of the routes to self-other transcendence because in this positive idealization, we are our better selves and affirm the best in the other. To recognize the weaknesses and the limitations of the other is not to impair but to enhance the relationship because the relationship is then founded upon reality.

LOVE, SECURITY, AND STATUS

The last facets of love to be discussed are security and status. Actually they are overtones of the sense of identity discussed above. Security is not being used here in the mundane sense of financial security, but, a deep emotional assurance that one can "reveal" himself to the other unconditionally. Mental reservations, strategies, or ulterior considerations are absent. What exists is the ability to be oneself in the presence of the other, with feelings of closeness, relaxation, and informality. The feeling toward the person and the body of the other is the same as the feeling toward oneself and one's own. Immodesty is impossible in the presence of the other just as one cannot be immodest with oneself.

An important aspect of such security is freedom. Not only is the individual free to be himself—his better as well as his worse self—but there is a freedom from social and psychological restraint. There is no fear of offense, suspicion, jealousy, envy, or misunderstanding.

A part of such freedom to be oneself and do what one wishes to do is a sense of responsibility toward the other. If the needs of the other are at variance with one's own, one can sacrifice or defer out of the intrinsic desire to do so, without the feeling of obligation, self-sacrifice, or self-restraint. Such freedom stems from the fuller understanding of the self and the other. To understand is to make allowances and to practice a kind of "high-minded resignation" to that which is at variance and cannot be changed. The insecure remain confused. They chafe and retaliate.

Status as an aspect of love is the sense of self-esteem and approval of the spouse that she (he) feels is accorded by others outside the marriage. We like to congratulate ourselves in the affairs of the heart.

Looking in retrospect at the larger meaning of love we can see that, despite the fact that Western Civilization has been striving to understand and to attain a greater capacity to love for over two thousand years, we seem to know much less about it than we have presumed. With the relatively late entry of the academic disciplines into the quest, we seem to have made substantial headway in two directions. First, we are defining forms of immature and neurotic love that can now be recognized for what they are. Second, the behavioral sciences are aiming more directly than before at the study of the circumstances of human growth and development that result in the maximal capacity to love another as the self, and kinds of marriages that provide the optimal context in which love can grow, continually transcending its less mature forms.

Part Two

DATING, COURTSHIP, AND ENGAGEMENT

Chapter 7

DATING

DATING AS we practice it today in the United States is in many aspects culturally unique, and is to be found in few other parts of the world. Among the older and larger populations of the East, marriages are arranged by the parents, often without the previous meeting or acquaintance of the couple. Romance does not enter in either as an expectation or consideration. Our conception of "romance" is uniquely Western and almost exclusively American. Europe and some parts of the East such as Japan are, however, undergoing rapid change from traditional courtship and matchmaking patterns in which marrying for duty, family status, the rearing of children, religious dicta, and other nonromantic reasons are of central consideration. This change has emerged very recently and is proceeding with rapid and often disrupting swiftness.

Recently we have witnessed the great debate in England over the romance of Princess Margaret. It was of serious concern throughout the British Commonwealth. Many believed that she should have married the man she loved, whereas others believed that she should sacrifice any romantic or other personal consideration and maintain her loyalty and duty to the precepts of the Church and the Throne. Many bitter words from the British press and pulpits characterized the tenacity with which any change in orientation toward traditional courtship and marriage mores was resisted by a large segment of the population.

Another commentary on the uniqueness of our American orientation toward courtship and the larger culture complex that surrounds it, is a letter received by the author from Kyoto, Japan, at the time of the controversy over Princess Margaret, the fall of 1955. A former Japanese-American student wrote of the tremendous impact that the American ideas of romance, dating, and courtship were having on Japan, primarily since World War II. He wrote,

> I have seen, heard and experienced quite a lot of Japanese society in its present mode. . . . To be part of the crowd in Riesman's sense of "other-direction" you must be able to say something as to how American culture is affecting Japanese morals. . . . Yet, strangely, American Jazz, fashions which bare more of the body, romantic movies and novels, etc., all of which flourished in Japan, are blamed for their undermining influence. Right now both Christians and Buddhists are concerned but are helpless to stem the tide. Japanese culture as a mass system and deeply traditional is changing so rapidly that people are confused by the strange, inconsistent and heterogeneous codes that are emerging.[1]

According to the new Japanese constitution young people may choose their own mates and by-pass the sanction of their parents. We of the West can only imagine the personal and

[1] Personal letter dated November 30, 1955.

social dislocation that has resulted from the introduction of romance and dating into the old sacred culture of the East.

Here in America dating as it is being practiced among young people is relatively new. One of the significant changes that has taken place largely since World War I is the emergence of dating among younger people as a social experience quite different in intent and purpose from that of courtship. In the present discussion we shall distinguish dating, whether casual or more steady, from courtship. Courtship will be regarded as the serious pursuit of another to marry. Not only is the distinction between dating and courtship warranted as a fact in the experience of young people, with early dating with no intention of marrying the "date" now nearly universal in American junior high schools, but the distinction also can serve to point up how inadequate a courtship is when based on a pattern of dating alone. This aspect of the problem will be taken up in the next chapter.

FUNCTIONS OF DATING

Among young people a date is someone of the opposite sex to talk to, to get acquainted with, to come to know, to serve as an escort to social functions. There is not the slightest implication that the couple is serious in intent or emotional involvement. Courtship does not necessarily enter in at all. There is no commitment beyond the immediate occasion. Dating is a way of expanding one's circle of contacts and friendships with the opposite sex, widening one's opportunity for social engagements, reducing parental influence upon heterosexual experience which includes one's choice of a date, and gaining new experiences that will enhance one's chances in the selection of a prospective spouse.

More recently another function of dating has emerged. It is what is often referred to in the marriage literature as *rating*. To be seen with a most desirable person is a way of enhancing one's prestige. It might be regarded as a form of sociopsychological "conspicuous consumption." As one fellow put it:

> The appearance of a girl on a date is very important to me. I like attractive girls who dress smartly. It does my ego a lot of good to be with a girl that gets glances of notice and approval as she walks by. Neatness and chic in dressing are my criteria for a date, rather than beauty. A large part of a girl's appearance is made up by her manners. I want a girl who knows how to conduct herself naturally wherever you go. Stage mannerisms or just the lack of correct social manners bother me. Any crudeness, vulgarity, or cheapness cannot go along with an attractive girl in my estimation.[2]

Note in this quote how much emphasis there is on external qualities such as dress, manners, and above all, social acceptability. The desirability of a date based on personal standards and appearances differs a great deal according to social class, age, and sex. Hollingshead, in his study of Elmstown, found that dating follows fairly well defined class standards, ranging from the "400" whose family backgrounds and manners are sometimes more important than their morals, to the lowest social classes where neither manners or morals are very important.[3]

DATING PATTERNS

For girls, there is a great deal of homogamy in dating, that is, they date boys much like themselves socially, economi-

[2] Ernest W. Burgess, Paul Wallin, and Gladys Denny Shultz, *Courtship, Engagement, and Marriage,* New York, Lippincott, 1954, pp. 29 ff.

[3] August B. Hollingshead, *Elmtown's Youth,* New York, Wiley, 1949, pp. 204 ff.

cally, educationally, etc. When they cross class lines they usually date "upward," i.e., boys from a higher social stratum. Whereas boys may and frequently do have two standards: girls like themselves whom they would consider marrying, and others who are one or more rungs down on the social ladder. Their behavior and their expectations on a date tend to be appropriate to the standards of the girl, with the girl of the lower station often being more sexually permissive.

Hollingshead found that dating patterns of persons in and out of school differed markedly. More of the out-of-school persons dated. They dated more frequently and more of them went steady. They generally dated other out-of-school youth, and they usually had premarital intercourse during their middle or late teens. At the time of his study 26 percent of those of high school age not in high school had married, usually drifting into marriage against the wishes of their parents. A high proportion of these unions were more or less forced marriages, with only 20 percent of the couples married before the inception of pregnancy.[4]

DATING ORIENTATIONS OF COLLEGE STUDENTS

In the main college women are in serious pursuit of a man to marry. This is nearly as true of freshmen as of seniors, though the graduating senior, quite understandably, seems to evidence a greater urgency. However, this is not necessarily true of men. Quite often a couple comes in for counseling who have been dating for some time, perhaps several years. Their question concerns a decision regarding a pinning and/or engagement. They have been having a number of inexplicable quarrels, provoked by all kinds of "little things."

[4] Burgess, Wallin, and Shultz, *op. cit.*, p. 37.

During such sessions the counselor frequently feels that the girl is serious, is emotionally involved, does want to move on to the planning of marriage, and wants the boy to commit himself. On the other hand the boy impresses the counselor with three orientations. First, he obviously likes the girl. He may even love her if he dared admit the implied commitment to himself. Second, he feels occupationally insecure and somewhat confused about the specialization, complexity, and competition in the occupational world. Sometimes his uncertain military status enters in. He acts as if he knows that he is going to have to "make the jump" sometime, but feels that he is being pushed and does not like it. Third, he doesn't want to have to think about marriage now, but he definitely wants to keep his girl and not have her lose interest and possibly break off their relationship. He recognizes, however, that he does have some obligations to her and feels quite ambivalent toward himself as well as toward her because he cannot have his unqualified freedom and still remain in the fray indefinitely.

True

Some men are still quite unprepared for the life that they have projected for themselves and will change in their orientation toward the girl with the gaining of greater personal maturity and occupational security. Others are financially and occupationally quite secure but have another girl "back home" and do not want to become emotionally involved with the present "date." Still others are not interested seriously in any girl for the present. They want to retain their unqualified freedom.

It is this writer's considered judgment that many college men are considerably less interested in marriage as a consideration in dating than are college women. This is understandable in the light of their respective positions, as well as their underlying motivations and considerations as mentioned above. However, this is not to imply that most college men are not interested in marriage. The great majority are, and seek in a date the kind of a girl whom they would consider marrying. Perhaps the difference between college men and women is largely one of timing. She is relatively ready for marriage while he is not. The age or academic class of the man would impose an important qualification here, whereas it would not necessarily in the case of the girl.

If these clinical impressions are substantiated by empirical research it would probably mean that college women are at somewhat of a disadvantage in their dating relationships with college men. Being more "serious" in her intentions she renders herself more vulnerable to exploitation by him. Being less involved he is freer to carry on the relationship on his terms. She, feeling that she has more at stake, does not want to "lose him" and thus is tempted to compromise more than she would otherwise be inclined to do. If both college men and women could understand this dating dilemma more clearly it would help them to be more honest in their intentions, with less consequent, inadvertent exploitation.

Preferences of College Students in Dating Behavior

In the Burgess-Wallin study of 1000 couples, it was found that college students have a rather clear-cut idea of what they prefer in the dating behavior of their companions. Since other studies bear out the findings of this Chicago study, let us look at them.

WHAT MEN LIKE IN A GIRL

I like a girl who:

1) can carry on a good conversation, especially on a first date when you are just getting acquainted. I don't mean that the girl should carry the full load of the conversation; she should

be able to listen as well as talk. I don't think that the fellow should always have to bring up the topic of conversation.

2) will make a definite choice if there is one to make as to what you will do. I don't like the "I don't care" type of girl. I myself may have a preference about what to do, but I think that a girl should have something to say about the matter also. This is especially true if you have dated the girl frequently before.
3) doesn't keep asking what time it is during the last of the evening. I think the girl should have a little trust in the fellow that he will see to it that she gets in on time.
4) wears good-looking clothes and wears them to the best advantage. I believe that a girl that wears smart clothes and knows how to wear them, can many times help to offset some of the beauty requirements she may not have.
5) doesn't mention other dates she has had or places she has gone.
6) does not collect things every place she goes. I strongly dislike the "I must have an ash tray" type of girl.
7) is reasonably attractive and desirable to other fellows as well as myself.
8) doesn't keep you waiting.
9) can adjust quickly to new people she meets on a double or triple date.
10) can have just as much fun roller skating as she can dancing at a hotel.
11) does not drink or smoke excessively.
12) has enough gumption to say "no" when offered a drink or a smoke if she really doesn't do either.
13) will draw the line at heavy petting, but isn't frigid. I do not dislike a girl who will not kiss you good night on a first date. But if you get the same reaction on a second date, I think that you should find another girl.

WHAT GIRLS LIKE IN A MAN

I like fellows who:

1) are not last minute dates.
2) arrive on time.

3) dress appropriately.
4) do not discuss other dates they have had.
5) meet a girl's family gracefully.
6) use good English.
7) take you nice places, not necessarily costly.
8) compliment you on your appearance.
9) do not talk loud and brag.
10) consult you in regard to the evening's plans.
11) do not honk to announce they are waiting.
12) do not act as if they are conferring a favor on you to date you.
13) are good talkers without having a "line."
14) are neat in personal matters—hair, nails, teeth.
15) omit vulgar jokes and swearing.
16) have good manners—stand when you enter, etc.
17) do not talk sex.
18) show respect for girls.
19) can talk on current affairs.
20) are good dancers.
21) do not criticize your dress or hair.
22) show reverence in church and other places where it is due.
23) are good mixers.
24) have good table manners.
25) know when they are not wanted.
26) enjoy sports.
27) devote themselves to their date.
28) are interested in good books, music, art.
29) are popular with other fellows.
30) are good at love-making but not always making love.
31) do not flirt with other girls to make you jealous.
32) have poise—take everything in their stride.
33) are not immoral.
34) are thoughtful.
35) are entirely dependable.
36) are good sports.
37) have a good sense of humor.
38) are not sissies.

39) do not try to neck on the first date.
40) are not routine petters.

Of course, no fellow is expected to measure up perfectly to all of these social graces, but those who come closest to it will be tops on a girl's list of favorites.[5]

Dating Codes on College Campuses

Dating has been a subject of scientific study on a number of American college and university campuses. A composite picture of morals, manners, and problems of college dating has emerged. However, it must not be assumed that the American college dating scene represents a homogeneous picture. There are some marked geographical differences, especially between some of the private schools of the East and our state colleges and universities. Eastern colleges and universities are less coeducational in tradition than are western schools, with eastern schools more like European universities in their dating and intersex social activities. "I am amazed at how much time American students spend in discussing dates and dating, as compared with students in my own country," commented an exchange student from Central Europe. "There we seem to play cards, drink beer, argue politics, and spend more time in groups—men with men and women with women. Furthermore, in America you seem to exercise more control over your students' personal lives than is obtained in Europe—closing hours, etc."

During the three years that this writer lived in Central Europe prior to World War II, he saw very little social interaction between college men and women on university campuses. One of the favorite pastimes of male students was

[5] *Ibid.*, pp. 48–50.

sword dueling even though it was forbidden by law, and there were no women observers.

The academic life of the eastern part of the United States has been strongly influenced by a noncoeducational tradition. Some of the drinking songs, traditions of the "Ivy League," are openly hostile to coeds. For the more important parties girls from outside the university are invited but the idea of campus coeds is frowned upon. This pattern seems to change considerably as one moves to the West Coast where, most frequently, the schools have been coeducational from their founding.

We can see that there are marked differences in student dating, orientations, and activities in our American universities. However, studies from the University of Wisconsin, Bucknell, Florida, Penn State, California at Berkeley, and other places indicate that a comparatively homogeneous, picture of coeducational state school dating codes is emerging.[6] The findings of Burgess, Wallin, and Shultz are quite representative:

THE MASCULINE CODE

My personal set of rules in regard to social dating is as follows:

Appearance. A girl hates to have a man come for her looking as though he were dressed to wash the car. Therefore, some of the items I have avoided when taking a girl out are soiled shirt, mussy suit, crumpled hat, socks that droop, and all articles which have definitely had their day. Fads or extremes in style not only make one conspicuous but are in bad taste. I believe it is better to be a year behind the style than a jump or two ahead.

Approach. There's a certain technique to making dates. I plan

[6] *Ibid.*, pp. 52 ff. See also, Robert O. Blood, Jr., "Uniformities and Diversities in Campus Dating Preferences," *Marriage and Family Living*, February, 1956, pp. 37–45.

to make my approach so as to get the best results. I ask the young lady some time in advance, allowing more time according to the importance of the event. This shows she isn't second, or third choice. I never call at mealtime or at ten minutes to eight and expect her to accept a date for that evening with enthusiasm. I believe a girl will always appreciate a hint about my plans so that she will know how to dress.

Behavior in public. The most all around statement covering public actions is "to be smooth about things." Act with dignity and reserve, being careful not to shove her around by the elbow, and not to walk on the wrong side of her. If I'm going to the theater, I try to get tickets ahead of time. This procedure will sometimes eliminate standing in a long line at the ticket window or trying to be comfortable in the last row of the balcony. One important thing I always remember to omit, and that is honking the horn raucously to let her know of my arrival. I always call for her at the door and help her into the car.

The farewell. My final responsibility for the evening is to see her safely home at the appointed hour. If her father said to get home before midnight there is just one thing to do: get home before midnight. I don't believe I have ever left a girl at the curb, or fumbling with her key or the night latch. The policy which is best to follow is to deposit her safely within her door. If it is late and the members of her family have retired I make sure that I don't disturb them.

THE FEMININE CODE

Before I became pinned I dated almost every week-end, and I had an unconscious set of rules that I had learned or had been told to follow in dating procedure.

When to refuse a date. One of these rules was that you should accept the first boy that asks you for a particular day or night. This is easy to say, but not so easy to follow. If a boy called me two or three weeks before an event (even if it was a Prom or some other special occasion) I'm afraid that I sometimes refused him even if I had not already been asked for that night. It always seems as if the boys you dislike most call you the farthest

in advance. What should you do? I have usually decided that if you definitely dislike a boy—yet he persists in asking you out—it is much fairer to him and you if you refuse. Eventually he will find out that there is no use calling. If you do accept a date with a boy you don't like because otherwise you would have to sit home that night, you should be pleasant and a "good date." After all, if you accept the date you must not take it out on him because you don't like it—it's your own fault you are there.
Breaking a date. I always felt guilty about breaking a date and always tried to be careful in accepting dates so I would not want to back down at the last minute with a feeble excuse. It's better to refuse in the beginning. This may cause complications, and I sat home many a night for the handsome hero who never phoned. If you are popular and in circulation it isn't bad to refuse dates, but otherwise it is good to be seen different places with different people.

The Sex Code

We know that there are a range and variety of sex codes even in the relatively homogeneous middle classes. However, there has emerged a pattern of expectation and behavior that tends to characterize our state colleges and universities and some private schools.

In the first place it is the girl who usually determines what is appropriate and where to draw the line. The boy tends to test the limits, as it were, but accepts her definition of the situation as long as he continues to date her. On the first date there is little if any physical love making. They may sit together and hold hands, but the good-night kiss is usually declined until the second or third time they have been out together. Many boys do expect a good-night kiss on their first date but are quite willing to wait, satisfied that the girl does have standards. Many fellows state that it is not her refusal that is important, but her attitude. If she is responsive to him as a person, affirming, and appreciative, he reflects these feelings and is satisfied. As one put it, "It isn't the notes that are played, but the tone that makes the music."

Depending upon the degree of emotional involvement that develops, the couple may move on to light physical intimacies—holding in the arms and kissing, referred to as necking. This usually happens on the subsequent dates if the couple are attracted to one another. This characterizes much of the dating up to the time of a deeper relationship which is often formalized by a pinning or engagement. During this later phase many couples participate in heavier intimacies—varying degrees of physical closeness, fondling, and body contact, referred to as petting. This is the limit for many couples up until the later stages of the engagement period when the deepest stimulation short of coitus is experienced, sometimes with accompanying orgasm by one or both. About half of the couples studied on the various campuses where these studies have been made, report that this is the extent of their physical intimacy, and that they enter marriage virginal. Less than half have sexual intercourse before marriage with their future spouse, but are not promiscuous.

There is little question about the near universality of necking as part of the college code. Notwithstanding evidence of considerable petting, it is, however, controversial. Some couples feel that it "is not right" and refrain because they do not want to bear the anxiety and guilt that is engendered. Others may refrain not so much on moral grounds but because of their desire not to become so caught up in, and thus preoccupied with, the physical aspect of their relationship. They say, in effect, that they wish to remain emotionally unencumbered so that they are freer to consider the other aspects of their relationship and to engage in activities that they regard as more developmental. Still others feel that they would be unable to keep within the bounds of their own standards and do not want to run the risk of a premature marital commitment or carry the emotional burden of feeling that they had violated their own standards.

For others, however, the problem is more one of reputation, especially on the part of the girl. She knows that some men discuss the details of a date during their bull sessions. She does not want to be an inadvertent victim of character assassination. She is quite aware of the fact that if she becomes known for her looseness that she will be popular with some boys, but, most frequently, not the boy she really wants. Uppermost in many girls' minds is the question of the man's sincerity, affection, and discretion. She is more permissive where these are assured.

Rating and Dating

During the 1930's Dr. Willard Waller, a family sociologist, wrote that there was a great deal of exploitation on college campuses, that much of the dating was superficial and treated like a game in which the so-called "line" was used to ensnare and exploit another, with emphasis on the materialistic and social climbing aspects of the relationship. Whether or not this was true at that time we do not really know. However, recent studies at Michigan and Pennsylvania State College indicate a definite shift from the materialistic and competitive aspect of dating to that of sincerity and mutual regard. This writer's contacts with students on different college campuses located in different parts of the country, and hundreds of autobiographies, would tend to substantiate the Michigan,

Pennsylvania State, and other studies.[7] There will always be a minority who are out for all that they can get and who are concerned about no one but themselves. They are to be found anywhere. However, It appears that the majority of college students date for fun, for growth and development, and as preparation for marriage.

THOSE WHO DO NOT DATE

Those who do not date might be placed roughly in two categories: first, those who want to date, but for some reason are unable to; and second, those who prefer not to date or to date very infrequently and casually. As to the first category, there are many reasons and combinations of reasons why some people cannot date, ranging from not having a requisite amount of popularity or inviting personal qualities, to deep psychological problems such as unconscious attachments to parents or parent figures. Theirs is a problem of developing intersexual competence and the skills of social interaction and communication, which may involve developing personal autonomy and emotional maturity—freeing themselves from neurotic attachments. The reasons these persons give for not dating are nearly always rationalizations which offer plausible sounding but not valid explanations. They often need help, but they can change once they face

[7] For one of the most recent and critical discussions of Waller's assumptions as tested empirically by Robert O. Blood, Jr., see E. E. LeMasters, *Modern Courtship and Marriage,* New York, Macmillan, 1957, pp. 70 ff. One of the better general discussions of dating is to be found in Evelyn Millis Duvall and Reuben Hill, *When You Marry,* New York, Heath, 1953, chap. 3. See also, Willard Waller and Reuben Hill, *The Family: A Dynamic Interpretation,* New York, Dryden, 1951, chaps. 8–12; Robert O. Blood, Jr., *Anticipating Your Marriage,* Glencoe, Free Press, 1955

their problem squarely and take steps to gain the necessary freedom and skills.

Those in the second category have no serious problem except to realize that as the years go by the field of available persons narrows. In the Chicago study by Professors Burgess and Cottrell, they found that marriage in the later 20's or early 30's was related to the best future marital adjustment, as measured by their tests. However, there is no close statistical relation between age of marriage and success in marriage after entering the 20's. Persons who are caught up in their work, or preparation for their future work, unlike those in the first group, sense no immediate or urgent need for heterosexual company on a more personal or intimate level. Often they are emotionally absorbed in some creative pursuit. They may or may not be sexually continent. However, sexual continence does not seem to harm one when it is the result of sublimation or high-minded resignation. Continence that is a result of the fear of sex is quite another matter, and is often emotionally damaging, perhaps not because of the continence but because of the fear. It is interesting to consider that sex is one of the strongest animal drives, yet one from which man suffers least upon deprivation.

Such nondating persons can and often do meet someone connected with their work and marry. Others become quite satisfied with their bachelor status and do not marry. However, rather extensive professional and personal experience would lead this writer to believe that most persons would prefer to marry if they could find one whom they regarded as capable of meeting their high standards and expectations. This can be a serious personal problem to the one out of ten persons in America who does not marry.

Chapter 8

COURTSHIP: ATTRACTION AND SELECTION

THE FAILURE of marriage can often be attributed to too superficial a courtship. It might be too brief an acquaintance or a relationship that had bogged down in immaturity or neuroticism in which the couple did not come to know one another's deeper needs, orientations, and expectations. One or both might have been vulnerable to being attracted to and selecting another on the basis of compensatory personal needs without taking into consideration their future compatibility and growth.

Our high divorce rate and the other indexes of marital failure are evidence enough that too many persons do not experience a thoroughgoing courtship in which they understand more fully their own personality and that of the prospective spouse.

In addition to the functions served in dating, courtship has other more complex and mature functions to be met before a couple can make any legitimate claim to marrying responsibly. These courtship functions include: (1) the more mature understanding of the bases of mutual attraction and the grounds upon which the other has been selected; (2) the testing of every conceivable aspect of the relationship not only for the present but for future growth and compatibility; and (3) the preparation for marriage, including the physical, economic, emotional, and spiritual foundations upon which a home is to be founded. Marriage, thus, will not be a running leap and plunge, but an imperceptible step across a threshold that has been well planned in advance.

Such an orientation may seem unromantic and thus objectionable to the immature. However, it seems to this writer as imperative as the intensive preparation for a successful concert tour by the musical artist. To argue that thoughtful planning will take the deeper satisfaction out of marriage is to argue that learning to play well takes the appreciation out of music. The immature rebel because it imposes on them the responsibility of marrying well, a responsibility that they are not yet ready to carry.

The purpose of this and the following chapters is to point up the phases of the courtship process cited above, to show how some couples fail to fulfill the possibilities of more adequate attraction and selection, testing, and maturing of their relationship; and, then move on to a discussion of the kind of courtship that portends future compatibility and growth.

IMMATURE AND NEUROTIC ATTRACTION

Some persons are attracted to others and marry for immature or neurotic reasons—to escape impossible home conditions, for romance or sex which they mistakenly think is love, to escape the demands of a job in a highly competitive and threatening occupational world and at the same time acquire financial support, for name or fame, to have someone to manipulate and control, for the ego enhancement to support faltering self-respect, to have someone to lean on and provide support, to have someone to hurt and exploit, and many other such reasons.

As the complex and varied as the reasons may be, there is scientific evidence that most faulty marriages fall into nine or ten broad categories, and can be described in terms of our theory of basic personality. In a pilot study made by Community Research Associates, Inc., in New York, it was found that most faulty marriages that they studied fell into typical "axes around which family relationships revolve." With modest caution they report, "The classifications . . . present a hypothesis evolved by a multidiscipline team of skilled diagnosticians with intensive thought after studying and analyzing case material . . ."

Two examples of these "axes" are: "(1) A dual immature dependency axis. A passive dependent man and a passive dependent woman. (2) A woman oriented anxiety axis. A controlling dependent woman and a passive dependent man."[1]

From these examples of faulty marriage it can be seen that the couples were attracted to and selected one another on the basis of their neurotic needs. In the first case, there were two socially and psychologically dependent people who could be two immature persons high in the A-component of basic personality. Since faulty marriage will be taken up in Chapter 15, only two "axes" have been cited here to illustrate the

[1] *Classification of Disorganized Families for Use in Family Oriented Diagnosis and Treatment,* New York, Community Research Associates, 1953.

point that many persons are attracted to one another in the name of love, but find later that the real basis for their attraction was the desire for support, mistaking the "responsiveness" of the other for "strength."

Sometimes one of a couple is immature but not neurotic and needs further experience to distinguish apparent from real maturity in the other, while the other may be neurotic with less promise of growth without professional help. The following is a case of a marriage in which an inexperienced girl fell in love with (was attracted by) a "dashing, handsome" young man.[2] He, needing someone to look up to his "great strength" was attracted to her attentive deference. As it turned out, however, he was quite neurotic which was not apparent during courtship, needing a wife-mother figure with whom he could compete, show off, and aggress against. In terms of our personality theory the girl might be regarded as high in the socially affirming A-component, with potential aggressive-ascendant B-component, while the boy was high in the socially aggressive-ascendant B-component with supplementary strength in the socially withdrawing C-component. Let us look at the case of Glenn and Vivian.

Vivian grew up in a New England home that was quite Victorian in orientation. Her mother was a quiet, efficient homemaker. Her father and two brothers owned and operated a store. Vivian was an active and rather dynamic girl who identified herself with her mother. She looked up to her father and brothers from some distance since they formed somewhat of a self-contained "male side of the house" unit. Feminine and masculine roles were distinct and separate in the family. Vivian wanted to work with them in their merchandising firm but they told her that she should do more

[2] This case is taken up again for fuller treatment in Chapter 15.

feminine things and be a homemaker. The family was close but not too intimate. They were friendly and coöperative with one another. When Vivian was 18 years old she met Glenn whom she thought was a handsome, dashing, and most eligibile young man.

Glenn came from a broken home. His parents had been separated when he was very young, and his mother had not remarried but had worked to support Glenn and an older sister. During his adolescence his mother's health began to "fail." She complained of a heart disorder and constant fatigue. During his adolescence his mother relied increasingly on his financial and moral support and he began to feel that she was holding on to him, restricting his activities with his friends, and making unreasonable demands on his time. Glenn rebelled by staying out late and coming home with the odor of beer and cigarettes on his breath which offended her. His mother's reaction was more complaining, even greater dependency, and more controls on him. Finally their relationship reached an impasse and he took a room down the street from where they lived. The mother and the sister then went to him in tears, told him that he was the father, husband, and brother in the home, and begged him to return. He did, in triumph over them. It was soon after this that he met Vivian.

Vivian was first attracted to Glenn's apparent "independence," and his active, "dynamic" personality. Looking up to him as she did to her father and brothers, she was in effect playing a deferent, admiring role. In turn he felt her adoring court and responded. Neither had had very much experience in dating or other heterosexual activities. They felt that it was love and were married.

As years went on Vivian went to work in a ladies ready-to-wear store where she advanced in human relations skills, received responsibility, and had an independent income. She made more demands on Glenn, expected more little courtesies in the home, and asked him not to spend so much time visiting his mother. He rebelled at "any woman making demands on me." Early on Sunday morning he would take off alone with his golf bag or fishing rod and Vivian would not see him until evening when he returned fatigued and complaining of "some possible heart trouble." This served to throw Vivian back into her more deferent, less demanding, and solicitous role until, after being coached by one of her friends, she told him that he could not "work this old gag" any longer. At this he packed a suitcase and went to stay with his mother.

Enough of Glenn and Vivian's problem has been given to illustrate Vivian's lack of experience at the time she met Glenn, which resulted in the projection of her orientation toward her father and brothers onto Glenn. This would have been all right if he had been able to respond on a more adult basis. In his background, however, there was a marked absence of masculine roles, a tendency to argue with and "win" over women, then "walk out." His adolescent dependency upon women, first his mother and sister, then his wife, failed after he had, perhaps quite unconsciously, used the same strategy of illness that his mother had used on him.

Without going into a deeper analysis of their relationship it will suffice to point out that Vivian's limited experience had not taught her the difference between apparent and genuine maturity. Glenn had never had an opportunity to receive and to return genuine love. He had only learned to compete with and attempt to dominate the women in his life, while depending on them to take care of him. Their attraction to one another was the reënacting of the social and emotional roles that each had learned in their families, meeting her immature and his neurotic needs. The failure of their marriage in one sense could be said to be the result of their faulty attraction-selection.

POSITIVE BASES OF ATTRACTION

Considerable research has been undertaken in an effort to find the underlying bases of attraction.[3] It has been found that one factor is geographic and occupational proximity. There is a tendency for people who live near one another and who work together to marry. This can have a favorable or an adverse effect upon the marriage. It can be favorable when one of the underlying bases of the relationship is social and cultural homogeneity and common interests which often obtain when a couple come from the same segment of the community or share the same work. It can be limiting and divisive when the circumstance is one of social isolation as in the case of a small town where the number of prospective mates is very limited. Here there may be a tendency to marry the one available rather than one more suited. This is especially true of the couple who marry then move to a community where there is a greater diversity of social types and personalities. It is something like trying to sell a large life in-

[3] Excellent recently published discussions of different aspects of attraction and selection are to be found in, Morris Fishbein and Ruby Jo Reeves Kennedy, *Modern Marriage and Family Living,* New York, Oxford University Press, 1957, pp. 50 ff.; Ernest W. Burgess, Paul W. Wallin, and Gladys Denny Shultz, *Courtship, Engagement, and Marriage,* New York, Lippincott, 1954, pp. 19 ff. See also, Judson T. Landis and Mary G. Landis, *Building A Successful Marriage,* New York, Prentice-Hall, 1948, chap. 4; Alan Bates, "Parental Roles in Courtship," *Social Forces,* XX (1942), 485–486; August B. Hollingshead, "Cultural Factors in Mate Selection," *American Sociological Review,* XV (1950), 619–627.

surance policy to one of six random prospects. To increase the number to 60 would increase the possibility of finding one with enough money to buy the kind of policy one wishes to sell. It is not always necessary to concentrate on one with a restricted income and be satisfied with the most obtainable under the circumstances. That is the point: extend the circumstances.

There are some persons who believe that seeking broad acquaintance is symptomatic of being fickle, insincere, and a "bargain hunter." Often young adults are advised to "go steady," with the intent of marrying the first person who is sufficiently interested to request it. More often high school students tend to form a pattern of going steady with only one or two others, resulting in narrowing dangerously the person's acquaintance with more prospects. This orientation confuses the difference between dating and courtship. It cuts off the range of social contacts at a time when it is easier to form friendships with persons of the opposite sex than it is later, due to greater social mobility and less critical self-consciousness. Also, parents who control the courtship of their children too closely run the risk of restricting the youth's interests in a broad range of individuals.

Perhaps the attitude of the bargain hunter ought to be assumed, if by the phrase one means seeking the best possible on the marriage market while fully expecting to pay a worthy price—give a full measure for that expected. If by bargain hunting, one means the sharp practice of misrepresenting what one has to offer, it can result in exploitation and disappointment. If this sounds unromantic, calculating, and undesirable, perhaps the need for growth is indicated: the story of Cinderella and her Prince Charming may be a pleasant dream fantasy, but we must learn to operate on a more realistic basis. Mature people do not take as many chances, but rather make more of their chances. It would be so much easier if one could fall into successful marriage; it would be so much easier if a young man could fall into a successful business without assiduous effort, planning, and preparation, but this doesn't happen.

Girls planning to do gainful work before marrying might consider more carefully their chances of meeting the greatest number of prospective men in one or another occupation. Teaching, social work, nursing, or any occupation that restricts contact with eligible men is less desirable from the standpoint of mate attraction than the sales and service positions.

Where one plans to live is an important consideration. For a more cosmopolitan minded young person, the small rural community contains many fewer prospects than the city. This also is true of small schools and especially true of noncoeducational and parochial schools. Newer areas of the country tend to have a higher proportion of men of marriageable age than do the older areas. The West Coast is better for the girl; the East Coast better for the boy. Cities tend to specialize in an occupational role; a high proportion of men to women in the industrial cities like Detroit; a high proportion of women to men in the political and cultural centers like Washington, D.C.

While these considerations may seem of remote interest to many, the high rate of mobility of young people within our states and from state to state indicates that they might be important during the courtship years when choosing a position, a place to work, or a school. However, in order to attract another, making oneself available is not enough. To attract the best prospect, a great deal of intelligent consideration should be given to personal and social development as well as appearance and manners.

Another basis of attraction and selection is a preconceived image or type of person. Research indicates that we are attracted more to persons like those we have grown up with and have learned to love, rather than the textbook or fashion-plate image of a universal ideal type. Often it is a composite of personal qualities that we have introjected or "taken in" as it were, in our past association with parents and friends. Thus a girl may be attracted to a person with her father's physique, her mother's warmth and perseverence, and brother Joe's sense of humor.

Often values, ideological outlook, and other expectations provide the mainsprings of attraction. They are set during the formative years and released when the person compatible with these orientations is met. For example, about one-half of the men and two-thirds of the women in the Burgess-Wallin study said that they would not marry another of a different race; about two-fifths of both men and women would not marry one of a different religion. Other differences reported, in order of descending importance, were educational status, markedly different political views, economic status, appearance, nonprofessional occupation, and not being a native American. Appearance was regarded as being little more than half as important by women as by men.

Research has found that affianced couples tended to be influenced in their choice of one another by the nature of their parental images.[4] Burgess, Wallin, and Shultz conclude that:

> Typical physical resemblances between the affianced person and the parent were in physique, posture, carriage, features and

[4] Bates, *op. cit.,* pp. 485–486; Burgess, Wallin, and Shultz, *op. cit.,* pp. 108 ff.

facial expression. . . . Occasionally a young man reported nearly all of the traits of his mother and fiancee to be identical. More often a few characteristics in his mother which he had felt important to him had been duplicated in his girl. Sometimes only one or two of the most significant traits in his mother appeared in his reports of his fiancee. Some of the more discerning young people decided upon reflection that the resemblances in physical appearance and personality were not as important to them as the feeling of loving and being loved, which was similar to the one sustained with a given parent, generally of the opposite sex, in childhood.

A second pattern, reported less frequently by engaged couples, is that of the "reverse" parental image. It is represented by cases where the parent image reproduced by the mate is not that of the parent of the opposite sex, but of the same sex.

While a third pattern, not as frequent as others among engaged couples, is that of the negative parental image, where the person reports being attracted to someone the direct opposite of the parent in one or more personality characteristics. Like the girl who stated that she was attracted to her fiance by his trait of dominating, which she desired in a husband because she disliked the passive role played by her father in his marriage . . .

A fourth and quite frequent pattern in mate selection is a combination of those traits of both parents which had made a deep impression in childhood. . . .

There is some evidence that in selecting a mate the tendency is to choose one that will continue to reproduce, as nearly as possible, the total home atmosphere, insofar as it has been a happy one. We regard parental image as more than a limiting factor. It is potent in turning thoughts toward a specific person in a group where all might be considered "possible."[5]

This writer agrees with these reseachers but does not think that they go far enough in their last generalization. As was illustrated in the case of Vivian and Glenn, individuals bring

[5] Burgess, Wallin, and Shultz, *op. cit.,* p. 110.

with them to marriage a whole repertory of social and emotional roles that have developed in their interaction with parents and siblings in their homes, the "negative" as well as the "positive" traits.

Another basis of attraction is homogamy, or "like marrying the like." The issue of whether persons tend to be attracted to persons like themselves has been clouded by some tendency in the marriage literature to assume a kind of "general" homogamy rather than to break the question into a number of parts and ask whether homogamy of choice with regard to physical characteristics or of values is necessarily related to a similarity in basic personality. Recent research indicates that there is a considerable tendency for persons to be attracted to others like themselves in some respects, but different in others.

In five of the six physical characteristics that Burgess, Wallin, and Shultz studied, engaged couples showed greater similarity than chance would accord statistically speaking. This was true also for health and physical appearance as reported by the individual and the affianced. Of the 31 personality traits studied, about 17 showed a greater than chance probability of being positively related. They found ". . . a strong tendency for persons with neurotic symptoms to be engaged to others like themselves. Correspondingly, non-neurotics unite with non-neurotics." They conclude with the statement that personality *need* appears to be perhaps the single most important factor in selecting a mate.[6]

Other studies such as those of Burgess and Cottrell, Winch, and Locke tend to confirm the case for homogamy of some social, physical, and psychological characteristics. However, recent evidence suggests that while homogamy of some psy-

[6] *Ibid.*, p. 115.

chological *traits* may obtain, such as two "friendly" people being attracted to one another, couples tend to attract one another on the basis of *complementary needs*. This is a principle more complicated than opposites attract or polar attraction. It is not merely that one is different, but different in a way that meets a need in the other.

In a study by Ktsanes he concluded that *patterns* of needs rather than single needs seem to be important in mate selection. After developing a personality typology, using the statistical method of factor analysis, he compared husband-wife teams and found that in no couple in the study did both members have the same personality type. The study concluded that there is a tendency for an individual to select a mate who is *different* in *emotional* make-up. The principle of polar attraction operated in some cases but not in others.[7]

The Ktsanes study lends support to the theory of selection on the basis of complementary basic personality and the studies of Community Research Associates cited above.

Thus it would seem that both of a couple could be friendly, but express it emotionally in quite a different manner, i.e., one quietly modest and the other more overtly demonstrative. This might suggest that we have *common* human needs, needs that are characteristic of all people, but *particular* and *different ways* in which these needs are expressed.

If this is true, it would seem to be important that a couple come to understand their deeper needs with a minimum of rationalization and with optimal reality sense. A clue to our needs lies in our understanding of basic personality and in

[7] Thomas Ktsanes, "Mate Selection on Basis of Personality Type: A Study Utilizing an Empirical Typology of Personality," *American Sociological Review,* XX, No. 5 (October, 1955), 547–551; Robert F. Winch, *Mate-Selection: A Study of Complementary Needs,* New York, Harper, 1958.

applying it to an analysis of oneself and one's spouse or prospective spouse.

In the discussion of basic personality in Chapter 2, needs including one's expectations, were discussed according to individual differences. However, there are human personality needs that seem to transcend the individual and might be regarded as universal. One useful formulation of such universal needs has been made by W. I. Thomas. He lists four. First, there is the need for recognition. This might be thought of as a less personal feeling that one is thought well of by those who are important to one. This provides the basis for much of the status striving in our society. Second, there is a more personal need for intimate response. Ego enhancement is less to the fore. More central is a feeling of closeness, of intimate relationship with another(s). Third is the need for new experience, whether it be a thrill of one sort or another, or the less emotional satisfaction of exploration and discovery—personal and impersonal. In courtship and in marriage this can be fulfilled by the physical and psychological intimacy of companionship or the discovery of life in the company of the partner. Fourth, there is the need for security in the foregoing three—security in the feeling that the regard of others is genuine, that personal response is honest and without ulterior motives, and that new experience is more deeply satisfying rather than merely momentary escape.

Fulfilling the general human needs posited above, as well as those stemming from the individual basic personality constitutes the *deeper substance* of contemporary marriage that seeks fulfillment in the reciprocity of the marital companionship. Thus, one of the tasks involved in the selection of a mate is to select one on the basis of total personality, rather than on the basis of segmental satisfaction of one particular need. One of the advantages of longer acquaintance and courtship is the greater opportunity to test not only for present satisfaction, but also for future growth and compatibility in all areas of personal need.

SCIENTIFIC PREDICTION OF MARITAL COMPATIBILITY

During the past 25 years there has emerged an area of scientific study of those couples who seem to succeed and those who fail in marriage. One of the knotty problems involved in any such pursuit is the definition of just what is being studied—in this instance "successful" marriage and "compatibility," one of the factors currently presumed to underlie successful marriage. Without attempting to define the successful marriage in any precise terms we may assume that not only the *present* nature of the relationship must be taken into consideration, but also its *future growth potential.* If the good marriage is thought of as one in which the deeper needs of both members of the couple are being met, continuing growth of the individuals as well as the relationship is one of the bases of successful marriage. The manner in which each couple pursue their marriage will differ. For some it may be a relationship experienced in an atmosphere of "communion." For others it may be more like a workout with foils on the strip, or attempting to better the time of the other as they ski into the slalom.

A number of marriage prediction scales have emerged from the study of marital adjustment. One most widely employed, is the revision of the Burgess-Cottrell "Marriage Prediction Scale." It takes into consideration aspects of the social and emotional backgrounds of each of the couple, their agreement or disagreement on a range of items that make up many of the day by day experiences of marriage, and finally, their future plans. A very recent development is a series of scales developed to measure the competence of persons in human relations skills. For example, one of the scales presumes to test the degree of "autonomy" achieved in relations with others. When this Foote-Cottrell "test" is completed it will consist of five scales which will constitute the test of "interpersonal competence."[8]

It is not assumed here that spouses can be selected scientifically, at least on the basis of our present knowledge. However, it can be of value to know what has been found to be characteristic of those who succeed in their marriage as compared with those who have only one chance out of four of remaining out of a divorce court—those whose scores on the Burgess-Cottrell test are in the lower 25 percent of the score range. The problem might be put a little differently as follows: In selecting a mate, what are the characteristics of persons and couples who have the highest chances of succeeding in marriage?

The Burgess-Cottrell "Marriage Prediction Scale" is made up of five parts.[9] Part One consists of items regarding the background of the individual, including health, marital status, education, work record, church affiliation and attendance, social participation in community organizations, the social status of the parental family, and the happiness of the parents' marriage. In general, it has been found that the

[8] See Nelson N. Foote and Leonard S. Cottrell, *Identity and Interpersonal Competence: A New Direction in Family Research,* Chicago, University of Chicago Press, 1955; Howard R. Stanton and Eugene Litwak, "Toward the Development of a Short Form Test of Interpersonal Competence," *American Sociological Review,* XX, No. 6 (December, 1955).

[9] For a presentation and discussion of the Marriage Prediction Schedule, see Burgess, Wallin, and Shultz, *op. cit.,* chap. 17.

person who has the highest chance for success in marriage is the one with higher education and a steady employment record except when in training, who is a member and participant in church and other community organizations, who comes from a respected family in the community, whose parents are happily married, who was close socially and emotionally to each of the parents, who received firm but not harsh discipline in the home, and who received his sex information in a context of understanding and affirmation at the hands of the parents.

The most important item in Part One is the nature of the relationship with the parents. This carries a higher predictive value than any others in the entire test.

Part Two consists of a list of personality traits that describe some of the characteristics of temperament and emotional maturity discussed in Chapter 5. In general the person who has a modest sense of self-respect, is somewhat easygoing rather than dominating, and has a sense of duty and a sense of humor, has the better chance for success in marriage. Ambitious, moody, dominating, nervous people rate lowest.

Part Three takes up the relationship of the person with previous men and women friends, the reaction of friends and relatives to the couple, the reaction to parents (in-laws) of the affianced, and the length of acquaintance and engagement. In general the person scores highest who has had many friends, both male and female, whose relationship (partner in the courtship) is approved of by friends and the parents of both, and who has had a long acquaintance and courtship (2 years or more).

Part Four takes up the interests, activities, agreement of the couple on a great range of topics including religion, philosophy of life, recreation, table manners, the demonstration of affection, etc. In general those couples who have the highest chances for success are those who have activities that they share, are affectionate toward one another and demonstrate it, who agree on matters of conventionality, money, etc., who settle disagreements by compromise rather than one or the other giving in, and who have an orientation of the permanence of marriage.

Part Five deals with the couple's plans for marriage—whether they plan a church marriage, the size of community in which they plan to live, housing, attitudes toward having children, and the like. In general the more conventional couples score the highest. They expect to be married in their church, be independent of their parents, live in the smaller or suburban community rather then the metropolitan city, and desire "very much" to have children.

It will be noted that this marriage prediction schedule deals more with individuals than with couples. As such it is more a measure of a person's suitability for marriage. If a couple could take the test and answer the questions with reference to one another, the scores could be averaged and then would be an indication of what the chances are that they will achieve a working adjustment in their marriage. However, the scores on any prediction schedule should be interpreted with great caution. While they are a statement of probability, there is much in two given personalities and their relationship that cannot be measured by any scale yet developed.

The purpose of introducing the general characteristics of the tests here is to acquaint the reader with an "inventory" of items and experiences that have been found to be related to future compatibility in marriage. They can help the person become aware of *some of the things that are important in selecting a marriage partner.*

Chapter 9

COURTSHIP: TESTING FOR SEXUAL COMPATIBILITY

In this chapter we shall consider the problem of testing for future sexual compatibility and the problem of continence during the courtship.

The teacher of marriage or marriage counselor is often asked how a couple might determine their future sexual compatibility. The question might be posed by the conscientious couple as follows: "If you advocate testing all phases of your future marriage, how can you test for sex compatibility if you do not have sex relations?" The answer has two parts. First, as to the desirability of raising the question, it is a consensus of professional opinion that the question of basic attitudes and orientations toward sex ought to be discussed by a couple as fully as possible during this engagement period. Second, what is the best way to test in experience the *potential* responsiveness of the other?

Since we have already taken up this subject in part during

the discussion of emotional maturity, and sex and personality, one can be brief: Future sexual compatibility cannot be tested by other than indirect means for the majority of our middle-income couples, because the circumstances after marriage are so different from what they are before marriage. This is especially true for women because the relationship is so bound up with a total consideration of love, permanency, home, desire for children, morality, and other such factors, that it is not a simple matter of testing a "gadget." It is a complex matter of testing a total way of life.

For many women the insecurity of the clandestine meeting and fear of discovery, the guilt over contraception out of marriage, the possible thought of the man's losing interest and abandoning her, pregnancy, and so forth, combine to make nonmarital intercourse anything but an adequate test of what could obtain under the circumstances of marriage. Research from Terman to Kinsey indicates that under the best of circumstances it takes most women time to learn to respond deeply to a sexual relationship, and that the initial conditions in which she is introduced to sexual intercourse have an important bearing on her future responsiveness. In marriage these are maximal. Out of marriage they are not, in varying degrees with different people.

Actually, trying to test future sexual compatibility before marriage can not only fail to be a true test, but it can have the adverse effect of being so unpleasant that a conditioning against the experience is established. At the same time it is only fair to both sides of the question to recognize that for many who do have premarital intercourse, the test seems to be adequate, and whatever problems are encountered seem to be worked through with a minimum adverse effect on the marriage.

In the discussion of emotional maturity, it was stated that one of the best indicators of a person's sex potential is the general, total personality. If a person is relatively mature emotionally, which includes autonomy from parental ties and being considerate, warm, affirming, and outgoing, this person will prove to be the most mature sexually, and will, under the right conditions, develop into a deeply responsive individual.

Without being dogmatic or moralistic, it can be fairly said that if the foregoing is not true we can throw 25 years of clinical and statistical research out of the window. This is not to assume that others who order their lives differently will fail. We are talking about the optimal circumstances for success.

The problem of chastity before marriage is a vexing one for many middle-class couples. There are others who do not regard it as a problem during engagement. However, we know that it is for at least one-half to two-thirds of our couples oriented in the traditional Judeo-Christian ideology of virgin marriage.

PROBLEMS OF CONTINENCE

The clinical case for premarital chastity and fidelity in marriage is the affirmation of the cultural ideal of Western civilization. Like any high standard it is achieved by relatively few persons today as part of a basic mode of living. It has been achieved in fact by many more than have achieved it in attitude and orientation, that is, there are some who are defensively chaste as a result of fear of themselves and of the community mores rather than as a result of understanding the social and emotional bases for chastity and accepting them with inner conviction. The case is like that of the adolescent who refrains from stealing watermelons because he fears getting caught, not because he has acquired inner controls. In other words, he does not understand the need for the protection and regulation of the rights of property as a prevention of social chaos and the exploitative law of the jungle.

The problem for modern youth and adults lies primarily in the difference between their own needs and those of others with whom they have to live. The difference between the problem today and in our grandparents' time, lies in the present attitude of moderate sex affirmation and freedom from community controls, as compared with the past attitude of sex denial and more effective community controls.

The problem is primarily a social one, but finally always a personal one. For example, it might be desirable to drive one's car down the street without regard for traffic regulations *if* no one else's welfare was at stake. But, some one else's welfare is always at stake. No amount of rationalization can deny the fact. The problem is to achieve the greatest personal freedom of expression commensurate with the general welfare. Freedom from control or the social effects of one's acts is but half the equation. One must also be free to participate in a community which always involves some necessary social restrictions and personal renunciation.

Having worked continuously for the past 25 years with middle-class youths in the United States and Europe, the writer feels that the great majority accept and wish to conform to the sexual code of Western culture. However, with the newer freedom from social control stimulated by the frankness of movies, books, and radio programs, the abandon of the car and access to liquor, contraception, some safeguard against disease, and the feeling of financial inability to marry early because of the long period of training for a complex occupational future, the majority of people have not lived up to their stated ideal. No less a factor in the deviation from present sex norms is the neurotic personality of our time which finds consolation and escape in the guilt-anxiety of forbidden sexual relations. To worry about sex problems takes one's attention from other conflicts. It is a way of unconsciously spanking oneself for guilt stemming from nonsexual frustrations, such as unfulfilled or unresolved relations with one's parents during the formative period of personality development.

For these and other reasons the writer does not believe that people are consciously transgressing, nor that they have abandoned their ideals. *They are caught in new expediencies of living;* are frustrated by the immediate desire to express their own sexual feelings while being withheld by the community's dictum to wait for years; and rebel inwardly at the felt but often not reasoned "injustice." Much rebellion, consciously or for the most part unconsciously, stems from the conflict between the needs of the individual and those of the community for its young citizens to be prepared for the responsibility of self-support and the rearing of children.

However, as practices change so do peoples' attitudes and orientations. With the rapid increase in premarital sexual intercourse during the past 50 years there has been an accompanying change in the mores of young people. The first reported research on premarital intercourse was published in 1923 by Davis.[1] Of the 1000 married women reporting, 93 percent had not had premarital intercourse. In the latest

[1] K. B. Davis, *Factors in the Sex Life of Twenty-Two Hundred Women,* New York, Harper, 1929.

study of a comparable group of women, 54 percent reported that they had not had premarital intercourse.[2] In an attempt to determine the reactions of this recent group to their premarital experience, over 90 percent of the men and women (92.6 percent of the men and 90.6 percent of the women) *said that it had strengthened the relationship.* Whether their premarital intercourse experience had a lasting effect as now felt, or whether they were reporting a temporary and spurious "strengthening" of their relationship we do not know. What is important is the way they said they felt, for it represents an attitude that may well contribute to a gradual change in the sex orientations and values of young adults.

THE FREQUENCY OF PREMARITAL INTERCOURSE

Before we can attempt to evaluate the meaning of premarital intercourse or continence, we should look at what is being reported as actually taking place today. The most recent and comprehensive study of engagement and marriage appeared in 1953.[3] It is based on a study of 666 couples, largely from our middle-income-education class. The Burgess-Wallin findings on the frequency of premarital sexual intercourse correspond closely to those of other major studies. Of those who experienced sexual relations, the great majority reported their frequency as "occasionally or frequently." When we look at the statistics we see an outstanding difference between the proportion of men and women who reported having premarital intercourse *with someone other than their*

[2] Ernest W. Burgess and Paul Wallin, *Engagement and Marriage,* New York, Lippincott, 1953, p. 330.

[3] *Ibid.,* pp. 319 ff. Chapter 11, "Sex and Engagement," is one of the most comprehensive and penetrating discussions of premarital sex intercourse to be found in the research literature.

spouse. Whereas one-half of the men had premarital intercourse with some one other than their spouse, this was true of only about one-tenth of the women.

Comparing the incidence of premarital intercourse of couples who had been going steady different lengths of time, it was found that the length of time the couple had been going steady was practically unrelated to whether or not they had intercourse. "When the 240 couples who had 'gone steady' over 26 months were compared with the 338 couples who had 'gone steady' under 26 months, the incidence of premarital intercourse was found to be almost identical in the two groups. Similarly no meaningful difference was found between those couples (135) who had 'gone steady' for 41 months or more and those (167) who had 'gone steady' 13 months or less." There was, however, a small positive relation between the length of the engagement and whether or not the couple had intercourse.

Burgess and Wallin found further, that whether couples were relatively young or old, or whether the man or woman was the older, was unrelated to the probability that they would have sex relations before marriage.

It was found that a significantly large proportion of the religiously active couples remained continent. Couples where the man was religiously inactive and the woman was active were more likely to have premarital intercourse than those couples who were both active.

As to why those couples who did not have premarital intercourse refrained, by far the most frequently given reason was that they did not believe it was right. This reason was given three times more frequently than any other reason by men and four times more frequently by women. Other reasons including the fear of pregnancy, hurting parents' feelings, or social disapproval, were mentioned by less than one in five of the engaged couples.

It was found that premarital intercourse most often was entered into after discussion and decision rather than "just happening." After it had begun the couple tended to have intercourse "occasionally" or "frequently," rather than "rarely."

AN APPRAISAL OF PREMARITAL INTERCOURSE

There is a strong tendency on the part of some people to think about premarital intercourse in terms of it being "right" or "wrong," implying that it is either all right or all wrong. In other areas of life, however, some of these same persons are quite willing to weigh the merits of a case by looking at what different people have done and evaluate the consequence of their different experiences. From the accumulated evidence we have from the study of the relationship between premarital intercourse and future success in marriage we can only conclude that the meaning and the consequences of premarital intercourse are different for different couples, and often different for each member of a single couple.

Let us take a number of different couples from the writer's clinical experience and try to see more clearly what the results seem to have been. The following cases represent different groups or classes of persons.

The first couple comes out of homes where emphasis has been placed on premarital chastity. The orientation of their parents has been strengthened by their religious affiliation and participation in other groups in their community. They feel that their warm companionship could develop into a full sexual relationship if they permitted, but they decided to wait until they were married. They *suppress* (consciously withhold) rather than *repress* (fearfully avoid) deeper sex stimulation by seeking to surround themselves with friends of the same standards, keep alive their common interests, avoid excessive stimulation of liquor and provocative entertainment, and see to it that they do not spend too much time alone. They build their companionship into a central theme by developing and extending their mutual interests and skills. Group activities are participated in, but their personal and more reflective interests are also developed—the art of conversation, books, recordings, activities, etc. If you were to ask them why they had chosen this course of action they might answer you somewhat as follows:

We look forward to sexual intercourse with warm anticipation, but in the meantime there are reasons why we cannot marry now. They include our mutual desire to test further the compatibility of our temperaments, interests, and values. We must finish our preparation for occupational and financial stability. We wish to be emotionally as free as possible to plan and achieve many details of our future together before we marry. We feel that the violation of our own conscience, the risk of a poor initial sexual adjustment under the circumstances of fear of discovery, the inadequacy of contraception, the possibility of pregnancy, and some threat to our mutual security in the thought of possible separation, combine into excessive weight of emotional luggage that we do not wish to carry. Of some consideration, also, is the quiet feeling of satisfaction in restraint that will give us personal assurance in the presence of a wider circle of acquaintances, thus greater social mobility that would be restricted by feelings of guilt and thus the avoidance of some persons and groups. Not least we do believe in the tenets of our church, and would like to participate in religious services and activities without distracting and painful mental reservations. In view of these and other considerations we shall try to maintain virginity as a basic *attitude,* willingly accepted out of our own conviction. The *act* of sexual intercourse as such is of much less importance; it is these meanings and broader orientation symbolized by the act itself that we shall husband.

It is the considered judgement of this writer that the "orientation of virginity" is an achievement and not a happenstance. It is a consequence of two people being able and willing to face their problem squarely and think it through to their own satisfaction, and who are mature enough to take a definite course of action. They do not achieve this high ground as a result of fearful indoctrination. Furthermore, there is little tight-lipped "will power" involved, but much judgement that is a product of experience and reflection. Their ability is a by-product of a stable background, one that has been emotionally warm, mature, self-contained, and intellectually honest.

The second couple comes out of homes of religious orientations much like the virginal couple above. They aspire to the same ideals as the former. They feel that they love one another and wish to marry but find that they cannot marry at present. They become caught up in the intensity of their mutual expression of affection and have sexual intercourse, but only with the future spouse. There is the initial feeling of guilt that is minimized by the feeling that the experience was one of mutual desire and consideration, that their intentions are honest, and that they are willing to face whatever problems of adjustment and responsibilities result.

If this second couple is relatively mature and compatible they will tend to be drawn closer together by their sexual experience, step up their plans for marriage, and marry at a relatively early date. The adverse effects of their premarital experience will tend to be minimal and carry relatively little residual weight in the marriage.

However, if this couple is relatively immature and each is at least half kidding himself and the other about his intentions, the relationship may be a passing romance that may fail because of its lack of inherent common interests and the other bases of stable marriage. The usual result of this circumstance is the gradual loss of interest on the part of one and a growing feeling of failure, rejection, and being abandoned on the part of the other. In the writer's counseling experience this seems to happen more often than mutual drifting apart. The rejected one can feel deeply hurt and be psychologically damaged, depending on his ability to make an independent adjustment. One or both may and frequently do feel somewhat "hardened" by the experience, and adopt attitudes of expediency in dealing with members of the opposite sex, or they may retreat from the fray to nurse their psychological wounds. In this case it must be assumed that the couple are relatively sensitive people who allow themselves to become emotionally quite involved in each other. They are "serious" people. Their intentions were "honest" enough, but they simply did not know themselves, their limitations, and their ability to rationalize their sexual needs in the name of love.

Some individuals can grow through their experience. If they come to understand wherein they failed, they may mature to the point where their second courtship will have a more substantial foundation. However, others are so emotionally immature, especially in their lack of reality sense and personal automony, that they do not benefit from their experience. They go on to another illusory and idealized romance with comparable, more severe consequences, often with some degree of depersonalization.

The third couple comes out of homes of religious orientations that *appear* much like the couples above. Their backgrounds, however, have been rather rigid. Their morality is one of indoctrinated shibboleths and cliches, with the controls of their conduct from without, and with adherence more out of fear than understanding and conviction. They tend to be rather unimaginative and provincial in emotional and intellectual experience, but "good" and "conscientious." Such couples tend toward a number of different orientations, but only two will be described here. One type of couple is usually reserved in their early sex approaches, unconsciously half curious and half avoidant. Following initial acquaintance they maintain the good intention of avoiding intercourse while becoming increasingly involved in heavy intimacies. They have not attained the "orientation of virginity" of the first couple discussed, but only awareness of the "act." They may remain technical virgins, i.e., experience heavy sexual arousal with the future spouse and others, and in some cases achieve orgasm through mutual stimulation of one sort or another without actually having intercourse. They carry initial heavy guilt but rationalize it quite easily with the thought, "I am still a virgin." After marriage such persons tend to remain withheld in sexual expression with continuing feelings of some degree of floating anxiety and impaired ability to abandon themselves to a deeper sexual experience. Their problem is not basically sexual, but relates to *the kind of people they are.* They might be said to have some of the scars of combat fatigue resulting from a form of psychological *coitus interruptus.* Their future sexual adjustment has probably been marred by a specific conditioned reaction—arousal-inhibition-attraction-involvement-avoidance—but their major problem is not that specific. Rather, they are basically restricted, withheld personalities who are afraid of themselves and of life.

The other pattern often found to be related to persons coming out of this third type of home and community is rebellion against parental and religious authority which may lead to a series of promiscuous sexual relations. This may be a passing phase that will mature into a monogamous relationship after the initial period of "blowing the top" or "proving oneself." However, promiscuity may become fixated (develop into a strong habit) on this level, leaving the person like the campus pet—friendly with everyone but unable to be deeply and genuinely personal with anyone.

In counsel the writer has seen two modes of reaction to promiscuity; one, a deeply repressed (unconscious) feeling of personal insecurity, with accompanying surface reactions ranging from reckless abandon to "sophistication," with periodic bursts of irritable aggression. The second reaction is an attitude of apparent "cheerful idiocy"—unaware of the other person's involvement in the affair, immaturely self-centered in the feelings of pride in the skill of the he- or she-wolf. The first seems to have a deeper emotional problem, with varying degrees of awareness in different persons. Promiscuity among the more sophisticated affords satisfaction of two sustaining neurotic needs: need for security-approval and for clothed aggression.

The fourth couple comes out of homes that are quite different from the foregoing middle-middle class in American culture. They come from the upper-middle and upper classes, or the lower classes. Their homes and moral orientations have not placed emphasis on virginity before marriage. Some parents encourage their older adolescent children to seek sexual experience as "discretely and responsibly" as possible. Some mothers have their daughters fitted with contraceptive diaphragms and teach their children of both sexes to avoid disease and pregnancy.

This fourth type of couple enter into intercourse without apparent feelings of violating their moral or ethical standards. They seem to take the attitude that it is a private affair and constitutes no problem. When this type of person is relatively mature he is not promiscuous in the sense of spending much time seeking sexual relationships with almost anyone, but tends to confine his sexual relations to a person, or a series of persons whom he is genuinely fond of, throughout the course of the courtship period. The less mature person would tend toward promiscuity and depersonalization.

The first three modes of sexual adjustment discussed are characteristic more of the middle-income-education levels in the United States than of the wealthier or poorer classes. The parental homes of the former tend toward the "protective," "moral" atmospheres. The latter tend to be less protective with regard to sexual patterns and expectations. There is little scientific data on the attitudes underlying the surface patterns of the upper and lower social levels. The published cases of psychiatrists, largely psychoanalysts, give an anomalous picture of the upper income groups, with generalization hazardous. It is probably safe to say that they are much less subject to the mores of the larger community; that their surface patterns are those of "sophistication," i.e., they are willing to grant highly personal, deviant, and unique patterns of expression to others, but formulate their own with two primary considerations in mind: the personal welfare of the couple itself quite independent of the traditional courtship mores and meeting certain "necessary" expectations as to outward form of the particular social set with whom they identify themselves. Sexual morality is not an important mechanism among the upper-income groups to maintain differences from others, to feel superior to others, or to maintain the internal picture of their social position.

As among those of the upper social levels, the lower status groups do not use sex as a symbol of achievement, superiority, or social distance. It is as if the person were saying to himself unconsciously, "I have nothing to live up to and nothing to live down." Consequently promiscuity is often the mode among young, unmarried adults of the lower-income groups. It is a less socialized pattern; it is the expression of self-assertion, pursuit, and "fun"; it is more natural (primitive) and does not carry the religious and ideological meaning and guilt that it holds for the middle classes. It is almost an entirely different experience in meaning.

The foregoing discussion of four general "types" of couples is far from complete or exhaustive. Enough has been presented, however, to illustrate the point that premarital sexual relations constitute a great variety of different kinds of experience and motivation, and with very different results. Relatively few American middle-class people would fall into the first and fourth categories—virginal in orientation as well as physical fact, or sexually permissive as a matter of honest conviction. For the great majority of middle-class Americans, and to a lesser extent lower-class persons, the dilemma of premarital intercourse is very real and often painful because a great many people have not been reared in homes and social sets where the problem has been so clearly defined and a given unequivocal stand taken. For a great many couples, especially engaged couples, the problem is an equivocal one, painfully so.

In recognition of this fact there have been a number of announcements of recent interest in the problem on the part of the churches. The following is an example, a statement published in 1954 by the National Student Council of the YMCA and YWCA, entitled "Faith, Sex, and Love."

> Every serious person is concerned today about the problems of what it means to be a person, to live with integrity and to enjoy creative relations with others. Most of us have asked ourselves, "How can we resist the pressures that society places on us to *use* other people, our education, ourselves, simply as means to some goal?" . . . This leads us to our second point. Because the body is good, because sex is a good gift of God and not the source of evil, it is to be used within certain limits.
>
> Notice what this argument does *not* say. It does not say that sex is evil and dirty and to be avoided by truly spiritual people, to be indulged in as rarely and under as limited conditions as possible. No, it is because it is a good thing that we say it can be better, more creative and exciting, when certain limits are observed.
>
> We admit this logic in regard to eating. Eating is a good thing. But although it is good, we do not eat all through the day. We leave some hours of the day free from eating, and when we do eat we appreciate it more. Without suggesting that sex and eating have any intrinsic relationship it should be clear that this emphasis on the limitations of sexual experience is derived from a high, and not a low, estimate of sexuality.

What are these limits that Western society, or convention, or religion, or whatever you will, place upon the exercise of sexual activity? Monogamy is one of them and, technically at least, this is pretty well established in our society. Young rebels do not rage into our parlors inveighing against the unnaturalness and puritanic restrictions of monogamy. We are a monogamous society, at least insofar as we admit that one ought to have but one wife at a time. Another conventional "limit" placed on sexual activity is the one of premarital chastity. Now this is far less popular than monogamy. Kinsey discovered that premarital intercourse varied widely with educational level. His figures look something like this . . .[4]

Since we have already covered this ground let us go on to a consideration of this official YW-YMCA statement on the question of sex relations during engagement. Sexual promiscuity is condemned on several grounds, including the possible exploitation of the other, but primarily because it does not represent and symbolize any declaration of mutual love or more permanent identity and responsibility.

The statement of the National YW-YMCA on sex relations during engagement is as follows:

Our definition of sexual intercourse as a special kind of knowledge and as a symbol appropriate only for a certain kind of relation rules out, then, these arrogant and imperialist forms of premarital promiscuity. But I can already hear you murmuring: How can such an analysis give a convincing "no" to sexual relations between engaged people? Appropriate symbol, you say? Isn't the sexual act an appropriate symbol of the relation that exists in the final months of most engagements? If so, on what basis can you put your defense of the traditional view opposing pre-marital relations?

This is a very important question. The problem of sexual relations within an engagement is a different problem, and in many ways quite a new one. Engagements are often long today. Graduate school, financial problems, military service, all these stretch engagements out. The conventional moralist in defending premarital chastity in these contexts often can do real damage. Suppose the couple decides to put off sexual relations until marriage. If they see a good deal of each other, this will be an extremely difficult and serious problem for them. Sex may actually become a divisive factor, a thing that keeps them apart, a thing

[4] *Faith, Sex, and Love,* National Student Council of the YMCA and YWCA, 1954, especially pp. 83 ff. See also Evelyn Millis Duvall and Reuben Hill, *When You Marry,* rev. ed., New York, Heath, 1953, chap. 7.

that limits their ability and desire to express their love to each other. Can a thing which before a marriage was divisive suddenly after a marriage become a principle of unity? The couple that has said "no" to pre-marital relations has indeed made a difficult decision and may have made difficult and prolonged the sexual adjustment after marriage. Yet it may be the case that the conventional defense of pre-marital chastity ought to stand nevertheless.

One remark ought to be made to the engaged couple who may feel that intercourse is an "appropriate symbol" for their love. Certainly there is true love between a man and a woman in engagement. But doesn't the sexual act express more than just love? There is another layer of meaning in the sexual act: responsibility, loyalty, willingness to accept the consequences of anything, utter dependence, self-giving. This is one of the very deepest things that sex means. Are these factors really present in an engagement? She may occasionally launder his handkerchiefs but it is not likely that she will wash his socks. He may take her out a good deal, but he isn't responsible for her board and room. No, there is a dimension of mutual responsibility suggested by the sexual act that an ordinary engagement does not know. Our "appropriate symbol" argument still may hold up.

But there is a deeper reason why the problem of pre-marital chastity between engaged people must be thought through in a fresh and honest way. In the past, conventional religion, fear of conception and fear of disease generally banded together to limit pre-marital sexuality. None of these three is any longer a particularly powerful deterrent. Since external fears are no longer doing the prohibiting, unless the Christian answer against pre-marital intercourse is clearly and honestly given, the general drift away from the ideal of chastity will continue. I have tried to throw some Christian light on the nature of the sexual act to show that the conventional "no" to pre-marital intercourse still has some powerful weapons on its side.

The important thing is that we must all be honest about these questions and think through to answers for ourselves. Professor Hiltner in "Sex Ethics and the Kinsey Reports" has made two searching and impressive comments on these matters:

"Against any possible libertine answer, the Christian view must simply testify to the radical and serious and therefore, in a sense, partly unpredictable nature of sex. But against a legalism that would simply condemn all sex relationships of such people, regardless of context and motive, the Christian view would raise a warning. The general question would be: Under some conditions, may sex limited be better than no sex, provided the radical and serious character of sex is not denied? We need some ethical wrestling with this question." (p. 231)

Dr. Hiltner also has some very interesting things to say about the dangers of pressing prematurely for a clear yes-or-no answer to this question of pre-marital chastity. He tells this amusing and instructive story:

"When I was once dragooned into leading a discussion on this subject for a group of male college freshmen, I presented the factors involved as I saw them, and stressed the importance of responsible personal decision. After the discussion period, every question and comment for an entire half hour was a variant of the question: But is it, in itself, right or wrong, yes or no? After about twenty minutes or so had passed, I began to despair of making it clear that something more was involved than a yes-or-no answer. So I turned on the rhetoric and analyzed for them what they would do if I said unequivocally no or unequivocally yes. If I said no, those who agreed would go down to their own house justified, and those who disagreed would set me aside so as to forget all I had said about the process of considering the question. If I said yes, those who agreed would wonder what claim I had to be a moralist but would probably report me gleefully in the college paper, and those who disagreed would be shocked and unable to think of the problem at all." (p. 84–85)

Our conclusion, then, to the question with which we began this section: How does being a Christian affect our sexual practice? would seem to be this. Being a Christian gives us firm grounds for a very high estimate of the goodness of the sexual side of life. The Christian has a deeply personal interpretation of the sexual act itself and, as a result of that interpretation, it is possible to wrest a redefinition of pre-marital chastity that may be convincing to the modern student. But it is more appropriate to point out that each of us must finally bring his faith and obedience to these matters and decide for ourselves. No pastor, no book, no church, no teacher, no parent, no student conference can decide for us. This is why it is such a terrible thing to be a Protestant.[5]

THE SEXUAL DILEMMA

The sexual dilemma exists largely for those who are confused in their orientation, and this includes many conscientious and thoughtful people. If they were not conscientious there would be no problem. If they were not thoughtful they would already have an answer, perhaps somebody else's answer and not one that they had thought through for and by themselves.

Those who have been reared in a social and psychological atmosphere that has developed over a period of years a decisive orientation that affirms or condemns premarital intercourse seem to have much less of a problem than those who find themselves somewhere between the two positions. Those whose "stand" has become a part of their way of life and not merely an acquired verbal conversion to one of the unequivocal positions will confront problems of sexual adjustment. But these persons will not necessarily carry the excessive emotional burden of a divided orientation and conscience. They may pursue quite different ways of life compared with other couples with different assumptions about a great many things. Contrary to the assumptions of some persons, we have no conclusive scientific evidence that one or the other—the continent or the permissive—will achieve the better marriage when premarital sex is entered into with the

[5] *Faith, Sex, and Love, op. cit.*, pp. 8 ff.

intent to marry, rather than as a test of future compatability.

The problems of the "equivocal" group are several, stemming from the fact that sex, to them, becomes a highly emotionally charged concern. It takes on weighty importance. Since it is forbidden but sweet it risks becoming surrounded with a combination of anxiety and a strong desire to pursue the unknown. They become preoccupied with it, something like the problem drinker who feels that drinking is fascinating but dangerous.

When sex thus becomes emotionally overcharged, the couple is less free to experience and to test the other aspects of their courtship. Feelings of sexual fascination are enhanced by the feelings of guilt and self-deprecation resulting in a tendency to idealize the partner without seeing the other's weaknesses and limitations. Furthermore, more time is spent by this couple than others in precoital sex stimulation. They "keep at it" (necking and petting) rather than resolving their present sex needs either by decisive renunciation or satiation. If they have sexual intercourse they do not relax and appreciate it, but are bound to the experience by some degree of guilt, remorse, and feelings of obligation. Thus, for the equivocal couple the role of sex continues to be an excessive pack of emotional luggage that imposes a weighty burden on their courtship. Such emotional patterns, with their overtones of feeling and meaning, tend to be carried into marriage. When such premarital experience is practiced frequently and over a period of time these "habits" tend to become interconditioned in the personality, becoming interrelated to many other experiences. The interconditioning of a habit makes it very difficult to change.

Not infrequently does the marriage counselor see a couple move toward marriage because they feel obligated to one another. Such feelings of obligation can stem from the feeling that a sexual commitment is a marriage commitment. If one feels that the other is losing interest following their sexual experience, he might say or imply: "I have given myself to you sexually. Now it is your obligation to marry me." It should be quite evident to anyone that obligation is not a substantial basis for lasting marriage. Herman Wouk in his novel, *The Caine Mutiny,* expressed the point well in a conversation between Willie and his mother. Willie had spent the night with his girl friend. He seemed preoccupied and troubled as his mother approached him in an attempt to draw him out:

"Give me a cigarette, please" . . . She continued, "Any man has a feeling of debt toward a decent girl with whom he has had an affair. Furthermore, he acquires a taste for her. All that is inevitable. The point is, any girl with a half a brain knows these things. And if she really wants a man, and feels that her chances are good, she'll risk it. It's the last throw of the dice."

Willie's cheeks became red, and he started to speak. His mother rode over him. "Willie dear, this is all a process, natural and inevitable. It's happened a million times. Anybody can get caught up in it. Only remember, a marriage shouldn't be based on a bad conscience, or a taste for a girl's looks, but on similar background and values. If you get married out of a guilty feeling, very well, the guilty feeling passes—to a certain extent—but what else have you got? Now, honestly—do you think you love this girl—or do you feel obligated to her?"[6]

Sex, like any other important and meaningful experience can be overvalued and thus serve to complicate a relationship. Couples with equivocal sex standards seem to be more vulnerable to this courtship pitfall than do others.

[6] *The Caine Mutiny* by Herman Wouk. Copyright © 1951 by Herman Wouk. Reprinted by permission of Doubleday and Company, Inc.

It is the writer's judgement that there is a sensible answer to the sexual frustrations for relatively mature couples: early, responsible marriage. Intelligent continence is possible without damage in the case of only a relatively few couples for reasons already given. If Western societies continue to regard virginity as of the importance it is accorded by our communities and their institutions, supported by a lifetime of the strongest personal and social pressure, then we must quit kidding ourselves about the ability of young adults to remain virginal very long. Ways must be found to make early marriage possible.

By "early marriage" the writer does not mean merely the purchase of a marriage license to make sexual intercourse legal, which may be more of a vice than a virtue, but marriage with mature intentions of fullness and permanency. This would entail considerable change of public opinion in the following directions:

1. Regard the preparation of young people for the founding of sound marriage as a serious obligation and dig deep into our pockets to activate highly professional education-counseling programs.

2. Assist young people to earlier adult status and adult roles. This would entail in-service education-work programs with financial remuneration; for some, early entry into occupation and earning, without experiencing opposition to an abundant labor supply by those who would gain by a scarcity of labor.

3. This may entail a program of governmental and/or private (family) subsidies for young couples, especially for those facing years of technical or professional education.

4. There would have to be economic planning that would permit low-cost housing and neighborhood nursery facilities

for young mothers who wish to spend some time in further education and community activity and service.

5. There would have to be adequate medical facilities, care, and additional financial assistance for young families with small children.

The problems involved in helping young adults marry well are prodigious and it will take time to solve them on any widespread basis. In the meantime individual couples can become aware of the important issues involved in responsible early marriage and plan for their own more substantial futures without waiting for the social lag to catch up.

Chapter 10

COURTSHIP: MIXED MARRIAGE AND FUTURE COMPATIBILITY

TODAY PEOPLE are much more mobile than they were during the time in American history when a high proportion of our population lived in smaller, socially and culturally homogeneous communities. This is especially true of our college students, many of whom meet and carry out their courtship on a campus where they mingle with others of different nationality, race, religion, and social status. Because of this relatively new circumstance many young people meet and are attracted to persons different from themselves in one or more important respects. Where people of such different backgrounds marry it is referred to in the marriage literature as a "mixed marriage." Thus, an American in our foreign occupation forces may marry a German or a Japanese girl, a Protestant marry a Catholic, a white person marry a colored person, or a student from Middle East marry a native born American.

In one sense the problems of adjustment encountered by all couples of different backgrounds are much the same from the standpoint of their relationship with one another because, most frequently, there is involved a difference in total way of life rather than some segment such as race, color, religion, or language. However, when there are visible elements of difference such as color, there is the problem of community acceptance in addition to the more subjective aspects of the relationship. In the case of the Japanese-American marriage not only are differences in religion and other aspects of culture involved, but also the contrast in racial characteristics.

In general, research shows that mixed marriages are more hazardous as marital risks than are those in which the couple are more similar in social and cultural orientations and expectations. In a study made by the American Council on Education, 12,000 young people reported on whether their parents were married, divorced, or separated.[1] It is of note that those coming from families of mixed religion reported two to three times as many broken homes as those whose parents were both Protestant or both Catholic. The percentages were as follows: Where both parents were Protestant 6.8 percent of the homes were broken: Where both were Roman Catholic, 6.4 percent were broken. Of mixed marriages 15.2 percent were broken. Where there was no religious connection there were even more broken homes, 16.7 percent. Childless marriages were excluded by the nature of the study. Otherwise the proportion of failures would have been higher.[2]

Such a statement of probability must not be interpreted to mean that mixed marriages cannot succeed. We know that

[1] Howard M. Bell, *Youth Tell Their Story,* Washington, D.C., American Council on Education, 1933, pp. 20 ff.

[2] Quoted from *If I Marry A Roman Catholic.* Copyright 1945 by the National Council of Churches. Used with permission.

some of them do. When they do, however, there is evidence that those marriages have not been the result of a casual and brief courtship, but one of special circumstances. In a study of 30 Japanese-American couples living in the Chicago metropolitan area it was found that a very high proportion were regarded as successful, with only one actually broken. The researchers became interested in why this should be, when the marriage literature would have led one to predict just the opposite. They found several factors present in these happy marriages that seemed to be related to the success of their marriages. In the first place the girls were quite autonomous persons. They were working when they met their future husbands and had become relatively emancipated from their parental families. In the second place these marriages had hurdled many obstacles that had provided insurmountable barriers to other couples who did not marry such as opposition from both sets of parents, religious authorities, and commanding officers and a general cultural orientation against mixed racial marriages. It was concluded that after running such a formidable gamut, the couple really wanted to marry. Another factor mentioned was unusually long courtships without the traditional Western barriers to coming to know one another very intimately. In general it might be concluded that these successful mixed marriages were more rigorously tested during the courtship than is often the case.

RELIGIOUS INTERMARRIAGE

In counseling experience with college students one of the most frequent types of mixed backgrounds that constitutes a serious question of whether or not to marry is that of difference in religion. The problem will be taken up here for two reasons. First, it is quite a widespread problem. Second, the questions considered in its resolution represent a kind of "mode of operation" which can be applied to problems found in other types of mixed backgrounds. This is not a discussion of theology or religion *per se,* but of some of the considerations confronting couples during the testing phase of their courtship.

Frequency of Religious Intermarriage

The frequency of religious intermarriage is difficult to generalize about because it is affected by so many other complicating factors such as the degree of orthodoxy of the couple, their parents' orientations and expectations, the cultural region of the United States in which they live, whether or not the religion of each is a minority or part of a larger group, whether or not the religion is related to ethnic patterns, and the severity of the sanctions against marrying out of the faith. For the United States as a whole, for the period from 1930 to 1950, 30 percent of all Catholic marriages were mixed marriages. This figure does not include Catholics marrying outside the church and it should be noted that the figures vary considerably in different regions of the United States.[3] Because of the severity of the sanctions against Catholics marrying outside their church as compared with Protestants, it would be reasonable to assume that between a third and a half of all American marriages of religious affiliation are interdenominational.

Of the three major religious groups in the United States, intermarriage is most frequent among Protestant denomina-

[3] R. S. Cavan, *The American Family,* New York, Crowell, 1955, p. 250.

tions, less among Catholics, and least among the Jews. Thus frequency of intermarriage is seen to be related to the severity of sanctions against intermarriage and the integration of the faith and ritual with the overall ethnic culture of the group. One of the most extreme examples is to be found among some groups of Jews in eastern Europe and old Spain where they practice the custom of regarding the one who marries outside the faith as dead. The death ceremony is held, and he is no longer considered a part of the family or the religious community. Likewise, the vigilance of the Catholic Church and family against marrying outside the church generally seems to be stronger than that of the Protestants. With the increasing mobility of American youth and the breakdown of ethnic distinctions it is probable that religious intermarriage will increase.

Severity of Conflict in Religious Intermarriage

Research indicates that certain combinations of religious intermarriage are accompanied by greater conflict than others. Where both members of a couple are of the same religion, Catholic or Protestant, about nine couples in ten report no religious difference and no conflict. Where the husband is Protestant and the wife Catholic about a third reported some conflict with nearly 7 percent indicating that their mixed religion imposed a "great" or "very great handicap." The difference is even greater where the husband is Catholic and the wife Protestant. More than two out of every five such couples reported that their religious difference was "some handicap" to their marriage; and one couple out of ten said that it was a "great" or "very great handicap." This represents considerable marital dislocation due to differences in religion in view of the relatively high proportion of Catholic-Protestant marriages.[4]

Bases of Conflict in Religous Intermarriage

Before discussing the bases of conflict in religious intermarriage, it should be made clear that some couples of different religious background recognize that as different in some respects as the tenets of the major religions of the world are, they hold much in common. This is especially true of Judaism and Christianity but we are not as far from the Islamic world and other Eastern religions as many think. The assumptions that people of different faiths hold in common are not irrelevant in testing religious compatibility, for the case is not all one sided. Some couples seem to be able to compromise on what they regard as the less important differences in theology and ritual.

However, for others within Christianity itself there are major differences in doctrine and worship that are not considered irrelevant or minor details, but differences which represent and symbolize divergent larger patterns of living. There are fewer of these major differences among the more closely related groups such as those churches that hold common membership in the Federal Council of Churches. Even here though, in apparent communality of thought, there can be some of the most divisive factional groups. As Harold Lasswell has brought out, some of the most bitter struggles between ideological groups can take place between two that are

[4] Judson T. Landis, "Marriages of Mixed and Non-Mixed Religious Faith," *American Sociological Review,* XIV (June, 1949), 405.

so much alike that they have to fight to maintain their differences.[5]

In the writer's clinical experience the following differences in religious backgrounds constitute hazards to the compatibility of a couple.

RELIGIOUS AUTHORITY

There are the differences in the degree of *authority* churches exercise. In some there is virtually no centralized authority, as in the case of the Unitarians or the Congregationalists. What different persons or congregations believe is derived in part from tradition, but also results from discussion, and meeting in convention. In other churches there is a direct line of authority from the supreme head of the church through a hierarchy of officers to each member. Roman Catholicism or Mormonism are examples. The former pattern of authority has been referred to as "open social organization" and the latter is designated as "closed social organization."[6] In the open organization even the most basic tenets of the group may be questioned, and different members may and frequently do hold different positions about such basic matters as the divinity of Jesus. In the closed organization the "first principles" are assumed to have been given through revelation or inspiration to the head of the church and passed on through official pronouncement to the member constituents.

[5] It may be that any comparison between political groups struggling for equality or for supremacy, and partners in marriage going through a comparable process is a matter of too loose a generalization. Let us grant that such comparisons are most speculative, but inviting of consideration. For a discussion of motivation underlying political "demands for equality and for supremacy," see Harold D. Lasswell, *World Politics and Personal Insecurity*, New York, Whittlesey House, 1935, chaps. V, VI.

[6] Karl R. Popper, *The Open Society and its Enemies*, London, Routledge, 1947.

For the devout of the two different kinds of churches there is the deepest ideological chasm permeating their outlook on a great many things, religious and nonreligious. The conflict may present itself in the clinic or pastoral conference as follows:

MARY: John, why do you always want to argue about those things that we should accept as a matter of faith? Marriage is a sacrament, not merely a civil contract, and as such it cannot be dissolved by mutual agreement. There is nothing to be gained in going over that ground again and again.

JOHN: Mary, I appreciate with you the importance of marriage, even its sanctity, but the marriage is intrinsically what you and I make of it. No one can put it together or take it apart but you and me. After a couple have tried to live together and have conscientiously attempted to reconcile their differences and can't, they should divorce.

Differences in the authority and authority structure of the church can constitute deep and painful dilemmas to the conscientious couple, especially to the devout rather than to those of a more equivocal position.

PARENTAL SANCTIONS

When the parental families of the couple are devout in their religion they will tend to feel strongly that their children should marry within the faith of the family. Families from the older cultures such as Italy, or from ethnic groups like the Mennonites or the Jews, have developed a system of religious worship and practice that is an integral part of their whole culture. This stands in contrast to some Protestant groups whose family practices and rituals are much like those of their neighbors or friends who do not belong to the same church. Marrying outside the religion of a strong culture group, then, would be socially and psychologically tantamount to breaking with the tradition of one's family and culture.

Such a contemplated or actual break with one's past can create a conflict in the person, deepened by the pressure exerted by the parents and religious authorities. The depth of the conflict can only be understood when we realize that the dictates of the superego or conscience of persons are established in the parental family. This substratum of the personality is partially, if not wholly, unconscious and as such not amenable to conscious manipulation or change. Conflict with established family values cannot always be handled in a purely rational manner. Being at variance with the family will produce a floating feeling of guilt and anxiety. In some persons it can be of almost overwhelming proportions, especially when accompanied by charges of "moral sinfulness" or threats of being ostracized by the family. Not infrequently the feelings of guilt will be added to by a parent's complaint of "what it will do to me with my weak heart," or "your mother couldn't stand it."

CHILDREN

In the mixed religious marriage the couple may agree to disagree about their own religion, even to go their separate ways. However, when the children come along it can be quite a different matter, even though they may have agreed beforehand that the children would be reared in one or the other of the churches. Verbal agreements about matters that are deep and personal aspects of the self do not carry the weight of feeling of actual experience. It is something like *talking* about bereavement as compared with what one *feels* when losing a loved one.

One couple had three children. She was a Protestant and he a Catholic. She agreed to be married in his church and underwent the requisite instruction. She signed the Catholic Ante-Nuptial Agreement, to be signed by the non-Catholic party in a mixed marriage, as follows:

I, the undersigned, not a member of the Catholic Church, wishing to contract marriage with ...., a member of the Catholic Church, propose to do so with the understanding that the marriage bond thus contracted is indissoluble, except by death. I promise on my word and honor that I will not in any way hinder or obstruct the said .... in the exercise of .... religion and that all children of either sex born of our marriage shall be baptized and educated in the Catholic faith and according to the teaching of the Catholic Church, even though the said .... should be taken away by death. I further promise that I will marry .... only according to the marriage rite of the Catholic Church, that I will not either before or after the Catholic ceremony, present myself with .... before a civil magistrate or minister of the gospel.

Signature ....

Signed in the presence of Rev. ....

Place .... Date ....[7]

They were married and subsequently had children. "Increasingly," she said, "I felt bound and trapped. When I realized that my children, a part of me, were going to be reared and educated in a faith that I realized I had not really accepted, I felt literally ill. . . . Any act on the part of my husband to take the children to church alienates me from him. . . . I fear that it is going to break up our marriage." One can appreciate the husband's feelings in the matter, or how he would have felt if his wife had tried to rear the children in her church. In clinical experience this writer has

[7] *If I Marry A Roman Catholic, op. cit.*

found that such a dilemma nearly always affects the children adversely because they tend to identify themselves with the parent they prefer and suffer feelings of guilt and anxiety engendered in their rejection of the other parent.

PLANNED PARENTHOOD

The use of a mechanical or germicidal agent to prevent conception in the voluntary spacing of children may become an issue in a Catholic–non-Catholic marriage. This is especially true when the health of the mother is vulnerable to a pregnancy and the couple does not feel certain about the rhythm method of contraception. When one feels, on moral grounds, that contraception is wrong, not only is guilt engendered in its use, but feelings of anxiety in its application serve to distract from the emotional setting of the coital experience, and provide the basis for partial or more complete sexual nonresponsiveness.

Therapeutic abortion may present another problem. If it is deemed medically necessary to take the fetus in order to preserve the wife's life, understandable anguish can arise due to possible differences in orientation.

FOOD AND DRINK OBSERVANCES

With the increasing widespread use of alcohol and tobacco there is probably less intense feeling on the part of those who believe in moderation or abstention in their use. However, there are the members of a number of religious groups who feel very strongly about the "moral" issue involved in serving alcohol and in using tobacco. With some people the issue is largely, if not wholly, a matter of mental and physical health. With others, however, abstinence from alcohol and tobacco has been woven into the basic tenets of their religions and has thus become a symbol of adherence and orthodoxy. To smoke or to drink may be regarded as signifying a break with the church. Dancing and other forms of entertainment, formerly frowned upon if not forbidden by a number of Protestant groups, have become less objectionable in the main, but still remain as divisive orientations in the experience of some couples. In general the sacramental Christian churches and Jews regard the moderate use of alcohol and tobacco as a matter of personal preference and consideration. The nonsacramental (many of the Protestant groups), the Mormons, and some ethnic groups range in orientation from "permissive nonpreference" to the strongest social and religious sanctions against their use in any form.

To one reared in an orientation of total abstinence, any use of alcohol or tobacco can be a matter of extreme displeasure if not a more major divisive factor in the relationship. Since people do not wish to seem prudish or impolite, there is probably a great deal of covert rejection and resentment on the part of persons who feel strongly about these food and drink observances and other social amenities. They are frequently major issues encountered in marriage counseling, and often serve as pegs upon which other grievances are hung. Of further significance, these can serve as the bases of acceptance or of the rejection of potential friends.

MINORITY GROUP DISCRIMINATION

Minority religious groups are sometimes discriminated against socially, occupationally, or professionally. One who has been reared in a particular in-group has usually been reared to accept it and to accommodate himself to it one way or another. The one from the out-group who marries into the minority group becomes identified with the group into which he marries. For some this constitutes little or no serious problem. Others brood over the injustice and seem unable to extricate themselves from feelings of unjust discrimination. Of central concern is one's ability to adjust to a position of lower status in the community with minimal personal and social dislocation. Another important factor is the individual's ability to identify himself with the ideology and activities of the minority group—to become one of them.

CONFLICT IN RELIGIOUS IDEOLOGY

One of the last considerations to be discussed but most important in a mixed religious marriage is that of theology and some of the epistomological foundations upon which the substance of beliefs are founded. There are so many possible combinations of conflicting theological "foundations," even within some of the churches themselves, that any attempt to characterize the major differences would be beyond the scope of the present writing. For some couples the more peripheral considerations in religion, discussed in the foregoing pages of this chapter, constitute the major differences standing between them. In the case of others, however, it is the theological and philosophical substance of their religions that constitutes an ideological impasse. Their different integrated assumptions, assertions, and aims stand at variance.

As one of a great many possible examples let us take a couple both of whom are working toward advanced degrees at State College. He is a student of psychology and philosophy. She is interested in human relations. They met in a "cases" course in human relations and found that they enjoyed talking with one another, and the challenge that each offered. As they continued in what had amounted to an intellectual companionship they found themselves thinking of possible marriage, but were troubled by "religious" differences. One of their conversations started with a discussion of the difference in what they chose to read. He had suggested that she read Jean-Paul Sartre's, *The Age of Reason.*

HE: *There* is reality . . . the two boys caught in the anguish of their homosexualism, with one trying to extricate himself in order to pursue his girl friend—the desperate search for some kind of personal meaning.

SHE: I agree, but why read such morbid stuff.

HE: I grant that there is a morbid aspect to it, but lots of reality is depressing. I think that one has to have the courage to look at all of life right down the barrel. Do you find that threatening?

SHE: I think not, but there is so much that is decent and good without all that psychological muckraking. Why Sartre, an athiest and quasi-Communist?

HE: O.K., let's talk about Kierkegaard, a Christian. Wasn't his anguish out of the same piece of cloth when he left Denmark and went down to Berlin where he hid out, brooded over the girl who had thrown him over, and wrote his *Sickness Unto Death?* It's the same point—a terrific struggle with the meaning of life and of faith—the love of Abraham for his son Isaac whom he was ordered by the Lord to kill as a sacrifice and a test of his unconditional faith. There was none of the sunny Philistine in that. It was more like a morbid struggle through the mud and shale of life to the horizon which was thought to be salvation, but, when attained, turned out to be only a step through an unexplored, infinite number of experiences that were sustained only by the faith that tomorrow or some morrow *must* hold the ultimate nature of the course and the purpose behind the struggle.

SHE: But, wasn't that Kierkegaard's feeling about the matter? Wasn't he trying to express what he felt to be Abraham's unshakable faith, what he, Kierkegaard, was struggling toward but had not attained?

HE: Yes, he seemed to be reconstructing how he, with less faith than Abraham and other "mortals" would react to such a dilemma. Yes, Sartre and Kierkegaard make strange bedfellows, but bedfellows they are—seeking to know themselves, willing to go to the depths of experiential reality in an attempt to make some kind of sense out of things. Your kind of faith seems to me to stand between you and God. You *have* it, as it were. You seem to me to have crawled into the lap of certitude which is incompatible with faith, for if you were certain there would be no need for faith. You would know.

SHE: Could you be rationalizing your own neurotic need to punish yourself? I don't care to struggle with God. To me he is personal and someone very close. I just can't buy your brand of pulling yourself up by your pessimistic bootstraps.

HE: I grant that what you say may be very true. I may be quite neurotic, but I think that more is involved—really a difference in the meaning of our faith. Has it occurred to you that your religion may be a kindergarten venture in the kind of social and community activity program that distracts you from the great soul struggle with its admitted transient feelings of utter loneliness, that your church is actually protecting you from the purpose for which it was founded—to sustain you in the struggle? As to the meaning of God, I don't think that he is less personal to me than to you, but in a different way. To you he is more like a loving father who will show you the way. To me he is more one who gives me the strength to continue the search. Truth seems to be much nearer to you in your orientation—just out there, as it were. To me, I can only work toward it, not expecting to achieve it, only to come closer to it as I, through experience, smelter out the untruth, leaving *more* of the pure thing.

SHE: Our ideas are so close, yet so distant. Indeed . . .

It is of note that this couple's preferences for art, literature, and music differed markedly. He enjoyed Grünewald's

Crucifixion in which Christ is portrayed as an emaciated figure on the Cross, or Van Gogh's *Starry Night;* she, a portrait of Christ in peaceful repose in the Garden of Gethsemane. He preferred to read Eliot, Auden, and Whitman; she, Christina Rossetti's *Sonnets*. They both liked classical music and jazz, but he preferred Bartok to Beethoven and enjoyed Brubeck "going way out" in his improvisation on the theme of "Take the 'A' Train"; she enjoyed Beethoven and Brubeck. However, it was the influence of Bach and Scarlatti that she commented on in Brubeck's improvisations rather than his musical idiom. She preferred Paul Laval and Henry Levine's NBC Chamber Music rendition of "Lower Basin Street" with its clear cut clarinet obbligato. In their respective visits to Europe their time was limited. He chose to spend most of his time in the Scandanavian countries; she, Italy and the Middle East. To him sex was a personal matter involving consideration and responsibility; she had a religious preference to enter marriage virginal. He preferred a dry martini; she a coke.

The foregoing is a composite "case" based on the reality of several cases seen in marriage counsel.[8] It is cited in some detail to illustrate the striking difference in the intellectual way each member of this couple pursued his religion; how their respective differences in religious and philosophical outlook were related to their aesthetic and other personal preferences. Thus, religion to each of them was much more than either theology or mode of worship. It was a difference in a larger *pattern* of outlook and way of life.

Testing for future compatibility in the case of this couple would be difficult and hazaradous without each knowing much more about the other. Some couples might go through

[8] See "Who's an Existentialist?," *Time,* July 16, 1956.

life enjoying the challenge of the other in the pursuit of their common interest hoping that the accommodation of their ideas would some day achieve some new assimilation. Others would experience such a relationship as a temporary interest and challenge, maybe over a considerable period of time, then move in different directions with each seeking more identity with his own.

PERSONAL INTEGRITY

Persons who have worked through a background of religious orientation to achieve a position, often at the cost of inner debate, doubt, and resolution, cannot change easily to accept the orientation of another. Those who have acquired a deep-seated faith in anything are not easily shaken in their faith. To find oneself in love with some one of a different position can present a painful dilemma.

Often the attempt to be "rational" about the matter only serves to intensify the conflict. Actually, far more than the intellect or the cognitive in personality is involved. This type of problem involves the feelings, sentiments, and emotions that have become associated with patterns of religious worship, ceremony, and aesthetic expression and appreciation. Frequently the position is strengthened by patterns of social and communal participation. To change one's "faith" would be tantamount to changing one's way of life. To repeat, people of integrity cannot do so without the deepest personal strife and internal division.

We hear it said, "I loved him (or her) so much that I was quite willing to change my religion and join his church." In this instance the one who changed may not have been deeply grounded in his own church, and gained something by joining that of the other. However, if an individual has achieved a conviction and identification with his own church and changes to compromise, there is danger of deep feelings of lingering doubt, anxiety, and the emergence of smaller forms of disaffection which can grow in magnitude to destroy the entire relationship.

MIXED SOCIAL AND ECONOMIC BACKGROUNDS

Crossing class lines in marriage introduces an additional hazard as is indicated by the marriage prediction research. Marriage adjustment scores of these couples who marry "upward" or "downward" are significantly lower than are those who marry one of their own background.[9] Dissatisfaction is especially characteristic on the part of one who marries another of lower socioeconomic status.

Much more is involved than financial income, as important as that may or may not be to the couple. It is a change in way of life—many social and emotional roles of expectation and need have to be altered and accommodated to the new circumstances. We have already discussed the different sex orientations characteristic of different social classes. Standards of entertainment may have to be altered. The further up the scale one goes the more social "imperatives" enter into everything one does.

The more apparent social amenities of dress and entertainment can be learned with much greater ease than the skill of a more responsible position in the occupational world and the community. Often marked differences in education and personal discipline are involved, leaving the less educated

[9] Julius Roth and Robert F. Peck, "Social Class and Social Mobility Factors Related to Marital Adjustment," *American Sociological Review,* XVI, 478–487.

confused by the expectations of the other, and the more educated disappointed at the inability of the other to respond. This can be especially painful for the couple when the one "born of the manner" is rejected socially by the friends of the one who is not. It is not only a matter of the couple's adjustment to one another, but one of social acceptability.

Not infrequently it is the parents of the one marrying "downward" who object. Sometimes their objection is presented in a subtle form of persuasion to "go away to school" or to postpone the marriage, in the hope that the relationship will break up. Often their open hostility is expressed with the strongest financial and other sanctions brought to bear. Some parents sense with validity that their children are locked in a romance that will not last because of the differences in their backgrounds. Other parents have set impossibly high standards for their children, or hold prudishly unreasonable expectations. Such a circumstance presents a painful dilemma. If the couple is mature enough to marry they will make their own decision. Those who are not autonomous enough from parental sanctions to make up their own minds and risk the threatened dire consequences, are probably not mature enough to marry.

Marrying below what one has become accustomed to economically can give rise to many frustrations associated with a curtailment of interests and activities. This is especially true for the woman with some ambition for a career or other activities who finds herself bound by young children she cannot afford to leave, or when she cannot afford to entertain her former friends in the manner in which they entertain her. She may feel that it is a reflection on her husband and an exploitation of her friends.

The role of the partner in such a marriage is of utmost importance to its success or failure. If a woman marries the "poor but talented" writer, his ability to meet her expectations makes the difference. If he is unproductive, procrastinates in getting his work done, or is easily discouraged, she may lose confidence in him. If he is the young mechanic who becomes a successful engineer, then the situation is reversed.

In testing for future compatibility when one is in love with another of different socioeconomic status, it is most important to be able to judge the potential growth and achievement of the spouse—whether one marries upward or downward. Failure of the one of lower status to meet the expectations of the one of higher status is nearly always disastrous. This is no risk to be taken by the immature and starry eyed who are vulnerable to misjudging the potential of the prospective spouse.

It is of greatest importance to recognize that economic position *per se* is no criterion by which to judge the culture and personality of the other. What is important is the *intrinsic* social, emotional, aesthetic, and intellectual *substance* of the other.

DIFFERENCES IN AGE AND EDUCATION

There is little conclusive evidence one way or the other that differences in age at the time of marriage and differences in the amount of formal education of the couple are related to success or failure in marriage.

Research evidence on age differences and their relation to successful marriage is conflicting whether it is the man or the woman who is older. This probably obtains because differences in maturity are not necessarily related to age. In general, age differences up to five years are not given serious consideration by the marriage counselor, whether it be the man or the woman who is the older. The research of both Terman and Burgess and Cottrell found a slight increase in marriage adjustment over other combinations when the wife was four to ten years older. However, we cannot generalize and conclude that because some couples find this difference desirable, that most couples would.[10]

In professional experience this writer has found that women generally want a man whom they can "look up to," who takes somewhat of an ascendant role. This may require a man several years older than she in order to meet this expectation. It seems to be a minority of women who want to be older and assume a more "mothering" role to the younger "son or brother." In counsel, one often sees a couple who, when they married, mutually enjoyed the woman's more ascendant and the man's more deferent roles. As the marriage goes on she may and frequently does outgrow this initial role and yearn for a more ascendant man. We must recognize that age *per se* may not be involved, but it is a matter of psychosexual roles with their different levels and combinations of maturity. It is most difficult during the testing phase of courtship to know what the growth potential of each of a couple will be, but it can be borne in mind as a consideration.

It is surprising to many that the relation between happiness scores of couples studied and differences in the amount of education that each had, is small and inconsistent. Furthermore, differences in education (number of years of formal schooling) are quite unrelated to whether or not the couple will divorce. It must be remembered, however, that homogamy of educational background most frequently obtains, and

[10] Louis M. Terman, *Psychological Factors in Marital Happiness,* New York, McGraw-Hill, 1938, p. 186; Ernest W. Burgess and Leonard S. Cottrell, *Predicting Success or Failure in Marriage,* New York, Prentice-Hall, 1939, pp. 162 ff.

the proportion of persons who marry another with four or more years difference in formal education is but one in five. Other factors in these marriages may outweigh the difference in education. We can only conclude from research literature that educational differences do not necessarily affect the marriage adversely.

Terman did not consider differences in education important enough to include in his marriage prediction scale. However, we should not assume that in a particular couple this difference may not be significant. The real question would be: How compatible is the "universe of discourse" of the couple and can they communicate and enjoy their common interests without divisive gaps in their respective skills and abilities?

Clinical evidence indicates that marked intellectual incompatibilities are evidence of neurotic needs, that some persons are attracted only to persons considerably above or below their own ability, such as an editor of a woman's magazine marrying a service station attendant with an eighth-grade education. This might fulfill the temporary needs of both the superior and the inferior, but would have little future promise.[11]

In testing for present as well as future compatibility it is well to take the time to experience in reality, rather than on the verbal level, the reactions of each to as many situations as possible that will be confronted in marriage. The considerations discussed in this chapter have not been treated exhaustively and there are many others, including things that are unique to each couple. However, they are problems encountered most frequently in counseling with college students as well as with others, and represent common problems of our middle-middle and upper-middle classes.

[11] See the case of Peter and Claire in, Karen Horney, *Self Analysis*, New York, Grune and Stratton, 1942, pp. 190 ff.

Chapter 11

ENGAGEMENT: PREPARATION FOR MARRIAGE

THE SUMMATION PHASE

It may now be assumed that the couple have completed the first three phases of the courtship process—have been attracted to one another, have made their provisional selection of a marriage partner, and have tested many of the facets of their relationship for present as well as future compatibility. They are now ready to move on to a commitment to marry. Such a commitment may be an informal understanding. In addition it may be announced to the respective families and a circle of friends. It may be a more formal engagement. The first three phases of the courtship have been completed and the couple now moves into the final phase, that of fulfilling their plans and preparation for marriage.

The summation phase holds the opportunity for growth together in the more personal aspects of the relationship—sentiments, emotions, understandings, and appreciations. It also allows the couple the opportunity to complete many of their plans for the founding of a home—physical, economic, occupational, social. In experiencing this dual purpose of the summation phase the couple will grow closer together. Their marriage will then be "an imperceptible step across the threshold" rather than a plunge into the unknown. With so much that is ordinarily undertaken after marriage out of the way, with the greater confidence in having worked through many potentially distracting, if not threatening, experiences, the couple is free, upon marriage, to continue the "unveiling process." Putting it differently, with many of the mundane details out of the way, and having moved closer together in the activity of preparing for marriage, they are free to undertake their companionship on a deeper and more profoundly personal level. They are neither encumbered nor distracted with "a million and one things yet to do."

This orientation stands in contrast to two other notions. In the past the bride-to-be was cloistered under heavy guard, working on her trousseau in feminine secrecy. It was presumed that all the early adjustments in marriage would be confronted stoically and somehow worked through. The contemporary extreme is to assume that this period between announcing the engagement and marriage is to be filled with prolonged necking punctuated by showers and bachelor parties. In contrast to these actions, the summation phase of the courtship, or engagement, is one in which the couple will continue to grow together in the kind of close relationship that obtains in working together, planning, arranging, building, and preparing for the founding of a home.

One of the purposes served by this summation period is that of announcing to the families of the affianced as well as to the community that the couple are to be married, so that others can assist, on the one hand, and leave them alone to work together, on the other.

One couple met in a fencing class. Their common interest led to a romance. During their courtship they were nearly always available for a workout on the strip. When they reached the summation phase of their courtship they let it be known to their relatives and friends that they were spending most of their free time together. They rented an apartment, made curtains, refinished furniture, remodeled their fencing vests, and reshaped the handles on their foils. Less time was spent in love-making, with the realization that there would be plenty of time for that after they were married. This temporary leave from their families and friends was not 100 percent, but it was a period of intensive preparation for their forthcoming marriage and living together. And it was surprising to them how many of their friends pitched in to help, without invading their privacy. When this couple married, their plans and preparations were so complete that their first weeks and months together were spent in deeper *personal* exploration and companionship—socially and psychologically *alone*.

THE ROLE OF THE CONSULTANT

The role of the consultant has become increasingly important in our complex and specialized society. Many of the details of planning for marriage and a home that in the past were presumed to be common knowledge, have become matters needing professional judgment and skill. Take housing for example. The problem involves not only considerable knowledge of different financial arrangements available, but such subtle considerations as the deeper, most often unconscious, personal needs for a particular architectural style, color combinations, utilization of floor space, landscaping, and the like, that have an important bearing on the emotional health and satisfaction of the couple. Such details might be left to hunches and chance preferences. Or, planning on a more sophisticated level can proceed so that individual needs will be satisfied. For example, persons with more expansive basic personalities would be able to achieve the effect of the "open" architectural style. Those who have a greater need for an emotional tie-in with the ancestral past might want the symbolic French, English, or American, provincial styles with all of the details appropriate to the basic mode.

One can already hear many young couples say, "How can we entertain such considerations when we'll be lucky to end up with a house trailer?" That may be true, but even a trailer can bear the personal tastes of the couple and be carried out on a sophisticated, if not expensive, level. In this event the special consultant would probably not be the home decorator, but magazines such as *Architectural Forum* or *Interior Decoration Personified.*

The financial problems of budget, buying, possible savings and investment, health and life insurance, etc., are important and worth prolonged consideration, often with counsel.

PREMARITAL MEDICAL EXAMINATION

Medical service and counsel and the opportunity for an expanded physical examination are available to most couples in their preparation for marriage.[1] The premarital laws in 34 states, together with the recommendations from pastors,

[1] One of the most recent, complete, and professionally reliable books dealing with the premarital physical examination and consultation is, Abraham Stone and Lena Levine, *The Premarital Consultation,* New York, Grune and Stratton, 1956.

priests, rabbis, and teachers of marriage courses, bring an increasing number of couples to their physicians for premarital service and counsel. These services have heretofore been sought largely by our middle and upper classes, but are being extended to the lower education and income groups through agencies such as the Planned Parenthood Federation of America, Inc.

Of the brides and grooms who seek the extended premarital medical service, about half are virgins. The other half have either been married previously, had sexual experience with their future spouse, have been promiscuous to some degree, or have had different kinds of precoital experience. Thus, there is much difference in their sexual orientations and experiences. Some brides know a great deal about their own physiology and anatomy; many do not, and have very little knowledge about themselves, the opposite sex, or the nature of coital experience.

Gynecologists report that most grooms are more mature in their sexual experience and knowledge. Their experience, however, most frequently does not include proceeding with a virgin, and differs greatly in their appreciation of the value of tenderness, consideration, and care in proceeding with their bride.[2]

The physician trained in this kind of premarital service is interested in the orientations and attitudes of his clients and remains alert to their reactions to the various steps in the premarital examination, especially evidence of guilt or anxiety. This is especially true of the pelvic examination.

[2] Nadina R. Kavinoky, "Premarital Medical Examination," *The Journal of the American Medical Association,* October 16, 1954. Dr. Kavinoky, a practicing gynecologist, is a former president of the National Council on Family Relations and a marriage counselor. The writer is indebted to Dr. Kavinoky for a considerable portion of the present discussion.

Steps in the Premarital Examination

The first step is the pelvic examination. After noting the appearance of the hymen and the size of its opening, its texture is established by palpation (touch)—whether it is thin and elastic or thick and fibrous, and whether it bleeds easily. In order to relieve any anxiety the bride is then taught to relax and contract the vaginal muscles. This reduces stress and prevents undue tension in first coitus. Furthermore, it prepares her psychologically for the second step if she is a virgin, that of helping her insert a well-lubricated Pyrex centrifuge "test" tube. This acquaints her with the vaginal opening and canal. After evaluating the depth and flexibility of the vaginal canal the tip of the tube is inserted and tilted to conform to the position of the canal. She is then instructed to insert it. This is an exercise in psychological as well as physical defloration. Dr. Kavinoky writes, "She is then asked to bear down as she inserts the tube. The rate at which she introduces the tube and her facial expression reveal any anxiety. The return of color to her face and her relief, as she discovers no bleeding and no pain, convinces the physician of the therapeutic value of this simple procedure. The bride learns more about her 'mysterious' sex organs in these few minutes than she could have learned in hours of talking and studying."[3] This is usually followed by a vaginal inspection and the fitting of the contraceptive diaphragm if it is desired. If she seems tense or fearful, the fitting of the diaphragm is postponed until the next visit. Following the fitting of the diaphragm, she is instructed in its proper application by the nurse. As a conclusion to this step, the bride is instructed in how to apply it and remove it in two 15 minute practice sessions. Prior to the third visit to her doctor the bride is in-

[3] *Ibid.*, p. 693.

structed to apply the diaphragm the evening before her office call, leave it in during the night, then return the next day to have it checked for proper application, comfort, and absence of any pressure or irritation to the vaginal walls. When she returns from the wedding trip she can return to have the diaphragm checked for size and the possibility of a larger fitting due to the relaxation of the vaginal muscles.

In some more extreme cases of anxiety, faulty orientations, or emotional instability the couple is referred for marriage counsel or psychiatric treatment, with the possible recommendation that plans for the wedding be extended, depending on psychological counsel. This has served as a safeguard against damaging psychological shock with resultant annulment or divorce.

Physicians are prepared in varying degrees of professional skill to give medical and psychological assistance to those proportionately few couples who need therapy. Some kinds of problems should be treated before marriage. Others may have to be postponed. However, unwarranted postponement can lead to the development and strengthening of anxiety which could be avoided by more expedient action. Some malformations of the hymen and vaginal canal can make the consummation of marriage painful if not impossible. The hymen may require minor surgery to reveal its sensitivity. The term "super-virginal" is preferred in reference to a vaginal opening that is "too small." Very small openings can be stretched, first in the office of the physician, then by the bride herself at home, using graduated dilaters and anesthetic ointment. These direct attacks on the problem, while sometimes disappointing to the patient, can forestall the deeper psychological trauma that often results when the problem is "left to nature." Initial uncertainty and disappointment are removed by increasing supportive therapy from the physician which can develop confidence and an orientation of warm anticipation of the consummation of the marriage.

Grooms often need the support of the physician to remove doubts and anxieties. Often there is fear of the size of the penis, usually associated with its small size. The size of the genitals has nothing to do with the adequacy of sexual intercourse, despite folklore to the contrary rampant in many different cultures including our own. Assurance, understanding, and the correction of fallacious assumptions discovered in the premarital interviews can prevent undue anxiety associated with the unknown, one of the most common causes of wedding impotence. Even a man of considerable sexual experience can feel very modest in the presence of his bride, contrary to what he might expect from himself from his reaction to the stories often told at the bachelor parties. Greatest understanding and consideration on the part of both can be counseled.

An important part of the extended premarital examination is a thorough systematic physical examination. In addition to the possible discovery of incipient physical disease, conditions which involve the endocrine system, the nervous system, obesity or malnutrition, etc., can affect the sex desire and/or capacity of the couple. Sometimes nervous exhaustion is evidenced and the person who is vulnerable to the enervating experience of the wedding can be counseled regarding food and rest.

PLANNING FOR PARENTHOOD

The Protestant, Catholic, and Jewish faiths are of one mind in the ideology of familism. They believe that couples should have as many children as they can commensurate with their ability to care for them and rear them decently. There is the further common belief that children should be planned for and the number of children limited under given circumstances. However, there are some striking differences between the non-Catholic and Catholic faiths as to *how* conception should be limited and the *circumstances* under which limitation should take place.[4]

The Protestant and Jewish Position

No single statement could characterize the position of all Protestants and Jews. However, the following is an excerpt from one that would be acceptable to many:

3. Because children are intended by God as a blessing and a reward (Psalm 127:3), every child may expect love, care and nurture from its parents. To be unloved or rejected by its parents

[4] The position of those opposing mechanical and germicidal birth control methods has been set forth many times, but perhaps nowhere in the marriage literature has a more vigorous stand been taken than in the recent book, Carle C. Zimmerman and Lucius F. Cervantes, *Marriage and the Family,* Chicago, Henry Regnery, 1956. They cite over 100 references to support their case.

The position of those favoring modern scientific methods of birth control is perhaps best set forth in the publications of Planned Parenthood Federation of America, Inc., with offices in all metropolitan cities. The following are some of their most recently sponsored publications (reprints): "Shall Science and the Democratic Process Be Shackled?," sermon given on Rogation Sunday, May 10, 1956, by the Reverend Arthur Lee Kinsolving, D.D., Rector in St. James' Church, New York City. His position is that of the Church of England and its counterpart in America, the Episcopal Church; Karl Menninger, M.D., "Psychiatric Aspects of Contraception," *Bulletin of the Menninger Clinic,* VII, No. 1; Regina Flesch, "The Problem of Diagnosis in Marital Discord," *Journal of Social Casework,* November, 1949. Miss Flesch is a caseworker in the Family Service Bureau, United Charities of Chicago; Lena Levine, M.D., "The Doctor Talks with the Bride and Groom," Planned Parenthood Federation of America, Inc., 1954. Dr. Levine is a gynecologist, psychiatrist, and marriage counselor.

The foregoing is not an exhaustive but an illustrative list of writers from different professional disciplines.

is a cruel tragedy which may forever mar the child's personality and may subject the parents to the dangers of the millstone the Saviour described (Matt. 18:6).

4. To enable them the more thankfully to receive God's blessing and reward, a married couple should so plan and govern their sexual relations that any child born to their union will be desired for itself *and in relation to the time of its birth.*

5. The means which a married pair uses to determine the numbers and the spacing of the births of their children *are a matter for them to decide with their own consciences, on the basis of competent medical advice* and in a sense of accountability to God.

6. So long as it causes no harm to those involved, either immediately or over an extended period, none of the methods for controlling the number and spacing of the births of children has any special moral merit or demerit. *It is the spirit in which the means is used, rather than whether it is "natural" or "artificial," which defines its "rightness" or "wrongness."* "Whatsoever ye do, do all to the glory of God" (I Cor. 10:31) is a principle pertinent to the use of the God-given reproductive power.

7. Scripture recognizes that a couple may wish for a limited period to practice marital continence as a religious expression, but cautions against its prolonged practice (I Cor. 7:5). Continence in the marriage relationship, however, when its sole purpose is the selfish avoidance of pregnancy, is equally as wrong as is the use of contraception toward this same selfish goal.

8. An unrestrained production of children without realistic regard to God-given responsibilities involved in bringing children up "in the discipline and instruction of the Lord" (Eph. 6:4) may be as sinful and as selfish an indulgence of the lusts of the flesh as is the complete avoidance of parenthood. God does not expect a couple to produce offspring at the maximum biological capacity. The power to reproduce is His blessing, not a penalty upon the sexual relationship in marriage.

9. In planning their family a married couple would wisely heed the Psalmist who pointed out the special blessings that may accrue to larger families and the rich joys from children born in

one's youth (Psalm 127:4–5). They are then more likely also to experience the truth that "Children's children are the crown of old men" (Prov. 17:6).[5]

The foregoing statement is clear-cut in condoning contraception, the spacing of children according to the conscience and judgment of the couple, urges larger families rather than smaller ones, and condemns an unrestrained production of children without realistic regard to the responsibilities involved.

The Catholic Position

The Catholic position would affirm the ideology of familism in the above statement of one Protestant Church, but would disagree as to method of limiting conception and the circumstances. The following does not necessarily represent the official Catholic position, but is one acceptable to many Catholics:

Moralists in distinguishing between duty and idealism, generally lay down three prerequisites for the practice of rhythm: (1) Both parties are willing; (2) Both parties are able; (3) Sufficiently serious reason. Under the third prerequisite we would have these examples of "sufficiently serious reason":

1) Childbirth would be dangerous, or one of the parents is too ill to help in the rearing of children (medical reasons);
2) The real likelihood of mental abnormality or serious hereditary defect in children, or mental weakness on the part of the parents (eugenic reasons);
3) Lack of housing facilities, overpopulation, the husband's em-

[5] A report given by Professor A. D. Mattson, Chairman of the Committee on Morals and Social Problems which presented the report on Responsible Parenthood, in June 1954, before the national meeting of the Agusta Lutheran Church. It was passed by their 95th Synod in Los Angeles, 1954. (Italics mine.)

ployment in a public office, such as military service, which is at least temporarily incompatible with family life (social reasons);

4) The inability to provide decently for children according to the papal standard of a family living wage (an economic reason).

Regarding . . . the economic reason we must think not merely in terms of frugal support but also of the possibility of moderate savings for the future . . . "a saving wage constitutes an essential part of the definition of a living wage." Those who so readily accuse (others) of seeking specious excuses for practicing the rhythm might well ponder how many of them actually get a family living wage. . . . It allows of the following conclusions:

1) To have more than four or five children is an ideal;
2) To use the rhythm to limit the family to four or five children is permissible, even without special justifying reasons, provided both parties are willing and able to practice it;
3) To use the rhythm to limit the family to less than four children requires a serious justifying reason.

The antifamilial implications of the contraceptive philosophy may be summed up in G. K. Chesterton's words that "Birth Control means No Birth and No Control."[6]

The foregoing is clear cut in its affirmation of familism, setting forth the conditions under which family limitation might be undertaken, its affirmation of continence or the use of the rhythm method to control conception, and its denunciation of the use of any mechanical or germicidal (medical) contraceptive devise.

It has been this writer's professional experience with the clergy of the Protestant, Catholic, and Jewish faiths, in referring couples for pastoral counsel, that religious leaders want their couples about to be married to understand as

[6] Gerald Kelly, "Duty and Idealism: Rhythm in Marriage." Quoted in Carle C. Zimmerman and Lucius F. Cervantes, *Marriage and the Family*, Chicago, Henry Regnery, 1956, pp. 332–333.

fully as possible their faith's stand on planning for parenthood. It is not the purpose of this book to make these differences clear in their details, but to suggest that these differences exist, to illustrate them, and to urge pastoral counseling when there is any question about planning for parenthood. The official literature of each church will be readily available. This is not something to be left until after marriage. Whatever the couple's position with regard to these considerations, there is no longer room for squeamishness and boorishness in confronting this aspect of planning for marriage.

Planning for Family Limitation

"Contraception" will be used here as it is defined in Webster's dictionary, "to prevent conception," rather than as defined by some special groups. Couples fall roughly into two categories: (1) those who want to get along with having their children and who desire no contraceptive information at the time of the premarital examination, and (2) those who desire to wait until they have completed their education, military service, or some other plans, or who desire to give themselves time to come closer together and to become weaned from their parents before starting their family. The latter will either believe in some mechanical and germicidal means of controlling conception or will not. Those who do will want to be counseled and served by their physician in the latest and best methods of contraception. The others will want to understand more fully what the rhythm method of limitation involves, and receive specific instruction in how to carry it out. Whatever the couple's orientation and request, the time of the premarital medical examination, several weeks before the marriage, is the time and the place when they can most propitiously be advised and served.

Research in contraception has moved forward so rapidly that physicians themselves have difficulty keeping up with the most recent findings. It is quite possible that at the time of the publication of this book new medical techniques will be in practice. At present it is a consensus of medical opinion that the contraceptive diaphragm used in conjunction with a germicidal "feminine hygiene" jelly most completely meet the criteria of the ideal contraceptive. However, recent research has developed a jelly which has been tested and found to have a high degree of contraceptive reliability.[7] It is five times as strong in its germicidal reaction as jellies heretofore used. It is applied with a plastic applicator, which is a simpler process than applying the diaphragm. Drugs taken orally are under experimentation but have not as yet proved efficacious.

The use of the condom or sheath worn by the male is not recommended except under special circumstances. Its visibility, its vulnerability to tearing, slipping, or containing slight holes, are against its use. Of greater negative consideration to some is the interruption of the love-making, often at a time of emotional absorption and heightened intensity, to apply the condom.

The diaphragm used in conjunction with the jelly has the advantages of greater safety and the fact that it can be applied before retiring and remain a matter of no further concern, whether the couple have coitus or not. Furthermore, neither can detect its presence. It is in no way obtrusive, does not detract from the naturalness of the experience, and

[7] "Clinical Effectiveness of a New Vaginal Contraceptive Cream," *Western Journal of Surgery, Obstetrics and Gynecology,* LXIV, 152–157.

provides a mild lubricant. It is not removed following coitus, leaving the couple uninterrupted in the prolonged caress of the "afterglow," which is to many couples as important as coitus itself, and a profound phase of their mutual expression of love.

Marriage counselors are of one mind when they recommend that no one should advise the couple and serve them but a physician or one of the reputable planned parenthood agencies that has its own staff of doctors and nurses. The nominal cost should stand in the way of no one as the complete service is available to everyone irrespective of the amount of their income, through the Planned Parenthood Federation of America, Inc., with offices in all metropolitan cities, and referral agencies in Massachusetts and Connecticut, the two states in the United States where contraceptive information cannot be given legally.

When the rhythm method or the "safe period" is to be relied upon, either alone or in conjunction with other methods, the couple should likewise have competent medical advice as to what it is and how it may be relied upon by a given couple. Adjunctive reading material can be obtained at any Planned Parenthood Federation office.

The foregoing discussion of contraception has been limited to a discussion of differences in orientations toward it, recent medical trends in its development, and some of its social and psychological implications. No attempt has been made to discuss the details of its techniques. The latter should be obtained from one's physician and the literature cited.

REVEALING THE PAST: LAST MINUTE CONFESSIONS

During the final stages of the engagement there is often the feeling that one does not know all about the past of the other, but should, and now is the time to find out. The motivations for such feelings vary greatly. It may be that one has no doubts, but feels as part of a learned orientation that "one should enter marriage with no secrets." Others feel guilty about a past love affair or some unpleasant previous experience and desire to confess. Still others have doubts about their own sexual abilities and are unconsciously curious about the partner's possible more successful experience with another. This is a kind of verbal voyeurism or "peeping," in which the person has been sexually damaged and, doubting his own ability, has to "watch" others, that is, listen to them tell about their sexual experience. Whatever the motivation, however, confessions are often a serious consideration and should be weighed carefully.

Some people are reared in an ideology of virginity and thus desire to know whether their prospective spouse is virginal. There will be varying degrees of emotional involvement in the matter. One reaction upon learning that the other is not virginal is initial disappointment which soon passes with the thought that "I love him (or her) unconditionally, and it is not a matter of continuing importance." Others, however, are obsessive about the matter and become preoccupied with it, unable to extricate themselves from feelings of anxiety and hostility. In counsel one hears it expressed, "I know that it shouldn't be that important but it is, and I can't get the thought of his having intercourse with another girl out of my mind." Clinical experience indicates that the person making such a statement generally is insecure and fears abandonment. Any thought of the partner having been intimate with another threatens the person's defenses against this fear and thus arouses anxiety. It does little good to try to handle such an orientation by presenting rational arguments. The orientation is a symptom of deeper personal insecurity that must be dealt with as such, often with the necessary help of counsel.

In the event that a person has had an adverse experience that he feels he should share, but does not want to burden the partner with unnecessary concern, he might discuss it with a minister, physician, or marriage counselor. This may be the better course if: (1) what has happened is not directly relevant to the present relationship, such as being a victim of a childhood experience, or (2) if it is not a matter of public knowledge, and thus, will not return at some later date through another informant. Into this category would fall such things as family disgraces, court actions, previous engagements, sexual experiences, and the like.

Sometimes verbal assurances are given that it is all right to tell all, based on one's present feeling. However, we cannot rely on how people *say* that they feel. They may react quite differently. Furthermore, when future difficulties arise they can be unnecessarily encumbered by bringing up the past.

In the case of past experience that is considered relevant to the present situation, such as a potential court action or the vestiges of a relationship with another, the person may feel that it is necessary to share the concern. In this instance the problem is one of timing and should be handled during the testing phase of the courtship so that it does not come at the last minute to cast some shadow on the marriage.

In general, the more mature the personalities of the couple the less concern will be shown for final confessions. Mature people can be honest with one another without damage. With the less mature, it is more likely that any confessions will be divisive wedges in the relationship. Curiosity, self-display, self-punishment, the expression of doubt, and other motivations should be recognized for what they are and not be rationalized in the name of "honesty."

Finally, confessions have both psychological and ethical import. Each person will finally answer the question of how much to tell according to his own standards. These cautions are raised for those who presume that there is some easy generalization such as, "Tell everything and let the chips fall" or "What they don't know won't hurt them." Couples should think more in terms of the *motivations* underlying raising the question in the first place, and the *effects* of the answers on *both* of the couple.

IS PLANNING UNNATURAL?

In an upper division university course in marriage this writer was giving, a senior woman who had listened intently to the orientation presented in this chapter came up after class one day and said, "Don't you think that all of this medical service and preparation is *unnatural* before marriage and should be left until after marriage?" The discussion that followed consisted mostly of an expression of feelings that she held, up to a point. Then the instructor asked the student what she meant by "unnatural" and why this procedure should seem so to her. It was pointed out that in the history of gynecology and obstetrics men had been burned at the stake for their medical interest in the delivery of a baby (at that time carried out solely by women), that anesthetics, surgery, and measures against infection had been and still are held by some people to be interfering with the "natural."

At the end of the term the students were invited to write an autobiography and this same woman student chose to write about her recent marriage and what had happened between the time when she asked the question and the end of the term. It is quoted in part here with her permission.

After viewing the film shown in class on "Dance and Trance" in Bali, in which these Balinese mothers teased their infants and children by taking another child to her breast and slapping her own, I was troubled even more by what I meant by "natural." My only conclusion could be that I had been confusing "natural" and "primitive". . .

When I reflected further on how modern medicine had reduced the death rate among infants and had increased the life span, eliminating many of the "very natural" virus diseases that caused so much tragedy, etc., again, I could only conclude that the gynecological and psychological fields could assist "nature." But how far they should go still bothered me. . . .

I was engaged to be married just before graduation, since his military commitment would have complicated things if we waited until graduation. . . . Still concerned about having to make some kind of a decision I shared my feelings with my fiancé, and to my great relief found him most sympathetic. The way he acted made me feel like I wasn't a silly, prudish girl. . . . One Sunday, shortly thereafter when it was very cold, we chanced to visit some friends in a neighboring city who maintained a tropical garden. I don't know what happened, but as I saw the beauty of this "unnatural" setting and felt the attentiveness of my fiancé, I felt, in a moment, that my dilemma had been resolved. . . .

The next week-end I went home and laid my cards on the table with my mother. She was at first a little surprised that "this sort of thing" was being discussed at school. Then, after some prolonged moments of preoccupation, she turned to me and said, "What have you decided?" I guess that it was the way she said it, but I felt lifted and that my decision to seek the complete premarital medical service was a right one. . . .

After my fiancé and I left the doctor's office we both commented on the informality, professional dignity, and, I added "naturalness" of the experience. Somehow I felt even closer to my future husband than I ever had before which I didn't think possible. . . .

Two weeks ago we drove to X-City and were married by our Priest in the Church at noon. We told only our immediate families and a few very close friends, who attended. Since we had to be back to school on Monday we had only the week-end to be together and we didn't want to contend with receptions, his imaginative and prankish fraternity brothers, or anything else. So we left immediately after the ceremony for "Tim Buck Tu." Actually we drove back to College Town on the assumption that that would be the last place that these same prankish friends would look for us when they got wind of what we had done. We rented a nice motel on the edge of town and there consummated our marriage. . . .

Words could never adequately describe the beauty of our relationship. . . . I feel that I had somehow worked through some vague concerns that I had been holding to prior to our marriage. . . . We were prepared and I felt so secure. . . . I don't know what to attribute what to . . . but here is a plug for preparing more thoroughly for marriage, and you have my permission to quote . . .

THE WEDDING AND HONEYMOON

Traditionally in the United States the bride and her family plan the details of the wedding and pay for all of the expenses. This is especially true of formal weddings. The mother and the sisters of the bride have a strong vested social and psychological interest in the forthcoming event, with the role of the father of the bride more one of financial underwriter. In quite a real sense, then, it is the bride's family who are hosts and the couple to be married the guests of honor, especially with regard to the reception.

Tradition likewise holds that the honeymoon is the exclusive concern of the couple, to be planned and carried out by them, often in greatest secrecy. Generally the honeymoon is paid for by the groom.

Where the parents of the couple and the couple themselves are in agreement as to where the marriage should take place, the details of the wedding and reception, etc., the marriage has optimal chances for success, other things being equal. However, disagreement between the couple and one or both sets of parents can be painful and divisive in the relationship between the couple themselves.

Sources of Conflict

In general the disagreement and conflict stems from several sources. One of the more common bases of difficulty lies in the fact that the parents of one of the couple have not accepted the spouse-to-be of their son or daughter. This obtains most frequently in the case of mixed marriage, especially when social class lines have been crossed. Or it can be a matter of parental dominance or overprotection resulting in the son or daughter feeling that the parents are planning the wedding to meet their own interests without regard for the wishes and expectations of the couple. In other cases the couple to be married have a preference for some kind of unconventional wedding whereas the parents have their hearts set on the "good old-fashioned like we have always had in the family including the wedding dress of the bride's mother." In still other cases the matter is simply one of not knowing or of misunderstanding one another's roles in the forthcoming marriage. And not infrequently, there is the possibility of differences in expectation and desire between the couple themselves, especially when their backgrounds or their basic personalities are markedly variant.

Regardless what the conflicts are over the plans for the wedding, it is important that the couple should not attempt to reconcile the differences by dealing with the surface issues before getting behind the symptoms to the deeper causes. For example, if it is a matter of the bride's mother having always made the important decisions for her daughter, the problem is one of lack of psychological weaning and not merely one of differences of opinion about the wedding. All of the arguing and harsh words in the world are not going to change these realities overnight. The bride in this instance may rebel, capitulate, or remain ambivalent. If the groom is of the same mind as his bride, the matter is simplified but not resolved. If not, then the conflict becomes a triangular struggle among the three.

The conflict can be fought out on the basis of each holding to his own assertions, with the strongest winning out in the end. Or, they can face the unpleasant reality of a dominating mother and try to reconcile it on the basis of a new power alignment with the center of gravity in the couple rather than in the parent. When such an issue is confronted with consideration for the parent in an atmosphere of conciliation, some parents are flexible enough to make radical changes in their expectations and demands. However, in some cases, no amount of conciliatory effort is fruitful.

Sometimes it is the young people and not the parents who take arbitrary stands without consideration of their parents' understandable interest in the forthcoming wedding plans. If they were more mature and could place themselves in the position of their parents, they could appreciate their parents' feelings and make some compromises without stress and the violation of their own integrity.

Some of the most emotionally involved and difficult problems in all human relations are those that emerge in the final stages of the social and psychological weaning process and may be played out in planning the wedding.

Elopement

One of the solutions to an impasse with parents regarding whom one should marry or plans for the wedding, is to elope. There are, of course, many other reasons why some couples elope, including a desire to avoid publicity, as in the case of an airlines stewardess who, while in the employ of most companies, is not permitted to marry; to avoid the expense of a big wedding; pregnancy of the bride-to-be; the sentiment of anonymity; and many others. In one study of elopements nearly half of the 738 couples eloped because of parental objection to the spouse or the wedding (45 percent). Other reasons were cited less frequently.[8]

There is some evidence that the chances for a successful marriage are less for those who elope than those who marry with the blessing of the parental families. It cannot be assumed, however, that elopement *per se* condemns a given marriage to less success than if the couple had been married in a more traditional fashion. Of greatest consideration are the motives underlying the elopement. When the bride is pregnant or the couple elope out of protest against parental disapproval the marriage is more vulnerable to failure than when the motives were less personal and more social, as in the case of economy or professional considerations.

Ascertaining Expectations

Perhaps the greatest consideration in planning the forthcoming wedding and honeymoon is for the couple to probe in detail the expectations of one another. The broader social and cultural orientations as well as unique personal desires

[8] Paul Popenoe, *Modern Marriage,* New York, Macmillian, 1940, pp. 222–227.

and expectations can come in for careful scrutiny. In counsel one bride of several months complained that her husband did not present her with a gift when they were married. "It is such a little thing," she said, "but when my family and close friends asked what he had given me I realized that it was just one of many things that made me feel that he was so insensitive to my expectations. It wouldn't have had to cost much, it's the idea behind it." In this case it turned out to be a difference in social orientation. He was unaware of the fact that persons of some social strata give one another wedding gifts. This provided a peg upon which other dissatisfactions and disappointments were hung.

The purpose of the present discussion does not permit a detailed treatment of wedding décor and etiquette. Books on good form are available at the bookstores and libraries. The point from a marriage consultant's point of view is simply but profoundly this: The feelings and sentiments of people about to be married are composed of so many generalized orientations and specific expectations, made up of a lifetime of experience and reflection about one of the biggest events in one's life, that no consideration of what would please the *other* can be overlooked.

Greatest of all considerations is the feeling of affirmation that is communicated in many small ways but most through attentiveness. Each of the couple can feel that the *other* is the center of attention, interest, and concern. It can be as if the couple were waltzing together in a great hall oblivious to all others, with everybody at the distance looking on, approvingly, admiringly. The adoration of her husband is the secret wish of every bride. It is an occasion when to exhibit one's love is in good taste.

The pair-centered orientation that can obtain at a wedding

stands in contrast to the wedding in which one or both of the couple takes the other for granted, plays a role of host or hostess to the relatives, friends, and possible "very important people," usurping the role of the bridesmaids, and leaves the spouse in some state of psychological abandonment.

The Honeymoon

The careful planning of the honeymoon as an extension of the wedding will result in rich rewards. Whether it is brief or more extended it should provide the couple with the opportunity to consummate their marriage in an atmosphere of "leisurely detachment, congenial surroundings, and complete freedom from responsibility."[9]

In contrast to the wedding in which the couple is the constant center of attentiveness from others, the honeymoon is best served by as complete psychological detachment from others as possible. This may take place in the presence of people, as in the case of a resort, but in social anonymity. There is probably nothing as distracting to the honeymoon as the presence of relatives or friends. Such counsel may seem trite, and yet it is astounding how often "the folks" suggest paying for the trip and going along as a part of a "too-long postponed vacation." This stems, as do some other faulty honeymoon plans, from the popular conception that a honeymoon is a kind of a vacation. It is not. In many ways it has nothing in common with long travel, sightseeing, hiking or golfing, and a movie. Its prime purpose is to permit the couple the atmosphere of complete abandon where they feel free to reveal and to discover one another and thus enjoy the deepest physical and spiritual communication.

[9] David Mace, *Marriage: The Art of Lasting Love,* New York, Doubleday, 1952, pp. 47 ff.

What constitutes congenial surroundings differs greatly from couple to couple. For some it may be the mountains or seaside; for others, the atmosphere of Las Vegas. Of importance, however, is the realization that most weddings are far more enervating affairs than many couples realize during the period of intensive preparation and the emotional buoyancy of the wedding itself. Even the most active couples are surprised to experience the exhaustion that sets in when they are away, alone, and let down. A part of the atmosphere for the surroundings, then, should be an absence of any feeling of haste, obligation, duty, strain, or any other extraneous consideration.

Part of the psychological preparation for the honeymoon is the realization that in our present society many of the details of personal hygiene are felt to be more intimate than sex itself. Often there is the greatest reticence in sharing toilet functions and the many details of living together. As we discussed in the section on emotional maturity, part of the more mature reality sense is the ability to feel toward the body of one's spouse as toward one's own body—with all of its weaknesses, limitations, blemishes, and intermittent dysfunctions. It is to be recognized that it takes some experience, thus some time to unveil these less lovely aspects of ourselves. To have a sense of this orientation can reduce embarrassment, disillusionment, disappointment, and the gradual accumulation of minor offenses. Also, there is the greatest obligation to one another to appeal to the aesthetic sense of the other in personal cleanliness with all of its delicate ramifications. To be natural with the other is not the same as being boorish.

Counseling experience reveals the most divergent orientations toward nudity. Current surveys indicate that the majority of young couples sleep with little or nothing on. This does not necessarily mean that that was the way they started their marriage. When we consider how secretive and clothed the dressing and toilet functions of women are as compared with the rearing of boys, we can appreciate the differences in orientation and habit that are carried over into marriage. Psychologically unveiling her body may take a period of weeks or months rather than a moment. The man might feel impatient and wish that she were different. However, he will be depositing pure gold in their future marital account if he will appreciate rather than deplore her modesty, and reciprocate in kind rather than trying to force her hand or "shock" her into his expectations by posing as the prancing, leering wolf. It is not a matter of who is right or wrong, modest or immodest. The problem is one of assuming a role with its appropriate orientation that will prevent unnecessary blocks and lead to the greatest fruition of mutual sexuality.

It should not be assumed that it is always the bride who is more reticent. Just the reverse may be true and she will be placed in the position of showing him the same consideration.

In counsel one hears a man complain of his wife's undue "prudishness." Sometimes it is a matter of sexual nonresponsiveness. Often, however, the problem turns out to be one of a rather basic difference in the preference for ceremony and ritual. It is comparable to the difference between eating and dining. One couple came in several months after their honeymoon for counsel. There had been an accumulation of small dissatisfactions that combined to threaten their marriage. It seemed that she wore too many clothes in their love-making to suit his taste. He had jumped to the conclusion that she was "prudish" (in comparison with other girls he had known), and had in fact called her that during one counseling session. At that she retorted, "You call me prudish because I have a preference for what you call these frilly things. Sometimes I think that there isn't an aesthetic bone in your body. You make love like you eat a hamburger. I have been responsive to you because I love you, but I must admit that the night of the wedding when I wore the gown that I had worked on, anticipating my marriage as every girl does as she works on her trousseau, and I sensed your lack of appreciation of something that added to the whole atmosphere, I was disappointed." Further evidence tended to confirm the fact that this was really no moral issue or problem of sexual responsiveness. It was, however, one of rather marked difference in basic personality. He was more direct, outgoing, literal, and demonstrative. She was more retiring, subtle in her ways of communicating, indirect, and "clothed" not only her body but her personality in intellectual and aesthetic ways. Coming to realize their differences in basic personality was painful, but they discovered anew their many common interests. This realization lifted the case from the arena of petty argument, charges, and countercharges, into the light of greater appreciation of one another. Had they known and anticipated these differences during their courtship, the early course of their marriage would have been less painful.

In this section on dating, courtship, engagement, and preparing for marriage, an attempt has been made to point up the great opportunity for couples to choose more wisely, to test more thoroughly, and to complete many of the plans and preparations for the marriage that will prepare the way for the longest enduring and most creative of all human relationships, with overtones of the greatest joy of which man is capable.

Part Three

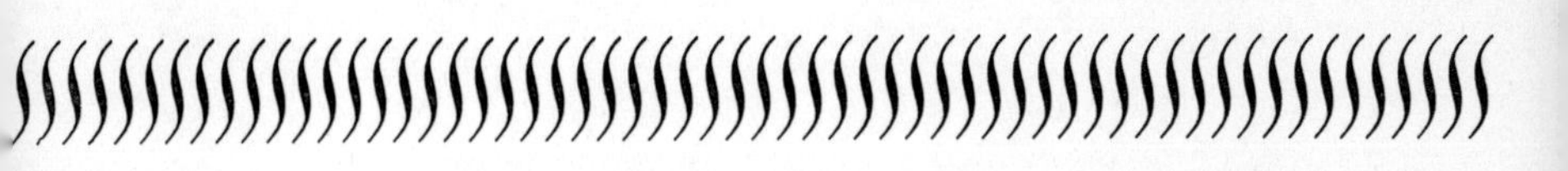

GROWING TOGETHER IN MARRIAGE

Chapter 12

EARLY PROBLEMS OF ADJUSTMENT

"SETTLING DOWN" to marriage is an inevitable process. It poses one of the first problems of adjustment to be confronted by the couple. No matter how thoroughly the marriage has been planned, two conditions obtain. First, the couple has been living on a level of heightened emotions, hopes, and expectations. Second, the reality of living with another person in a relationship as intimate as marriage is never fully what was anticipated. To some this period of adjustment is a new phase of a creative relationship with only minor "dislocations." To others it is a rude awakening. For all, however, it involves turning from the recent, exclusive pair-centeredness of the courtship to the world of a workaday reality which is punctuated by, but not preoccupied with, romance. "Romance" now takes up a smaller part of the day and night, not all day and much of the night as in courtship. The honeymoon is over.

The phase of the marriage following the honeymoon has been described by psychiatrists and marriage counselors as the disillusionment of settling down to marriage or the scaling-down process.[1] To the romantic and inexperienced such phrases and their implications may sound extremely pessimistic or iconoclastic but just the opposite is true. What is meant here is "constructive" disillusionment, that is, moving to a higher plane of reality where, mindful of the danger of immature idealization and projection, the couple are freer to build their relationship on a foundation of reality.

We sometimes hear a couple say how perfectly adjusted to one another they were right from the beginning. That may be true, but one often wonders what kind of uncomplicated persons they must be, or when they are going to let down the guard and cease the unconscious pose. Two people, both of whom have differentiated and sensitive personalities, will probably have to take much more time to work through the myriad contrasts and differences to common grounds.

Take for example Linda and Dick. Just married, Linda was a pretty little temptress, the apple of Dick's eye. He loved to watch her sit and brush her long, black hair. Exquisite in her negligee, the time taken seemed like hours but Dick enjoyed every minute of it. Even *Dragnet* on TV ran a poor second. Her temperament was quiet and deep, while Dick was quite different. He bounced in and out of the many events of the day. Here is a situation they confronted during the first days of their marriage. In brushing her teeth at night Linda characteristically replaced the cap on the toothpaste with ceremony and one last twist. Dick bouncing into the

[1] See John Levy and Ruth Munroe, *The Happy Family*, New York, Knopf, 1938, p. 67; David R. Mace, *Marriage: The Art of Lasting Love*, New York, Doubleday, 1952, pp. 51 ff.

bathroom in the morning characteristically grabbed the tube of paste and squeezed it. But lo! That blankety-blank cap was not only on, but tight. He had never put the cap on his toothpaste. Later, when Linda brushed her teeth she thought, "Gee, that hard crust on the toothpaste, why can't he just put the cap back on when he has finished."

It wasn't disastrous. They had a sense of humor. That evening Dick placed another tube of toothpaste in the medicine cabinet with the comment that he did not like the flavor of hers anyway.

A great many such differences in personal habits come into play following marriage. Some represent small but significant differences in basic personality. When the couple love one another these will be amusing episodes that can be resolved with mutual satisfaction. When there is little substance to the marriage, however, such little things can form a larger pattern of irritation and dissatisfaction which can be evoked by the most inconsequential experience.

LOOKING BEHIND THE SYMPTOMS

The majority of early marital problems that are regarded by the couple themselves as being of a more serious nature emerge as symptoms of deeper problems. Failing to understand this a couple are likely to become preoccupied with the painful psychological skin rash rather than looking at the source of the infection, the virus in the blood stream. When quarrels or suppressed hurt feelings center around the symptoms—an array of psychological ghosts—the relationship bogs down in misunderstanding and name calling rather than rising to a resolution of the difficulty.

Take for example the so-called mother-in-law problems.

Frequently they turn out to be problems of lack of psychological weaning and dependency upon a strong parental figure. Remove the mother from the marital scene and the problem is not resolved because the spouse will have to find some one else for ego support. Sex problems, as we saw in the preceding chapters, most often are problems of emotionally constricted or labile people who have been unhappy in their more intimate personal relations, or they may be problems of insensitivity and boorishness that can express itself in nonsexual situations. Money problems most frequently turn out to be symbols of "holding on to" or "reckless abandon and irresponsibility," traits which can be seen in the whole gamut of personal reactions to people and things. We must bear in mind, then, that many if not most of the serious problems of adjustment in marriage cannot be accepted at face value, but must be considered in terms of their deeper import.

THE SCALING-DOWN PROCESS

Let us look at one area of personal adjustment that confronts all marriages in varying degrees. It is what we referred to above as the *scaling-down process.* It can be relatively painless and constitute an extended growth experience. Or, it can be painfully disillusioning and represent deeper incompatibilities with divisive consequences. The scaling-down process is the intellectual and emotional "movement" from the idealization of the unknown, the untried, the not yet experienced, to the testing of the new reality. One or both members of the couple may now relax and revert to their prior-to-courtship habits and thus become, to some degree, the persons they were in their parental homes. It might be regarded as a return to the kitchen-self rather than the ballroom-self. There no longer seems to be a need to be "on best behavior." As one woman put it, "When I married Frank he wore his dashing pajamas. Now he comes to bed in his underwear. I guess that is the way he slept for the first 20 years, and maybe I'm not going to change him. But it makes me feel like my sheer nylon gown is a harlot's costume. He doesn't sense, and he doesn't seem to care."

The degree to which this scaling-down process is involved depends to a great extent on the degree of integration of the levels of one's personality, that is, how consistent one's personal roles are in different situations. Where both members of a couple have learned to maintain a high level of "morale" in their personal habits, such as being dressed with hair combed, teeth brushed, and perhaps a dash of cologne before breakfast, not as a pose or a concession to the bride or groom, but as an evidence of genuine fastidiousness, there is much less scaling down that takes place during the early part of marriage. The example of breakfast décor seems small and inconsequential, but multiplied by the many personal situations that make up the couple's days and nights, it can be symbolic of a total relationship.

However, of greater importance is the honesty or frankness in revealing one's deeper personality. Simply put, it means this: To what extent is an individual after marriage, the person who was met, courted, and known before marriage, or was the person courted more or less a conscious (or unconscious) pose? One can remain immaculately groomed and still act inconsiderately and insensitively to the needs and expectations of the other.

Categorically speaking, the most serious problems of early adjustment are those of conflicting basic personalities. This happens when one or the other has not been himself during courtship, and then after marriage, when the halo effect of the honeymoon has faded, it is discovered that former appearances have no substance. Let us recall the three theoretical modes of basic personality. Take the socially affirming person. Before marriage this person could *act* lovingly and affirmingly, as a part of putting his best foot forward. Remember, he was on good behavior. Now, if this behavior was not genuine, he may "let down" after marriage and become dependent, unusually demanding, and clinging. Or take the socially ascendant person before marriage. He may seem to be an active, "strong," assured person with confidence in himself and life. If this was an unconscious pose to win the fair person, he may become a dominating, demanding, overriding spouse after marriage. Finally, take the socially retiring person before marriage. His emotional austerity and the lure of wanting to "discover the unknown" may be very attractive to another during courtship. However, after marriage he is vulnerable to emotional disengagement, withdrawing into his books, science, the occult, and other solitary pursuits, leaving his partner lonesome and abandoned.

These examples are admittedly too neat. But by looking at them for their theoretical import and translating the *idea* into reality, one can see some of the most important bases of real incompatibility. The incompatibility may lie in two directions or a combination of the two. First, the two basic personalities may be genuinely incongruous. The couple awake to the fact that they see, feel, interpret, and like very little in common. Or they may be potentially compatible but too immature to know it. It is the writer's opinion that the latter obtains more frequently than the former, that a given person can learn to be compatible with quite a number of other persons if he or she is mature enough to grow in the same direction and not bog down in a rut of neurotic demands and expectations.

As we saw in the case of Glenn and Vivian, one was immature and did grow. The other, Glenn, was neurotic and did not change. This is an example of how individuals can meet, court, and marry an illusion, the projection of what they would like the other to be. Their relationship called for painful reëxamination on Vivian's part after the honeymoon—sometimes regarded as the shake-down cruise. Like the shake-down cruise, a couple may discover only minor adjustments to be made in the craft which will prove basically worthy on the sea of matrimony. Some prove to need partial redesigning and basic overhauling. In a few cases it seems fruitless to have to buoy up the empty hulk when it may need to be scuttled. These words may sound harsh, but they are realistic, and scuttling may be preferable to letting the relationship drift out to sea as a ghost ship.

AREAS OF ADJUSTMENT

Before returning to the subject of working through and resolving the more basic problems of personality incompatibility let us consider some of the areas of adjustment reported in research literature. The following are typical results of a number of comparable studies of middle-class families. Landis reports that the 409 couples in his study agreed that they were adjusted in certain areas from the beginning of marriage as follows: sex relations—slightly over one-half (53 percent); spending the family income—nearly three-fifths (57 percent); social activities—about two-thirds (67 percent);

in-law relationships—about seven out of ten (69 percent); religious activities—about three-fourths (75 percent); mutual friends—about three-fourths.[2]

This study was based on the reports of couples who were the parents of college students. Thus the results are somewhat more favorable than would obtain among other classes in our society, because the people in this sample were persons who had remained married a long time and had children in college.

We cannot regard any one area of adjustment as more important than another. Actually their importance varies among different couples. We can note, however, that the more personal areas of adjustment, such as sex adjustment or agreement on the spending of money, were areas of great maladjustment than were their social relationships with others at the time of marriage.

Sex Adjustment

Studies of the sex complaints of those who experience a less successful initial adjustment have been made by Terman, Burgess and Wallin, and others. One of the most frequently cited complaints is that of differences in sex appetite, with about one-fourth of the men desiring coitus more frequently than their wives, and about one-sixth of the women having intercourse "far beyond desire."[3]

As important as any research is, these statistics are far from a revealing statement of the problem. In counseling experience problems in sexual relations are often found to be not

[2] Judson T. Landis, "Length of Time Required to Achieve Adjustment in Marriage," *American Sociological Review,* XI, No. 6 (December, 1946), 666–677.

[3] Clifford Kirkpatrick, *The Family,* New York, Ronald, 1955, p. 439.

a matter of coitus *per se,* whether it is too much or too little, but a matter of *how* it is entered into. Of course, one does see some rather chronically "hungry" persons—people who say that they would prefer more coital outlet. However, getting to the heart of the problem it seems to be one more example of what we might call the *inadequacy of the response patterns* of the partner. More specifically it is not a problem of *how much,* but of *how.* Let us look at a number of examples that are so common they could be found anywhere in our society.

This is a woman speaking:

My husband works hard at a desk all day sometimes six days a week. When he comes home he is tired. He eats, flops down on the davinet, and watches television. He just doesn't notice me when he comes through the door. Knowing he has had a hard day, I can appreciate that for the moment. But during or after dinner there is never that spontaneous nibble on the neck, or his arms around me. When I do get a kiss I have come to interpret it as a peck on the cheek, signifying that he is leaving, or a kiss which means that he wants to have intercourse. It doesn't seem to be *me* as a *person* that he is interested in, but only himself. *I wouldn't mind his expectations, as frequently as he desired, if I felt that it meant any more to him than a biological urge . . .*

Here is a characteristic statement from a man. It is like a fugue with the theme expressed in an infinite number of variations, but unmistakenly the same theme:

I can't understand why my wife thinks that I'm such a "leering, prancing wolf," interested only in sex. I think that she got the idea from the Kinsey report. But she thinks that *that* is all men are interested in, implying me, I guess. . . . But I really think that if she would respond and not conjure up so many ways of putting me off, that I would be less demanding. She can stand and cold-cream her face for what seems like an hour, especially when she knows that I am anxious. Frankly, it burns me up.

She regards the moments of preparation for coitus as a major task that ought to be rewarded with a mink coat. . . . I really believe that my expectations from her have become demands, and that there is more than a bit of hostility behind them. If she acted like she was really in there pitching, I wouldn't be so demanding . . . *a little of the real thing would go a long way.*

Here is still another frequent complaint from a woman: "My husband is so direct in his approaches that I just seem to tense up. I don't know why I should expect to hear an ear full of pretty nothings and a bit of playful flattery as preliminary to our love-making, but I do, and I don't believe that I'm just a prudish and silly girl."

The foregoing examples of so-called sexual problems in marriage could be multiplied many times, but they, and many others, should be recognized for what they are—illustrations of a lack of understanding, consideration, and care. A couple can tamper with the sex symptoms, can be the most sophisticated readers of sex techniques among different cultures, can blame one another until red in the face without getting at the roots of the difficulty which may, to repeat, not be sexual at all, but sexual symbols and symptoms of a faulty personal relationship in the whole gamut of their marital interaction. When this is understood, the way is clear to work through these problems and to learn to be more genuinely understanding and considerate. Perhaps at first it might be a pose. Then as competence comes with practice, a couple can move into a relationship where sex is not merely a biological outlet, but the deep and meaningful communication of what a couple really mean to one another.

One aspect of sex adjustment is an orientation related to the scaling-down process which could save unnecessary tears and disappointment. Some couples have the mistaken assumption that anything less than "every time" spells sex failure. Actually the satisfaction or completeness of the experience may vary a great deal in a given couple. When we reflect on the complexity of sex as a medium of communication we appreciate the many things that can affect the nature of a prolonged embrace. There will be the intermittent "highs" when it turns out to be an incomparably memorable event. There will be intermittent high anticipation that results in failure. There will be periods of feeling emotionally "disengaged" or distant from the spouse. Lowered and heightened mood levels are a part of the swells, the ebb, and the tide of life. To accept the reality of the matter is to prevent unnecessary self-recrimination and projection of failure and blame.

There are, of course, the more serious problems of sexual adjustment. The following are forms of incipient or overt sexual inversion: persons who have to dress like members of the opposite sex before they can become aroused; such extreme narcissism that a person cannot respond to anybody but an audience or a mirror; exhibitionism or display of the self; hostility associated with the sex act in which a person must hurt or be hurt; continuous rather than transient impotence or frigidity; fetishes in which sex has to be expressed in unusual and bizarre forms such as the person who could respond only to another (any person) dressed in highly polished boots; and forms of sexual rejection such as a spasm of the vaginal muscles. However, these and other deeper sexual symptoms are not common and do not enter into the sex problems of the majority of people to any disrupting extent. These, also, are not merely sex problems, but symptoms of deeper neuroses that need psychiatric treatment.

At this point it is desirable to mention another sex problem often experienced early in the marriage. It is one that is sensed and defined usually by the woman rather than the man: "My husband seems to take an interest in variations in position in coitus and to employ different techniques in foreplay. Some of these I can't help feel are perverse and it worries me."

It is the consensus of professional opinion that mature people are not bound to a single English-American (man above, woman below) position in coitus. They feel free, increasingly, to employ different positions and to stimulate any part of the body that is responsive, orally and/or manually. However, with mature people, there is a relative absence of *preoccupation* with the unique. There is no constant striving for something unusual or bizarre.

Some persons reject almost any variation, making love in a lighted room, nudity, etc., in the name of modesty. This may represent a stage in the unveiling process. When this continues, however, this person may be too immature or neurotic to move on to an orientation in which he or she regards the body of the other as one's own in which an act of immodesty is impossible. Sexual immaturity defends itself by feeling squeamish. To be more fully responsive is to threaten the defense against the fear of sex and is experienced as some degree of anxiety. It is much like the primitive who fears touching the taboo object. To push him toward it is to arouse anxiety which will be proportionate to the importance of the taboo.

What is appropriate and in good taste in sexual behavior is extremly variable in our society. Couples vary greatly in their feelings about many of the details of their erotic experience, expectations, and desires. It is fortunate when they are of one mind about the matter. It can be very painful and personally threatening when they are not. Many couples go through a number of successive stages of increasing intimacy to the fullest extension of the self to the other. When they do not and seem unable to work through their orientations to what to them is some reasonably common ground, professional assistance should be sought. Even though it is a minority of couples who need help, there are too many who let their maladjustment drift into more serious problems that require extended treatment or wreck the marriage. It is a common assumption on the part of marriage counselors that anything in the sexual relationship that is pleasant and enhances the total relationship might be regarded as acceptable and desirable by the couple themselves. What any one else thinks or does is quite beside the point.

Extramarital Attraction

Another problem of the early adjustments to be made in marriage is one that enters into the scaling-down process. It concerns glamour outside of marriage. It may be a facetious comment about the attractive figure of another woman, a little flirtation at a cocktail party, or teaming up particularly well with your best friend's spouse at bridge or on the fairway. Two particularly vocal people, both of whom married more retiring basic personalities, often find themselves enjoying extended conversation.

To some couples these are natural, normal, desirable bases of association with other couples. To many others, however, any more personal "exchange" is a threat, especially to one who is high in the socially reticent component of basic personality, or one who has suffered feelings of social ineptitude and rejection. In marriage we tend to reënact the social and emotional roles that we learned during childhood and adolescence. If a person has been particularly secure in his relationships with others, the spouse's "engaging" manner with the couple's friends of the opposite sex will not be threatening. If a person has not been secure and feels somewhat insecure in the marriage, almost any personal gesture will be interpreted as a "pass" at someone and evoke feelings of ambivalence toward the spouse and toward the other person. The offended spouse may act with considerable politeness and deference but at the same time harbor feelings of jealousy and hostility. This can be very painful and disillusioning, especially during the early part of the marriage when it first emerges as a problem to be dealt with.

In the best of marriages one or both members of a couple may have an eye for glamour outside the marriage. The familiarity of living in such proximity as in marriage cannot help but reduce the high pitch of romantic feeling of the honeymoon. The "pursuit of the unknown" is a widespread latent, if not active, interest of a great many men and some women. It will express itself as a fleeting thought or a passing gesture in the case of the good marriage, with a prevailing, shared sense of humor. Levy and Munroe believe that a man who can appreciate the figure of another woman is more appreciative of his wife's than one who cannot:

> There is also the question of glamour outside of marriage. An old song runs:
>
> If in your heart one corner lies
> That has no room for me
> You do not love me as I deem
> True love should ever be . . .
> You do not love me, no!
> Bid me good-bye and go.

To this exacting young lady I reply: "Bushwah." No man is so deeply in love with his wife that he loses his eye for a pair of pretty legs wherever he finds them—unless he's the sort of man who never notices his wife's legs either. A lady with a worried air said to me: "Whenever I'm feeling particularly keen about my husband I start behaving like a schoolgirl with other men, kissing in the moonlight and that sort of nonsense. I fall for sweet nothings like a ton of bricks. Does that mean I don't really love my husband?"

Not at all. Happily married people are by no means impervious to the romantic attractions of outsiders . . . the most highbrow literati are not above chuckling over an ephemeral paragraph in the *New Yorker*.[4]

Levy and Munroe go on to say, however, that when a marriage is really stable, extramarital attractions are not compulsive and do not have to be pursued. They are of passing interest and do not threaten the marriage.

The foregoing orientation will be offensive to the moralist. He will counter with the idea, "But think of what it could lead to." Here we have a dilemma. It is a dilemma that our society has dealt with most unrealistically. Traditionally we have said, "There should be no attraction to another outside marriage." That may be true. It may be possible that some couples could achieve such a complete oneness in their relationship that romantic thoughts of others could not possibly cross the threshhold of their conscious or unconcious minds. Even granting that as a possibility and an ideal goal, the problem still remains. Being what we are, how do we achieve psychological monogamy? To deny the thoughts categorically would be one possible course of action. This is as difficult as the task that Tolstoy set for himself as a boy when, to acquire the coveted green stick, one had to stand on his head in the corner without thinking of

[4] Levy and Munroe, *op cit.,* pp. 78–79.

a white rabbit. Another possible solution would be to recognize that man is part of the animal world and thus is capable of some promiscuous thinking, but suppress any gesture of expressing it—always remaining proper though not necessarily stiff and staid. Another orientation would be the one expressed by Levy and Munroe above that we might paraphrase as: "What's the fuss about. What's wrong with finding others attractive or engaging. It's no reflection on the marriage. I love my spouse and wouldn't trade him or her for anyone whom I have seen. Let's be honest about the matter, not try to kid ourselves, and above all, not become enmeshed in a complex of anxiety and self-recrimination. As a matter of fact the stimulation one receives from others might enhance the marriage, actually making one feel keener toward the spouse and express it in more ardent love-making at home." Still another orientation would be the opposite position of the moralist, one of overt promiscuity: "Monogamy in any sense of the term is outmoded, and a lot of people are missing a great deal. Love is a game that should be pursued with ardor and with any attractive person who is willing to play. The important thing is to be discreet about the matter."

The first and the last of the above orientations are more representative of the lower and upper classes in our society than of our middle classes. The firm and resolute stand against the expression of any attraction to another outside marriage is quite characteristic of our lower-middle class—the most "moral" segment of our culture. The Levy-Munroe position of "tolerant restraint" is not necessarily characteristic of our upper-middle class, but would find a large proportion of adherents among them.

We have as a society been so preoccupied with the question

of ideals in marriage that we have paid too little attention to the developmental experiences that people might have to go through to achieve successively higher forms of conduct, however we may define them. In the main we are quite permissive with our children during their dating and courtship experiences, allowing milder forms of intimacy as preparation for the deeper intimacy of marriage. Can we expect what has become and amounts to a great deal of psychic promiscuity during the rating-dating phase of adolescence suddenly to change with the marriage ceremony? Our high divorce rate, especially during the first year of marriage, together with the other evidences of marital incompatibility and dislocation stand as powerful challenges to us to consider what we might do in orienting ourselves to that kind of rationale and those practices that will be conducive to the continued growth and strengthening of our Western ideal of truly monogymous marriage, thus narrowing the wide gap between what we think that we ought to do and how we act in reality. How long can we allow ourselves the moral luxury of escaping the responsible question by hiding behind moralistic cliches? To seek perfection may not be the same as presuming to be perfect.

We have been much more sensible about personal matters that have not become moralistic issues in our culture. Take the toilet training of our infants for example. At first we impose no controls. Then, when the child has matured to the point where he can begin to achieve bowel and bladder control he is trained in an understanding atmosphere. We accept regressions when he is ill or insecure, knowing that patient guidance will eventuate in mastery. We know enough not to frighten him, use anxiety as a weapon, or reflect undue preoccupation and concern. In the main we have no problem.

The "moral" dilemma is not black and white in nature. It is neither one of morbid, tight-lipped denial of human nature, as when some of our forebears branded their erring daughters on the forehead with a hot iron; nor is it a question of irresponsible personal freedom. The question is one of how to achieve the greatest personal freedom within a society (and thus within a marital relationship) commensurate with necessary renunciation for the good of the other.

However, many in our society are in no position to think through any moral dilemma and tend to seek one of two avenues of escape: compulsive conformity or flight into irresponsible self-indulgence. Both means of escape are accompanied by deeper feelings of boredom, loss of spontaneity and capacity for critical thought, and a feeling of aloneness.

Though the context of the moral dilemma described above is "marital" and the problem is one of "sex," the origins of compulsive conformity or of self-indulgence lie quite outside the marital relationship itself. Many persons in our society have been the victims of faulty psychology, education, and religious training, leaving them emotional, intellectual, and moral cripples.

Many children's spontaneous interest in learning has been stifled by the kind of educational system which assumes that the "strict discipline" of gathering information is the same as learning to reflect deeply and think originally. Academic browbeating, didactic teaching methods, "facts" meted out in a drab "intellectual" atmosphere that could not possibly stimulate the child's imagination often combine and are rewarded by the citations of some administrators. And often enough, the product is the kind of walking encyclopaedia one sees on the television quiz program whose daily bread is earned by doing menial, routine jobs. Of course, creative thinking cannot take place in a factual vacuum, but doses of facts given to children outside of some larger, and to them more meaningful, context can not only clutter up the mind but also stand in the way of true learning. Finally, our curricula were first developed to further the mastery of our material welfare, to be enriched by adding the fine arts. A gesture of importance was accorded those fields in the humanities that were well expergated, noncontroversial, and emotionally anesthetized. The social sciences and clinical arts have just begun to get their foot in the door of primary and secondary education.

There are those religious leaders whose preachments are a far cry from the liberal currents of Judeo-Christian thought and tradition. They play upon the fears, anxieties, doubts, and loneliness of people rather than inspiring them to new horizons of awareness, ethical concern, consideration, and self-transcendence. Sometimes they appear in the role of the charismatic leader, similar to their political counterparts in state dictatorships, "inspiring" masochistic subjection rather than mature dedication. They are preoccupied with hell-fire-damnation rather than with love and the dignity and integrity of human personality.

These are among the more potent forces in our society that have played such a central role in robbing people of their capacity to weigh the new problems of sex morality in a context of the changing and emerging circumstances of each new era. To recognize our social ills and their sources is not to condemn our society, nor is it to minimize the many liberal forces now operating in our homes, schools, and churches. Such recognition, however, will help us to confront our moral problems with greater maturity and to minimize those social and psychological circumstances that keep men in immoral and amoral bondage.

Chapter 13

EARLY PROBLEMS OF ADJUSTMENT IN MARRIAGE (Continued)

RELATING TO PARENTS AND IN-LAWS

WHEN A couple marry they enter a new relationship with their parents and the parents of the spouse. For many this emotional transition from the parental families to the pair-centeredness of marriage is unhampered by parental expectations, demands, or lingering dependencies on the part of the children. For many others, however, there are problems of varying degrees of seriousness that are carry-overs from the courtship period, or emerge unexpectedly for the first time.

We often see young couples who have been and are very close to their parents. Such a condition is very favorable to the success of the marriage when the closeness is a result of mutual confidence, shared activities with family rituals that give the families a sense of uniqueness and identity, and a mutual sense of care. Where this kind of closeness has obtained between the person and the parents, the process of psychological weaning from the family continues after marriage, with the extension of these meanings and sentiments to the spouse. One turns less to mother or father for advice, guidance, and shared confidences and gradually the spouse takes this "parental" role. The process is gradual and does not take place all at once. There is probably never a complete transference, because the person who has been close to his family always retains a feeling of regard, love, and respect for the parents. However, the center of emotional gravity shifts with marriage from the parental family to the spouse. As the couple grow together their identity becomes closer and fuller as a pair. The transition from the parental family to the marriage is imperceptible and there is no problem. One can visit the parents without feeling it a duty or obligation. The spouse is not threatened by such visiting and sharing of some confidences. A close relationship continues with the parental family, but on a psychologically autonomous rather than a unilateral basis.

It takes time for this transfer of sentiment and identity where parental ties have been strong. Relatively mature young people can be patient with one another and not expect all of the coin of sentiment to be withdrawn from the parental family account at once, and deposited to the account of the new marriage. The visits or phone calls to mother will decrease as will the transient feelings of nostalgia for the safety, comfort, and lack of responsibility experienced while a fledgling in the family nest. The reward of waiting for the more complete pair identity to emerge in marriage is well worth the price. It is infinitely more promising than the marriage in which one has little or none of the identity of the parental family to vest in the marriage.

Let us now turn from this optimal parent—child—in-law relationship to the problem cases. In counsel the most serious problem is overdependence on parental expectations, sanctions, and aid. In this case the child harbors a gnawing ambivalence toward the parent even though it may be quite unconscious. In such a case it is the spouse who has a sense of being displaced. Often one hears the complaint, "I feel like I am playing second fiddle," or, "I feel like the fifth wheel on the wagon." It may be the man who is bound to an ascendant, dominating mother or the long-suffering "dependent" parent. The sex combinations in this kind of "octopus" love are unimportant. Either of the couple can be dependent upon mother, father, or other parent figures.

Here is how one woman states the problem:

My husband and I seemed so close when we were first married. I guess that it was me who felt close and assumed that he did too. However, things changed gradually and then suddenly, when his father died. He visited his mother every evening after work and it didn't seem to matter whether I had a hot dinner waiting or not. When he finally came in he would pat me on the shoulder and say, "You know how lonesome mother is, with dad gone and all, you shouldn't mind me calling on her." Then I'd feel guilty and selfish and all. . . . Recently his mother asked us to come and live with her but I just can't bring myself to do it. I wouldn't really mind if she were a different kind of person, but she seems to ignore me if not resent my being around. I just don't feel like I possess my husband at all.

Often money constitutes one strand in the silver cord. It might be the estate or the farm that has been left and the surviving parent is using it to buy the child's continued care and deference. In other instances ill health and loneliness are played up, and these can be the most lethal of all psychological weapons, for they make the son or daughter feel so guilty about "callously ignoring mother," or "failing to appreciate all that she has done for me."

Overprotection, ease, dependency, money, and feelings of obligation often serve to cement the child to the foundation of the parental homestead. This is the kind of situation that Strecker found in his study of several thousand men who were rejected for military service. They were suffering from what he called "momism" by which he meant the overprotection by the parent of either sex.[1] They might also be regarded as marital 4-F's.

Sometimes such parent-child relationships are very subtle and difficult to see for what they are. The following case is an example of a woman who is caught in a swirl of emotional entanglements with her mother. She is neurotically preoccupied with the symptoms of her problem and quite unable to understand the bases for her deep ambivalence toward her mother.

My mother goes to church alone. While Phil and I are still half asleep, I hear her moving softly in her room across the hall. She is always afraid of disturbing us—always careful.

I ought to get up, I think, uneasily, I ought to go with her.

I have been thinking this for more years than I like to remember, and very occasionally I do go to church with my mother. At such times I am conscious of all the good that is promised and needed. It is her eagerness which defeats me—her hair swept up like a cloud from her face, and her blue eyes shining too brightly.

"Mrs. Truax, this is my daughter." She will cross the church to introduce me, after services.

And then, the lingering handclasp, the welcoming note. "So glad to have you with us—wasn't the sermon splendid?"

What happens to me then? What blind, stubborn thing sets itself hard against them, refusing to become a part of this weekly ritual, even to please my mother? The conflict is deep, and I

[1] Edward A. Strecker, *Their Mothers Sons,* Philadelphia, Lippincott, 1946.

have never understood it. There are so many things I believe, but not in the way my mother believes, and I cannot force myself. I have read countless books on religion, I have studied the Bible, I have listened. I am not an atheist, either, or a true agnostic. For there are these things I believe, and there is one thing I know: that my mother exemplifies most of them. Yet each Sunday morning I am awake before she leaves, and I almost never get up and go to church.

After all, I never miss an Easter service. She knows I would do anything else for her—anything in the world. It is the kind of rationalization at which I have become adept. David (my son) will take her to church. He'll call for her later on—she doesn't really mind.

For a long time, now, we have dispensed with Sunday dinners. We have usually been out late the night before, and none of us are hungry before eleven. Only, my mother must eat something before she leaves.

Dressed in slacks and a long-sleeved blouse, I pass my mother's room without really looking. I run quickly down the sun-flooded stairs, and into the kitchen. But once inside the door, I stop. She has left her cup and plate in the sink. The water from the faucet drips down on them with a curiously empty sound. I move them aside, and brush some shreds of dry cereal from the breakfast table. She has set three places—the ice water is made, the orange juice squeezed; and in front of the coffee pot there is a brief, scrawled note: "Darling—please leave the dishes until I come home."

On her dresser stand three little pictures in dull gilt frames. They are arranged like a vanguard of perpetual innocence—my own slightly forward, since I am the oldest, my sister's set back a few inches, my brother's last. All of them were taken when we were not more than five. They face the bed where my mother sleeps, and in their round, solemn eyes there is no hint of questioning. They seem to reflect my mother's faith, and nothing on earth can shake it. Though my brother is dead, now, and neither my sister nor I have fulfilled that first promise, my mother's life is still one of service, and she prays on her knees every night.

More than once I have gone to her room, my footsteps intentionally deadened, some uneasiness drawing me . . . I don't know. I have stepped through the doorway to find my mother on her knees, her face concealed between outstretched arms, the shining plait of hair lying motionless between her thin shoulders. I stand there for a minute, looking down at her; I glance at my brother's picture, and I think, next Sunday I will go to church with her. It is such a little thing, and there are only two of us now. I will go to please my mother.

It is early spring. The trees outside are a bright, stabbing green, and all the pretty things with which my sister and I have thought to delight her catch the sun and somehow mock me. There is, among them, the cheap little paperweight on her bookshelves. A replica of a cathedral shines up through the glass—each window and dome is inlaid with iridescent mother-of-pearl. My sister and I found it in a secondhand store near New York. Twenty-five cents, I think, and she likes it better than anything else in this room. Only the pictures mean more to her; and the Bible, frayed on the edges. I pick it up from the floor by her chair. Is it my fault? I cry silently. Haven't I done the best I could? Going to church is not the only answer—it's what you are and believe.

I am nearly always reading in the living room when my mother comes up from the basement garage. It is my way of hiding from myself, more than from her. Elaborately casual, I glance up from the paper, and something inside of me contracts. Is it just my imagination, or are her eyes faintly bleak? It seems to me that I can detect some weariness about her—something lonely and asking—and the roots of my tongue begin to ache. Instantly I point to the bulletin she holds—I am ready to blame the church. Now, as she moves about the kitchen, I think of this and of how, at times, my mother blames herself for having failed her children. I hear her open the oven door, and I fling my paper aside and go out to help her. I edge around, so that I can see her face. She isn't crying. Her mouth does not tremble at the corners, but there is such open sorrow in the lines at either side that I am stricken with shame and self-loathing.

"Look," I press my cheek against her. "I'll go with you next Sunday, mother, I give you my word."

"You needn't do that—I believe you," she tells me.

"I don't know what makes me so hateful."

One wet hand reaches up to my hair. "You're not," she says, "you're my sweet fine girl."

I draw back as if she had burned me. "Don't say that. You know you think I'm lost. A heathen," I cry, bitter as gall, "just because I don't go to church. Because I can't believe the way you do, no matter how I try."

"I don't think any of those things," my mother says gently. "If I give that impression, then I am sorry."

"You mean you really think there's hope for me?"

"I know it," she says, and though I am prepared to mock and gibe, a strange thing happens to me then. For a moment, I move backward in time. I am a child, unburdened by the weight of years—a little girl kneeling beside her mother, with her head bowed in trustful imitation. The next instant I see myself as I really am, and the taste in my mouth is acid.

"Now you've got something to look forward to—for a whole week!"

My mother hides any grief she may feel. "You needn't go on my account," she remarks quietly. But I must. I have promised, and all through the week I am conscious of this, if only because she never quite lets me forget it. Though she never actually says a word, there is about her some added tenderness—a hint of joy that closes my throat, and makes me sharp when I notice. I find her pressing my street dress on Saturday, and I exclaim impatiently, "What's that for?"

"Nothing, I just noticed it was wrinkled."

Then comes Sunday morning. "Now, you run along and dress—I'll fix a little breakfast. I've already made some cinnamon biscuit for later on," she adds. "We'll have a nice, hot breakfast when we come home from church."

So, even before we leave the house, I am robbed of any comfort I might have had—any possible complacency over going to please my mother. She betrays her longing in these little ways, and each of them is a reminder. No last-minute rush—no listening, as she must, for David to wake . . . no tension. This is the way it should always be, I think, driving over the glistening streets at exactly ten-forty-five. Here we are, early enough to find plenty of parking space. Here is my mother, exquisitely neat, her blue eyes suffused with some inner radiance, a small purse clasped on her knees. She looks across at me, smiling, and I give the car a savage swing, and scrape the tires on the curbing. I try not to notice her moving lips, or to think of my brother and sister. But they are here with the choir which files toward the left—each white-surpliced boy has my brother's eyes, each rosy girl is my sister. She has never seen us any other way, I think. She comes to find us every week, and none of us is here. There is not one who seems to worship alone, yet every Sunday of her life my mother sits in a space by herself, and prays for the strength to guide us. She stands erect, as now, and repeats the Scriptures with boundless faith, for whether or not we live by them, in this respect we have failed her.

But then, with the last hymn, I look at my mother, and her thin, luminous face is too much for me. I see her quickly gather her things, and I long to rush out ahead of the crowd, for I know too well what is coming.

"Good morning—how are you, Mrs. Estes? You've met my daughter, haven't you?"

"Why, of course! So nice to have you with us today."

We shake hands, and move slowly up the aisle. There is no hurrying my mother now—she must stop and greet each person she knows, and always with her hand on my arm. "Mrs. Lockridge, this is my daughter—my oldest daughter—you remember my daughter." Oh, see, she is here. She has come with me to the house of our Lord. Be warm and friendly—be kind to her, for she is confused and in need. "Let's cross over, darling, I want you to meet the Theilens."

Pulling tighter within myself, I smile and smile. "How do you do? Yes, wasn't it? Just wonderful."

After church, "Sometimes I feel a little tired," my mother confesses, "but today it was lovely, wasn't it?"

I just nod. I want, more than anything, to assure her—to say that I will join her every Sunday after this—but I can't bring myself to promise—not so soon. Instead, I heap her plate with omelet. I read in her room, during the symphony hour; I take up her supper on a tray.

"Phil and I are going out for a little while, mother. We'll be home early."

"That's all right—you have a good time."

"Here are the New York papers, and some magazines."

She reaches for them—I see the paperweight half concealed in her hand, and I just go blind, for a minute.

Her room is dark when we come home, and I have to stop and listen. There is no sound. I am afraid of disturbing my mother's rest, but still, I must turn the handle of her door, and look inside, as always.

She is lying on her back—facing the mirror where the three miniatures glint softly in the light from the hall. One thin, white arm is curved around the pillow, the other lies over her chest. Her body seems flat and very still, and watching until the covers rise, I bury my face in my hands.

I tell you, I am afraid . . . I don't know. She seems so little and pale in the shadows. She isn't very young any more, and in a way I have helped to age her. I want to fall down on my knees and pray—I want to beg her, and promise. But my back is rigid with the habit of years—I stand there waiting until a clock strikes twelve, and then, on Monday, I buy her a dress, or a hat trimmed with pretty cloth flowers.[2]

In this case we see the pronounced ambivalence that the daughter feels for her mother—love and appreciation for what her mother has done for her, but deep and quite unconscious hostility because of the binding obligation that is inadvertently exacted by her mother. Every time her mother clutched her Bible, uttered a silent prayer, pressed her daugh-

[2] Henrietta Daniels, "Sunday Morning," *Ladies' Home Journal,* November, 1950.

ter's dress for church, the daughter felt that she *had* to meet her mother's expectations or hasten her mother's ill health or even death. She could not come to her religion and church in her *own* way and *own* time. She was struggling desperately for her personal autonomy. Not being able to strike back at the emotionally smothering expectations of her mother, her hostility and aggression came out in disguised form such as swerving the car into the curb, "heaping" her mother's plate with omelet (to choke), appearing on Sunday morning in slacks, etc.

The conflict was not over religion. Church attendance was not the real issue. The same struggle for autonomy on the part of the daughter and for dependence-security on the part of the mother could have been expressed in many different forms. The context could have been politics, in which instance the mother would expect the daughter to belong to her party and "fulfill her citizenship duty" by attending political meetings. The daughter would have found politics distasteful, the mother's party too conservative, and rebel by silently wishing that she were a member of the radical party.

It does no good to blame either or call them clinical names. The mother, widowed, lonesome, could not form her own friendships and enter into church activities as a member of the group. She worshiped alone. Her daughter was all that she had, she felt, all that she had to "hold on to." The daughter was struggling for her personal autonomy, to cut the strings of obligation and duty, and to be herself. If her mother could have understood, could have really let her make the break from parental ties, the daughter quite possibly would have returned of her own volition to meet her mother's expectations without rebelling inwardly.

We can imagine how her husband must have felt about

his wife's constant preoccupation with hurting her mother. He did have an "in-law" problem, but it was really a problem of lack of psychological weaning on the part of his wife. To remove the mother would not necessarily remove the problem. It was a matter of unresolved dependency that the daughter would continue to carry in her repertory of expectations toward any parental figure who fitted the role that her mother played in her life.

Like most such cases the principals here are completely unconscious of their real problem. Furthermore, they all mean well. Such is true of many disturbing, neurotic problems. If they were asked to define their problem, the mother would probably deny that any problem existed. The daughter would probably blame herself and say that she had a religious problem, then go into a highly intellectual and irrelevant discussion of humanism and insist that she is not agnostic.

Note, in this case, the classical symptoms of the prototype of many, if not most, serious in-law problems: (1) There is a neurotic binding relationship between the parents of one spouse and that person. (2) The relationship is loaded with guilt, self-recrimination, and resolutions to "do something about it." (3) They are caught in a quagmire of symptoms, unaware of the deeper, underlying personality problems involved. (4) The child feels strong ambivalence toward the parent—appreciation, on the one hand, and on the other, unconscious resentment at the obstacle the parent imposes against growing into greater personal autonomy rationalized in self-deprecation. (5) The spouse resents the other's being bound to the parent. This makes it an in-law problem. The spouse might acquiesce and pass as it were; or, might rant and rave, depending upon his or her basic personality and the circumstances. The marriage is suffering a severe case of in-law combat fatigue resulting from a running, unconscious battle of parent-child relations.

There are, of course, other kinds of in-law problems. Sometimes a person has become quite autonomous, but a parent will continue to hold on and try to control. This is usually not serious from the marriage's point of view, since the child can handle the parent one way or another. It may be a nuisance or of some concern, but it is not a serious disruption. In this instance the situation is reversed, and the child may have the task of weaning the parent.

One such couple sought premarital counsel. They were graduating together. He was younger, but had already spent some time in military service. His mother strongly disapproved of the match on the grounds that a man should be older than his wife. His mother disapproved so wholeheartedly that she threatened to cut her son off from his share of the estate which ran into five figures, if he married the girl. In counsel the couple were seeking to determine whether the differences in their ages would give rise to problems of adjustment later. They loved one another, had been going together several years, and had no doubts in their own minds about the future of their relationship. They were seeking the opinion of a counselor regarding his mother's assumptions. After being assured that age differences of three years were inconsequential the couple phoned his mother and told her of their intentions to marry after graduation, six weeks hence. After they listened to her protests and repeated threat to disinherit them they affirmed their intention to marry as planned. "Mother banged down the receiver," he said, "jumped into her car, drove to Campus Town where I had an apartment, stormed in, and read me the riot act. I called Betty and we confronted mother together.

We told her that we intended to marry regardless of what she did, that we would like nothing more than to have her blessing, but that we could not break our engagement for anybody, when we loved one another as we did. When I finished speaking mother rose. Without saying a word and wearing a grim look on her face she stalked out."

On the way back to her home, some 75 miles away, something happened. His mother turned her car around, drove back and found the couple where she had left them. "I've been an old fool," she said, opening the conversation. "I can see now that I have run your father's life and tried to run my son's. You were kind to me when you spoke as you did and I respect you for having gumption enough to know your own minds. I am sorry and I insist on paying for the wedding as the least I can do."

The outcome of this case is unusual, but not without precedent in the writer's experience. The couple showed unusual autonomy, especially when so much money was involved. Whatever the mother's motivation, she was flexible enough, and apparently loved her son enough to make a dramatic change. It is noteworthy that the initial conflict was not between the couple themselves, or within either, but between them and his mother. This stands in contrast to the case in *Sunday Morning* which is a much more painful and serious "in-law" problem. It is fortunate in the present instance that the couple faced up to his mother and resolved their differences before the wedding, rather than circumventing a show-down, leaving the conflict to confront them anew later.

We are prone sometimes to place all of the blame on parents. Often they are partially if not entirely right, and it is the son or daughter who, in immature projection, is seeing the spouse or spouse-to-be through rose-colored glasses and the parents through smoke-colored glasses. The parent wants the child to avoid a faulty and perhaps tragic marriage, but often their advice is largely ignored if not resented. This case is one of immaturity and the person is probably not ready for marriage. This problem of emotional immaturity we have already discussed.

Looking with some perspective at the relations of young married couples with their parents, we know that the majority of middle-class couples do not have serious in-law problems, but enjoy continued parental support and assistance. There is probably nothing in life that parents want more for their children than happiness in their marriages. By realizing this the young people will not be excessively independent, robbing their parents of the many pleasures of continued familism, including the grandchildren as they come along, and whom you might expect mother and dad to "spoil." But such transient extravagances of the spirit will do the grandchildren little if any harm, and will provide the grandparents with one of the greatest of life's satisfactions —the feeling that they will live on in their children and grandchildren.

PATTERNS OF SOCIAL AND EMOTIONAL ROLES

Another aspect of the scaling-down process is that of achieving the pattern of social and emotional roles that constitutes the "mode of operation" in the marriage. In the chapter on the meaning of love we discussed the meaning of surrender and indicated that the achievement of increasing *oneness* involves a mutual dependency while, at the same time, each assumes roles of ascendance appropriate to the "department" in which each is in charge. We have already discussed the traditional division of labor in the family and the fact that the roles of men and women were quite rigidly defined in the early patriarchal home. During the courtship and often the engagement period young couples assume more or less traditional social and emotional roles. If the girl is inclined to be rather "bossy" she probably plays down this role and assumes one of greater deference to his male ascendance. He may have tended to play a passive and dependent role in relation to his mother in his home but during courtship, he will help his fiancée with her coat, seat her in the car, and place her order at dinner.

After marriage this can all change. They may relax quite suddenly into the social and emotional roles that they learned in their relation to parents and sibs of the opposite sex. Another closely related aspect of the problem is the dramatic change in the roles of both men and women in American society, so that in addition to the more personal and unique needs and expectations of a given couple there is the influence of the confused expectations of our "equalitarian" orientation conveyed through magazines, advertising, and all other media of mass communication. We can see this problem in the titles of articles and books such as *Woman, The Lost Sex, Woman, The Third Sex,* and *Have American Women Forgotten?* This copious literature is indicative of considerable psychosexual disequilibrium and quandry. It might be characterized as modern woman's (and man's!) search for a sense of personal identity. When the cultural definitions of the social and psychological division of labor in the courtship are at variance with the personal needs and expectations of the couple after marriage, they constitute disillusioning experiences and the couple are confronted with the problem of reconciling them. The following is one woman's statement of the dilemma:

And I don't see why I always have to get all dressed up, while *he* appears in his old blue suit. The modern couple is an immaculate, split-personality model living area, hand in hand with a muddy old shoe.

Did it ever occur to anybody to let me be Common Woman for a while?

Everybody was always picking on Hamlet and Faust, and everybody is always picking on me. It's partly because I'm a sitting duck. You can't criticize anybody who belongs to a minority group, but women are equal now. This makes them practically the only group that is, and a nice big group to criticize.

One of the things everybody has against me *is* that I'm equal. Let's get this straight. I didn't ask to be emancipated. That was my great aunt Melusina. Let's let bygones be bygones. We're in this together, men. All right, all right, I know I never wrote a decent symphony.

One of the reasons I haven't is that I spend so much time thinking about men.

Anything I am, I'm a type, and not one of them is good. If I say "Darling, I love you more than life itself, and I can't live without you," I'm possessive and sucking the man's blood. If I say, "Let's have fun and let the chips fall off the old block where they may," I'm an aggressive specimen of the lost sex, incapable of loving. If I don't let them make love to me, I'm repressed. If I sit with my hands folded and let them, I'm passive. If I leap enthusiastically into their arms and make love to them, they say they like women who are hard to get.

If I'm sick, it's in my head. If I have something in my head, I'm supposed to give *him* the idea that it was really in his all along.

If, inspired by those photographs, I serve my husband rich delicious meals, next month they tell me I'm killing him by making him overweight. Honestly, has the cat got his tongue? Why doesn't he just say, "No more Marshmallow Surprise," instead of going behind my back to the editor.

If I work, I'm competing with men and I'll have door-key children. If I don't work, I'm not providing for the long lonely years when the tiny feet have taken their door keys and pattered away.

If I love my son to distraction, I turn him into a homosexual. If I love him with restraint, I turn him into a juvenile delinquent. The little bastard. I'm not supposed to have a little bastard, but even a sitting duck may be somebody's mother. If there's any question of it, I'm supposed to have him, give him up for adoption, and Seek Counseling. Then, eventually, I will meet a man who Understands.

If he does, I hope he'll explain it to me.

But I have a feeling he won't. No matter how otherwise brilliant and original they may be, men serve up any old tired cliché when they talk about women. After I tell him my mournful tale, he'll say "Momism."

(The appalling thing is I go right on wanting to cook Marshmallow Surprise for him. But I'm thinking up a new recipe. I add gin.)

It's NOT that I want anybody protecting me, or supporting me, or giving me his seat in the subway. I just don't want them spitting in my eye the whole time. I've given up hope of having time to have a soul, but can't I have one tiny foible? My unemancipated great aunts had a great advantage: they could be eccentric. Right now, there's not one young female character in the whole vast breadth of these United States. A few old ones, mostly toothless, persist: everybody loves them and talks about them continuously. I want to be a character, too. I want to save string. I want to be scared of the telephone. I want to let my heels run over and not wear gloves. I want to make scenes. I want to write occasional verse. I want to be rude to fools, while I'm still young enough to do it without being described as a naughty old lady. I want to have crackpot notions, little ways, and one of my moods.

It's not my world. I just washed it, and I can't do anything with it.[3]

We can partially understand young Mrs. America's dilemma in view of the fact that she has not moved too far away from her Victorian grandmother's definition of femininity and the maternal, domestic role of the woman in her presumed-to-be rightful place in the home. And, while she has *not* flung her house apron into the corner or let the kitchen fire go out, she has, indeed added to her own traditional expectations of herself and those of her husband.

To put it more succinctly, she is no longer the emotionally and intellectually withheld woman that she was in the past. With this recent emergence of greater freedom to come and go, and do as she wishes, she is often confused. This confusion expresses itself in her relationship with her husband, often with overtones of some degree of anxiety, guilt, a sense of futility, boredom, feelings of unimportance, resentment, and regret over wasted ability, punctuated by spasms of social service, housework, and doing special things for the family, a network of truly mixed orientations and emotions.

Every generation has had its own problems of reconciling the present with the past. It is quite probable that the present psychosexual dilemma is now more painful and disruptive in marriage than it was in other generations due to the rapidity and extent of recent social change. Few, however, would trade their present freedom and opportunity for

[3] Sylvia Wright, "Whose World? . . . and Welcome to It," *Harpers Magazine,* May, 1955, pp. 38 ff.

self-expression for the lot of their grandmothers. The pain and dislocation are inevitable and they may be a fair price to pay for the gain. This is a problem to be recognized and dealt with as a part of growing together in marriage.

Research has shown that couples who are flexible in their social and emotional roles, rather than rigid and unyielding, have the least difficulty in effecting the transition from engagement to marriage.

Such persons do not remain deferent or ascendant, submissive or dominant, but are capable of shifting their psychosexual roles appropriate to the expectations and needs of the partner. This applies to both men and women, as compared with the stereotyped roles assigned by the culture of the paternalistic past, in which the man was supposed to be dominant and the wife submissive. Why *should* a woman have to choose between the extremes of domination of or complete submission to her husband's every wish? Neither seems to fit our emerging ideal of husband and wife as equalitarian in their regard for one another, and flexible in their assumptions of roles of ascendance or deference in the many different situations they confront as a team in their division of labor. If it is a matter of décor in entertaining she may be the "expert," whereas he may be chairman of finance. During periods of illness or discouragement the one least affected might carry the weight of responsibility, assuming the more ascendant and supportive role.

In all events, this kind of working relationship emerges during the early years of marriage, through the *experience* of confronting new situations that could not possibly have existed before marriage. It is in experiencing, testing, defining, and laying out informally the ground rules of marital interaction that conflicts can and in most marriages do arise.

To one reared in an atmosphere where it is presumed that only loveliness and light *should* prevail in marriage and that conflict is divisive and should be avoided in all cases, any disagreement takes on magnified concern. To one of a different orientation, however, conflict can be regarded as necessary to the growth of the relationship.

Many sociologists believe that much if not all growth stems from the resolution of conflict or of opposing forces. It is a process of the "old" coming into conflict with the "new" whether it is in growth within one individual or conflict between the expectations of both members of a couple. An example of the personal growth process is the passivity of the unborn fetus. With birth the "force" of passivity is confronted by the "force" of birth and the necessity to breathe, suckle, eliminate, and adjust thermally, on one's own. The first cry is regarded by some clinicians as a "protest" against giving up the dependency of the prenatal period, or as a symbol of the old state vs. the new. With time the infant "adjusts" and assumes an omnipotent role in the home. This exclusive possession of the mother is soon interrupted by the arrival of a brother or sister. The psychological security and passivity of the infant is then thrown out of equilibrium. A new force has entered the infant's life to push it out of the number one position. There is protest. When handled well, the conflict within the child between possessing the mother exclusively and becoming more independent is minimal. In some families and in some cultures the conflict between the child and his mother, and within the child himself can be so severe that the child's emotions can be fixated on this early oral level, binding the child to this level of emotional maturity. Mother is still around and keeps reasonable peace in the family with the child's gradual acceptance of the new sib. This equilibrium, however, is upset one day when the child must leave his mother's protective custody and enter the relatively impersonal atmosphere of the school. Each of these experiences of the child involves a painful relinquishing of the old for the temporarily threatening new. Each is accompanied by some disruption and dislocation of the past and is at first undefined and thus to some degree threatening. If it were not, we would not protest no matter how welcome the new experience may be. It is important to realize that this process of moving into the new only to find that it is too small, then partially tearing it down to remodel and enlarge, is inevitable to growth. Without it one would stagnate and die. In social and psychological experience there is no such thing as standing still.

As we mature we learn the skills of making these inevitable adjustments incident to growth with a minimum of dislocation and pain. We learn to confront some things and work them through. We learn to struggle with some things realizing that the outcome is uncertain. We learn to resign ourselves to still other things realizing that nothing within our power can change them. In this way, we learn to live with the conditions imposed by reality.

The skills necessary to implement this orientation to conflict, change, readjustment, and growth, are not part of our biological heritage. They are learned as love is learned through social and psychological experience. Marriage can be a prolonged experience in which this process of conflict with its possible resultant growth can take place giving rise to higher forms of accommodation and assimilation. It is like tempering steel. The raw ore must undergo heat and pressure to give the blade its fine edge. However, early in marriage the creative role of conflict can be dissipated if the conflict is too intense. It can destroy a relationship rather than strengthen it. Thus, conflict can play either a constructive, growth-promoting role in marriage or a disruptive and destructive role. The results are not a matter of chance by any means. The foregoing orientation can do much to help one use conflict constructively and avoid much of its painful and disruptive influence in marriage.

We can understand how the naïve person entering marriage with the idea that it is all going to be a bed of roses is going to react to the differences, the pressures, the revival of adolescent brother-sister rivalry, and the out-and-out conflicts of presumed legitimate self-interest. This kind of a person will be tossed like a hand full of feathers in a tornado, a victim of psychological forces that he cannot handle. Some will say, "But who could be that naïve?" However, many accept verbally the inevitability of conflict without being oriented emotionally and intellectually to the creative role that conflict can play in maturing a relationship to a point where a couple have gained the ability to resolve their differences with the skill of a team approach to problem solving.

THE RESOLUTION OF CONFLICT

Let us consider some of the techniques that other couples have worked out as part of what we might regard as the art of "interpersonal competence," or human relations skills.

We must first look behind the complaints, charges, and countercharges, or from what the argument is on the surface to the underlying issues. We have said that causes of quarrels are seldom evidenced in the surface symptoms. This was illustrated in the case of sex, money, in-laws, and the like. When the man fails to appreciate the dinner that his wife has prepared and even accuses her of spending all afternoon playing bridge, when she could not possibly have been out all afternoon and prepared such a dinner, her reaction might be something like this:

I know that I am right and that he is dead wrong. Perhaps I would like to play my vantage and mow him down with one prolonged, delicious burst from my psychological burp gun. But I cross my fingers, count to ten, and say to myself, "Who in the world has crossed you today." After a minute's reflection my better judgment tells me that there is a pecking order at the plant. When the Board chews out the vice president in charge of production, the vice president in turn takes it out on Dave. Dave, being quite human, and for understandable reasons can't yell back, so I, his devoted wife, am the next in line of yelling order, and so the wind blows. I know very well that it was inconsiderate of him to speak as he did. I also know that the roaring lion is hungry, angry, and embarrassed and will settle down to purring like a kitten about a half hour after dinner. I guess it really isn't hard to assume a deferent if not actually a self-effacing role in this situation. If I lash back and tell him that he is just like his crotchety old man then I'll have an in-law problem. He might cut my allowance, or make me come to the office for the grocery money. Then I'll have a money problem. He might even pack his bag and check in at the club for the night, then I'll have a sex problem. I guess I just can't *win.*

What could be quite a nasty evening can become a growth experience in which, after I swallow my pride and let him calm down, I can draw him out and serve as a challenging sounding board against whom he can throw his production problems, talk it out, get a new angle, and confront, on the morrow, the vice president anew—even though I didn't understand half of what he said, I could *listen.*

I can hear some women and even some men say, "But, why should I? The gal is right and ought to stand up for herself." *If* that conception is right, that a thing is right in and of itself, irrespective of circumstances and consequences, then my only alternative would be to draw blades and learn the hard way, but I really can't go for that.

I do not believe that it is *always* I who should "understand," defer, make the concessions. The shoe will be on the other foot often enough. When he comes home at six, having fought the traffic bottleneck at Interstate Bridge, but otherwise has had an up-and-coming day, he might find me reading a novel, no dinner on, my hair frazzled. He would be fully justified in clouding up and raining all over me. But no, after crossing his fingers and counting to ten he realizes it is the 28th day of the Lunar month and that I often feel fit to be tied at such times. It then occurs to him that we haven't been out to dinner alone together for some time, and that I would enjoy getting out . . .

It is astounding how many of the day-by-day squabbles are as inconsequential as the foregoing, but how often they loom as mountains rather than as molehills, and how, by capitalizing on a potential conflict situation to show that one understands and cares, another link is welded in the silver chain of matrimony.

The following discussion of techniques for the resolution of conflict and the facilitation of adjustment in marriage is contingent upon the orientation that one must be honest and of unconditional good faith in looking behind the appearances—the symptoms of the difficulties—and handling them on a reality level.

In our folklore and tradition, and in some of our marriage literature of the pink and blue variety on how to live happily forever after, there are a number of clichés that are handed out as suggestions for the resolution of conflict and achieving adjustment. As Kirkpatrick brings out, such devices are gimmicks that largely fail. Here is a typical list: (1) Never get angry at the same time . . . which usually means that it is you who is angry. (2) Arbitration by friends and relatives . . . whose friends and relatives? It is something like saying, let's compromise and do it my way. (3) Arouse jealousy . . . the strategy involves the assumption that it is better to make him jealous than to get him angry. (4) Alternate dominance . . . which means, just wait until next week when I'm boss. (5) Repeat marriage vows every year . . . which is all right with me, but it makes me wonder what I meant when I said them the first time, and besides, it makes me feel foolish. (6) Think of pleasant things about the marriage . . . that's O.K. too, but I'm too mad just now. (7) Heap coals of fire by being so nice that only a moral imbecile would fail to respond in kind . . . there's only one thing wrong with that—the spouse sees through it.[4]

These strategies should be seen for precisely what they are—strategies to *win*. This leads to a second orientation. While one may seek to win a round in the fight, he should never seek to win the fight itself, that is, avoid the total personality rejection of the spouse. Do not deal in the traffic of ego destruction. If things are that bad, professional help is indicated before deep-seated hostility and rejection boomerang and destroy the marriage. Limited constructive quarrels can clear the air, focus upon problems to be confronted and worked through, and serve to reveal some hidden feelings that one or the other did not dare express until provoked by the heat of the argument. But this is not the same as an insidious desire to win—to dominate, to control, eventually to destroy.

A third orientation involves the planning and spacing of

[4] Clifford Kirkpatrick, *The Family,* New York, Ronald, 1955, pp. 450 ff.

the events that are shared and those that are undertaken alone or separate from the spouse. Brief as well as more prolonged separations from one another can be provided for preferably when things are going well. Vacations from the marriage, when the couple can afford it, can serve to preserve autonomy, prevent the marriage from settling into a humdrum routine, and serve to renew the uniqueness of the relationship. It is a good thing for all of us, now and then, to realize how indispensable we are to one another. This is difficult to realize when a couple are together all of thc time. Separations can be carried to an extreme, and what is moderate separation for one couple might be extreme for another. However, this is one device for preventing excessive possessiveness, dependency, and taking one another for granted.

A fourth orientation would be that of periodically undertaking a course of self-study and self-revelation. As we grow through the years we emerge as somewhat different selves. Our occupations, increasing skills, and different activities add new dimensions to our older selves. New or reformulated roles appear in one's repertory of roles that make up the self. To illustrate this, choose any person whom you know and compare what he was at the time of his marriage with what he became at successive stages in his life. This is not only a practice in self-discovery, but it is one in self-revelation to the other. People can, and often do, grow inward rather than outward and apart. Stocktaking is an antidote for that. Furthermore, self-searching can be fun.

A fifth orientation with regard to the resolution of conflicts in marriage is that of involving as few other persons as possible. Sometimes a confidant whom you know will be discreet about your problem, can be of assistance when you seem to have no one to turn to. However, it is nearly impossible to find unbiased persons who will do more good than harm. Nearly everybody who has been married and some who have not, tend to regard themselves as experts by virtue of their experience. When you inadvertently enlist a host of others to help you out of your marital problem, you have the vexing task then of dissociating your marriage from their continued, well-intentioned interests. It is much easier to deal with one than with ten. It should go without saying that a public display of marital difficulties is to multiply them ten times ten.

This leads to the last point of orientation to be discussed here, namely, that of utilizing more fully the diagnostic and treatment facilities of professional people. If it is a personality problem it might possibly be caused, contributed to, or precipitated by poor physical health of one kind or another—anemia, endocrine dysfunctions, or a host of possible aggravating factors. Your problem might be one of deeper need for personality diagnosis and psychological or psychiatric treatment.

Counselors often see a marriage in which the physical and mental health of both of a couple are relatively good, but the marriage itself is suffering and in need of professional counsel. Professional marriage counseling has emerged during the last two decades and has become a specialized field requiring high standards of training and experience from members of the American Association of Marriage Counselors and professional social work agencies such as the Family Welfare Society. Other professional services such as the clergy, law, and medicine can be borne in mind. Too many people believe that it takes a doctor to set a bone, but that almost anybody can advise about mental and marital health.

It is not so. Couples locked in serious conflict should seek professional assistance before they reach a crisis rather than after. It is much easier to save a marriage than to try to raise a dead one.

It is a consensus of professional opinion that the function of the marriage counselor is to save the integrity of two individuals rather than the marriage itself. If the marriage can be saved, so much the better. However, there are some couples who may be better off apart. In that case even they can be helped to understand what happened and why, so that they do not jump from the frying pan of an unhappy marriage into the fire of divorce, without having learned through the experience. This must not be misunderstood as advocating easy divorce. Divorce is to the marriage as surgery is to the practice of medicine, to be undertaken only after all other possible treatments have been conscientiously undertaken and have failed.

Chapter 14

PARENTHOOD

IN THE early American family it was assumed that the signing and sealing of the marriage contract took place almost simultaneously with the placing of an order with the stork. There were fewer intruding considerations of more education to be completed, higher standards of living to be secured, time to be allowed for the couple to become more fully weaned from their parental families and grow closer together as an uninterrupted pair, women wishing to become established in some occupational pursuit or career before junior arrived, and so forth. Furthermore, in our patriarchal society it was an important male prerogative to strut his virility before a large family, which meant that the couple had to get started early. Of consideration, too, was the fact that our grandparents married considerably later than do couples today. Chronologically speaking, they were more ready for children than many young persons today. Furthermore the idea of contraception was regarded as obscene. And not least, each mouth to be fed in those days was not proportionately related to the family income since most of what was consumed came directly from the farm enterprise and not from the corner grocery. Another potential farm hand was an economic asset to the family. Finally, there was the strong religious sanction of "Multiply and replenish the earth."

Today much has changed in the baby department of marriage. Young couples are confronted with these new considerations and many conclude that it is not incumbent upon them to have children as soon as they are married. How recent and dramatic this change has been is illustrated by the public's attitude toward the practice of birth control. In 1936, 63 percent of all women polled in a *Fortune* Magazine survey said that they believed in the teaching and practice of birth control. Of the Catholic women polled, 43 percent were favorable. By 1943, the same polling agency found that 85 percent of all women polled were favorable and the proportion of Catholic women favoring birth control had jumped to 69 percent. Among college graduates it had risen to 93 percent. That was fifteen years and two wars ago. These figures stand in sharp contrast to the federal law of 1873 which identified contraceptive information with obscenity and forbade the use of the mails to transport information or devices.[1]

This change is not to be interpreted as evidence of an attitude of increasing negation toward having children. In 1954, there were about four million babies born in the United States which represents a very high birth rate as compared with the years during which the changes in attitudes toward birth control just cited, took place. The import seems to be

[1] Herbert Yahraes, "Planning Your Family," *Public Affairs Pamphlet,* No. 136, 1948.

this: We Americans want children, want more of them than we have in the recent past, but we want them when and in the number that we choose as a part of a larger orientation of voluntary, planned parenthood.

This leads to a consideration of the aspirations of American couples. There is evidence from varied sources that Americans say that they want about three children. According to our 1952 census, the average number of children born to married women was 2.35, with a discrepancy of about two-thirds of a child between what people say they want, on the one hand, and what they get, on the other.[2]

But what of the deviations from this "ideal" number of children? This is more difficult to determine. People often are so influenced by what they feel they "should" believe, that it is difficult to get at the real facts and underlying orientations. Evidence from a study made in Indianapolis indicates that many couples were disappointed when they learned of the wife's first pregnancy, which usually resulted from their failure to use contraceptives. "A large percentage of couples were unsuccessful in the use of contraceptives, and a large percentage of conceptions occurred in spite of contraception. Yet the proportion of these couples who clearly had more children than they desired was only 26.5 percent."[3]

A number of separate studies made in such different states as Utah and Indiana, indicate that between 10 and 20 percent of the first babies born to married couples are conceived out of wedlock.

Perhaps more serious, however, from the standpoint of frustration in marriage is the incidence of involuntary sterility. In 1952, of the American women who had ever married,

[2] Clifford Kirkpatrick, *The Family,* New York, Ronald, 1955, p. 475.
[3] *Ibid.,* p. 474.

about 19.4 percent had never borne a child. Best estimates indicate that at least one-half to two-thirds of all childless marriages are due to involuntary sterility. However, of the million couples in the United States today who think they cannot have children, at least 30 to 40 percent could conceive if they would undergo diagnosis and treatment for their temporary disability. As research in the field of involuntary sterility progresses, as it has done in our medical centers with the support of planned parenthood societies, we shall certainly be able, increasingly, to help those couples conceive who think that they cannot have children.

The frustration of many such persons is deep and painful, but such a personal matter that it seldom is discussed or becomes otherwise evident to others. The reasons are many, as we shall discuss when we come to a consideration of why people want children, a subject far from obvious as it may seem. However painful as this failure to meet a marital expectation may be, there has been an increasing number of people who have sought artificial insemination. Even so, it is still not very popular. Of persons polled in 1949, 70 percent had heard of "test-tube babies" but only 27 percent approved of it. In a poll of college students, one study showed that about 90 percent approved of artificial insemination with the husband as semen donor, whereas about 52.4 percent approved of it if another were donor.[4] The possibilities and the issues surrounding artificial insemination are so new that the legal and religious issues have only begun to emerge, let alone be crystallized and formulated into policies.

Following is a summary of some of the facts surrounding fertility:

[4] *Ibid.*, p. 475.

1. The fertility of a group fluctuates and is quite closely related to such social circumstances as war and the business cycle. Peace and prosperity are conducive to the higher birth rate.

2. More babies are born at certain times of the year than others. In general, there is a higher birth rate during the summer months, especially August and September. That places the period of highest conception sometime between Thanksgiving and Christmas.

3. Fertility in terms of the number of births decreases with age, and with the working of women, but not with men. Employed men have more children than the unemployed.

4. The relationship between income and number of births in a given family is changing. In 1949 there was a direct, inverse correlation between family income and number of children under 5 years of age. In other words, as income went up the average number of children per family went down. However, recent evidence indicates that where family planning is undertaken aided by contraception, there is a positive correlation between amount of income and number of children. In Sweden this was found to be true, and also in the Indianapolis study cited above.

5. Fertility seems to be negatively related to social status and achievement among men. However, with the emergence of planned parenthood there is evidence of a reversal of this trend. This is not true of women. College women and career women have a considerably lower rate of reproduction than do their less educated and less career-oriented sisters.

6. Finally, people living in the country have more children than those living in cities, with those who work with things having more than those who work with symbols.

It is beyond the scope of our consideration here to go into the social implications of these differences in fertility, but it may be noted in passing that as responsible world citizens our consideration of the implications of parenthood planning as a part of a larger population policy is very important. Now that the scientific control of much disease has cut deeply into the death rate and has increased longevity, there is grave danger of multiplying beyond our resources. This has already occurred in widespread sections of the Middle East and the Far East whereas in Egypt, India, and Japan poverty, sickness, and almost unbelievable circumstances of life obtain. In Japan where 90 million people are crowded into an area the size of the state of Montana there are as many legal abortions each year as there are births, in addition to the illegal abortions.

The better educated in our own culture, men and women of cultivated abilities including child training and human relations, are having an increasingly higher proportion of our children. It may be true that the chain of culture is as strong as its weakest links. If so, planning parenthood has every promise, based on scientific evidence, of strengthening the quality of our children.

MOTIVES UNDERLYING PARENTHOOD

Emotional attitudes toward having children seem to run the gamut from elation to despair. In the main our culture is a parenthood-affirming culture, epitomized in such phrases as "the blessed event." Now and then the picture of a large family is the feature of every newspaper. Often reactions to such pictures are, "Wouldn't it be wonderful to have such a fine large family if one just had the health or the money to see such a project through." Some couples undergo months or years of medical treatment in order to have a baby. Adoption agencies tell us that the waiting list of couples desiring to adopt a baby is long and that the supply is much less than the demand.

There are other couples, however, sometimes only one of the couple, whose attitudes toward having a baby range from uncertainty and mild ambivalence to outright feelings of being unequivocally trapped. One study of 1444 relatively fecund couples indicated that about one-fourth (27.1 percent) had planned and spaced their pregnancies, a little less than one-sixth (14.1 percent) had planned but not spaced their children. Nearly one-third were classified as "quasi-planned." About one in five couples said that they had "one too many," and less than 10 percent reported two or more too many.[5] Taking these data at their face value we can see that somewhere between one-third and one-half of the pregnancies reported in this Indianapolis study were "quasi-planned, unplanned, or unwanted," which is some indication of feelings of ambivalence toward pregnancy. Other studies of Landis, Christensen, and Philbrick, tend to bear out this generalization. This should be qualified, however, by taking into consideration the timing of the pregnancy, the health and welfare of the parents, and the number of children already in the family. To say that up to half of those parents were ambivalent in their feelings about the pregnancy is not to say that they were ambivalent about having children. As we have already indicated, some young couples wish to finish their education and become somewhat established before having a child. If they were to have one before, at first they might feel quite insecure and thus to some extent ambivalent, but they feel quite differently later.

[5] *Ibid.*, pp. 463–464.

The consideration of why different couples feel differently about having children is much more in the realm of speculation and hidden motives than is the relatively objective fact that some are affirming, some are ambivalent, and some are rejecting.

One of the prime motivations for having children, whether it be conscious or unconscious, is that of love of the spouse. It is expressed in a desire to perpetuate this deep feeling in and through this most intimate extension of the self in coitus, the nine months of planning and preparing, and the visible symbol of this literal extension of the self—the child. This is the embodiment of the oneness of the marriage. Such is one means of self-fulfillment and of self-trancendence. The psychoanalysts have written about love being closely associated with the desire to have a baby by the loved one.

For some, having a baby is a means of "self-validation," as Winch has pointed out with some empirical evidence to support it.[6] In the competition of a male-oriented culture some women want to retreat from the competitive fray but still feel important. Having a baby is one way of accomplishing it. Vicarious achievement through children may be a part of the self-validation. The parents may feel they have not accomplished a great deal in life, but dream of the promise of their children where they failed. Putting it a little differently, Kirkpatrick expressed the parental feeling "in terms of an extension of *having* rather than *being*."

For some persons a child may provide a substitute symbol of a love object, such as a spouse who fails to satisfy a craving for greater closeness, or feelings toward the child may reflect fear of losing a spouse and wanting something that is "part of him." We hear this especially during a war. More often,

[6] *Ibid.*, p. 458.

however, it is an attempt to hold a spouse where it is feared that one may otherwise lose him or her.

Still others want children for the sense of power that it seems to give them. Such children may be treated benevolently or may be the objects of manipulation and control.

Hostility and a desire to control a spouse is another motive. It is expressed in the "keep them barefoot and pregnant" philosophy. It is a way of thwarting social activities or more immediate plans for a career.

Some couples have children because it is expected by the community, especially in small towns where everybody knows everyone else. The motivation underlying such an expectation may be an expression of a cultural orientation stemming from the Bible. Or, it can be an expression of envy and jealousy. One woman in counsel said that she and her husband were happy and wanted to have children eventually but not at present. "I came from a large family that I virtually raised by myself because my mother was ill," she said. "Now I want to work for a while and have a rest from the constant demands of children, but my friends tell me that I am selfish. They remind me so often and make me feel so guilty that we would move if my husband didn't have such a good job." She was seeking to determine what effect quitting her job and having a baby would have on her attitude toward her child and her marriage.

The last of these more personal motives for having children to be discussed here, is the assumption by some persons that having a baby will bolster up and save a faltering marriage. We sometimes hear it said, "And if they had a baby they would be too busy to think of themselves," or "Having a baby would bring them together."

Among the less personal motives for having children are

those of religious and/or ethnic ideology, especially among minority groups who are conscious of their small numbers and desire to become larger and stronger. Explicit in many religions is the dictum already cited, "Multiply and replenish the earth," as part of a broader assumption that it is the duty of men and women to give others, namely their own children, the experience of life. With regard to ethnic ideology, we see some of the smaller nations like England and Ireland expressing grave concern about their relative positions in the world of nations. This idea of size, thus power and influence, underlies the thinking of the constituents of many minority groups, be they nations, religious bodies, or ethnic groups.

WHY PEOPLE DO NOT WANT CHILDREN

Consideration of the reasons why people do not want children becomes more complex. High on the list of reasons that people *give* is that of real or fancied financial obstacles. According to a national poll taken in 1941, 57 percent of the persons questioned stressed economic reasons while 20 percent said that it would interfere with their freedom.[7] We cannot discount the role of finances in rearing children, especially when we have such high standards projected for them. One study showed that it costs about $15,000 for a couple with an income of $5,000 to rear a child. On the other hand one can question the validity of the economic argument when, as is quite often the case, a couple say that they cannot afford to have a baby because they need a new car.

It seems that the economic argument against parenthood is more valid as a limiting rather than an eliminating factor. Closely related, however, is the desire for women to pursue

[7] *Ibid.*, p. 461.

activities and careers outside the home or in combination with homemaking. Often this tends to amount to a so-called financial problem. A woman says to herself, "I would have children if I could afford to have them taken care of part of the time, but I do not want to be tied hand and foot myself." This, however, may be more of a problem of planning and spacing than anything else. The writer has known couples who wanted to have two children close together, then wait a number of years to have two more. This was their way of avoiding what they felt would be too many too fast, and still have their projected four, with some time in between for the mother to "catch her breath."

During the recent past we went through a period when the pursuit of money, prestige, and productivity, on the part of both women and men took many persons outside the home often at the cost of children. There is some evidence that the pendulum has swung back, not to earlier extremes, but to a position between that of having five to nine children and none. A larger proportion of women than a decade or two ago are choosing college majors in home economics, nursing, and elementary education, quite satisfied with a projected ideal of combining related professional and domestic skills. Every now and then, however, we hear about women like Clara Schuman, the wife of Robert Schuman, who had a brilliant career as a concert pianist and, at the same time, raised 12 children.

Research has come up with another factor that tends to be associated with fewer or no children, and that is the presence of differences and disagreements in the marriage. For example, marriages lacking unanimity in religion tend to be relatively low in fertility.[8]

The emotional acceptance or rejection that a child experi-

[8] *Ibid.*, p. 462.

ences in his parental family is one of the most important influences on his later attitude toward having children. Women who, as children, identified themselves closely with an unhappy mother, may tend to reject their own feminity and not want to have children. In contrast, we see women who have wanted and loved each one of their children and talked with enthusiasm about, "when you all grow up and bring your babies home." Such children enjoyed being children themselves and tend to want children.

Some fear of pregnancy is reported by a high proportion of women but cannot be taken as an attitude toward having children. It is understandable that the physical, economic, and social sacrifice incident to having a baby, together with the added responsibility, give many couples at least a momentary feeling of wanting to avoid it all. For most couples, however, this is a passing feeling and fades into the satisfaction of anticipating the rewards of having children.

CHILDREN AND MARITAL HAPPINESS

How does the presence or absence of children in the family affect the happiness of the parents' marriage? Research has thrown considerable light on this question and we have a composite picture that has been summarized by Kirkpatrick: "There seems to be an association . . . between desire for children, successful planning, lack of frustration by obstacles, presence of children, and marital adjustment. In other words, personality adjustment with respect to parenthood, as defined in terms of aspirations, is associated with marital adjustment. Persons with clear-cut aspirations for children and free from frustrations can apparently have them in substantial numbers and yet achieve marital adjustment."[9]

[9] *Ibid.*, p. 481.

The foregoing generalization is based on a satisfactory marital relationship. Whatever the dislocation of other plans and strain, such couples seem able to make new adjustments to the changes in their lives occasioned by the baby and in the whole process find that their marriage has been intensified and deepened. In this new coöperative endeavor mutual sacrifices and satisfactions add a new dimension to the marriage.

Where either of the couple or both feel that the child is an unwelcome burden for any reason, the child does not strengthen the marriage but serves as a divisive influence on the relationship. If some marriages are strengthened by the presence of children, others seem to be weakened. The effect of children on marriage might be a test of its solidarity.

All of the research to date indicates that it is not so much the presence or absence of children in the family that is associated with happiness of the marriage, but the attitude of the couple toward children. Those couples who want children have the highest happiness ratings on the marriage adjustment scales, whether they have children or not. Thus, the absence of children need not have an adverse effect on the happiness of the marriage if the orientation and attitudes of the couple are parent affirming. Their capacity for loving children will probably find an outlet and be manifest in some other ways.

The higher divorce rate among childless couples is frequently cited as evidence of greater marital happiness among those couples who have children. Such a generalization is not warranted. It is during the first year that marriage is most vulnerable to divorce. These couples have had less of a chance to have children than others who have been married for a longer period of time. It is likely that couples who harbored doubts about their marriage would avoid having children and would be more likely to divorce than other couples. Thus it is not the childlessness *per se* that is related to unhappiness resulting in divorce, but some other underlying factor. Couples can be quite unhappy but not divorce because of a feeling of responsibility to the children, including the feeling that a divorce would have an adverse psychological effect on the children.

SOCIAL AND PSYCHOLOGICAL ASPECTS OF PREGNANCY AND BIRTH

It is of interest to note that until the seventeenth century, obstetrics was the sole charge of women. As late as the sixteenth century one Dr. Wertt of Hamburg was burned to death for disguising himself as a woman in order to attend a delivery.[10] Today, in contrast, not only are the majority of obstetricians men, but increasingly the fathers are being invited to participate in the entire prenatal education of the expectant mother and to be present during labor. Notwithstanding much insidious folklore regarding the gremlins of pregnancy and delivery, the facts are that it is safer to have a baby today than it is to take a spin in the family car, and that a woman of childbearing age is healthier in having a baby than in not having one.

Preparation for Parenthood

Paralleling the advances in the medical aspects of obstetrics has been an emerging orientation regarding pregnancy and

[10] F. W. Goodrich, *Natural Childbirth,* New York, Prentice-Hall, 1952, p. 1.

delivery that is indeed recent. "Within the past twenty-five years an advance has been made which has enabled women to find that pregnancy and labor can be rich, satisfying and meaningful experiences. This advance constitutes a different approach to childbirth which its originator, Dr. Grantly Dick Read, has called natural childbirth. Reduced to its essence, natural childbirth is best described as intellectual, physical and emotional preparation for childbirth, to the end that mothers realize their potentialities and in so doing enjoy the bringing forth of their babies."[11]

The physical pain and discomfort of pregnancy and delivery with overtones of a general floating uncertainty, as well as specific fears, combine to form a physical and emotional burden that is largely unnecessary. Despite great advances in gynecology and obstetrics with magazines, newspapers, and now television increasingly candid in presenting the new advances to the public, there remains with us a great deal of ignorance and provincialism in this area.

Anxiety and doubt can be the bases of much *physical* discomfort during pregnancy and pain during delivery due to the tenseness of the whole body musculature. A general orientation must be borne in mind: One cannot fight anxiety directly with pep talks, mustering of will power, and resolution. Such a course of action treats the symptom, the anxiety, rather than the real cause which is the *fear of the unknown*. The thing to do, then, is to supplant the halftruths, untruths, and areas of ignorance with understanding and thoroughgoing preparation—psychologically and emotionally—for each successive stage of pregnancy and delivery.

There are, first, the physical and emotional changes that can normally be expected—physical changes within the body

[11] *Ibid.*, p. 2.

and the changes in the husband-wife relationship and with friends. For example, during the first stage when there are changes going on within the body that manifest themselves in morning discomfort, a period when sexual intercourse normally continues, there is little change in the outward relations between husband and wife and with friends. A second phase when the fetus is fully formed and has its own blood stream and heart beat, is one when the wife is obviously pregnant and shows it. At this time the woman can be relieved of much possible anxiety by knowing in detail what changes she might experience physiologically. Her physician and nurse can advise her, but frequently they are either so busy or are presumed by the patient to be too busy to "bother." In some areas classes in maternity are held for expectant mothers and fathers where illustrated lectures are followed by group discussion. This is not only informative, but allows an opportunity for the exchange of experience, especially feelings, with resultant confidence and emotional serenity. Many possible sources of normal discomfort can be partially if not entirely anticipated and avoided—such as constipation, heartburn and flatulence, numbness in the extremities of the body such as fingers and toes, rashes and the development of pigmentation or baring of minute skin veins, etc. However, it should not be assumed that this phase of pregnancy is one of prolonged discomfort. Such is not the case. Where these physical changes and the reasons behind them are understood, this can be a period of only temporary, minor, and intermittent discomfort. Adherence to proper diet, exercise, care of skin, etc., together with the confidence resulting from understanding what is going on, can and does leave most women in radiant good health during this second phase.

Increasingly important from this point to delivery is the

understanding that a husband and wife have between themselves with regard to the physical, social, and psychological aspects of the pregnancy. By participating with her in the entire prenatal orientation program he will be aware of what she is experiencing, and can support her in her possible doubts. For example, one area of possible defensive feelings on the wife's part is that of her appearance. She might take pride in the fact that her pregnancy shows, but be quite sensitive about her skin pigmentation, especially if she has always harbored some feelings about the texture and color of her skin. This is but one of many possible sources of sensitive feeling, which, if understood by him, can result in his emotional support. He can anticipate her expectations and needs and avoid excesses in his demands on her in social activities, pace of living, frequency and mode of sexual intercourse.

During the final phase of pregnancy when her feelings of physical discomfort may increase, there is even greater need for mutual understanding, and the opportunity for a more thorough preparation for the delivery than often obtains. Coitus is undertaken with care so as to prevent rupture and a premature dilation of the cervix with the possible risk of infection due to the tremendous concentration of blood in the uterus. During the last few weeks when coitus is ordinarily discontinued she can understand his needs and expectations which differ markedly in different men. If she is outgoing and affirming of him, his sexual needs will be less urgent. Where they have achieved a good sexual relationship prior to her conception she will continue during the latter part of pregnancy to recognize his need for continuing intermittent outlet and assist him with affection and possible manual stimulation to orgasm. If sex has been associated with negation in her thinking and feeling she may use the latter part of the pregnancy period to disclaim his needs and expectations by refusing to have anything sexual to do with him. She might rationalize her attitude by thinking or saying, "If I am making this supreme sacrifice to bring a baby into the world the least you can do is abstain." He probably will, *with her*. If he genuinely accepts her definition of the situation there is no problem. If not, it can be the continuation of a deepening marital rift.

Men and women are sensitive enough about feelings of sexual rejection during the normal course of marriage. During pregnancy where new adjustments and personal sacrifices have to be made, emotions become heightened and feelings more sensitive. Any gesture on her part to use her pregnancy as an excuse to reject him sexually will be met with deepest hostility, hurt deference, or psychological withdrawal, according to his basic personality. Any act of boorishness or lack of consideration on his part will be most deeply disillusioning to her and she will react according to her basic personality. It is not so much the adequacy of the sexual response and satisfaction *per se* that is important, but the couple's respective attitudes toward the other's sexual expectations at this time.

During the final phase of the pregnancy there is the possibility of the wife becoming so preoccupied with details of the forthcoming event that she may inadvertently forget that she has a husband, or take him too much for granted. It must be realized that he may be very sensitive to "maternal" rejection. His childhood experience with his mother when she was to be delivered can be revived, feelings that have long been forgotten but which lie as mainsprings to be released in the reliving of an old situation. Expectant mothers can afford psychologically to realize that they may soon have two youngsters on their hands as sibling rivals!

It should go without saying that the final preparations for the delivery should be made with thoroughness—such things as visiting the hospital and checking on its facilities, filling out the admittance questionnaire, arranging for the payment, determining the exact location of the receiving ward and possibility that some entrances may be locked at certain hours, and arranging for a room where a wife and her husband can be together with as much privacy as possible during the period when the uterus is dilating preparatory to actual labor. If hospital facilities permit a visit to the delivery room, meeting the nurses, and becoming acquainted with the physical facilities and surroundings prior to admittance for delivery, it can serve to eliminate doubt and wonder later. The foregoing considerations together with many others are anticipated by persons who plan their lives. It is often astounding, however, how many couples leave everything until the last minute and then bungle their way through a maze of unanticipated details that confuse, bewilder, and render her so tense that labor becomes unnecessarily prolonged and painful.

Provisions are being made increasingly for the wife to lie in a private room with her husband present during the period just preceding labor. He can rub her back to relieve discomfort, part of his role as a psychological ally. Often with this assurance she will fall off to sleep knowing that he can get help when it is needed. When she is finally taken into the delivery room she knows that he is near. This can serve to elicit from him an important psychological vestment in his wife and child. His role does not have to be one of weighty sentimentality nor of fussy solicitation, but one of buoyancy with a sense of humor.

So that "expectant" fathers will be able to play this role genuinely rather than as posed roles of pep coaches, they are being invited, increasingly, to attend classes given to couples in the physiology and sociopsychology of pregnancy. Sometimes these classes are offered by community agencies, nurses, medical groups comprising clinics, or a combination of these groups. In a number of midwest communities medical teams have formed, offering a number of specialized services in their medical practice. For example, one group of doctors representing general practice, internal medicine, pediatrics, gynecology and obstetrics, surgery, and psychiatry formed a clinic with their own medical building. Their latest addition to the staff of medical doctors and nurses was a specialist in marriage and family relations who does personal counseling as a clinical and social psychologist and offers a series of classes for groups of patients who have common problems. One of these groups is comprised of the clinic's obstetrical patients *and their husbands*. The purpose of these classes is twofold: (1) to acquaint those attending with the facts of pregnancy and birth—"matrology" and "patrology," and (2) to provide group counseling in which feelings can be expressed and examined, providing a cathartic experience in which latent insecurities and anxieties can be worked through to conscious understanding and acceptance. The goal is preparation of both the wife and the husband for the more mature role of personal sounding boards against which each can cast his doubts and anxieties, and have them resound with genuine assurance from one another as a result of understanding on a reality level. They do not have to resort to meaningless pep talks which can amount to transmitting the feeling that one is whistling in the dark. Their mutual quiet assurance will enable them to talk sense and thus assure one another on a deeper level.

Bringing about greater participation of husbands and wives in this larger learning and communication process will take time, facilities, a change in public opinion, and a reorientation on the part of some physicians who feel that they have neither the time for or interest in such psychological "frills." The experience of any marriage counselor will attest to the fact that for many couples these are not frills but very genuine needs.

Results of Faulty Preparation for Parenthood

Research has been accumulating rapidly on the influence of the fetal environment on the growing fetus and early infancy. Studies of the impact of war on the fetal-maternal relationship have contributed to the emerging larger picture of the environmental influences on the prenatal development of the infant. The negative results of the attempt to control the weight of the fetus by controlling the mother's caloric intake have lulled some expectant mothers into complacency about prenatal dietary factors. Because infants appear normal at birth the mother may not recognize that a vitamin D deficiency can result in rickets a month after birth, or that a vitamin C deficiency can result in scurvy in the infant. Vitamin adequacy is but one aspect of the larger dietary consideration, but a very important one illustrating the influences of the mother's body chemistry on the developing fetus. In studies comparing mothers, all of whom were on deficiency diets during pregnancy, one group received large amounts of supplementary vitamins. The results showed that the infants of the latter group, ". . . showed better growth during the first year of life and much less illness, and in general were healthier children than those of the mothers whose diets had not been supplemented by vitamins. An additional fact of interest was that the labors of the mothers on supplemented diets were easier and shorter than those of the women whose diets were unsupplemented."[12]

As important as these and other dietary factors are, they are outside our present consideration except to illustrate the influence of biochemical factors on fetal development. From the point of view of the social psychology of pregnancy a more direct problem concerns the effects of emotional states and activities of mothers on the developing fetus. We know that there is no direct neural connection between the mother and the fetus. They have independent nervous systems. Their blood systems are also separate. The chemical composition of the mother's blood does filter through the placenta to the fetus, however, and has a direct if often delayed effect on the growth and development of the fetus. Our interest is in the profound changes which may occur in fetal development due to maternal fatigue and emotional reactions.

During emotional states such as fear, rage, anxiety—often so repressed as to be unknown to the person experiencing them —chemicals such as acotylcholine and epinephrine are released into the blood stream and affect parts of the central nervous system. Dr. Lester W. Sontag and his coworkers observed an increase of several hundred percent in the fetal activity of mothers undergoing emotional stress. Exercise of the fetus results in reduced weight, using the fat that would

[12] Lester Warren Sontag, "War and the Fetal-Maternal Relationship," in R. F. Winch and R. McGinnis, *Selected Studies in Marriage and the Family* New York, Holt, 1953, pp. 172 ff.

otherwise go into growth.[13] The postnatal effect of severe maternal emotional stress is to increase the total body activity of the infant with symptoms of hyperactivity, irritability, squirming, crying, need for more frequent feeding, and feeding problems due to gastrointestinal disturbance. Such an infant is born with a reduced birth weight, but not body length.

While the results of severe emotional stress are more evident in the behavior of the fetus and infant, the effects of maternal fatigue, being subjected to sudden loud noises, and other enervating experiences also result in increased fetal activity. Studies of the effect of German and British bombing on expectant mothers indicate a resultant development of unstable nervous autonomy of the fetus.[14] These general conclusions have been supported by the research of Dr. Margaret Ribble. She concludes that the brain metabolism of the mother is affected adversely by excessive emotional experience and by fatigue, and result in convulsive disorders that are connected with disturbances in the functions of the liver and kidneys.[15] Dr. Ribble goes on to caution women whose pattern of work or activities is demanding and fatiguing, to spare their energy by making any necessary changes in the pace or intensity of their activities. Women high in the active B-component of basic personality are more vulnerable to this excess, especially if they are under some compulsive pressures.

Severe emotional shocks during the early stages of pregnancy are known to be related to radical alterations of the development of the fetus. For example, there is a low but positive correlation between emotional shock at about the third

[13] *Ibid.*, p. 174.
[14] *Ibid.*, p. 176.
[15] Margaret A. Ribble, *The Rights of Infants,* New York, Columbia University Press, 1946, pp. 106 ff.

month of pregnancy and resultant mongolian idiocy, a form of permanent growth impairment and feeble mindedness.

These findings should not frighten us any more than any of the other possible unpleasant facts of life, but should encourage us to do whatever we can to avoid them. There is the inevitable emotional impact upon all of us when, as young prospective parents, we realize "all the things that can happen." After wincing with this psychological inoculation we must pass on to the higher level of greater awareness and thus greater security, in the assurance that there is much that we can do to make the period of pregnancy one of greatest safety and future promise.

Part Four

PATTERNS OF MARRIAGE

Chapter 15

PATTERNS OF FAULTY MARRIAGE

In part iv, we shall consider first the bases of faulty marriage as seen in *constellations* of symptoms, or modes, stemming from the underlying immaturity and incompatibility of representative couples. The illustrative case histories might be regarded as sociopsychological portraits of faulty marriages. Then we shall examine a number of other marriages which have achieved unique patterns of growth, productivity, satisfaction, and ways of meeting the difficulties and crises of life.

This writer has felt for a number of years that many, if not most, faulty as well as more successful marriages fall roughly into predictable modes. Until recently, however, there have been no tested diagnostic classifications of marital interaction. In 1954 an interim report of a "Classification Project" was published by Community Research Associates, Inc. based on a pilot study of disorganized families in St. Paul, Minnesota.

The interdisciplinary team conducting the study sought constellations of symptoms and causes underlying family disorganization to serve as a theoretic, diagnostic, and prognostic frame of reference. The team was made up of skilled diagnosticians from the social work and mental hygiene fields, including clinical psychology and psychiatry. Their main hypothesis was that the causes of faulty marriage "must be sought in the emotional axis created by the interaction of two marital partners whose needs are excessive and unhealthy."[1] Their research resulted in the provisional identification of ten "typical axes" or patterns of marital interaction:

1. A dual immature dependency axis: passive-dependent man—passive-dependent woman.
2. A woman oriented anxiety axis: anxious-adequate woman—passive-dependent man.
3. A woman dominated dependency axis: controlling-dependent woman—passive-dependent man.
4. A woman dominated competitive axis: controlling-belittling woman—vulnerable-susceptible man.
5. A man dominated competitive axis: controlling-belittling man—vulnerable-susceptible woman.
6. A man oriented self-depreciating axis: pain seeking-long suffering man—troublesome-ineffectual woman.
7. A woman oriented self-depreciating axis: pain seeking-long suffering woman—troublesome-ineffectual man.
8. A dual emotionally detached axis: detached-ineffectual man—detached-ineffectual woman.
9. A man dominated hostile axis: hostile-aggressive man—vulnerable-susceptible woman.
10. A woman dominated hostile axis: hostile-aggressive woman—vulnerable-susceptible man.

[1] *Classification of Disorganized Families for Use in Family Oriented Diagnosis and Treatment,* Second Draft, Community Research Associates, Inc., December, 1955. It should be noted that these axes were preliminary formulations and have been revised and reduced to four basic types of family pathology to be presented in *Family Diagnosis and Treatment of Psychosocial Disorders,* to be published in 1959.

With continued research these interim postulates have been tested further for their validity and refined. Such a diagnostic frame of reference with its prognostic implications would be of great importance in working professionally with disorganized families. It has still further significance. It could be applied by persons in looking at their own courtship or marriage.[2] The clinical foundations and implications of the theory would be admittedly difficult for the untrained layman. To acquire such a foundation, however, would not be beyond the ability of a great many persons provided they had skilled educational guidance. We teach high school students Latin and trigonometry. They have to work to get it. The same effort in the development of skill in human relations would seem to have great promise.

A DIAGNOSTIC FRAME OF REFERENCE

The theory of basic personality developed in Chapter 2 grew out of the writer's application of academic theory in marriage counseling experience, and is directly applicable to the analysis of faulty as well as successful marriage. It must be remembered that this theoretical formulation is still very much in the stage of working hypothesis and lacks empirical verification. Aspects of it are supported by the pilot study cited above. The possible combinations of each of the three theoretical modes of immature or neurotic basic personality result in ten combinations of basic components:

[2] See Rex A. Skidmore, Hulda Van Steeter, and C. Jay Skidmore, *Marriage Consulting*, New York, Harper, 1956; Emily H. Mudd, *The Practice of Marriage Counseling*, New York, Association Press, 1951; Carl R. Rogers, *Client-Centered Therapy*, New York, Houghton Mifflin, 1951; John F. Cuber, *Marriage Counseling Practice*, New York, Appleton-Century-Crofts, 1948.

PRIMARY CHARACTERISTICS

Male	*Female*
I. A man high in the A-component Passive-dependent	1. A woman high in the A-component Passive-dependent
	2. A woman high in the B-component Hostile-aggressive
	3. A woman high in the C-component Inadequate-withdrawing
II. A man high in the B-component Hostile-aggressive	4. A woman high in the A-component Passive-dependent
	5. A woman high in the B-component Hostile-aggressive
	6. A woman high in the C-component Inadequate-withdrawing
III. A man high in the C-component Inadequate-withdrawing	7. A woman high in the A-component Passive-dependent
	8. A woman high in the B-component Hostile-aggressive
	9. A woman high in the C-component Inadequate-withdrawing
IV. A man high in all three components, ABC Dependent-hostile-overly sensitive	10. A woman high in all three components, ABC Dependent-hostile-overly sensitive

Since it seldom happens that a person is high in one component and lacking in the other two, the other two blend with the dominant component and might be thought of as secondary characteristics. Thus a man might be dominantly passive and dependent (A-component), but at the same time relatively high in the B-component. Such a person would tend to be passive and dependent upon a partner, but harbor considerable hostility and aggression. Or, if he were dominant in the B-component and had considerable strength in the A-component, he would tend to be outwardly hostile and aggressive while lacking in self-confidence and initiative, and would tend to need someone upon whom he could lean. From this, eight theoretical types of persons can be derived (see Chapter 2):

1. ABC	5. aBC
2. ABc	6. aBc
3. Abc	7. abC
4. AbC	8. abc

If each of the eight possible types of men is paired with each of the eight possible types of women there would be sixty-four combinations of the two personalities. Twenty-four are listed here as examples:

1. ABC—ABC	9. ABc—ABC	17. Abc—ABC
2. ABC—ABc	10. ABc—ABc	18. Abc—ABc
3. ABC—Abc	11. ABc—Abc	19. Abc—Abc
4. ABC—AbC	12. ABc—AbC	20. Abc—AbC
5. ABC—aBC	13. ABc—aBC	21. Abc—aBC
6. ABC—aBc	14. ABc—aBc	22. Abc—aBc
7. ABC—abC	15. ABc—abC	23. Abc—abC
8. ABC—abc	16. ABc—abc	24. Abc—abc

It is beyond the scope of this book to develop completely all the ramifications of this theory. However, it is this writer's conviction, stemming from clinical practice, that this frame of reference which is as yet crude and in need of rigorous validation and refinement, *can serve as a valuable tool in the fuller understanding of patterns of marital interaction with their deep underlying motivations.*

ANALYSIS OF CASE HISTORIES

The cases in this section will serve to illustrate a number of the more common patterns of basic personality interaction in faulty marriages. The description of the couple will be punctuated with analytic comments pointing up the deeper needs and expectations of both members of the couple and the bases for their frustrations.

The Case of Glenn and Vivian Carter

The Carters had been married for 14 years when Vivian went to her attorney to file for a divorce. After listening to her story the attorney felt that there was a chance of saving the marriage. He referred them for marriage counsel.

> [*Even when the marriage cannot be saved, marriage counseling can serve to help one or both to understand the deeper bases of their problem. A most important consideration is to help each retain his integrity on as much of a reality basis as is possible.*]

Vivian made the initial contact.

> [*In most cases it is the wife who feels that she has the greatest stake in the marriage and makes the initial contact.*]

She was a woman in her early 30's, medium in height, somewhat rotund but not heavy. She walked with a springy gait and shifted from relaxation to an upright posture while seated.

> [*In body shape and structure Vivian was relatively high in both the A- and B-components, low in the C-component.*]

She dressed with good taste, on the smart side, with a somewhat tailored effect. She was employed as a buyer of ladies' ready-to-wear and a departmental manager in a department store.

[*An occupation fitting her basic personality—friendly, outgoing, active.*]

After telling briefly of her contact with the attorney Vivian launched into a vehement attack against Glenn.

[*The complaint factor. The charges and counter-charges cited early in counseling virtually always turn out to be the symptoms of deeper need and expectation frustration, complaints about selfishness, inconsideration, sex, in-laws, money, and children are patent symptoms of many faulty marriages. Vivian is quite unaware of the deeper bases of their incompatibility.*]

"He thinks of no one but himself," she said. "When it's a pretty day he's either golfing or fishing. I wouldn't mind so much if he didn't dash off to his mother's as soon as he changed his clothes after returning . . . He won't let me have any children. It's always the car to be paid for, more clothes, or save for a vacation . . . I don't like his attitude toward our personal relations. If he would just not constantly bring up the girls he knew before we were married and brag so about his prowess as a wolf. He even talks about us to the boys at the plant. One day my father heard about it and I was afraid of what he would do to Glenn if he had seen him . . .

[*Her basic personality is revealed in her hostile, aggressive charges—B-component. There is, however, the warmth of conciliation—A-component. There is little reflection and introspection—C-component.*]

Glenn's mother has never accepted me. Somehow, I feel that she is his only confidant."

[*She wants to move closer emotionally to Glenn—A-component.*]

Glenn was a man of medium height, muscular but wiry. He was pale, tense, and punctuated his remarks with taut gestures.

[*Morphologically Glenn was low in the A-component, high in the B-component, with some of the C-component.*]

His aggression was contained as he talked with a quality of emotional detachment. After expressing his resentment at "the whole affair" (Vivian's insisting that he see a marriage counselor), he launched into his version of their problem.

> [*He was not only hostile but quite bitter. He showed little if any conciliation in his attitude—B- and C-components.*]

"I can't do anything I want to do," he said. "It is always how inconsiderate I am of what she wants to do . . . There is too much of her family in it to suit me—always celebrating birthdays, dinners, picnics.

> [*Glenn is trying to extricate himself from a feeling of being bound or controlled—C-component. He does not have a feeling of need for emotional closeness either to Vivian, her family, or any family—C-component, low in A.*]

She insists on my going along to listen to the endless talk . . .

> [*Here he cannot play the ascendant role—B.*]

I don't like the way she reminds me of how much money that she's earning . . . In our sex relations she is too aggressive.

> [*Her financial autonomy is a threat to his need to feel ascendant, as is her active sex role.*]

Things aren't like they ought to be . . . She has changed so much since we were married. She's nothing like the kid she was . . ."

> [*He wants her to play the more passive role (A), with the deference characteristic of the early part of their marriage.*]

Vivian's parents were of New England background. There were two older brothers. The family was close in many ways.

> [*The cultural backgrounds of the family provide clues to the psychosexual roles the parents assumed and thus the pattern of orientations set for the children.*]

They had spent much time together at mealtime and observed special occasions with sentiment, gifts, and festivity.

> [*Love of polite ceremony—A.*]

It was a male-centered family.

> [*Typically New England at that time.*]

The father and two brothers owned and operated a small but prosperous business. They were active men who fished and hunted together and participated in the activities of the community. Vivian said that they formed what she called a "small closed psychological corporation" and would not let her in.

[*A stable family, affirming of one another—close but not intimate, with some emotional austerity as part of a culture pattern.*]

She wanted to work in the family store but they told her that a girl's place was in the home.

[*The pattern of a traditional definition of femininity; encouraging expression of the A-component, withholding the B.*]

They were affirming of Vivian but excluded her from their activities.

[*Emotional security, but the thwarting of a wish that becomes a mainspring of action later.*]

Vivian's mother was a quiet, mild-mannered woman who believed that a woman's place was in the home. She was an efficient homemaker which took up most of her time, though she did participate in the activities of her church. During Vivian's early years she identified herself closely with her mother.

[*Personality strengthening effect of identification with parent of same sex, further definition of feminine role.*]

As she grew older, she participated more and more in school and church activities and became a leader among her girl friends. During adolescence her experience with boys remained quite limited and consisted largely of group dating until the time that she met Glenn.

[*Expression of the A- and B-components.*]

Vivian's childhood was a happy and active one, close to her mother but not intimate. She looked up to her father and brothers with modest deference, seeking to be closer to them but never achieving it.

[*In the frustration of her wish to be closer, another mainspring of future action has been coiled—her need for close emotional affirmation from the male figure.*]

Glenn's parents were separated when he was very young.

[*Glenn came out of an unhappy home. There was no father figure with which he could identify.*]

His mother worked to support him and his younger sister until his mother's "health" no longer permitted her to work. She was a dominating woman, long suffering and complaining.

[*Primarily a pattern of neurotic invalidism, seeking security through manipulation and control—hostile dependency.*]

Glenn's sister succumbed and became her shadowed image.

[*Weak ego development of sister.*]

During Glenn's early childhood he was held in check by her complaints, pleas, and threats of ill health if Glenn "did not mind."

[*The feeling of duty and obligation rather than love strengthened emotional separation from a mother (female) figure.*]

During adolescence he rebelled increasingly and spent more and more time with his gang of boy friends.

[*His reaction under stress was to strike back and then withdraw—B- and C-components. He was not close to his friends, but competitive—low A and C, high B.*]

When he returned home late she insisted that he kiss her good-night. Invariably he would have the odor of beer and tobacco on his breath. He knew that she strongly disapproved on religious grounds and would reproach him.

[*Continued hostility toward female figure.*]

During the ensuing argument she would cry, tell Glenn that he was driving her to her grave, and then clutch her breast as if having an "attack."

[*Attempt to use pity, guilt, and anxiety to hold and control. He takes this in as one of his repertory of roles—B- and C-components. The attack is a psychosomatic expression of repressed hostility and anxiety —C-component.*]

During early adolescence Glenn felt very guilty about disobeying his mother and feared that he was hurting her. Later he felt more and more indifferent toward her. Finally he broke completely with her and took a room down the street from his home.

> [*Strengthening of emotional separation and withdrawal and of his competitive aggression.*]

At this, his mother's role shifted to one of deference to him and complaining self-recrimination. She told Glenn that he not only was the man of the house but their "daddy and brother." Glenn returned home. His mother's praise made him feel important and needed. From his account, he seemed to have enjoyed the triumph of winning a series of psychological victories over her.

> [*Narcissistic satisfaction in praise—he wins over the female figure.*]

Later, when he married, Glenn said that his mother made him feel like he was abandoning her.

> [*Feeling of being trapped and bound—B-component, with some C-component.*]

During his later adolescence he attended school, spent his evenings with his boy friends, and fished and hunted on weekends, usually alone. He seemed to be close to no one.

> [*Restive striving in his relations with others—B-component, but a basic pattern of social and emotional withdrawal—C.*]

The pattern of Glenn's attitudes showed two extremes: one, a kind of aggressive, impersonal "gang" behavior, and the other, outdoor seclusive pursuits.

> [*This is the core of his neurotic basic personality—high in aggressive hostility, outwardly dominating, while inwardly dependent and withdrawing.*]

He had many acquaintances and "friends" but no intimates. His association with others was more competitive and demonstrative than genuinely friendly. He said that during his early adulthood he developed a "pre-ulcer" and that his health was not good despite the fact that he was active and seemed able to carry out any activity that he chose, between "spurts of energy and fatigue."

[His psychosexual development has remained immature. He is excessively self-centered, exhibitionistic, and unable to relate to anybody—especially a woman.

Glenn was never loved, only "disciplined" by guilt and anxiety.

His unconscious anxiety comes out in alternate B-component restless striving and C-component fatigue and withdrawal, with the symptomatic digestive disorder.]

Glenn and Vivian met during their senior year in high school. He was "dashing, well-dressed, and a good dancer." Vivian was inexperienced with boys and responded to his attentions. She commented, "I guess I was a naïve kid lifted three feet off the ground by his palaver." Likewise, Glenn had had little experience in dating. After a brief whirlwind courtship they were married.

[Note here the repertory of social and emotional roles that each brought to the courtship, each with his needs and expectations, partially if not wholly unconscious. Vivian had experienced warmth and affirmation, emotional security, and the discipline of a fairly strict New England family. She was, however, inexperienced in affairs of the heart and could not see through Glenn's unconscious pose. She could not discern the surface cavalier behavior from the neurotic personality that it concealed. He appeared outgoing, strong and, ascendant, like her father and brothers. He was on good behavior. She was flattered by his pursuit (which she always wanted from her father and brothers). In her immaturity (but not neuroticism) she was vulnerable to mistaking romance for companionship in love.

Vivian was warm, outgoing, and deferent but not clinging, the opposite of Glenn's mother. He was flattered by Vivian's solicitous court—a role that she learned in relation to her father and brothers. Little did he realize that he was still bound to his mother despite the appearance of autonomy. He seemed free from her on the surface, but carried the need to compete with, control, show off, and depend on a woman. These were role-patterned needs that were deeply and securely laid in his formative experience.]

They seemed to be "supremely" happy. Vivian looked up to his "great strength" while he enjoyed her adoring deference. She kept up the rented apartment and restricted her activities with her girl friends. Together they entertained often but modestly since he was working as a mechanic. Their entertainment consisted largely of bridge and attendance at an occasional dance. This continued at a diminishing pace for the first several years. Then, Vivian decided that she wanted to get a job. Glenn had been against having a baby, which she wanted, on the grounds that they needed to get a car paid for, get some new clothes, and do some traveling first. Glenn did not object to her working though he felt that his income was adequate. With this go-ahead signal Vivian found a job as a sales lady in the ready-to-wear department of a local store.

Vivian rose rapidly in the firm. She liked people and enjoyed serving them. Her income soon equaled and then exceeded that of Glenn. It was at this time, several years after marriage, that their difficulties were said to have begun.

[*Vivian entered marriage projecting her romantic image of a man on Glenn. With the fulfillment of her early dream of working she developed more autonomy, more responsibility with money and with people. With the development of the B-component of her personality, her expectations, when frustrated by the increasing sense of Glenn's neuroticism, became demands. It was at this point that she became for Glenn a nagging, tying, demanding "mother" figure. Glenn's reaction was to revert to his pattern of reaction to his mother. His deferent, worshiping "little girl" had changed.*]

With increased experience, responsibility, and self-assurance, her latent initiative began to develop. She had become more autonomous and ascendant in her relations with people. As

Vivian commented, "That's when the difficulty began. Glenn couldn't take any of my suggestions . . . he seemed to resent any demands that I made on him." At first there was subtle, *sub rosa* contriving to see who could gain the upper hand in their little sallies and arguments. Later she began to tell him of his short comings, how she was through "worshiping at his shrine," that it was his turn to pay her a few respects and to give more consideration to her interests. Glenn used the same tactics on Vivian that he employed against his mother. He left and went home to his mother for a few days.

[*Glenn reacted to Vivian as he had learned to react to members of his parental family.*]

Vivian then "came off her high horse" and in deference and tears went to him and begged him to return. He did.

[*The A-component shows through in her attempt to reconcile their differences, to compromise, and to try to resolve their difficulties. She wants to recapture the feeling that she projected into the marriage in the beginning.*]

Things went smoothly on the surface for a while and then the difficulties would break through again, each quarrel becoming more serious. Vivian received moral support from her girl friends at the store who coached her in attitude and strategy.

[*She confided in friends while Glenn remained completely self-contained—the difference between A-component and C-component reaction to stress.*]

"Finally," she said, "I called his cards. I told him that he couldn't get around me by throwing one of those ulcer attacks . . . that if he was strong enough to chop up the golf greens like he was doing on Sundays, he had strength enough to hand me my house slippers on Saturday night. Needless to say, it burned him up."

Their initial sex adjustment had been good. Vivian was responsive. It meant much to her and as she said, she was "very romantic." Her role was passive. Her response seemed to be affirming to Glenn. His role was that of the initiator and he was very demonstrative with the kind of "prancing self-display" that at first was somewhat embarrasing to Vivian.

[Their sex life is a miniature of their whole marriage. Vivian's early adjustment was evidence of her emotional maturity and changed with her increasing sense of Glenn's sexual immaturity, i.e., his inability to participate in an other-centered relationship. It served first as a medium of self-display and then later as a projection of hostility.]

As their marital difficulty developed Vivian's role became more active, or as Glenn described it, "more aggressive."

[Vivian's active role is a threat to Glenn's masculinity.]

At the same time she was increasingly "disgusted" with his "sexual exhibitions." She had come to feel that it was not meaningful as a relationship. To her it was more "physical release and satisfaction." "I somehow withdrew my love at this time and had much less interest in sex. When he made his 'demands' as he seemed to do more frequently as kind of a way of showing me, I simply held out. Some of our most bitter quarrels followed, then he just seemed to draw more within himself and retreat . . ."

[Vivian had finally realized that Glenn was not affirming her in his sex role, which was deeply disillusioning to her. Her sex needs had been developed and sought satisfaction, but the relationship now without her projection had become largely physical.

Sex withholding is deeply offensive to the partner and provokes feelings of retaliating hostility.

Their sex relationship mirrors their larger marital pattern of interaction.]

More of the details of the marriage of Glenn and Vivian would not add materially to understanding the pattern of their marriage. They were caught up in a struggle against one another in which each attempted to needle, barb, and hurt the other while jockeying for the upper hand. Unaware of what was going on underneath and what their deeper needs and expectations were, their relationship reached an impasse.

[At the time of seeking counsel neither was aware of what had happened since their initial, mutual feeling

of romance toward one another. They had not awakened to the fact that their romantic projections could not stand the changing reality of Vivian's maturation from the deferent, admiring "little girl" role to the autonomous woman that she had become. The more the ascendant, active B-component developed through her work, the more she resembled his "demanding" mother. She had no way of knowing that his attention to her was not affirmation, but a display of his self-centered personality. He was quite unaware of his unconscious identification of Vivian with his rejected mother.]

In counsel Vivian rapidly came to recognize that she had been attracted in courtship to the *appearance* of a more mature person, later to discover that he had never been loved nor disciplined, and that he had no capacity to love another; that he was locked in what was preponderantly a compulsion neurosis with a secondary pattern of anxiety. Vivian had been hurt in her marriage but not seriously damaged. She was able to understand without excessive defensive rationalization and projection. With new insight, her feelings of hostility and blame subsided. She felt sorry for Glenn. As she attacked her problem from these new perspectives she began to consider alternative actions that were open to her. She might return to her former role in the hope that Glenn would return to his former "affirming" role, and then she could help him to mature. However, after considerable reflection she concluded that their marriage had been a "tragic mistake of mutual ignorance" and reluctantly divorced him. Later she met a man considerably older than she. He was much like her father in appearance and basic personality. She married him, quit her job, and became content with a role much like that which characterized her later adolescence—primarily domestic, with civic and religious activities.

Glenn had been so deeply hurt by life that he was not secure enough within himself to understand what had happened either in his childhood or his marriage. This understanding might have been achieved through intensive psychotherapy. He reacted by vacillating from feelings of projected blame and anger, to feelings of confusion, followed by long verbal explanations of the situation which served to hide his feelings from himself. He accepted the divorce and the loss of "mama" reluctantly. Later he married a girl whom he had known since adolescence. She was passive in basic personality but "made a good home" for him, waiting on his needs. He had not changed at the time of last contact several years after his divorce and remarriage.

In the case of Vivian and Glenn, there was potentially an alternative to divorce. If the couple had received help earlier and not let the marriage deteriorate to the extent that it did, they might have saved it. From what we know about their basic personalities Vivian and Glenn had many potential common interests, including golf and bridge, and hunting and fishing which she had idealized in her brothers. These interests could have been pursued with a different attitude of companionship rather than adolescent rivalry and display. They were apparently unable to accomplish this on their own, though they might have been able to with professional help. The potential compatibility of their temperaments, their intelligence, their present and latent skills, and the recapture of some of the early bases of their romance could have been assets in saving their marriage.

Vivian had an early interest in children. If Glenn could

have matured enough to bear the responsibility and imposed restrictions of a family—which is often a shock and depressing threat to the exclusive possession of one's wife—Vivian then might have attempted the dual role of the domestic and the "professional." However, starting a family before they had proved their compatibility over a period of time might have had a harmful effect. For her to discontinue her work completely probably would have built up unconscious resentment within her without providing an outlet for this important need in her personality; also, it might have made Glenn feel anxious in his inability to match her sacrificing gesture. Often, to keep one's finger in the fire is the best way to become desensitized to the heat—if the fire is not too hot. Vivian could have accepted a more domestic, feminine role because of her early identification with her mother. Although she was more interested in the boys' work, there was a minimum of early masculine protest. This combination of feminine and masculine elements in her personality could have been of considerable importance in this case. Glenn needed a certain amount of support that his mother had given him, but in a more mature manner, which Vivian could have done because of her temperament and business experience in dealing with men.

It should be noted that the complaints regarding sex, money, and in-laws have not been considered separately in the case of Glenn and Vivian. After gaining some understanding of the underlying factors in their case, they did not mention these symptoms again, nor were they regarded as of primary importance by the consultant. Later it was pointed out that moderation in the whole range of these personal habits would have tended to heighten constructive idealization and prevent the lowering of mood that caused both to be thrown back on the old patterns of adolescent conflict; expression rather than exploitation would have helped.

The Case of Fred and Margaret Mansfield

The case of the Mansfields represents another pattern of modern marriage. The same basic mode can be seen in many different couples, with infinite variation of surface details.

Margaret went to her physician with a chronic skin rash, complaints of colitus, and marked restlessness. After a thorough examination and temporary relief of the symptoms, he told her that she was disturbed and that her emotional tension was expressing itself in these physical symptoms. She was referred for marriage counsel.

> [*Margaret accepted her physician's suggestion that she seek marriage counsel with some reluctance. At first she felt that she could "work it out" herself. He told her that the psychosomatic symptoms were evidence of prolonged, unresolved emotional stress. He facilitated the referral by making the call for the first appointment, with her consent. Part of such resistance is occasioned by an unconscious refusal to accept conditions imposed by reality and the responsibility of renouncing that which is desired.*]

Margaret was in her 30's. She was pretty, medium height, generally athletic in appearance, with rather distinct and angular features.

> [*Morphologically she was dominantly B-component, with evidence of some of the rotund (A) and considerable (C) that was manifestly overt.*]

She dressed with good taste and was dynamic, engaging, expressive, and frank. She said that she liked to read but found little time. She had "tried her hand at writing short stories."

[There was evidence of aesthetic ability. She was preponderantly active and direct in temperament (B) but socially engaging rather than competitive.]

Her rapid-fire description of her childhood gave evidence of a talented and active personality.

[Her childhood was active, happy, and oriented toward people and their activities. She was very versatile and ascendant rather than passive in her relations with others.]

She could be in there pitching with the boys in their ball game, or she could take part in the more feminine interests of her little girl.

[Margaret showed evidence of considerable empathy, but was not too sympathetically inclined.]

She enjoyed experimenting with details of homemaking, entertaining, and traveling with her husband. She was a good chairman of meetings and participated widely in civic, religious, social, and business activities.

[In most matters including some of Fred's business activities she assumed an ascendant role to him and most other people. There was little evidence of competitive aggressiveness, more, of the vigorous, and dynamic. Her religious activities had little spiritual meaning. They were only another source of social participation.]

Fred was two years older, heavy, rotund, and a "hail fellow well met." He was neat and appropriate in his dress and appeared to be well coördinated in his movements, relaxed, and somewhat inattentive.

[He was preponderantly rotund in physique with a secondary muscular component (Ab). The strength of the C-component, morphologically, was not determined.]

From the story of his background one gathered that he was a rather easy-going, pleasant, moderately successful salesman. His easy way with people had won him many friends both in the community and among the people with whom he carried on his business.

[Margaret described him as "genuinely liking people," and responsive to people in a somewhat impersonal way—a kind of adolescent "gang" behavior. He played poker periodically with a small group of personal friends.

In contrast to Margaret, Fred read little. When he did he preferred adventure or mystery stories. He had a moderate interest in sports, having played guard on his high school football team.]

Fred and Margaret had been idealized by those who knew them for their "fine family and contributions to the local church and community." They had two boys and a little girl all under 10 years old. A high standard of material comfort had been established in their home.

[Standards of achievement in their middle-middle-class environment were not too high or demanding. There was little social competition or striving. Living up to the community's expectations of being "good, honest, and industrious, participating in and supporting civic and religious organizations" assured them a respected position in the community.]

The Mansfields had never faced any serious difficulties nor had there been any conscious question in their minds about the success of their marriage until after Fred was called into military service early in World War II.

[A pattern of considerable social participation together with raising the children allowed little opportunity for reflection and introspection. Considerable ideological provincialism prevailed. The prevailing middle-class mores prevented any extramarital attractions, thus any possible discovery of deeper compatibility or incompatibility.]

His leaving was a "shock'" to both of them but they seemed to have taken his leaving "gracefully."

[The "shock" seemed to be more one of suddenness than of deeper psychological impact. The more personal and intellectual aspect of their possible relationship had not developed.]

Margaret had the children and many friends, some of whose husbands were also in the service. She continued her many activities in the community. As the months of Fred's absence wore into years their little girl, the last of the three children, entered school. It was at this time that Margaret decided that she would like to work.

> [*To Margaret, Fred's leaving was more like losing a comfortable roommate or office partner than a spouse. It was more of a social than a psychological dislocation. The social dislocation was temporary. Margaret's social mobility soon carried her into a changed pattern of activities—work, new friends, and much more freedom from her domestic role.*]

She took a position as a saleslady in a firm where she had worked part time before her marriage. Some of her former friends were still there.

> [*Margaret fitted into this new role easily. She had known most of her fellow employees as well as the management for many years. Her active and socially affirming basic personality fit her well for this new role. She felt secure in it.*]

Three years had lapsed since Fred had left. He had been home on several short leaves. Margaret said that during the periods of his absence she did not feel as lonesome for him as she had expected, and she expressed some guilt in not having missed him more.

> [*It had never occurred to her that her marriage lacked any deeper and more personal import. Against this emerging awareness stood the feelings of guilt and anxiety as a defense against having to face such an unpleasant reality. She recognized only the symptoms.*]

One night the employees of the firm held a picnic. During the dancing that followed Margaret found that she was the "partner" of a previous boy friend, one of the department managers. He saw her home. He started seeing her home from work, then later took her out to dinner and for drives in his car. Soon they were seeing one another often.

[Margaret had not consciously sought out her new friend. If the circumstances of war and Fred's absence had not arisen it is probable that she would never have discovered the incompleteness of her marriage.

The absence of a sex partner was an unconscious factor in motivating her to respond, if not inadvertently initiate, aspects of the affair. Her feeling of a desire to be close to someone was not recognized as being in part sexual. Such an orientation at this stage of their relationship would have been threatening to her feelings of morality and self-respect.]

At this point in her story she became evasive and continued, "I have more of the things that really count than 95 percent of the women I know. When my thoughts wander as they do now and then when I don't keep busy, I feel like a cad. Fred is all that any woman could want, but . . ."

[The depth and pain of her conflict is evidenced in her evasiveness. In denying to herself the reality of her feelings she is repressing her conflict with the resulting physiological (psychosomatic) symptoms. The strength of her conscience, oriented to the most traditionally moral segment of her community, makes it very difficult for her to recognize and thus deal with her dilemma.]

"My family," she continued with evasion, "was a good family, but never very close. Mother and dad didn't seem to have a lot in common but there was little conflict. It was that they were constantly on the go, often in different directions . . . I loved my parents but was never very close to them.

[Her parental family was a stable one with few conflicts though lacking any depth of intimacy or communication. Margaret had a feeling of security.]

Dad was cute, a lot like Fred. He would take me on his lap and rock me but I could never confide how I really felt.

[In being attracted to Fred she felt the comfort and safety that she experienced with her father. This was interpreted by her to be "love" since she had experienced no deeper sexual or intellectual needs. The A-

and B-components of her basic personality were being developed, but the C-component remained latent.]

Mother was active in everything. I rather think that she ran the household too. Mother saw to it that I had nice clothes, and she liked me to have lots of girl friends in our home . . ."

[*This was primarily an extroverted home in its interests, activities, and interpersonal relationships.*]

As Margaret lingered she realized that she had left the subject. She burst into tears which she quickly subdued with her handkerchief.

[*Further evidence of her dilemma and its underlying, unresolved conflict.*]

She said chokingly, "I guess that I really love the so-and-so, but what can I do about it? There are the children, there's Fred, there is our prominent role in the church, there are our friends . . .

[*She is now confronting the bases of the symptoms of her stress, but still does not understand the bases for the difference between her "love" of Fred and her attraction to the other man. Her attempt to be rational about the matter consists of a verbalization of what she "should do." In this instance she has ceased to deal with her feelings.*]

Furthermore I don't think this fellow is worth a minute of my attention . . . I suspect him of insincerity but all this doesn't alter my desperate desire to pull up my stakes and go with him."

[*In a recurring dream, related later, she saw herself in a distant city, sitting with the other man on a curb "with my shoes and stockings off, wallowing my feet in the water that flowed in the gutter." Her self recrimination and guilt feelings evidenced in "wallowing in the gutter" are strong. She actually knew virtually nothing about him but suspected him, possibly projecting her feelings about herself in this situation.*]

Margaret's new infatuation was a man somewhat older than she, greying, immaculately dressed, quiet but responsive, and "considerate of my every wish. At dinner his attention isn't on the crowd. I seem to be the only one who counts."

[In striking contrast to Fred's impersonal approach to her, the other man struck her as being very attentive and affirming of her in an intimate way. Absent was the gang behavior characteristic of Fred, or the preoccupation with his business. Such personal affirmation of a woman is sexually stimulating to her. Margaret came to recognize this later but not at this time. Such an orientation was too threatening to her already tarnished moral conception of herself.]

At the same time he seemed to hold her at some emotional distance by canceling dates the last minute, taking extended business trips without confiding any of the details, and by not making any sexual advances or discussing their possible future together. This inconsistent treatment seemed to intrigue and at the same time infuriate her. It became evident as her story continued that she had become deeply involved emotionally while he seemed to remain noncommittal.

[Holding her at some distance proved challenging and stimulating to Margaret. He was not "so evident" as was Fred. This B-component need was being met. This also served to stimulate her reflection and introspection (C-component) hitherto unawakened.

During the periods of his absence she was almost constantly preoccupied with thoughts of him. During this time she had such strong feelings of sexual attraction toward him that she recognized them for what they were. She began to think about how far she should go sexually, and under what circumstances the opportunity might arise. "To look at him," she said, "gave me a tingling feeling that I had never experienced before."

The strength of her feelings of ambivalence is evidenced in her "infuriation." It was at this time that her physical symptoms became more pronounced and painful, especially the skin rash.]

Asked about her earlier experience with Fred, Margaret talked about their courtship.

[She was temporarily relieved in getting away from

facing her problem. The "release" in returning to the security of her early marriage was seen in the near exuberant way in which she expressed herself.]

She talked enthusiastically about the small group of couples who were their friends and with whom they picnicked, went to the movies, danced, and attended church. They spent little time together alone.

[*Her courtship was almost as superficial as teen-age dating. She had no way of knowing what her own personality potential was. Their relationship was "nice, comfortable, and secure." It was largely a reënactment of her relationship with her parents. Furthermore, it met the moral expectations of the community. It was an expected and approved pattern of courtship.*]

She had often wished that Fred might find less interest in the group and a little more personal interest in her. In her dreams she had pictured Fred more like "Clark Gable or Humphrey Bogart" and silently wished that he were more aggressive and direct and that he "knew what he wanted."

[*These latent wish frustrations were not evoked by any other person she knew. Had someone like her new infatuation been on the scene to compare with Fred, the entire course of her life might have been different.*]

Sex was taboo, though they did kiss each other good-night. Margaret felt that their church teachings plus "always being in the group" had left this area of their courtship unexplored. She felt that Fred was steady and had a "heart of gold," that people liked him, and that he would be a "swell dad." She felt that marriage with him would mean a good home and the security that a great many women never have, even though he seemed too preoccupied with his friends and his work.

[*Her B-component needs were strong and sought fulfillment that was partially achieved through social activities. The personal element was lacking.*

The superficiality of the testing phase of courtship, due to the relative lack of insight into basic person-

ality needs and their potential development, constitutes a problem that contemporary society does not recognize in any articulate way. Moralistic opposition to a more realistic approach to education for marriage has resulted, in effect, in our saying to our youth: "Hang your clothes on the hickory bush but don't go near the water. Please, however, learn to swim before you take the plunge."

She reacted with a repertory of role-expectations that were developed in her parental family. Experience had taught her no others. If her parents had been more reflective, introspective, and personal, it is likely that she would have sought more in Fred.]

They were married. They had their three children close together. Fred rose rapidly in the ranks of his company. Much of their time together continued to be spent in the company of their friends.

[*A woman feels a deep sense of fulfillment and achievement in having a family under the circumstances of community affirmation of familism. There was little occasion at this time to have doubts about the deeper aspects of the marriage.*]

Returning to her immediate problem Margaret continued, "It was then [after Fred had been away and she had begun to see the other man] for the first time that I realized what had been lurking beneath the surface of my personality. A part of myself had been submerged with activity during courtship, the work and responsibility of the early years with the children, and Fred so good . . . We had just never had the chance to take a good look at ourselves and our marriage.

[*After expressing considerable feelings of anxiety, guilt, and self-recrimination, Margaret was emotionally free enough to recognize that she had been thrown by circumstances into a situation that she had not consciously sought; that there was no planned intrigue of infidelity; that, in a real measure, she was reacting as any normal, moral human being would; and more im-*

portant, that she had tried desperately to deny what was a part of her real, more mature self. With this more rational definition of her situation she was now able to look at what had happened; ask herself who she really was and what her deeper needs were and why.

Her next insight was an emerging sense that the other man was not necessarily "the one"; that she had projected many of her needs into a situation that had served to evoke what lay within herself. As she said at this time, "Am I in love with him or with a part of myself that was evoked by him?" She concluded that she knew much too little about him to love him; that she had been personally and sexually stimulated by "that type of a person."]

"My attitude toward Fred had not changed. I have always loved him and always will. He [the other man] knows that. He couldn't offer me the stability and home for my children that Fred has provided.

[*Her strong sense of loyalty to Fred and her children was ever present during her infatuation. If it had not been she would have experienced much less physical and mental anguish.*]

His wife and children are also involved. He will never settle down. I guess it is my imagined flight with him that is as intriguing as anything else, but there's no pay off in that . . . If Fred could just be more dashing and not so darned evident. I don't know how I stand with him [the other man]. Maybe if I did, the whole thing would go up in a bubble, but it is intriguing."

[*During the first part of her relationship with the other man, she thought only of him—not his wife, children, and marital situation. Now she is thinking more in terms of future reality and must take all of these larger, less personal considerations into account.*

With new insight into the basis of her involvement her problem was not solved, but it was becoming less personal and less urgent.

She did not enter into a sexual relationship with him. If she had and it proved to awaken her to deeper sexual experience, her problem would have been more complicated. It would have served to heighten her dilemma and provide new and more profound feelings of guilt that she would be less able to rationalize than her "painful but nevertheless innocent affair." If, on the other hand she had had sexual intercourse with him and it had proved disappointing it might have served to resolve summarily her feelings for him, if not strengthen her resolution to remain loyal to Fred.]

During the subsequent sessions Fred returned from service. Margaret said that he seemed to sense from her moments of preoccupation that something had happened. She decided not to tell him because she did not want to hurt him. She had not completely resolved her conflict, but her decision was becoming clearer. She could say, "As I think about the whole thing I have a rather tragic feeling that things might have been so different in my marriage, but the die has been cast. Marriage is more than romance. Fred and the children mean much more . . . It is now for the first time that the meaning of a quotation I read in an English course penetrated: 'Human understanding matures in the tragedy of caressing with a touch what might under other circumstances have been grasped and held.' "

[*The psychosomatic symptoms had disappeared. Margaret was facing her problem on a conscious, rational level. Her feelings toward the other man seemed to be much less personal and intense. He had become more of a symbol of "the things that might have been so different."*

In this kind of renunciation and resignation she is dealing with her problem on a reality level, not denying her deeper feelings as she did earlier. Despite moments and perhaps periods of regret in not having married a man who could fulfill more of her basic personality needs, this kind of "high-minded" resignation can serve to turn her interests from herself to her family and others, actually strengthening her personality. She is no longer repressing her wishes but accepting and redirecting them—sublimation.]

Margaret does not necessarily have to renounce part of her personality. The war confronted many men with new and more serious problems of human relations, and tended to make them more reflective and introspective. This may have happened to Fred (though we do not know if this was true in this particular case). Sometimes a personal crisis serves to jolt a person into self-examination with the resultant development of the C-component of basic personality. This has been known to happen as a result of the discovery that a spouse is having an affair.

In this case Fred might have benefited considerably by counseling or psychoanalysis. Some persons, and Fred may have been one, are too insecure to confront, accept, and deal with the more intimate in themselves or their relationships. To discover their own deep motivations is threatening to many people. Their defense is to minimize their importance, sometimes by deprecating clinical orientations, clinicians, and the human relations fields, and by avoiding depth psychology.

There was evidence that Fred was potentially able to mature into the kind of person who could meet more of Margaret's needs for companionship on the deeper level. This and many other cases like it are not consigned to marriages of mediocrity, but may provide greater fulfillment. Margaret's affair may have turned out to be a blessing in disguise, as painful and potentially disastrous as it was at the time. It was the beginning of greater growth in her and possibly in her husband.

The Case of Greg and Georgia Alden

The case of the Aldens is another pattern of marital interaction that is seen quite frequently by the marriage counselor.

The tensions that the couple experience are not regarded by either of them as constituting a marriage problem. Georgia was referred by a gynecologist who found that a feeling of chronic fatigue, a low backache, and low metabolism and blood pressure seemed to have no physiological basis. It was suggested by her physician that the difficulty might lie in their marriage relationship. In referring the case, he reported that this was quite a shock to Georgia, as she said that she "loved her husband dearly" and that "he was the only person in the world."

Greg and Georgia came in together for their first consultation.

> [*Their attitude seemed to be one of mutual interest in working out Georgia's health problem. Both were cordial and coöperative.*]

When asked to tell about any possible problems in their marriage, Greg spoke up.

> [*Greg's ascendant role soon came into play. Georgia's role was one of quiet modesty but not passivity.*]

He said that he knew of none except that Georgia acted "panicky" when he left on any kind of a trip, even to go fishing with his friends for the day. "On such occasions," he said, "she suggested that she either go with me or that I stay home, always with some reasonable sounding excuse." Most frequently he left her at home. When he returned she seemed to be happy at his return and showed no visible anxiety at his having been away.

> [*This pattern emerged almost immediately as a theme in their marriage that was evidenced in almost everything they did, at every point in their relationship. He was more or less taking her for granted and throwing himself into an extroverted world of activity. She sensed his lack of exclusive emotional involvement in her and reacted by trying to hold him. She was not aware of the depth of her feeling of anxiety, rationalizing her desire to feel that "all is well" by focusing on how happy she was upon his return.*

"The return" became a symbol of his moving emotionally closer to her.]

Georgia confirmed Greg's statement and then added that she had experienced "desperate" feelings of loneliness in his absence, often accompanied by dreams of something happening to him. When she awoke from such nightmares she would turn on all the lights in the house and try to read to keep from "feeling so anxious." Then she added, "But I don't see what this could have to do with our marriage."

[*They were both curious as to what her physical feelings could have to do with their marriage, or with marriage counseling.*]

Georgia was medium in height and thin; but with fairly broad hips. She had fine features and soft-textured skin. Her skeletal structure was small with little muscular development.

[*Morphologically Georgia was high in the C- and A-components. She was markedly lacking in strong bone and muscle structure.*]

She dressed neatly in a somewhat matronly style and wore no makeup.

[*She showed good taste in her dress, distinctly feminine with a touch of the old-fashioned.*]

She was quiet and retiring, but friendly. During the counseling sessions she remained somewhat passive but rallied at times with a flash of her eyes as she spoke.

[*Her temperament was consistent with her morphology. There was no evidence of compensatory or false assumption of a temperamental pattern inconsistent with her basic personality. Her responsiveness was more social and intellectual.*]

Greg, on the other hand, was quite the opposite in basic personality. He looked like a tackle on a football team—tall, broad shouldered, solidly built, and strong. His voice was resonant and modulated and he used enthusiastic gestures as he spoke.

[*He shifted from a dynamic to a relaxed role. There was some evidence of the C-component in his physical features.*]

He said that in the winter when he was going to school and not working in the forest he gained a great deal of weight. When Georgia was talking he often interrupted her or attempted to paraphrase what she had just said. If she interrupted him to add some detail, some irritation was evident but it soon passed. Often during the counseling sessions she turned to him for confirmation of what she had just said, or asked him to state the point more clearly.

> [*He reacted with some irritation at her slower and more methodical way of expressing herself. This was evidenced in his restless shift in his chair and his interruptions. She did not appear offended. He tried to be polite and not override her, but when they were together he did most of the talking.*]

When asked to tell about her childhood she described with mixed emotion her "happy" home.

> [*She seemed at this stage of counseling to be quite unaware of her deep ambivalence toward her entire family and continued to rationalize her fear and disgust with an excessive emphasis on "love and goodness" which she wanted but received only intermittently in the form of parent favoritism, ice cream, and temporary peace in the family.*]

Her mother was quiet, retiring, efficient in her housekeeping, and an ardent church worker. Georgia said that her mother was a very "good woman" who worked hard and attended to her church duties even when it was physically difficult for her to carry on.

> [*Her mother came out of a very paternalistic, church-oriented background. She tried to compensate for what she lacked in her marriage and family with near compulsive church participation. This served to quiet her anxiety created by her unpredictable egocentric husband and the ambivalence of the children toward him.*]

If Georgia or her two sisters were late in returning from school in the evening her mother complained that they should have been home doing "their share" of the housework.

> [*Housework was a ritual in the home that created an*

atmosphere of "all is well since we are all working together."]

She "sat on her emotions," Georgia said, "maintaining a silent grouch." The mother and daughters were together a great deal but usually engaged in housework. There was little evidence of companionship or common interests among them.

[*Georgia identified herself to a considerable degree with her mother during her earlier childhood. However, rather than real closeness, the "love" in the family was a period of quiet in the midst of psychological turbulence—something like the negative satisfaction derived from scratching a healing wound.*]

Georgia's respite from the work and her mother's complaining was to take her paints to the nearby beach and sit alone painting the rocky coast as she listened to the breakers.

[*This pattern of withdrawing emerged later. During the younger years it was one of "close apprehension."*]

Georgia had a number of girl friends during adolescence to whom she said she felt close. The tragic death of one of them drove her more to her painting which she pursued avidly at the time.

[*This reinforced her unconscious feelings of morbid apprehension of what could happen to a loved one —a member of her family.*]

Georgia's father was described as a robust "windmill" who talked with sweeping gestures. Except when he was troubled in his unstable occupation he was assertively jolly. At times her mother became "exhausted" and could not make the children mind. Then she would call on him to assert his authority which he did by using abusive language and becoming harsh with the children. He often threatened to "kick some sense into the kids" though he seldom did and there was a minimum of corporal punishment in the home. When he felt good he would take his family out for a ride in their car and buy them ice cream.

[*Of European background and of patriarchal religious orientation, he was using arbitrary disciplinary measures with his children who were born into the*

American jazz age. Their early home experience with authority stood in dramatic contrast with that of their peer group as adolescents. He could not understand this "new" generation. He was not occupationally unstable, but his business was subject to wide fluctuations due to an unstable market at that time. He was confused. The more his five rebellious children taunted him the more harsh he became. He loved his family in a patriarchal way.]

Georgia was the oldest of the five children. She had two brothers and two sisters. She was favored by both her parents which caused the younger brothers and sisters to rebel, especially against their "old man." This worried Georgia a great deal as she feared that they would provoke their father and that he would become harsh, lose his temper, and hurt them. He had administered several sound spankings.

[*Georgia's quiet personality expressed itself in deference to her parents' expectations. She excelled in school and assumed responsibility in the home. Part of the rebellion of her sibs was indirectly aimed at her favored role in the family. She was active in church, as were her parents. This became an object of their hostility. Whatever their parents' moral expectations, they managed to do just the opposite and succeeded in hurting their mother while infuriating their father.*]

After the death of her friend she worried more about her brothers and sisters who were bordering on delinquency.

[*Georgia's reaction was one of inner suffering, a sense of a personal loss, feelings of marked confusion and anxiety.*]

When an argument arose in the family Georgia would plead with them not to provoke their father.

[*During these family arguments she would stand and wring her hands. Occasionally she became very angry but seemed to repress it.*]

"I would do anything," she said, "to smooth things over." Thus her childhood and adolescence was characterized by feeling "close" to her family while very apprehensive about their welfare. At times she was so anxious about them that her stomach would be upset for several days.

> [*This gastric reaction was directly related to the periodic flare-ups in the family. Her first reaction would be nausea and vomiting, followed by lesser stomach discomfort.*]

A recurring dream during her adolescence was of a large dark object coming through one of the windows of the house to hurt members of the family while she, in panic, struggled powerlessly to go to their assistance.

> [*Following the discharge of extreme anxiety in a dream she felt exhausted and was socially withdrawing and silent for the next several days.*]

During later adolescence the children seemed to turn to Georgia for advice and guidance, a role that she had been playing and continued to assume.

> [*At this time Georgia got a job which, together with her school work, kept her away from home most of the time. Her brothers and sisters identified her less and less with their parents. She took their part more, realizing that her father was very arbitrary on occasion, while her mother ineffectually withdrew more into church activities.*]

Greg's father was a prosperous mill owner and operator, a rough-and-ready man who enjoyed getting a double-bit axe in his hands and felling the biggest tree in the stand. He was in effect a harsh disciplinarian though not from intent, who had great expectations for Greg's future.

> [*Greg's father came from a landed European family that had rebelled and come to America. His grandfather was a talented and skillful man but a heavy drinker who would be harsh at one moment and seek sympathy another. Greg's father rebelled at his father and ran away during his adolescence, but returned*

later to take over the mill that the grandfather had built as a pioneer.]

Greg's mother was a sociable, easy-going woman who let Greg do just about anything that he wished. She strove to please her husband and exacted little from Greg except to "do as his father wished." She was highly approving of her son's every achievement.

[*Greg felt close to his mother during the early years. He shared every confidence with her including the details of his adolescent sex experimenting. When Greg felt that his father was exacting too much from him in hours of work at the mill his mother would intercede in Greg's behalf. Her leniency in raising Greg was sometimes the basis for arguing between Greg's father and mother.*]

Greg took to the ways of the logging community and its rough-hewn men. He literally fought his way through childhood and adolescence.

[*Being husky, healthy, and well coördinated in body movements, Greg fared very well in the many physical contests and fist fights that took place in his peer group. He was aggressive in an assertive rather than hostile way.*]

The demands on Greg were to work hard and "get the goddam timber out." Little else was expected.

[*Greg worked well with his father who took an interest in his development. Their only differences were over what Greg sometimes regarded as excessive hours and the boredom of some of his jobs.*]

Greg and Georgia met during their first year in college. He said that he was attracted to her "warmth and feeling of closeness when with her. She was so open and held nothing back. The first time that I saw her on a date we were double dating. The way that she cuddled up to the fellow she was with really did something to me. I guess that it was love at first sight."

[*Greg referred several times to her "modest" lack of*

inhibitions. He was apparently strongly attracted to her physically. His reference to her figure, complexion, retiring manner was expressed in a tone of strong affirmation.]

At first Georgia was not attracted to Greg. She felt that he was too demonstrative and somewhat boorish. Even though she accepted his invitations to go out she continued to date another boy. Greg pursued her ardently and constantly. She finally accepted his ring and agreed to go steady with him.

[*Later in a flicker of insight, Georgia indicated that Greg was so much like her father that it "rather scared" her, and that his presumed "boorishness" was a defensive reaction that served to rationalize her ambivalence toward him. His continued affirmation of her broke down the defense enough for her to become increasingly involved in him.*

The ring was not regarded as a token of engagement at this time. It served more as a "pin" on a college campus.]

"As I came to know him," she said, "I found that I admired his strength and his ability to get things done. I felt that he was ambitious and would get somewhere. At first I was somewhat afraid of him as he had a reputation in the community of being quite fast. He always respected me though. I must admit that I liked the way he pursued me. In his arms I felt so safe and came to respect the many things that he could do." The following year they were married.

[*They were both becoming seriously involved, now spending most of their time together alone. She had come to admire his aggressiveness and pursuit; he, her "warm" affirmation. Whatever Greg's threat to her as a symbolic parental figure, or that his reputation might have posed, it soon passed and she seemed to respond to him without reservation. At this time their plans for marriage crystallized rapidly.*]

They both said that they were "supremely happy," until several months later. As Georgia expressed it, "Greg was too impetuous to wait for the draft so he joined up." (This was during the early part of World War II.)

> [*Both felt that their initial adjustment had been very good. However, the scaling-down process set in early. Some of their personal needs were being met but there were other social and psychological needs that were not being fulfilled. Part of his "impetuousness" was due to the pressure of the community, and not wholly a reflection on his continuing need for challenging new experience in the marriage.*]

He took the action over her wailing protests. As the bus pulled away Georgia's tight-lipped resolution not to show her feelings broke through and she fell limp into the arms of Greg's father. The following days and weeks she described as a "living hell," with her recurring childhood dream to provoke restless and tearful nights.

> [*The action that Greg took was a shock and a blow to Georgia. She felt deeply ambivalent toward Greg and the "military." Her old fear of being abandoned was revived. On the one hand she felt that Greg had acted hastily and that it was not necessary for him to go at this time. On the other hand she felt that it was his duty to go sooner or later and that she would have to accept the fact.*]

When he returned on leave she said that she was "supremely happy" again.

> [*They both regarded his brief leaves as reliving their honeymoon. His parting was very painful but she was more able to control her emotions on the surface.*]

During the years Greg was in service Georgia gradually took hold of herself and went to work as a secretary in her father-in-law's mill.

> [*In Greg's presence Georgia was forced by the weight of his assertive, dynamic personality into the social and psychological background. In his absence she was much more autonomous and socially and psychologically adequate.*]

During this period she turned more to his parents than she did to her own family.

> [*With Greg gone his parents turned to Georgia and treated her as their own child. She felt their affirmation, on an adult level. They took her out with them and included her in their weekend house parties. Greg's parents were very permissive with Georgia. She thrived on his mother's affirmation of her. His mother played much the same role to Georgia as she did to Greg. Georgia continued to worry about her own family, but much less.*]

She described her feelings during this time as "suspended," having no particular interest in anything, not even her painting that had once provided a refuge. However, she found new girl friends at the mill. By the end of the three years that Greg was away, Georgia had gained considerable emotional poise and autonomy in handling her finances and other personal matters.

> [*With her girl friends Georgia seemed to feel not only equal to them but somewhat ascendant, taking considerable initiative in planning and carrying out their activities.*]

Greg returned from foreign service. He seemed to have changed little on the surface except for increased restlessness and recklessness. He was drinking "lots of beer" and driving faster. During this period of readjustment he often felt like he "just had to get out of the house and have a beer with the boys."

> [*Greg's restlessness worried Georgia. It was related to his leaving to spend time with his war buddies. when they entertained it was usually his friends who came in. The pattern of their entertaining was one of beer drinking and endless talk about their war experiences. Georgia felt left out.*]

Georgia quit her job to "take care of Greg," spending most of the day anticipating his return in the evening. When he did return he gave her very little attention. Often he was home only long enough to change his clothes and leave for the evening. She dropped her friends and had no interest except him.

[It was at this time that Georgia "often felt desperate" with all of her early feelings of being abandoned returning. She wondered if he loved her.]

She seemed to Greg to be content in her domestic role.

[Greg seemed to take Georgia for granted as he had his mother. His prior-to-marriage gang pattern had returned. He did not sense her feelings.]

When he told her he was "going out" she protested with pleas and tears, then with uncontrollable anger. Greg left just the same. He described it as follows:

"When I'd get fed up with things I felt like I just had to get out with the boys. Then she would start clinging and telling me how much she loved me. I insisted that a fellow ought to have some time of his own.

[Greg had not been close to anyone in this particular manner. His relationship with his mother was one of confidence, but he had learned to bounce in and out of his parental home at will and with no explanation. None was expected. In his early emotional relationships there was none of what he called "this holding." He did not feel consciously hostile toward Georgia, but confused and bound.]

Then she'd get kind of a wild look in her eyes and tell me that she wouldn't let me go. One night when I walked out on her she ran out of the house to where I was standing in the middle of the street and took a swing at me.

[He said that at times she became so wrought up that she would partially lose consciousness and ask in a panicky voice, "What shall I do, what shall I do . . ." When deeply provoked Georgia would retreat psychologically into panic, when, most of the time, he would try to console her and change his plans. Characteristically she would "come out of it." Now and then she became very hostile in an emotionally disorganized way, with little control.]

Somehow I felt bound—trapped—and just had to pull away. When I got home she would have the windows and doors locked and all of the lights in the house on. For several days following one of these rounds she seemed very quiet and tried hard to please me."

[*Greg said that he did not want to hurt her, but that he "could not always give in to these tantrums."*]

When Georgia was asked about this period following Greg's return from service she looked somewhat startled and concerned. "I worried a lot about Greg," she said. "I love him so much." When she was asked if she thought that he loved her she stared out of the window a moment and then said somewhat evasively, "I guess men just don't love as deeply as women do."

[*Georgia felt so insecure that she could not recognize how dependent she had become on Greg. His occupational future was unsettled as he felt that he should have more education whether he remained in the mill or did something else. He was not satisfied with the mill as a way of life and seemed to seek some intellectual interests though quite unaware of the fact at this time. Furthermore, the pace of the war met his need for action and new experience which was being stifled by Georgia's expectations.*]

Georgia said that they wanted very much to have a baby but had not succeeded in conceiving though she had undergone medical treatment in the hopes that it would be possible.

[*Their sex life continued to be one of mutual satisfaction and a mutual bond. Georgia was described as very responsive, probably because her need for affirmation was partially satisfied in the sex relationship. Likewise it was an emotionally expressive experience for Greg, serving perhaps, as an emotional safety valve and pacifier, and as an outlet for his assertiveness.*]

About a year later a girl was born. Georgia felt that the child's arrival meant much to both of them. Greg had regained his interest in the mill and expressed a desire to go back to college on his G.I. allotment.

[*Greg had been encouraged by his parents to go*

back to college. This tradition and expectation was in their family background.]

Georgia seemed to have become deeply engrossed in the baby, expressing less possessiveness toward Greg.

[*Georgia visited her family occasionally but had continued to grow away from them. Greg's mother and Georgia now spent considerable time together.*]

He, in turn, felt less compelled to run out and leave her. There was some evidence that he was threatened somewhat by the baby's presence, by her demands on Georgia's time and energy. The total marriage relationship had improved.

[*He felt that she should leave the baby more and be free to go out with him. He seemed to have remained quite insensitive to Georgia's expectations that he "help more with the baby and relieve me a little with the house work." The baby was somewhat of a pawn, an object of their pulling in different directions—she holding on and he pulling away. However, their total relationship had improved considerably.*]

Approximately 15 months had passed between the time the baby was born and Georgia's first consultation with the writer. When asked about the present situation Georgia said that things "were going quite well but . . ." and then hesitated.

[*Both Greg and Georgia seemed to be vaguely aware of the mutual frustration of their deeper personality needs but were still dealing with their problems on a surface level with little insight into the deeper bases of their difficulty.*]

"Maybe I expect too much of Greg and I guess that it's my fault, but I don't seem to be able to get him to help much around the house. . . . He is interested in the baby but acts like he is more interested in fishing and hunting than in either of us when he gets a day off. I somehow feel that I don't quite possess him.

[*The pattern of her clinging and his pulling away was expressed in virtually every aspect of their marital interaction. They had their moments of release from the emotional bog, but the continued frustration was now beginning to express itself in physical symptoms. Georgia's health was "just not good." Greg continued to express his frustrations in restless striving.*]

Things are much better than they were a year ago but he's still restless and seems disappointed if I can't get a baby-sitter on the spur of the moment so that we can go out. We seem to be going out all of the time. I just wish that we could spend more evenings home together . . .

[*When they did go out it was Greg who made the arrangements. She went willingly for the most part, but took no initiative socially. She would have preferred to go out much less.*]

He likes his work at the mill all right but I don't think that he is satisfied because he gripes a lot about labor conditions. He had a run-in with a labor leader one day and came home confused and angry.

[*With greater responsibility in his work it had become more challenging but also more frustrating.*]

The fellow must have had quite a line. Since then, Greg has talked about going back to school and getting his law degree."

[*This was one of the precipitating factors that led Greg to reënter college later. The assertive and competitive in his personality had been challenged. It also provided a stimulus to his "intellectual" awakening.*]

She then returned to herself and said that perhaps some of her fatigue was due to her worry about their future.

[*She was not worried about their financial future, but their relationship. She felt that she had made little headway in her desire to win Greg's deeper involvement in her life.*]

After speaking of her fatigue she asked, "Do you think that having sexual intercourse nearly every night could make me so tired?" She indicated that it was pleasant and that she "responded" nearly every time and had "no complaints whatever" except that she had "learned somewhere" that frequent intercourse could be enervating.

[*She seemed to have no real doubts about their sex relations but used them in an attempt to find a reason for her feeling of fatigue, without having to face the painful reality of the deeper bases of their relationship.*

In both their backgrounds was a rather strong moralistic orientation with regard to sex which could provide some "theoretical" doubt that was largely erased by their sex adjustment.]

Later Greg said that, "Everything in the sex department is O.K. She is very responsive. I must admit though that any good looking dame gets another look . . . I kid the girls in the office at the mill and Georgia sometimes acts a little jealous but she knows that there's nothing to it . . . I don't think there's any problem here. It's my restlessness that worries her and, as she says, she doesn't feel that she possesses me."

[*If she had not been responsive and affirming sexually it is quite possible that their marriage would have had little basis for continuing. This adjustment apparently served to carry them through many difficulties. Neither was aware of the possible compensatory element in their sex relationship.*]

The relatively full account of their backgrounds was made possible by the fact that both were sincerely and deeply interested in getting at the roots of their problem. They came in for consultation together for most of these early sessions. The functions of the counselor during this period were largely support and diagnosis and there was no attempt to deal with deeper feelings or orientations at this time.

As counseling continued and they felt that they could talk more freely, their deeper feelings came more to the fore. At this time they decided that Greg should remain in the mill on a part time basis and work toward his law degree. Georgia was encouraged to leave the baby with the good help that was available, and decided to take courses in her art and in child development at the university near the mill town. She had been a good student in high school and responded readily.

If they had been in a community where clinical treatment was available and had they been aware of this possible source of help, they could have both benefited from psychotherapy. With a relatively few weeks of marriage counseling they had become self-confident enough to take the remedial steps that they did. As they discussed their marriage they recognized increasingly the deeper bases of their mutual frustration. There was no pattern of divorce in either of their backgrounds, and there was no pattern of infidelity among Greg's friends. These facts eliminated two possible complications which might have arisen. On the surface this marriage will appear to be a good one to their community. Beneath the surface it will have its ups and downs. The more they come to understand the deeper bases of their difficulty in a context that is assuring rather than threatening, the less vulnerable they will be to their former more extreme feelings. The more they understand one another's deeper feelings and what has caused them, the more they will avoid those situations that would provoke these remaining latent reactions, and the more they will work toward genuine mutual autonomy on the one hand and genuine mutual dependency in their pair relationship, on the other. Their training and experience at the university could well provide further social and psychological confidence, support, and increasing insight.

It is the belief of this writer that if Greg and Georgia could have understood the deeper bases of their own and one another's basic personalities, and the social and psychological backgrounds of their development, they could have undertaken corrective and ameliorative steps much earlier. Considerable pain and marital dislocation might have been prevented and avoided. Such understanding is not beyond the ability of relatively intelligent people, who have not been too emotionally disturbed, and who have the opportunity and the will to learn.

BASIC PERSONALITY AND MARITAL INTERACTION

The foregoing patterns of marital interaction, illustrative of the theoretical "ideal types" postulated at the beginning of this chapter, will be found frequently on the American marital scene. The details vary widely from case to case. Some marriages that correspond to a given mode may be made up of relatively provincial and boorish persons. Others of the same mode will be cosmopolitan and sophisticated. The identity of the mode is apparent.

In the case of the Carters we see a socially affirming, potentially aggressive, immature girl and a self-centered, competitive, aggressive, neurotic boy meeting one another's role expectations at the time of their marriage. In the scaling-down process following marriage she became more autonomous and aggressive. Their marriage drifted into a pattern of mutual, competitive hostility.

In the case of the Mansfields we see two relatively immature but not neurotic persons, she socially affirming and ascendant, while he was socially active and emotionally passive. He failed to meet her emerging dynamic and intellectual needs. Frustrated, she inadvertently sought another, whose basic personality seemed to fulfill her expectations. Finally she resigned herself to what appeared to be a marriage of partial fulfillment. There was frustration and anxiety but little hostility involved in their relationship.

In the case of the Aldens two rather immature and somewhat neurotic persons were attracted on a basis of mutual dependency, his active, assertive outward manifestation of basic personality notwithstanding. Her pattern of morbid anxiety was drawn toward his compulsiveness, and vice versa. Both needed boundless intimate affirmation, but neither was able to offer this kind of love. Incipient aggression was occasioned by mutual frustration of needs and expectations, but their marriage was not one of hostility (on an intermediate rather than depth level of analysis). Their marriage was moving more toward social and intellectual interests and satisfactions rather than social striving and activity.

This theoretical frame of reference, which considers the basic personality of each of two persons in marital interaction, provides a means of anticipating deeper personality needs and expectations that might otherwise remain hidden beneath socially manifest roles. Furthermore, knowing the make-up of basic personality provides clues to the *latent and potential needs* as well as the growth potential of the couple as individuals and as a pair. And not least, theoretical knowledge of the *immature and neurotic accompaniments* of modes of basic personality provides invaluable clues to the nature and meaning of the frustrations of the individuals in a marriage, and the nature of the incompatibility, i.e., what the individuals are striving for and how they fail to achieve it through one another.

Experience in teaching college students to apply this theory in the analysis of premarital and marital interaction has shown that there is a typical sequence of student reaction and growth. First, there is a tendency to place persons in neat categories—A-type, B-type, or C-type. The second stage of analytic growth is indicated by a change in language, with increasing emphasis on *strength* of component A, component

B, and component C in *each* of the pair." A third stage is seen in the student's search for the anticipated *and* the more unusual characteristics of components in a larger *pattern* of "total" personality. What starts out as a grossly oversimplified classification of types and then traits, develops into the ability to see *patterns* of personality (more extended roles) in *dynamic situational contexts.* Of course, the degree of competence attained by persons in the analysis of marital interaction varies greatly from student to student, depending on intellectual and emotional maturity, motivation, and human relations skills.

As a final consideration, it should be said that the purpose of developing skill in the analysis of marital interaction is not to make everyone a clinician. It is to help persons to deal with marriage realistically and effectively by considering not only what is *manifest* in what people say and do but also the *latent* meaning of their actions.

At first, the art of not accepting all things on their face value but moving to the deeper truth of the matter, may seem to result in undue introspection and preoccupation with the search for hidden motives in the analysis of others. But this is a passing phase. Like with a child learning to talk, each new word will be over-repeated and indiscriminately applied and then pass into its rightful place in his vocabulary. It is comparable to the first serious introduction to the study of medicine. There are the thoughtful and often sleepless nights wondering about the new disease syndroms just introduced and the inevitable question, "Have I got it?"

To look at the deeper (often more primitive) motivation in ourselves is at first threatening. This will pass through the following stages: (1) critical "analysis" (suspicion?) of the hidden motives or latent meaning of others; (2) critical "analysis" of one's self; (3) deeper understanding of others and the self resulting in an orientation of "objective compassion"—a deeper appreciation of the nature of and acceptance of the weaknesses and limitations of oneself and others, accompanied by a freedom from defensive or morbid preoccupation with oneself or with others.

Such is a significant step in freeing the human spirit in its intellecutal and emotional development. This is a significant step toward placing marriage on a higher level of reality, free to be experienced with greater spontaneity and creativity and less encumbered by the blind forces of the more primitive in human nature.

Chapter 16

PATTERNS OF PRODUCTIVE MARRIAGE

WE GROW through one another. The sociopsychological portraits of the marriages presented in this chapter illustrate the patterns of living that characterized each couple as they moved through life, and the growth and development of each as a person in the marriage. They are marriages in which each person achieved personal autonomy, productivity, and a cosmopolitan outlook, and in which patterns of living developed with distinctive kinds of pair unity. The marriages and family relations portrayed here are not presumed to be examples of the "successful" or "ideal," though they may be regarded as such by some people. They are, however, examples of real rather than fictional couples who confronted and worked through the kinds of experiences that have destroyed many marriages, and, through the struggle, achieved patterns of living that resulted in the production of much that is judged by many to be a significant contribution to the world.

These individuals had to struggle against almost insurmountable social, psychological, and ideological obstacles. They experienced the highlights and the shadows—tragedy bordering on despair on the one hand and the widest acclaim ever accorded by a world citizenry, on the other. And, not least in choosing these particular couples to present here, they honored and respected one another in the pair relationship without sentimentality or idealization of the marriage, recognizing with modesty the many weaknesses and imperfections inherent in their marriages.

It may seem unfortunate to some that the people presented here are controversial figures in nearly every respect. But, so were the prophets! We may disagree on the value of the contributions of their lives. However, this should not blind us in our attempt to understand more fully the different patterns of their marriages and their growth and development as persons through the marital relationship.

ELEANOR AND FRANKLIN DELANO ROOSEVELT: AN "OFFICIAL" FAMILY

The marriage and family life of the Roosevelts is not unlike an increasing proportion of families of upper-middle-class Americans who are becoming "official" families in the social and psychological sense of the term—business and industrial executives, members of the professions including the clergy, officeholders in state and national government, career military personnel, and others. Some have concluded that marriage and family responsibilities are incompatible with their projected "official" roles. The great majority have not, and they have married and had families. They have faced and will continue to face many of the problems of growth and adjustment that confronted the Roosevelts. The marriage and family relations of the Roosevelts will have relevance for many couples, not only as an example of an "official" family, but also as a "private" family.

Eleanor and Franklin D. Roosevelt were both born into old American upper-class, landed families in central New York State where the family patterns were traditionally patriarchal.

Franklin was born and buried at Hyde Park, his ancestral home. The land was the heritage of his father. The sea nearby, which became so much a part of his early life, was his heritage from his mother's side, the Delanos. His childhood and youth are symbolized in his spacious study which he filled with mounted birds from the nearby forest, models of ships sailed by the Delano china merchants on the seven seas, and books that lined the walls. He was close to his father until the latter's death when Franklin was still very young. His mother looked on proudly and affirmingly at her son's active and expansive development. There was a strong sense of familism rooted in both the land and the sea. Hyde Park was home. That is where the families from both Eleanor's and Franklin's side met. As Eleanor remarked recently, "It is a house that feels like it was lived in."[1] It was there that they met as children, where her early memories as a small child are of him carrying her around the ancestral halls "piggy-back."

Eleanor was also a Roosevelt, Franklin's cousin once removed. Her early memories are of her mother whom she regarded as a very beautiful woman. Characteristically, during the early period in her life, she remembers the late afternoons

[1] This is one of a number of statements Mrs. Roosevelt made recently in expressing her feeling about the importance of a homestead "rooted" in the tradition of family sentiment. "Wide Wide World," National Broadcasting Company program, January 6, 1957.

when her mother would have the three children in to spend some time with them. "Little Ellie" and her younger brother adored their mother and never had to be reproved. They called the baby, Hall, Josh. He sat upon his mother's lap contentedly during these visits.

Eleanor always felt a curious barrier between herself and the other three, despite her mother's great effort to make her feel a part of them. She read to Eleanor, had her read in return, encouraged her to recite her poems, and had her linger after the two boys had been taken to bed. But Eleanor has always remembered standing in the doorway, apart from her mother, and the look in her mother's eyes and the tone in her voice as she said, "Come in, Granny." Her mother often commented on Eleanor being such a ". . . funny child, so old-fashioned." Eleanor felt so sensitive, so ashamed, and set apart from the boys.[2] In spite of this she admired her mother greatly and sought to sleep in her mother's room when she dressed to go out so that she might be allowed to watch her and to touch any part of her mother, "the vision which I admired inordinately."[3]

Thus, attention and admiration were the things that Eleanor wanted and sought throughout her childhood. She felt conspicuous and that nothing about her would bring her admiration.

In contrast to her husband, Eleanor's childhood was one of social as well as emotional austerity and unhappiness. When she was about 8 her brother whom she described as "angelic" died of diphtheria. This was followed soon by the death of her beloved mother and then, two years later, the death of her father. She became a young orphan in the charge of her ma-

[2] Eleanor Roosevelt, *This Is My Story,* New York, Harper, 1937, p. 17.
[3] *Ibid.,* p. 13.

ternal grandmother. Her upbringing was firm, proper, and emotionally austere in the extreme.

It is family legend that Franklin first met Eleanor when she was about 2 years old and they played together in the halls at Hyde Park. A remote cousinly relationship continued for many years though they met very infrequently. While at Groton Franklin once wrote his mother that his cousins Teddy Robinson and Eleanor Roosevelt might be invited to a house party. He said that they would ". . . go well and fill out the chinks." They met again about two years later in a Pullman en route to Hyde Park, and talked together. Later they met intermittently at family parties and at dances.

Franklin was attracted to Eleanor and became fond of her. At this time when she was about 18, she had an interest in slum children and helped out at the Livington Street Settlement House. There, to her own amazement, she taught calisthenics and fancy dancing. She regarded herself as "a serious young lady." On occasion she would allow Franklin to call for her there. The children crowded around them curious to know if he were her "fellar," an expression that meant nothing to her at the time. Franklin was still at Harvard but saw Eleanor intermittently.

It was in 1903 that Franklin discovered his love for her, and later that year asked her to marry him. She accepted at once.

There loomed, however, one obstacle to their marriage. It was his mother. Not that she disliked Eleanor. On the contrary, Mother Roosevelt was fond of her. It was simply a matter of her being unable to imagine anyone taking him in the springtime of his youth—her precious, blossoming, only son! Even though Franklin was 21, he was too young, she thought, and so Mother Roosevelt set out in a most patient and tactful way to break the engagement or prevent them from actually marrying for as long as possible. In December, 1904, a year later, Mrs. Roosevelt accepted the inevitable. Official announcement of the engagement was made.

At the time of the wedding Franklin was studying law at Columbia. Immediately following the wedding the young couple stayed at Hyde Park for a week. The honeymoon was postponed until the following June when they spent several months in Europe.

Upon their return from Europe the young bride found that she was to be completely taken care of by her mother-in-law. Mother Roosevelt had planned, arranged, and furnished their new living quarters down to the last curtain rod and dishpan. Furthermore, the matriarchal role did not concern itself only with the mundane. Eleanor discovered that every aspect of her life was now to be dominated by Franklin's mother.

Shortly thereafter the young couple moved to a house of their own on East 65th Street in New York City, but Mother Roosevelt was not to be outmaneuvered. She had bought the house for them and the one next to it for herself. She had the two brownstones connected with a vestibule and interconnecting rooms upstairs. To complete her project she furnished both houses completely.

Mother Roosevelt had a strong feeling about holding the family together in matriarchal style. She wanted her children and grandchildren about her. Eleanor had long been inured to such expectations, and became completely dutiful. She never "dreamed of asking for anything" which would not meet with her mother-in-law's expectations.[4] Mother Roosevelt did

[4] John Gunther, "Roosevelt in Retrospect," *Omnibook,* December, 1950, p. 112.

not act overtly as a tyrant. She loved her children in her way. She worked indirectly to achieve her ends. The manipulation of money was one of her chief strategies. She believed that her children should work, but she wanted them home under her guidance and supervision. Keeping them financially dependent, she thought, was one way of keeping them near, whether they stayed with her or she went to them. She was generous in giving Franklin and Eleanor anything that she felt was necessary even though both had independent incomes of their own. She was even more generous with her grandchildren as they came along. Though she disliked extravagances of any kind she was often extravagant with the grandchildren. Later when Franklin was struck with polio his mother was unbounded in her generosity, but there was still a string attached—her desire that he, in return, would retire to Hyde Park with her.

Franklin's mother never seemed to accept the personal autonomy of either Franklin or Eleanor. She often complained that she never saw Franklin alone, though they disagreed when they were by themselves for very long. Following the first years of their marriage, there was evidence of their movement away from his mother's psychological orbit into that of their own marriage. As time went on Franklin became more annoyed at his mother's attempt to direct his every thought and deed. He was more impatient when she reminded him of his coat and rubbers as he left the house or asked whether or not he was wearing his sweater. When she wanted to entertain old friends whom Franklin did not particularly like, she would invite them to dinner and not tell him until they had arrived. Then it was too late to do anything about it.

As the years passed Franklin became more determined to

do what he wanted, though he always maintained great respect and love for his mother. The pattern of the relationship, however, did not change, even after he had become President. Eleanor tells a story that characterizes it: The King and Queen of England were having dinner with the Roosevelts. They were sitting in the library at Hyde Park waiting for their guests. Franklin had requested that a tray of cocktails be prepared. They were ready, set before him. Mother Roosevelt was sitting opposite him, near the fireplace, looking most disapprovingly at him and the cocktails. Finally she suggested that the King and Queen would prefer tea. "My husband," recalls Eleanor, "who could be as obstinate as his mother, kept his tray in readiness, however." Finally the guests arrived. "As the King approached my husband and the cocktail table my husband looked up at him and said: 'My mother does not approve of cocktails and thinks you should have a cup of tea.' The King answered, 'Neither does my mother,' and took a cocktail."[5]

Franklin chose the opposite course in bringing up his own children. He had the strong feeling that his children should be allowed to make their own decisions and learn by their mistakes. So extreme was he in the matter that friends suggested that he might give them more guidance than he did, but he insisted that they must find out for themselves.

Eleanor's psychological separation from her mother-in-law emerged gradually from the complete deference to her during the early years of marriage. Mother Roosevelt was distressed when Eleanor was not always available as she had been when they were living in New York. Eleanor wrote her fewer letters, asked fewer questions, and shared fewer con-

[5] Eleanor Roosevelt, *This I Remember,* New York, Harper, 1949, pp. 195–196.

fidences. She was thinking things out for herself and, she felt, becoming more of an individual. However, there was no overt protest or retaliation, quite the opposite. Eleanor joined the Monday Sewing Class of which her mother-in-law had always been a member. The ladies met to sew, talk, and enjoy one another's company. It gave them time together on a definite basis that served to quell Mother Roosevelt's feelings of being abandoned or of losing her young brood. As Eleanor commented, ". . . I had begun to realize that in my development I was drifting far afield from the old influence. I do not mean to imply that I was better for this. Far from it, but I was thinking things out for myself and becoming an individual. Had I never done this, perhaps I might have been saved some difficult experiences, but I have never regretted even my mistakes. They all added to my understanding of other human beings, and I came out in the end a more tolerant, understanding and charitable person. It has made life and the study of people more interesting than it could have been if I had remained in the conventional pattern."[6]

When FDR was elected to the New York State Senate, the family moved to Albany. "For the first time I was going to live on my own;" writes Eleanor, "neither my mother-in-law nor Mrs. Parish was going to be within call. One did not use the long-distance telephone in those days as we do today. I wrote my mother-in-law almost every day, as I had for many years when away from her, but I had to stand on my own feet now, and I think I knew that it was good for me. I wanted to be independent. I was beginning to realize that something within me craved to be an individual. What kind of individual was still in the lap of the gods!"[7]

[6] *Ibid.*, pp. 325–326.
[7] *Ibid.*, p. 171.

It was at this time, just as their marriage was being launched under its own colors, that fate in the form of polio struck and Franklin was rendered what he thought to be a helpless cripple. In his anguish and despair he was torn between the advice of his wife and the tugging of his mother. His mother wanted him to retire completely to Hyde Park where she could take care of him personally. Eleanor, with the help of their good political and family friend, Louis Howe, convinced Franklin that his discouraged outlook on life would be changed if he could keep in contact with politics. Through her interest in the League of Women Voters, the Women's Trade Union League, and the Democratic State Committee, she was maintaining and expanding the political contacts that they needed. The last great issue with her mother-in-law had been won.

During these fateful years when Eleanor was preoccupied with her husband and his future and the expectations of his mother, her two younger sons were maturing to the point where they commanded more of her attention and concern. There was the matter of their English nursemaid who, Eleanor felt, was keeping them well enough, but was too strict. She resolved this problem by finding a young Swiss girl who turned out to have a "wonderful" influence on the boys. Franklin was struggling with tremendous determination and effort to do a great many things that would enable him to be more active. He was in no position to assume the active role of father to his sons. Eleanor realized that she would have to assume the responsibility of seeing that they learned to swim, hike, ride, and do the other things that boys did. She had never done any of these things and had no confidence in her untried ability in physical activities. She concluded that there was but one thing to do: learn. She started by taking driving lessons. Some time and two accidents later she felt confident enough to take them on a camping trip. At the same time she was learning to swim at the YWCA. "Through sheer determination" her self-confidence grew until she felt that she had become proficient enough to be "a good deal more companionable and more of an all-around person than I had ever been before." With the arrival of spring she packed the two youngest boys in their car, together with a maid, two tents, a stove, pots and pans, a Red Cross Kit, a few clothes, and headed north through New York State into Canada.

Eleanor Roosevelt has always blamed herself and indirectly her husband for the personal and domestic problems of their children. Many factors were involved—the severity of their nurses, their early enrollment in boarding school, their father's physical disability with the restriction of his activities and his ties with his mother, their frequent moving, and later, the fact that they were an "official" family with virtually no opportunity to live as a family.

Regarding nurses she commented, "The mistakes I made when my children were young may give some help or consolation to some troubled and groping mother! The fear I had of my very well trained nurses which led me to allow my children to be punished very often far more severely than would have been the case had I been taking care of them myself, is something which I hope many young mothers will remember. It is not only fear of the nurses but one's own timidity as a nurse which makes one do things against one's better judgment."

By the time their youngest son, John, entered Groton, Eleanor had come to feel quite ambivalent about boarding schools. "I had by then come to feel that once a child went to boarding school there never again could be the ties and the dependence on the family that had existed up to that time. I had never been a convinced advocate of boarding school for the twelve-year-old boy, but it was a tradition . . . I still believe it is too early an age and a loss both to the parents and to the children . . ."[8]

During the years of Franklin's governorship and presidency, especially the years of national emergency and war, Eleanor was confronted with the personal problems of the "official" family. She noted that he found it increasingly difficult to take time for his boys' interests, to participate in their guidance, and to give them the advice that they sought. "One after the other, James and Elliot learned through bitter experience, and it was a bitter disillusionment as well."[9] In order to talk to him privately the children had to get an appointment with their father. On one occasion one of the boys had something important that he wanted to talk over with his father. He obtained an appointment. When he was finally admitted to the President's study he found his father absorbed in a paper he was holding. The President was "kind and gentle as he always had been with the children," but was preoccupied with the document. Finally, the boy asked his father if he was listening and his father answered "Yes" but remained silent until the boy paused and then looked up at him, handed him the paper that he was reading, and said, "This is a most important document. I should like to have your opinion on it." Franklin's son looked at it, commented briefly, then rose and left the room.

The boy was indignant. His mother tried to assure him and

[8] *Ibid.*, p. 43.
[9] *Ibid.*, p. 17.

help him understand that his father was deeply engrossed in a peace message to the world, and that he had paid his son a great compliment in attempting to share it with him. The boy was not to be reconciled, however, and closed the matter by saying that he would never again try to discuss anything personal with his father.[10]

Another of Eleanor's concerns as wife and mother of a family in public life was the fact that she felt her husband to be wholeheartedly hated by some persons and loved just as strongly by others, and that these attitudes would of necessity be projected onto the children. She was disturbed that they should be the objects of extended special privilege on the one hand, and of envy and malign gossip on the other.

"I quite understood their dissatisfaction," she wrote. "Their early marriages came about largely because they were not really rooted in any particular home and were seeking to establish homes of their own."[11] Eleanor seemed to be speaking about "roots" in the literal and figurative sense. She felt that Franklin had never quite made the break with his mother and had thus never felt the desire to build a home of their own. When they entered the White House, she felt that their personal life as a family largely had come to an end.

Eleanor Roosevelt had always placed duty ahead of personal preference and felt that she should dedicate herself to her husband's interests and concerns. Dinner in the evening was about the only time that she saw him, and their conversations were largely concerned with affairs of state. He came more and more to seek her judgment and opinion, but there was so little time. She learned to save anything personal

[10] *Ibid.*, pp. 19–20.
[11] *Ibid.*, p. 18.

that she wanted to tell him until he was in bed. If she found anything that she thought would interest or benefit him she would place a copy of it on his bed stand.

Reflecting on this latter part of their marriage she wrote:

> Before we went to Washington in 1933, I had frankly faced my own personal situation. In my early married years the pattern of my life had been largely my mother-in-law's pattern. Later it was the children and Franklin who made the pattern. When the last child went to boarding school I began to want to do things on my own, to use my own mind and abilities for my own aims. When I went to Washington I felt sure that I would be able to use opportunities which came to me to help Franklin gain the objectives he cared about but the work would be his work and the pattern his pattern. He might have been happier with a wife who was completely uncritical. That I was never able to be, and he had to find it in other people. Nevertheless, I think I sometimes acted as a spur, even though the spurring was not always wanted or welcome. I was one of those who served his purposes.
>
> It is hard for me to understand now, but at the time of Franklin's death, I had an almost impersonal feeling about everything that was happening. The only explanation I have is that during the years of the war I had schooled myself to believe that some or all of my sons might be killed and I had long faced the fact that Franklin might be killed or die at any time. This was not consciously phrased; it simply underlay all my thoughts and merged what might happen to me with what was happening to all the suffering people of the world. That does not entirely account for my feelings, however. Perhaps it was that much further back I had had to face certain difficulties until I decided to accept the fact that a man must be what he is, life must be lived as it is, circumstances force your children away from you, and you cannot live at all if you do not learn to adapt yourself to your life as it happens to be. All human beings have failings, all human beings have needs and temptations and stresses. Men

and women who live together through long years get to know one another's failings; but they also come to know what is worthy of respect and admiration in those they live with and in themselves. If at the end one can say, "This man used to the limit the powers that God granted him; he was worthy of love and respect and of the sacrifices of many people, made in order that he might achieve what he deemed to be his task," then that life has been lived well and there are no regrets.[12]

When their basic personalities are considered we see them as diametrically opposed in many ways, yet complementary in other ways. His early, outward zest for life and abundant self-confidence stand in contrast to her overt lack of physical and social skill, feelings of self-insufficiency, lack of autonomy, and almost completely reflective approach to life. The intimacy of their companionship was always impaired and sometimes threatened by his unresolved relationship to his mother, their mobility, and his official duties during the national emergencies when he served as President. The emotional and intellectual austerity of their marriage would not seem a likely basis for the kind of "happiness" that is thought by many Americans to be essential to the good marriage. Personal loneliness, lack of deeper communication with her husband, the inability to establish the "roots" of family that she always so deeply cherished and strove to achieve, constituted her life largely up until the time of his death. Through all of this her personal growth and development continued as did her devotion to service. After his death, her interests turned to the underprivileged countries of the world where her tireless travel, lecturing, and consultation has continued at a pace that has worn out her retinues. Finally, she has been elected The Woman of the World of the Year by the United Nations.

[12] *Ibid.*, pp. 348–349.

Franklin was cast early into the strongly extroverted role of the doer. He seemed never to sense the more intimate needs of his wife. His work was cut out for him and he did it with the help, honor, and respect of his wife who devoted herself to the children and his projected goals.

They were both born into a social environment of ideological contrasts and became involved in the needs of others at early ages. Their lives were oriented to serving others, to duty without apparent feelings of obligation. Whatever their marriage may have lacked in intimacy and more personal communication, it seemed to have made up in a mutual sense of purpose, as articulately stated by both of them. Though they often worked unilaterally rather than coöperatively, they supplemented and complemented one another's needs.

EDITH AND HAVELOCK ELLIS: THE MARRIAGE OF TWO LITERARY ARTISTS

This was a marriage of triumph and tragedy. In the following sociopsychological sketch of two literary artists, we see a couple who attained an unusual degree of personal autonomy, intellectual companionship through which each struggled toward greater maturity, and creative literary productivity in the expression of a broad range of interests from medical psychology to the ideologies of Europe. This marriage had its weaknesses, limitations, and defects bordering on pathology, of which both Edith and Havelock were painfully aware. The account of their backgrounds and their marriage is seen largely through the eyes of Havelock who wrote his autobiography during the last 20 years of his life.[13]

Havelock was born into middle nineteenth-century Vic-

[13] Havelock Ellis, *My Life,* Boston, Houghton Mifflin, 1939.

torian England, the son of a ship's captain. At the age of 7 he sailed around the world on his father's ship. One of his early memories was being on board the ship, singing to the accompaniment of a piano, and enjoying the applause of the passengers—a role so incongruous with all of the rest of his life.

His early relationship with his father was one of social but not emotional closeness. His father was protective but permissive. He granted Havelock his wish to remain in Australia during his early adolescence, thousands of miles from his parents and his native England. There, as he later recalled, he was cast into the sea of life alone to sink or swim. "Naturally," he wrote, "I swam."

His early relationship with his mother was one of intermittent contact due to their way of life as a family with the father almost always at sea. He was close to his mother, felt an intimacy with her, and identified himself with her to a considerable degree. He described his mother as a person who was "outwardly dignified and impressive, was beneath the surface congenitally emotional, shy, nervous, diffident, anxious, frequently uncomfortable in the presence of strangers, and only able to meet many ordinary eventualities of life with an effort of will and, I believe, secret prayer."[14] He felt this to be his temperament also, only to a more marked degree.

There was little early attachment to any home or community in any geographical, social, or psychological sense. He was, however, very strongly influenced by the intellectual and ideological climate of his native England as portrayed in the many books he read while in Australia—trunks full of books that he carefully selected and were delivered by his father.

[14] *Ibid.*, p. 45.

When full grown Havelock was 5 feet 10½ inches tall and "never thickly developed," averaging about 150 pounds. He was an extremely introspective person, even at an early age. Reflecting on his early adolescence he describes himself as predisposed to extreme physical and social sensitivity. At night he experienced such "nervous excitement" that he had difficulty falling asleep though he was not disturbed by "any definite morbid impulse, phobia, or obsession but the mother liquid out of which such things crystallize is forever flowing in my veins." Throughout his life, and especially during this early period he was painfully shy, blushing from "light causes or no cause at all." To look another in the eye was painful, intimate, and gave him a "slight nervous shock causing his lips to twitch involuntarily." He found any personal display that might attract public attention very embarrassing and for him quite impossible. During his entire life he never made even a short speech in public. He found ordinary sociability in a group of strangers difficult, oppressive, absurd, and even depressing.

His physical coördination was always poor though he played the active games of children. He felt that his awkwardness was not the result of faulty training or experience but an organic lack of nervous stability. Later he often observed that the larger muscles of his arms and legs were in frequent involuntary activity.

Havelock Ellis spent most of his adolescent years in the wilderness of the Australian bush where he served as a teacher in a one-room school. Half adult and half child he taught during part of the day and then turned to his books with which he was now almost constantly preoccupied. The saucy little maidens who were his pupils were quite as mature as their tutor and in affairs of the heart precocious in comparison. He recognized transient, generalized feelings of arousal in their presence as they taunted their teacher who was so shy and reticent in response to their coquettishness.

His first feelings of more localized sexual arousal were experienced while reading alone in the bush. The fascinating new intellectual world that was revealed through his books stimulated him emotionally, with overtones of sexual response. This confused and worried him. He had read many Victorian "treatises" on the sinfulness of masturbation and the evils of sex. Though he felt his environment was one of calm routine and an external atmosphere of peace and beauty, he experienced intervals of intense unrest bordering on misery and despair. Problems of sex and religion troubled him. He felt that his mother's simple-hearted religious faith did not meet his own intellectual sense of validity and reality. Yet, the mechanical coldness of Friedrich Strauss's *Old Faith and New* impressed him as holding no faith at all and it repelled him. This, together with Drysdale's writing in *Elements of Social Science* on the dangers of seminal emissions during sleep caused the sensitive youth to brood over the problems of sex and the meaning of life. As he strode down a garden path one day he concluded that the only outcome of his dilemma would be death or to become a monk. However, he recognized this as a mood, and it passed.

We can see his great intellectual and emotional struggle with this new world that was emerging before him. At the height of this painful struggle he read Hinton's *Life in Nature*. He read it calmly without undue expectation, but in reading it again he became conscious of what he could only call "in the precise and full sense of the term, a revelation." The intellectual content of his view of life had not changed, but a profound sense of unity with nature had suddenly and unexpectedly emerged. He trod on air. Everything he viewed seemed to take on meaning and significance. The diverse intellectual and emotional channels in his personality had achieved a unity which was to remain with him throughout the rest of his life.

Havelock Ellis now recognized that this period of self-exile was a temporary but necessary retreat into isolation in order to find himself. He regarded these fateful years of mental conflict and depressed moods as important because they added intensity to his emotional nature and critical awareness to his intellect. He had experienced continual growth in his intelligence and a constantly emerging, deepening appreciation of the arts. These he regarded as more important than attaining a comfortable position or making money. This phase of his life now complete at the age of 19, he left Australia for England.

Back in England Havelock was faced with the mundane problem of making a living. His quest for knowledge remained undiminished, however, and he decided to enter school to study medicine. During the years at the university he was so caught up in his work, which he regarded as pleasure, that he suffered feelings of chronic fatigue, brought on by long hours of study and his limited reserve of energy. His mind ranged freely as he enjoyed viewing life through his own eyes rather than through the eyes of tradition. He had a tendency to synthesize knowledge though his medical studies demanded analysis. Interestingly, science *per se* held little interest for him, then or later.

He finished his medical degree but, again, this was merely a phase in his preparation for life, as he decided against practicing medicine. He felt that his "tendency to nervous apprehension and intellectual doubt" would serve well in a diagnostic role, but that he was not given to swift and decisive action which he regarded as important to the practice of medicine. Furthermore, he felt that he had too much "faith in Nature" to want to practice on her.

Toward the end of his student days Havelock met a dynamic and vivacious girl by the name of Olive Schriner. This was the beginning of a very intimate companionship. She, too, was a writer of extremely liberal ideological outlook and they found they had much in common. They attended the Lyceum Theatre where Shakespeare was frequently played, visited the London museum, took long walks together along the Strand, "joyously oblivious" to the world. They would spend much time in her apartment where they enjoyed endless conversation. Olive, quite without inhibition, introduced Havelock to sex, and was very affirming of him. He always felt it fortunate that he had such an initial partner.

For a time the thought of marriage was considered but soon dismissed. Havelock felt that she had such a powerful and physically passionate temperament that he was not fitted to play the responsive part that her personality demanded. He seemed never to regret that "inevitable" decision. Though they each married, they continued to correspond for the next 25 years, with the full awareness and acceptance of their respective spouses.

Havelock first met his future wife, Edith Lees, on one of the occasional excursions of the Fellowship. The Fellowship was made up of a group of young intellectuals interested in social reform. On this occasion Edith asked a mutual friend who "that" man was, pointing to Havelock. "That is Havelock Ellis," was the impressive reply. But Edith was not impressed. It seems that she did not like his "ill-made" clothes, about which she always remained sensitive. They were introduced and talked of indifferent subjects. Havelock, for his part, was not impressed with Edith's appearance. She had pale blue eyes and he had never found blue eyes particularly attractive. It was an inauspicious beginning for what proved to be a lasting intellectual companionship that grew in intensity throughout her life and 25 years afterward in Havelock's memory.

Havelock described Edith at the time of their meeting as a ". . . small, compact, active person, scarcely five feet in height, with a fine skin, a singularly well-shaped head with curly hair, square powerful hands, very small feet, and—her most conspicuous feature on first view—large, rather pale blue eyes . . . It was always her beautiful voice that most appealed to me, and when I came to know her more intimately, the lovely expressiveness of her eloquent underlip, as I used to call it."[15]

Edith's childhood was socially and emotionally austere in the extreme. Her mother died bearing her. Her father inherited 20,000 pounds from his grandfather, and attended the university where he acquired intellectual tastes and a love of books. He was a man of limited energy, constantly preoccupied with presumed ill health. Plunging in and out of unsuccessful business enterprises he managed to lose his entire inheritance. He was described as irresponsible, harsh, rejecting, inconsistent, morbid, irritable, nervous, and torturing.

Edith's father set out to break her sensitive will with force and punishment, but his actions only served to set her against him and heighten her individuality. He later married a woman of mediocre abilities who gave Edith no love and who employed "cutting sneers" in her relationship with the "wayward" child. Later Edith went to live with her grandmother

[15] *Ibid.*, p. 244.

who neglected her in every way, even to the extent that she suffered from malnutrition. Edith worked hard, with spurts of energy followed by nervous fatigue.

As a result of this early experience Edith hated her father and seemed to fear and resent any man who attempted to become personal with her, or imposing in any way. She also learned to become cuttingly sarcastic when deeply provoked, a personality characteristic that she never outlived.

When she was 12 her father sent her to a Catholic convent. There she experienced love and tenderness for the first time. She loved the kind and gentle nuns, and felt at peace. She decided that she wanted to join the Roman Catholic Church and become a nun. When her father learned of her intentions he flew into a tantrum and demanded that she dismiss all such thoughts. Though she did, Edith always regarded the Roman Catholic Church as the only possible form of Christian faith.

During this early adolescent period Edith was sent to a girls' school operated by a German lady. The school was geared to an ordinary and perfunctory level of education, but the school mistress aroused in Edith an intense interest in literature, especially Shakespeare and Byron, whom she was said to resemble in appearance. Together the girls read and dramatized the plays, Edith always choosing to play the male roles. She liked to act and make speeches, and to improvise a repertory of dramatic roles.

Later she returned to her grandmother's and the hard and energetic life. There she organized a small school and went about teaching her pupils in their homes. She undertook this project with "sanguine enthusiasm, reckless expenditure of energy, and lavish thoroughness."

Whenever she received any money she spent it lavishly,

always including gifts for people she loved, a characteristic that she carried through her life.

During her later adolescence and early maturity a number of young men declared their love for her, but without success.

At about the age of 21 Edith left for London where she organized a girls' school. It was an arduous struggle to make financial ends meet. During this period she spent hours in the British Museum reading room and gave lectures at the Crystal Palace School of Art on the writings of Mrs. Browning. Her intellectual restlessness resulted in overwork and nervous exhaustion. Finally after two or three years she had a severe nervous breakdown. The period of prolonged despair that followed was broken by two women. One, an elderly lady, heard of Edith's financial plight and helped her. The other, Honor Brooke, the daughter of the well-known clergyman, Reverend Stopford Brooke, took Edith into the Brooke house and nursed her along the road back to health. It was while here that she met many well-known, cultured, and refined people of London—artists, writers, clergymen, and social reformers. Reverend Brooke was himself one of the most liberal clerics of that period. His home was the meeting place for this miscellaneous group of intellectuals. As Edith's health returned, she reveled in the atmosphere, and spent her "renascent" energies doing social work in the slums. It was here that she solidified her lifelong friendship with Honor Brooke, and met Percival Chubb who was later to be the link of contact with Havelock.

The courtship of Edith and Havelock was slow in developing and never reached a high pitch of ardor in the romantic sense. From intermittent, chance meetings the relationship grew into a sympathetic companionship. They attended concerts and the theater. Much of their time together was spent in long walks.

Edith began to initiate little intimacies, as the time when she told him of another man whom she had met at the Fellowship meetings toward whom she was attracted. (Her interest was not returned by the other. It was the only man toward whom she had been attracted before meeting Havelock.) On the surface, and in the physical sense, there was little attraction for Havelock. His untidy appearance and social awkwardness in group gatherings continued to offend Edith. It was her dynamic personality and social aptness that engaged Havelock, not her appearance. However, they were discovering beneath the surface a warmth of intellectual intimacy. Even before meeting Havelock, Edith once remarked to a friend, after reading Havelock's book, *The New Spirit,* "I love the man who wrote it."

As they approached the question of possible marriage there were long discussions of their mutual, unconventional needs, orientations, and expectations. They were both fierce champions of individual freedom from any restraint, including possible restraints in marriage. They both believed in complete social and financial equality and independence in marriage. They shared a mutual feeling about the sanctity and indissolubility of marriage though they thought that it was not necessary to have it sanctified by a church wedding. While the possibility of a common-law marriage entered their considerations, they both felt that the state had a legitimate interest in the social responsibilities of marriage and therefore legal control was necessary. In regard to the affectionate aspect of their relationship Havelock wrote:

It may seem to some that the spirit in which we approached marriage was not that passionate and irresistible spirit of absolute acceptance which seems to them the ideal. Yet we both cherished ideals, and we seriously strove to mould our marriage as near to the ideal as our own natures and the circumstances permitted. It was certainly not a union of unrestrainable passion; I, though I failed yet clearly to realize why, was conscious of no inevitable passionate sexual attraction to her, and she, also without yet clearly realising why, had never felt genuinely passionate sexual attraction for any man. Such preliminary conditions may seem unfavourable in a romantic aspect. Yet in the end they proved, as so many conventionally unpromising conditions in my life have proved, of inestimable value, and I can never be too thankful that I escaped a marriage of romantic illusions. Certainly, I was not a likely subject to fall victim to such a marriage.

The union was thus fundamentally at the outset, what later it became consciously, a union of affectionate comradeship, in which the specific emotions of sex had the smallest part, yet a union, as I was later to learn by experience, able to attain even on that basis a passionate intensity of love. It was scarcely so at the outset, although my letters to her in the early years are full of yearning love and tender solicitude. We were neither of us in our first youth. I was able to look on marriage as an experiment which it remained to the end, and a unique and profound experience which she never outgrew. Yet, had anything happened to prevent the marriage, it is not likely that either of us would have suffered from a broken heart. The most passionate letters I wrote her were, as she realised, not written until some years after marriage. I can honestly say that, by a gradual process of increased knowledge and accumulated emotional experience, I am far more in love with her today than twenty-five years ago.[16]

A final consideration before their marriage was the possibility of having children. Neither Havelock nor Edith expressed any strong desires for children of their own, though Edith "was sensitive to the beauty of motherhood." At the same time she had no patience with children, though she was inexhaustible with the care of animals. When Edith went to

[16] *Ibid.*, pp. 270–271.

her physician before their marriage, he told her that she should not have children, that her background of nervous instability constituted too great a threat to her mental health should she risk motherhood.

Edith and Havelock were married in a civil ceremony attended by his sister and a number of her close friends. They bought the wedding ring together, each paying half as symbolic of their agreement to remain financially independent. They both cherished what Havelock called the "independence of their spiritual lives." Their separate financial endeavors characterized their marriage throughout, though they came to one another's financial assistance from time to time as neither ever had much money.

Both Edith and Havelock felt that the "beauty and intimacy" of their relationship was founded upon, and maintained by, their mutual independence and frequent separations. They spent about half of each year under the same roof. During the early part of their marriage they did not share a common dwelling in town, but met frequently. Edith told some near friends the story of a couple of strangers who had traveled to Cornwall in the same carriage as the Ellis' and inquired later of mutual friends who they were. Upon being told one exclaimed, "Oh, they could not have been married! They were so interested in each other, and he was so attentive!"

This central quality of a need for mutual independence is seen further in one of Havelock's letters to Edith:

My wife,

I lay on my couch this morning so happy reading over and over my letter that was so full of love. You mustn't have too good an opinion of me, darling, but you may be quite sure I have the merit of loving you! And it's rooted very deep down and I don't know what could tear it up. I don't think you need fear, Edith, that I should ever try to sap your independence; because, you know, I take quite a selfish delight in your independence; it somehow appeals to the woman element in me—and I think to the man part too. I can't imagine myself with a wife who was just my shadow without any character or will of her own. No one who liked a dependent woman would come in your direction!

I have sometimes seen in marriages of devoted couples who are never separated that when one of them dies the survivor, beneath a real grief, experiences a current of relief, able at last to go freely his or her own way without the perpetual burden of little constraints. In our relationship we were only dependent on each other for a peculiar comradeship and affection, a special mutual understanding. The things we gave each other were the unique things that no other person can ever give.[17]

Ellis further described their relationship in these words: "Yet from the day of that first kiss I hid nothing from Edith; there was never, then or later, the slightest deception, and never a stolen interview. Any such lack of openness towards the woman in the world who was nearest to me would have been impossible; it would in any case have been unpardonable when she was absolutely open to me. Whatever the difficulties might be, we met them squarely, both Edith and I, and conquered them as well as we could."[18]

The heart of the Ellis' marriage was their companionship that consisted of conversation and writing. Characteristically they would sit in their deck chairs at Carbis Bay, thinking, conversing, writing, and evaluating one another's work. They had few close friends and went out little. Edith's plays, produced on the London stage, were widely received and appreciated, but their views on social conditions, politics, and sex met with a great deal of opposition and outright hostility by

[17] *Ibid.*, pp. 291 ff.
[18] *Ibid.*, p. 318.

a Victorian England. They were hauled into court again and again though never convicted. They left England temporarily in protest, but returned to carry on their work.

Edith had never enjoyed good health. During the latter part of her 25 years of marriage her health began to fail and became progressively worse. Her long trip to America, the 6 years of separation from Havelock since he felt that he could not stand the trip, and her pace of traveling and lecturing, had weakened her. Her sexual inversion and his companionship with a mutual friend, Amy, were deeply painful to them both and probably contributed to her increasing mental confusion and physical decline. During much of her prolonged illness Havelock attended her day and night as her nurse, though he was not her doctor. He lived for about 25 years after her death.

Now and then Edith expressed to Havelock doubts about her ability to be attractive to him and to be a "fit mate." She wondered if their marriage had been a mistake and whether it might not be better for them to separate so that he might marry someone else. She never seemed to doubt her love for him. But Havelock was never convinced that their marriage was a mistake and "never at any moment" desired separation. As he wrote:

Even if in some respects it might seem a mistake, it has been my belief, deepened rather than diminished, that in the greatest matters of life we cannot safely withdraw from a mistake, but are, rather, called upon to conquer it, and to retrieve that mistake in a yet greater development of life. It would be a sort of blasphemy against life to speak of a relationship which like ours aided great ends as a mistake, even if, after all it should in a sense prove true that we both died of it at last. Each of us exhibited a constant process of spiritual and intellectual development during the whole of that quarter of a century of close intimacy. My own work in life had been more or less definitely planned before I knew her, yet it was altogether carried out, and to a more triumphant conclusion than at the outset I had even imagined, during my fellowship with her.

She on her part was developing during all that period and she only attained the complete adult maturity of her spiritual and intellectual powers a year or two before the end . . . She was far more to me than a "liberal education" to enrich, she was also a constant discipline to fortify. The presence of her naked and vital spirit moved my more dreaming and aloof spirit to a realization of the fundamental facts of living which has been beyond all estimation . . . She was my champaigne, while I was her opiate.[19]

The Ellis' will probably be remembered longest for their writing about love and sex. The following is a statement from the conclusion of his autobiography written by Havelock not long before his death:

On her voyage to America in 1914 she [Edith] formed a friendship with a woman passenger who, as her swift instinct speedily divined, was secretly engaged to the captain and later married him. "She always talked of you," this friend wrote to me after her death, "with such pride and such affection, as though the first freshness of married life had never become dulled. Perhaps you realise how much she idolised and idealised you, perhaps not." And whether I fully realised I can never myself know. But I know something of all that was expressed in the cry from the hospital at Hayle: "Havelock! Havelock!" of which after many years the echo still rings in my ears. "There are no voices that are not soon mute; there is no name, with whatever emphasis of passionate love repeated, of which the echo is not faint at last!" I know it. The beautiful voice was soon to be mute. But the emphasis of passionate love in that name repeated in the distance still leaves an echo, only to die when I am dead. That constitutes the great discovery in love that I have made. Passion

[19] *Ibid.*, pp. 271 ff.

transcends sex. I shall never belittle the great roots of sex life. I know I could not love any man as I have loved this woman. But I have discovered that the sexual impulse of physical attraction may pass away and give place to a passion that is stronger than it. That is a discovery with a significance for life and for the institution of marriage which has not yet been measured. And I smile when I see the ephemeral creatures of a day sneering at love. We who are not the creatures of a day, who live greatly, and do the work of the world, we are moved by love. So that rather than belittle love, we would even see a sense in the final extravagance of Dante, and end, as he ends, on the omnipotence of love, *"Lamour che move il sole e l'altre stelle."*

. . . To an outsider who contemplates the life we led, it may seem at times an unnatural, uncomfortable, defective, and abnormal life compared to that of all the married couples who, to outward view, lead so placid an existence of smooth routine. Yet, when one is privileged to see beneath the surface of these lives, one realises that they are for a large part dead, with boredom gnawing at the core, unreal, paralysed, selfish, fruitless. How few must the exceptions be! We at least were alive. It can rarely, indeed, have happened before that a person of the same vibratory emotional sensitiveness has been mated with a person of the same poignantly acute and manifoldly radiating energies. If we missed the placidity of inertia, we gained a greater measure than is given to most of that joy and pain which are the essence of life and we were spending our strength for what seemed to each of us the greatest causes in the world,

"to enrich
The whole world with the sense of love and witch
The heart out of things evil."

Is it not enough?[20]

Edith's capacity to "surrender" herself to Havelock, occasioned in part by her longing for him during their separa-

[20] *Ibid.*, pp. 629–630.

tions and her dependence on him during her illness, emerged during the last few years of her life. Havelock's fuller realization of her emotional need for him seemed to have emerged many years and many regrets after her death. In a sense their marriage achieved its fruition two decades after Edith had passed and just before Havelock died.

CHARLES AND EUDORA VAN DOREN: A FAMILY-CENTERED MARRIAGE

The following portrait of the Van Doren family has been drawn largely from the writing of the eldest son, Carl, in his autobiography, *Three Worlds*.[21] The Van Dorens represent a *family-centered* marriage, with their way of life deeply rooted in the farm lands of Illinois, "in a close-knit affection which the later scattering of the family has never weakened." Each of the five sons distinguished himself in some creative field, with two of the brothers winners of the Pulitzer Prize for their writing. "The Van Dorens represent a tradition of people . . . like Thoreau and Emerson. They have their roots in the 19th century. They are content and confident in themselves."[22]

Charles Lucius Van Doren was the descendant of self-reliant Pieter Van Doorn who immigrated from Holland in the 1650's. Charles grew up on the farm lands of Illinois. Like his Van Doorn forebears he felt that he must own land, and like most of them, followed a profession so that he could buy more land. He finished a medical degree at Chicago, supported in part by food sent him from home, and first began to practice by assisting his brother Silas, in Pennfield.

[21] Carl Van Doren, *Three Worlds,* New York, Harper, 1936.
[22] *Time,* February 11, 1957, p. 44.

Pennfield was a team's haul from the small community of Hope where Charles was later persuaded to go by his grandfather and a handful of other men and where he set up his first independent practice. He arrived in Hope with his entire fortune, consisting of his clothes and medicine kit, lashed to the saddle of his black horse.

The new country doctor was a "kindly" looking person and industrious, but so young in appearance, and an outsider, that he felt neglected by the community. However, whatever doubts the community had about him soon passed. Within two years he had met and married Eudora Butz, a young woman with an ambitious, dynamic temperament.

At the age of 10 Eudora had ridden a horse across the prairie to "fetch" the mailbags for her grandfather, the village postmaster. At 15 she had become the village schoolmistress, though she had attended normal school for only one year. At 20 she was the best educated woman in the village and Charles the best educated man.

With their hands, education, good health, and zest for life, they built a house in the village where their first two sons, Carl and Guy, were born. During the early years of their marriage Charles' medical practice grew as did his wife's household duties, but not enough to meet their challenge. They had saved enough to buy a farm on the edge of Hope, moved onto it, and there had their three other sons, Mark, Frank, and Paul.

The Van Doren family was now complete. With the farm income supplemented by what Charles earned practicing medicine they established a comfortable standard of living—a commodious "home instead of a shack . . . and drove a carriage instead of a wagon." Sometimes they had a "hired girl" to help in the home, but Charles worked hard alone to build fences, erect barns and sheds, increase his livestock, plant trees, and replenish his soil. His medical practice was of secondary interest, pursued as a matter of necessary service as he was called from the field to saddle his horse and make a call. Eudora valued his profession and wanted him to devote more time to it, but he remained absorbed in his land and its future with "stubborn optimism."

Carl, the eldest, was 5 years old when the family moved from the village to the farm. In his autobiography, he describes the meaning that this new way of life had for him and his brothers, the significance and the bearing it had upon his entire life: "For the whole decade of the nineties we lived there almost as independent of the world at large as if this had been still the eighteenth century." The village general store could supply many of their needs—staple groceries, overalls, bolt cloth, and sometimes even oranges or bananas were hauled in. An occasional trip by their father to a distant larger town would reward the family with fresh meat in the summer and sundry luxuries. Everything else came from the farm.

We had beef when the winter cold would keep a slaughtered steer till we, and probably some other family who shared the cost, could eat the whole of it. . . . When I was fourteen I could kill, skin, clean, and hang a wether in thirty minutes. . . . No day of the year ever stirred my brothers and me more than the day we butchered. The men built a fire under a cauldron standing on iron legs in the barnyard, and set up a wooden platform beside it. The hogs, dragged from the pen, squealed wildly while they were stuck and bled. Bloody hands plunged the fat dead bodies in the boiling water, lifted them on the platform, and scraped the bristles off with the edge of a corn knife . . . It took the whole household days to dispose of what the men got ready for us in half a day . . .

Bakers were as far away as butchers. Our own oven furnished all of our bread, which we liked best to eat when it was so hot that butter would melt into it as into a sponge. So with all kinds of biscuit and corn bread. The oven was never idle. Cakes and pies poured out of it. The pantry—always called the buttery—had a special box for cakes, a rack for pies, and a stone jar for cookies. My brothers and I were not supposed to cut a cake or pie without permission, but we had the run of the cookie jar.

Our green season began with the first rhubarb, of which we knew although we usually called it pie plant. After a winter diet, rhubarb was such a delight it seemed a tonic. Then in turn, radishes, lettuce, young onions, peas, string beans, wax beans, tomatoes, celery, parsnips, cabbage, turnips, from the vegetable garden, and from the truck garden strawberries, raspberries, blackberries, new potatoes, and roasting ears. From the earliest cherries to the last winter apples some fruit or other was always ripe. And at the end of the season there were pumpkins between the rows of corn.[23]

During the fall pits were dug for the storing of vegetables. Fruits, tomatoes, pickles, and relishes were canned; grains were stored to be ground into cereals—all in preparation for the long winter months when the family would have to be entirely self-reliant for its food.

Mother Van Doren was, for the most part, her own dressmaker. While the boys were young she sewed for them, sometimes with the help of a visiting seamstress. As they became older she continued to make their shirts and knit their wool socks, but they bought their overalls, winter coats, fleece-lined caps, and other articles of clothing at the general store. Occasionally they ordered from Chicago. Their mother was a stickler for neat appearance and appropriate dress. She ordered smart tweed suits with button shoes to match from Lilliputian Bazaar in New York, but the boys were too em-

[23] Van Doren, *op. cit.,* pp. 33–36.

barrassed to wear them often in the presence of their rougher shod, not so appreciative peers. As clothes were outgrown they were handed down to the next in size. The household was distinctly masculine in dress. Mother Van Doren seldom wore a dress. She had feminine clothes as her husband had his fedora and Prince Albert coat, but their days were made up of long hours of hard work and they dressed for it.

Father Van Doren had his office on the lower floor of one wing of their house. He saw his patients in one part of the room and put up his medicines behind a partition in the corner. His practice included everything from pulling teeth and relocating joints to delivering babies, surgery, and doctoring sick cattle. He was sometimes assisted by a young doctor just out of medical school. Most of the time, however, he worked alone. Later, Carl helped by whittling out splints or dropping chloroform on a mask preceding a tonsil operation.

Living by the seasons, so close to the soil, gave the family an intimate sense of oneness with nature and one another. They were completely caught up in living together.

My life on the farm seems to be not so much an experience ten years long, as a spacious moment in which everything happened at once. . . . I had a happy childhood in a happy family. My father was not tyrant. My mother, while sharp and quick in punishment, did not nag. And though my brothers and I often fought together, we fought, not sulked, and never carried a grudge over to the next fight. If I had to go today to a lone island with one companion, there is no living man I should prefer to any of my four brothers—though I should not know how to choose which one of them. The years at Hope, remembered more intently, seem less like a single tide than like a slow, steady wheel, turning through the seasons.[24]

As the boys grew up it was taken for granted that they would put their shoulders to the wheel, and working long,

[24] *Ibid.*, pp. 41–42.

hard days gave them a genuine sense of responsibility and identity with the family enterprise.

> I remember early days in June. Along with the whole family I got up at dawn. My father, if he had not been away all night, as he often was, rode over the farm or made plans with the men. My mother set about breakfast. The little boys rushed out of the house to play. Guy did various chores, and I went to drive up the cows, my special chore. In those fresh dawns nothing was pleasanter than to find a cow still lying down and, after I had roused her, to step from the cold grass into the warm spot where she had lain. I followed the cows at their sluggish, wandering gait to the cowshed, where they went to their own stanchions and waited ruminantly for me to milk them.
>
> To have to milk two or three cows morning and evening is to be a slave to them, I know, but I felt my slavery less than my pride in being the eldest brother and bearing this responsibility. And I enjoyed milking, even the cantankerous, tough-uddered old Shorthorn and the Jersey that kicked like a horse. Milking would give me, I had been told, a strong grip. Milking was a good time for oratory. Squatting on a three-legged stool, my head pressed against the cow's flank but my eyes alert for her lashing tail, I made up patriotic speeches, rotund and magniloquent. "By the might of his own intellect," one sentence began with a rising inflection, "and by the power of his own will," it went on with a dying fall, "Abraham Lincoln rose to the highest level in the land," with a ringing statement. I remember no more of it.[25]

Carl took his full pails to breakfast, finished eating by six o'clock, then left for the barn to hitch up the team for hours of ploughing barefoot in the "deadly sun." After twelve hours of ploughing, broken intermittently by going to the shade of the hedge for a drink from the jug of water, the boy and the horses got a second wind, ploughed the last few rows at a quickened pace, and then returned for supper on the trot. Supper, however, had to await unharnessing and feeding the

[25] *Ibid.*, p. 43.

team, milking the cows that the little boys had herded in, and finally turning the cattle out to pasture. "I must have been tired as I sprawled on the grass under a tree beside the house, but I remember only a gorged, happy languor in which my mood expanded with the shadows. Not even the close, hot nights of Illinois kept me from sleep when I went to bed at eight."[26]

The sex education of the Van Doren boys was twofold—their first-hand observation of the potent deeds of the farm animals, and the more didactic school in the barn. The barn was the men's house, seldom frequented by women. On the rainy days when it was too wet to work in the field the boys and the hired men gathered in the barn. There the hired men joked in bawdy, expansive pleasantry. There was nothing morbid or anxious in their manner. By the age of 10 the boys had had quite enough experience with animal reproduction to understand comparisons with human behavior. By this time they had about as much scientific theory as they ever would get. From their mother the boys got the impression that "love" was a sacred prelude to motherhood, and from their father that it was one of the intermittent and harmless pleasantries of marriage. Nevertheless, the talk in the barn stirred feelings and relieved curiosity and tension in the boys. They heard of the occasional couple who "got into trouble," listened to the gossip, and learned of the community forgiveness if they "married and cut out their foolishness." Adultery was practically impossible in such a close-knit community. The hired men kept everybody informed about the few in the village, some married and some unmarried, who occasionally went to Danville to drink, gamble, and have a woman.

[26] *Ibid.*, pp. 43–44.

The religion of the Van Dorens consisted more of a reverence for nature than a preoccupation with theology. It was taken for granted that they would attend the community church that had developed from their Grandmother Butz' organization of the first Sunday School in Hope. The church was served by an itinerant minister. It lacked the evangelical fervor of some other areas and was more of a community center where the families of Hope gathered on Sundays to socialize.

The boys virtually never left the farm except to attend school and church. There were few cars, no radio, movies, or telephone, and so the family entertained itself. There were the rare occasions when their mother's twin brothers came with their vivid and absorbing tales of eastern cities, college, Indians, railroads, and the booming, expanding country. "They were like windows in our plain walls," wrote Carl. Much of their leisure time was spent in reading together as a family or alone, except in the busiest planting and harvesting seasons. The boys can hardly remember when they could not read. Few new books reached Hope until Carl discovered that he could get books from Chicago through the mail. Books were the most frequent gifts for birthdays and Christmas. Their reading interests ranged widely and uncritically. The boys liked Dickens and Mark Twain best. When Carl was 9 years old, he won a five volume set of Green's *History of England*. The vivid word pictures of the Anglo-Saxons always stood out like old photographs in Carl's mind. They had the works of Scott, Dickens, Thackeray, James Whitcomb Riley, Shakespeare, and Holmes. Their mother read to them a great deal from the time they were very young. Before entering school Carl remembers his father being "tickled to tears" at the humorous verses of Holmes, and how he, Carl, cried when his mother read the story of Evangeline. And the boys stole into their father's medical library more often than he surmised, since medical books seemed to have something to do with sex and were thus held in the guarded realm of the clandestine.

When the boys were old enough to go to high school Charles and Eudora decided they would have to leave the farm and Hope so that their sons might continue their education. They had long since concluded that all five boys would have a college education.

The day of their departure arrived. Their goods were packed and loaded. Carl was driving one of the wagons. He slept heavily, then arose before dawn with the feeling that he was not leaving the land, but being torn from it, leaving a part of himself imbedded in the soil of those transcendent years at Hope. He walked out across the fields that had played such a crucial, formative role in his life and to which he would never return, then, to the barn, again to feed and harness his team. "What I felt now," he wrote, "was not the general night and day, earth and sky, but the farm itself, and the familiar ways of living there. On every rod of land I had worked or played, and I could have found my way blindfolded anywhere. The farm was in me. I had eaten it as food. I had been sheltered by house and barn and tree, in every weather. The animals were hardly less kin to me than my family. My hands knew all the tools. Some of me would stay behind. The filaments of habit and memory which bound me were tougher than I had ever realized. Even in my dissolving ecstasy I felt the pain of separation and half-foresaw a long homesickness."[27]

Their departure from Hope was marked by a surprise party

[27] *Ibid.*, pp. 55–56.

when the whole town descended upon the Van Doren farm in wagons and buggies, carrying their covered dishes. The entire lane leading from the road to the house was filled; horses were hitched to wagon gate; there were long tables of food in the yard outside the house; and of course, it was a time for nostalgic memories.

Idyllic Hope stood in vivid contrast to the comedy of errors that characterized the family's early adjustment to Urbana. The first Sunday in Urbana they went to church, the meeting house, "by familiar instinct." It was just assumed that church was the place where people get acquainted. But the boys were soon to learn that the classless society of the village, where people had the same set of friends for weekdays as on Sundays, was quite unlike the situation the family now faced. After going to church a few times the boys came to dislike it. The pastor and his sermons had never been the main attraction in going to church. They went to church to meet their friends. And when they discovered that their friends went to another church the boys rebelled. Their mother wanted to remain, thinking that it would be a snub to the pastor as well as the people who had welcomed them. Their father was not concerned but their mother was torn between her conscience and the fuss the boys were making. Reluctantly she gave in and they decided on another church.

This was the beginning of a new orientation for the family. Where their association in Hope had been on a family, neighborhood, and community basis, and a man had to be pretty much like his neighbors in order to get along with them, life in Urbana was quite different. It had its distinct groups, if not social classes. There were the townspeople, business and professional people most of whom had been born and raised there. There were the retired farmers. Still another group was the workers who lived near the railroad yards. And there were the teachers and students who made up the University of Illinois. The Van Dorens never really felt a part of any group. In a sense they were retired farmers, but the retired farmers living in Urbana had not become part of the community. Many of them had moved to town so that their children could attend the University. Their father was now a practicing physician but the family did not feel a part of the townspeople. They were, and they felt like, a family uprooted from a rural community, somehow resisting being transplanted. They felt detached, and this was the beginning of a split in the family of which they were, as yet, not conscious.

Their father remained in Hope during the first winter in Urbana, wanting to round out his first 20 years of practice there. Carl entered high school while his brothers went to grade school in another part of town. They were no longer going to the same school, with the same teachers teaching all of their subjects, but to different schools with different subjects taught in different rooms by different teachers. Their new friendships were being formed with the boys they went to school with, not with neighbors as formerly. They continued going to church until Carl was in his middle teens, but the people he met at church were not his friends, and he finally lost all interest in Sunday School. This grieved his mother very much, especially when she sensed that Carl's attitude was influencing his younger brothers. She felt that she had a bunch of little heathens on her hands.

Commenting on this period Carl wrote, "Within a few months my brothers were almost strangers to me. Except for Frank and Mark, who had started to school in the same class and stayed together to the end of college, my brothers were equally strangers to each other. We ate and slept in the same house and acknowledged the authority of the same parents. Against hostile outsiders we would have united quickly enough, if there had been any. But, left to ourselves, we took our own ways in brotherly independence. I know next to nothing about what the others did or thought or felt during the eight years I lived in Urbana. We became acquainted only after we were men."[28]

The change from farm ways to town ways came at a time when Carl was entering a period of adolescent rebellion. As the eldest, and first in so many other aspects of their family life, Carl spearheaded the boys' revolt against their parents' expectations. As usual, however, in matters of manners and morals their mother flexibly but firmly spelled out the rules for the family, with their father standing by much less concerned. Soon after they arrived in Urbana, Carl was elected president of his class which surprised him, being a newcomer. He soon took up the ways of his peers, feeling at home with them. They danced, played football, and did other things that Mother Van Doren thought frivolous, dangerous, and even immoral. Pioneer dancing in Hope was nothing like the close body contact dancing in the Urbana high school. Sprained ankles and wrenched necks resulting from football were dangerous and seemed all so unnecessary to her. But these activities were indispensable to being accepted by the group. These were more sophisticated town ways that stood in contrast to the rustic village ways.

Since Carl was elected leader of his class and had never learned to dance, he was deeply embarrassed and humiliated. When he attended parties he made up plausible excuses but he knew they were not the real reasons. His mother disap-

[28] *Ibid.*, pp. 62–63.

proved, but while he loved and respected his mother, he just had to win as a matter of moral principle. In the end he won out over his mother. She not only permitted but encouraged him to dance since she recognized that Carl was withdrawing more and more from social activities despite his participation in football, with his share of bruises and sprains. Carl had won his independence, clearing the way for Frank and Paul who played football and danced as natives to the tempo of a new way of life.

The wounds of the rebellion had served to change Carl from the boy who was completely absorbed in the ongoing stream of life, to the young man who was now sitting on the bank, observing its flow, and trying to express the meaning it held for him in writing. During the last year in high school, his intellectual interests gradually manifested themselves though there was no intellectual atmosphere at Urbana High. His friends' interests were social and muscular. He could not confide these intellectual stirrings. Some of his friends went on to the University for a while then dropped out to marry. Others married their high school sweethearts and settled down comfortably in their fathers' businesses. And, while Carl had stirrings of feeling, they were for the greater part subdued by his quest for knowledge. The seeds of intellectual curiosity had been sown years before and were now coming to fruition. His parents had set the stage and Carl, with his brothers to follow in turn, was playing a role that he had learned throughout his formative years.

Young men who are not bound to their families in neurotic dependency become restless during their later teens. Despite the closeness of the Van Dorens, Carl found himself sometimes clashing with his father and angry at his good humor.

Carl recognized, however, that it was less a conflict between him and his father and more a feeling of being too close to his family for too long. Writing about his family, Carl felt that, "With nothing but love for any of its members, I had outgrown the thing itself, and I was cramped for want of room and exercise. I wanted to live alone, with my own hours and habits, without any household." Then, following his graduation, at the age of 23, Carl decided to leave. It was the beginning of the end of the family under one roof.

The train left Urbana late at night. He was sure that his family would not make a ceremony when its eldest son left. But what was he to expect, this being another first, a new experience, the eldest setting out to find his fortune?

Supper was very quiet. Guy, now a student in architecture at the University, seemed to pay no attention to the event. Frank and Mark, both in high school, kept staring at me with their bright brown eyes. Paul, only nine, sat close beside me, fidgeting and crowding. My mother ate nothing. My father self-consciously cleared his throat.

As soon as the meal was ended, Guy got his hat. Of all of us he was the most firm about avoiding scenes.

"I'm sorry. I have to go down the street. I guess—" and his voice trailed off in a sound of apology without words.

We shook hands, and both tried to be matter-of-fact.

The evening dragged. Paul, though he was to stay up for the train, went to sleep in a chair in the library. Frank and Mark had half a dozen scuffles. My mother disappeared. My father and I talked, neither of us saying a single thing that was on his mind.

I went to look for my mother. She was lying on a sofa in her bedroom, without a light. When I came near I found she was sobbing. I did not ask her why, but stooped to whisper to her. She suddenly threw her arms around me with the strength of an emotion I had never seen in her or anybody. Her sobs seemed to me to rise from some frightening depths I did not know.

"You are the first to go away," she said. "They will all go away."

I could not comfort her. When I had to leave I felt that I was tearing myself like a tree from her breast.

Paul woke up, sleepy but clamorous about going to the station. On the platform, Frank and Mark tussled over my baggage. My father laughed at them. The train came, noisy in the night.

I shook hands solemnly with my father, who looked as if he would like to say something, many things. But he only straightened his neck, pulling in his chin in a shy way he had, and said goodby. Frank and Mark were excited. Paul put up his small face to be kissed.

I got into the train so unstrung and dissolved that after a time I could almost feel my frayed nerves slowly knit together.[29]

When World War I struck, all of the boys but Paul had left. Carl had married and achieved distinction for his teaching and writing at Columbia University. Guy, regarded as the most humorous one of the boys, had been graduated in architecture from Illinois in 1910 and settled with his uncles in Oklahoma. He had married a Danville girl and had a daughter. Mark was finishing his doctorate at Columbia under Carl and was regarded by his older brother as the most "gifted [poet] and charming of us all." Frank, the "handsome" one, followed in his father's footsteps and became a farmer. Paul, then 18, the most "shrewd and worldly," was in his first year at Illinois.

The war did not touch the Van Dorens closely. None of them had any crusading illusions about it. Mark was the first to be drafted. He hated war but did not protest. He served as an officer at Camp Pike until after the Armistice. Paul enlisted in the Marine Corps at the end of his year at Illinois.

[29] *Ibid.*, pp. 85–87.

He ended up guarding German prisoners in France and returned to the states after the war "suave and silent." Guy and Frank were drawn into the economic boom and were no more affected by the war than to suffer the effects of the agricultural depression that followed. Carl felt that being the oldest he should have gone and let Mark and Paul finish their studies. He shared the entire family's aversion to the war but felt very guilty about not taking steps to become involved in it. Mother Van Doren accepted with stoic resignation the possibility that one or more of her sons might be killed but said that she could stand it as well as other mothers. Father Van Doren held more illusions and seemed to be hurt most by the war. His attitude toward the boys entering bordered onto crusading. "Go to war, young men, and protect your fathers," he said. He was caught up in the land boom and soon parleyed his holdings into a fortune, invested in land, banks, and an electric railway. Instead of cashing in on his holdings, paying his debts, and banking a small fortune for each of his sons as he later planned to do, he bought more and more land. When the farm depression of 1920 hit, he could sell none of his land, could not meet his taxes, and was unable to raise enough grain or livestock even to pay the interest on his holdings. Despite the stark reality of it all, the only definition of America he would accept was that it was Eldorado. He fought doggedly but was economically inundated by the financial tidal wave that swept the country. The more personal anxiety of the war years passed for members of the family and the wounds of the postwar depression soon healed with the upturn of the business cycle during the 1920's.

Late in the fall of 1933 Mark received a telegram from Frank with the news that their father was dead. To the last of his 76 years, Charles Van Doren maintained a sanguine outlook on life. Of two views, he would almost always choose the more optimistic. Toward the end he was very tired, bothered by a hernia, and increasingly feeble. The boys suspected that he had cancer though it was never discussed. His mind, however, remained agile. He enjoyed listening to lively conversation and was especially amused when the boys and their families visited and argued in stimulating discussions. The fact that he voted for President Roosevelt in 1932 despite his lifelong, staunch Republicanism was evidence that he could change his mind. Flexibility in thinking and changing with the times are signs of an active mind.

Of the many mourners who came to the funeral, those from Urbana were outnumbered by their old friends from Hope. "By some unconscious tact," Carl wrote, "my mother had asked men who were a kind of index to my father's friendships," to serve as pallbearers. One of them was a professor at the University, one an athletic coach, a county official, a mechanic, a school superintendent, and a retired farmer, all of whom Charles Van Doren had helped in their careers. Of all those present at the cemetery only the minister was somber. "The sun shone sweet and warm on the green grass and the harlequin leaves, the flowers of the funeral were gay, and on the faces of the mourners friendly smiles were more often seen than tears," as he was lowered into his grave.[30]

Of the five boys, Carl was best known for his stimulating teaching at Columbia University. Among his many writings the biography of Benjamin Franklin is perhaps the most widely known, having won a Pulitzer Prize in 1939. Together Carl and Mark became editors of *The Nation*. They had both married girls who could write, edit, and cook. Carl died in 1950. Mark, now at Columbia University, is a literary critic

[30] *Ibid.*, p. 296.

and poet. One of his eleven volumes of *Spring Thunder* won the Pulitzer Prize a year after Carl won his. Guy, now 69 is semiretired as a consulting architect and is running a prosperous antique business in Clinton, Michigan. Frank, now 65, is a retired farmer and agricultural expert, in Tuscola, Illinois. On his bookshelves are 64 volumes written by "the Van Dorens." Paul, 57, is now an investment banker in New York. Together, the five brothers had nine children and the Van Doren trust continues with seventeen grandchildren and possibly more to come.

Part Five

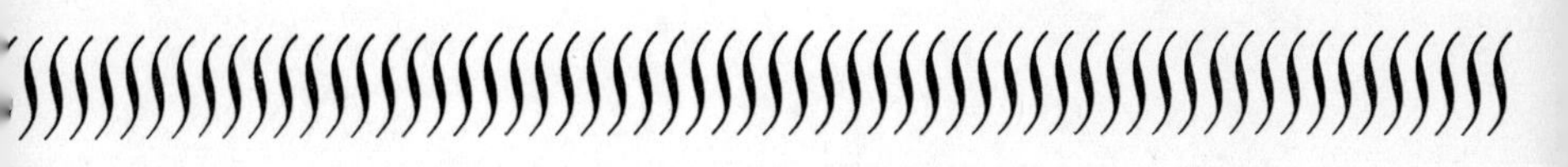

DISORGANIZATION AND RECONSTRUCTION

Chapter 17

DIVORCE

IN SHEER numbers of judicable actions, marriage termination constitutes the biggest business of our American courts. Taking the country as a whole over the past several years, the total of divorce, annulment, and alimony cases exceeds the total of all other court business combined. For example, in Dayton, Ohio, during the years 1944–1947, divorce petitions represented 80 percent of the total of all civil cases filed; in Columbus, Ohio, during the same period, 75 percent. In all Ohio cities with populations of 25,000 or over, for the years 1947–1952, this ratio ranged from 55 to 65 percent. Court reports from other states contain similar figures, though somewhat lower in the South and Northeast, and somewhat higher on the Pacific Coast.[1]

In the United States today there is one divorce granted for every three to four marriage licenses issued. In addition to the divorces granted are the couples who are disturbed

[1] Ralph Bridgeman, *Marital Discord, Divorce and the Family Court,* Lucas County Family Court Center, Toledo, Ohio, 1955, p. 3.

enough in their marriages to file for a divorce suit that is later dismissed, estimated at one-fifth to two-fifths of all divorce suits filed.[2] In order to get a more complete picture of the number of marriages that are pronounced legally dead, we must add legal separations and annulments to the divorces granted and dismissed. During the past several years about 350,000 couples have been legally separated each year. In spite of the fact that more than half of these marriages are childless, in the United States there are about a million and a half children under 18 with divorced parents and this number is increasing 333,000 a year.[3]

The present volume of marriage terminations represents a leveling off since the highest peak in American history, 1946, when the relocations resulting from the war boosted the divorce rate so high.

Regional differences in American divorce rates stand in considerable contrast to one another. The rate is lowest in the middle Atlantic states and increases as one goes west, with the highest rate in the mountain states and only slightly lower on the Pacific Coast. The rate in the mountain states is over four times as high as it is in the middle Atlantic states.[4] These differences are due in part to differences in the law, since every state has different divorce laws. However, the divorce laws do reflect differences in religious and economic backgrounds, with the East Coast being relatively conservative in its laws and the West very liberal. Part of the con-

[2] Quintin Johnstone, "Divorce Dismissals, A Field Study," *Kansas Law Review*, I, No. 3 (May, 1953), 245 ff.

[3] For an excellent, brief summary of the detailed statistics see, Mabel A. Elliott, "The Scope and Meaning of Divorce," in Howard Becker and Reuben Hill, *Family, Marriage and Parenthood*, Boston, Heath, 1955.

[4] *Vital Statistics Special Reports*, Washington, Public Health Service, Federal Security Agency, 1951.

servatism of the South is due to its general financial position, with possibly a higher proportion of persons who would divorce if they thought that they could afford it. In New York State, with its large Roman Catholic population, the only grounds upon which a divorce can be obtained is adultery, whereas in New Mexico, a couple can obtain a divorce on the grounds of "general incompatibility." Until 1948 divorce was not granted on any grounds in the state of South Carolina.

Notwithstanding the high figures, we have a legal situation in the United States that prevents as high a number as would obtain if people were free to do as they wished. Stricter divorce laws seem to have a depressing effect on the divorce rate. This is due in part to the fact that relatively few couples leave the state of their legal residence to obtain a divorce. This writer made a study of 2400 consecutive divorces that were granted in Multnomah County (Portland), Oregon, in 1942.[5] Comparing them with divorces granted in southern Washington, just across the Columbia River Bridge from Portland, where divorce was easier to obtain than in Oregon, there was virtually no difference in the divorce rates. Phony residence could have been established if couples had wanted to take advantage of changing residence. Having worked professionally in this field on both the East and West Coasts this writer's experience would bear out the generalization that seems warranted by the statistics: the dramatic differences between states of high divorce rates and those of low divorce rates does not mean that the marital

[5] Lawrence S. Bee, "A Partial Analysis of 2386 Divorces Granted in Multnomah County (Portland), Oregon, During 1942," *Research Studies of the State College of Washington,* XVII, No. 1 (March, 1949), 18 ff.

health of one area is better than another. It seems to mean that people in different areas handle their marital problems differently.

Looking at the volume of the divorce traffic a little differently, the state of Kansas, with a population of two million, stands in a median divorce rate position in the United States. There is a divorce action filed on the average of one every hour, 365 days a year.

In general, as social status goes up the divorce rate for a given group goes down. It is lowest for persons in the professions, farm owners, and farm managers, and highest for service workers, salesmen, farm laborers, and foremen.[6] Divorce tends to be related to social mobility, however, almost irrespective of occupation. In general divorce goes down as formal education goes up, but this must be qualified by noting that almost twice as many college-educated women divorce as compared with college-educated men. In one study of men and women graduates from many colleges and universities, after 40 years of age only 1.7 percent of the men were divorced or separated in contrast to 2.9 percent of the women. Finally those who divorce have fewer children, or most characteristically, no children.

A high proportion of divorced persons remarry. This affects greatly any generalization that one might make about divorce-marriage ratios, since most divorced persons remarry and have a score of one divorce to two marriages. A survey made by the Bureau of the Census in 1948 indicated that three-fourths of all persons who had been divorced during the 5 years preceding the survey, had remarried. Of those who had obtained a divorce 5 to 14 years prior to the survey, 85 percent had remarried. It is estimated that at age 30, the

[6] Clifford Kirkpatrick, *The Family,* New York, Ronald, 1955, p. 529.

divorced woman has 94 chances in 100 for subsequent marriage during her lifetime; the widow, 60 chances, and the unmarried woman, 48 chances in 100. Girls at the age of 30 who are not married still have a 50–50 chance.[7]

There are three kinds of legal separation that can be effected. One is annulment. This is a nullification of the marriage if it can be proved that it was contracted by force or deception. In this instance it is assumed that the marriage never in fact took place. Then, there is a legal separation which provides for the separation of the couple in every respect—property, custody of the children, nonaccess for cohabitation. It is like a divorce except that neither is free to marry again even though they should remain apart the rest of their lives. Finally, there is divorce which does not negate the marriage as in annulment, but recognizes its end.

Theoretically divorces are granted only after a contest in which the innocent party charges the presumed guilty one on the grounds recognized in the state in which they live. According to legal precept, the divorce is supposed to reward the innocent and penalize the guilty. But this is a farce. Actually 85 to 90 percent of the divorces granted in the United States are uncontested. But of the 10 or 15 percent who file a cross-petition, that is, contest or challenge the one who files first, all but 2 or 3 percent withdraw their cross-petitions. Thus all but 2 to 3 percent of all divorces are uncontested. If one does contest a divorce, it may become very involved, legally and personally. Ralph Bridgeman, Chief Marriage Counselor and Supervisor in charge of the marriage counseling service of the Lucas County Court Family Center in Toledo, Ohio, describes the legal situation as follows:

[7] Ruth S. Cavan, *The American Family*, New York, Crowell, 1953, p. 486.

Fractionated, overlapping, and conflicting jurisdictions between courts in different states and among different courts in the same state are made to order for those partners and attorneys who have reasons for wanting to prolong litigation. In New York, for instance, only the Supreme Court can grant a divorce decree, but questions of custody must be decided in a lesser court where evidence not admissible in the higher court may be used. Not long ago one New York family found itself involved in four different courts. After the mother's Nevada divorce, the father absconded with the child to another state. In order to get the matter of custody into the jurisdiction of a New York court the mother secured a writ of *habeas corpus* from the Supreme Court, and in due time recovered her child. Whereupon the father refused to pay for the support of a child he did not possess, so the mother had to go to the Family Court for a support order. Proof of the father's ability to pay, however, had to await a verdict of the Children's Court which had a very full docket. While all this was going on, violence flared one night when the ex-spouses happened to meet. Thereupon ex-wife hailed ex-husband before the magistrate's court on a charge of assault and battery. Meanwhile over these two to three years, the child shuttled from parent to parent, school term by school term. One can imagine the effect of all of this upon the peace of mind and the emotional stability of these three impaled souls.[8]

This case is cited to make the point that though most uncontested divorces are easy to get, often averaging five to ten minutes actually in court, one can become deeply entangled in legal proceedings if the other spouse wishes to prolong the hearings for whatever vindictive or other reason. The illustration above also points up the absurdity and antiquity of much of our domestic relations legal machinery. To say that it is archaic would be to compliment it.

We know that not all unhappy marriages end in divorce. Mr. Bridgeman, who has also worked closely with the Federal

[8] Bridgeman, *op. cit.*, p. 3.

Council of Churches, believes that there are as many "psychological" divorces as there are legal divorces. This view is supported by Dr. J. Louise Despert, psychiatrist, who for many years treated and studied the children of "emotionally" divorced parents.[9] The evidence of the amount of marital unhappiness clearly places it in the position of being one of America's greatest social problems.

CAUSES OF DIVORCE

Legal Grounds vs. the "Real Causes" of Divorce

The legal grounds cited in the divorce decree are seldom the same as the social and psychological factors underlying and leading to divorce. In all states, grounds for divorce include adultery, and in most they include the inability or unwillingness to perform the act of coitus, fraud in representing the self to the partner before marriage, and desertion with whereabouts unknown for a specified period of time. In addition, many states include an array of other grounds such as loathsome disease, joining a religious sect disbelieving in marriage, felony, and the like. Today, however, the charges have become almost stereotyped and are most frequently listed as "cruel and inhuman treatment and mental abuse." Sometimes "physical abuse" is added. In some cases these are valid descriptions of the actual relationship. In others they are quite irrelevant. In still other cases they are anything but true, as in the cases of couples who agree to disagree and continue as friends after they have become divorced. The public is rapidly learning that the legal grounds for divorce cited in the decree may mean anything or nothing. As to the underlying factors leading up to the divorce, they are often

[9] J. Louise Despert, *Children of Divorce,* New York, Doubleday, 1953.

very complex and most frequently quite unknown to the couple themselves, as was illustrated in the chapters on faulty marriage where immature and neurotic personality patterns underlay the surface symptoms.

Social and Personal Factors Related to Divorce

The rapid social change that Americans experienced during the first half of this century has had a profound influence on marriage and family relations—the break from conventional ties to authority; the emergence of more equalitarian roles of the sexes making it psychologically and economically possible for a woman to divorce a man if the marriage does not meet her expectations; property and other forms of wealth now more negotiable; a husband or wife being less indispensable than in a frontier economy; women working outside the home and meeting eligible men; intersex competition, status striving, and "hardness" incident to urban living; reduced social and religious stigma against divorce; earlier marriage which often means that the couple is too immature; emergence of a code of liberalism which champions individual choice and freedom; greater racial, cultural, and religious heterogeneity; and, perhaps not least, *divorce* as a cause of divorce, the bandwagon effect of the high divorce rate, the divorce courts sending the divorced into the marriage market, and children imitating divorced parents.

These are all important factors in our social life. They have dramatically altered the ground rules of marriage. We are a part of an intricate social system and as such are influenced by it. As individuals, however, we are not rigidly bound by it. We must consider then, in addition to the social factors, some of the more personal factors which give rise to divorce.

In one sense we have been dealing with this problem throughout the book. We described people who married when they were so young and inexperienced that they were caught in the web of romance without being mature enough to choose a mate wisely and to achieve a responsible marriage. Some of these couples matured through one another and achieved relatively full marriages. Many others did not. Some of them matured, but in different directions, and found themselves "hopelessly" incompatible.

We have also discussed and illustrated some of the neurotic bases of marriage. When we review this material we see that the motives of some persons were so deeply egocentric and compensatory that they were in no position to respect themselves or love anybody else. As important as this ground is we cannot repeat it in detail here, but we should keep in mind the several presentations on predicting success or failure in marriage.

This discussion should not be interpreted as an indictment of those who divorce. There are many people, divorced and not divorced, who grow apart in meeting and adapting to changing circumstances of life. They become aware of themselves as being painfully different in their deeper needs and expectations of one another. No one may be to blame, as it were, any more than oil could be blamed for not mixing with water. They might have chosen one another more wisely to begin with. However, they might have chosen well under certain circumstances, but the circumstances may have been too limited or may have changed. Such couples can sometimes reweave the threads that brought them together by taking stock and facing up to real problems of adjustment. Others seem to be quite unwilling or unable to go on together. What we need in the whole consideration of divorce, whether as a social problem or as a personal problem, is more information and enlightened analysis and less self-righteous or "do-gooder" fervor.

A Case History

Let us turn to the more personal and subjective aspects of divorce. Couples will vary a great deal in the reasons for their difficult marriages, and in their personal thoughts, feelings, and reactions to the crises leading up to separation. However, it has been this writer's experience in marriage counseling that many couples contemplating divorce experience many common reactions to their spouses and in a predictable sequence. The following case is illustrative.

The husband grew up in the industrial section of a city where his father had been employed as a supervisor in a manufacturing plant. When the war broke out, the husband signed up with the services and was sent overseas as a member of an engineering crew. He returned after the war to enter State University where he worked toward a degree in engineering. With his income from the GI Bill and under no pressure to rush his education, he dated considerably, falling in and out of love with several girls. He was sociable and engaging and reflected a feeling of self-confidence in his major field since much of what he was studying he had already encountered during the war. As he put it, "I guess I cut a swathe with the girls and dated the more responsive ones, playing the field, since I was in no hurry to marry . . ."

During his last year of academic training he met a girl who, as he said, ". . . threw me for a loop. She was tall, stately, and had the bearing of a queen." At Christmas they were pinned and then later announced their engagement to be married following graduation. He described her at this time as being engaging but somewhat "aloof" which seemed to intrigue him as the other girls he had known had been "too urgent" in their expectations.

Following graduation they were married and moved to a small city that was within commuting distance of a metropolitan city. He had been employed as an engineer with an excellent starting salary. During the next several years they became well acquainted with a circle of friends most of whom were working for the same firm. They participated extensively in the social and religious affairs of the community, with his wife taking the initiative in gaining and maintaining the social contacts. During these early years of their marriage they had two children. The community came to regard them as an "ideal couple and ideal family," but underneath they were having their problems.

When he married he said that he was marrying for love and a family, and that sex was relatively unimportant. His previous amours had been emotionally responsive, even flattering, but he found little continuing interest in them. His wife was much more emotionally self-contained. He said that he looked up to her and put her on a pedestal, rather than engaging her more closely.

About five years after they were married, his wife happened to be brushing his hat when a contraceptive dropped from where it had been lodged under the rim. Stunned, she went to her best friend and confided her discovery. After listening intently her friend turned to her and said, "Look, Fran, everybody in town knows that Mark has been stepping out when he goes to X-city as frequently as he does 'on business' and leaves you home. It is one of those former flames that he went with in college. Nobody wanted to be the first to tell you . . ."

Stunned, confused, and then angry, she returned home. "I felt half stupefied, half bereaved," she said, "as if I had lost him in an automobile accident. Despite the evidence, I still half denied that it could be true." Her next reaction was a feeling of failure accompanied by an emotional "void," a feeling of being completely rejected. As she said later, "How could he do a thing like that if I were half the woman I thought that I was?"

When he returned that evening she flew into "a nearly uncontrollable rage" and accused him of having an affair. He denied it, confronting his wife with studied innocence, while she settled into a reaction of icy indifference. After listening to his story about "all of the gossip nowadays," she interrupted him to tell him what she had found in his hat and asked him if he had anything more to say.

The community rushed in to side with her. Their relatives on both sides told him to his face what a cad they thought he was. And, as often is the case, she was advised on every hand to divorce him. Surely if these were not grounds enough what more was needed? And so she divorced him and received custody of the two children with visiting privileges and most of their assets. Out of feelings of guilt and humiliation he did not wish to contest anything.

His reaction was a mixture of stinging regrets, of confused ambivalence, and of amazement that she should feel the way she did. As he said to the counselor later, "I loved her, I still love her. Nothing has happened that hadn't happened long before. I don't love any other woman . . ."

He persisted in trying to see her, but she refused. During this period when he was living alone in a small apartment, he kept telling his friends that his feelings about his wife were still there. Then, after several months of unsuccessful attempts to "talk things over with her" he sought marriage counseling.

He was urged to reflect on why he did what he did, and to try to understand how differently men and women often feel about extramarital relations. He finally reconstructed his feelings, many of which he had denied or ignored. He discovered the basis for a genuine feeling of hostility beneath his love, toward what seemed to stem from a felt favoritism on the part of his mother for his older brother. Furthermore, his wife was quite the "queen," not only somewhat sexually aloof, but not as overtly affirming of him as he really desired. Not only had his professional success gone to his head more than he realized with several unexpected advances in his company, but the responsiveness of other women in his life had flattered his male ego. He felt with half-conscious awareness that his wife had been "withholding," though he did not understand that he was reacting to his wife as he did toward his mother, with hurt jealousy and hostility. He knew that he did not love the other woman, but he did not recognize that his "affair" was more than tinged with revenge against his wife. He said later, with emerging insight, that he had often daydreamed of his wife discovering him and the other woman together and, with a smile, "the look on the old lady's face when she caught us."

Upon discovering some of these needs, expectations, and strivings hidden beneath the surface of his personality, with their counterpart of motivating him on to success, his outward debonair role changed to one of conversative sociability and modesty. His wife had not remarried, though she was miserable. She had never sought counsel. She was pursuing a career and had little financial need of a husband.

He was urged to try to engage her in conversation and to go back over the old personal account with her, discussing quite frankly and dispassionately their mutual expectations. He was assured that her "aloofness" had some deeper basis, and that once it was aired the ground would be laid for the first time really to talk sense about the whole matter. He succeeded in getting her to talk with him. Sometimes she seemed quite reasonable to him, and there seemed to be promise of getting together again. At other times she became very angry with him and would summarily order him to leave. He recognized that she was expressing some hostility that had been there long before the marriage and that could come out with righteous indignation only after the divorce. She had always competed with men in her professional training and later activities. His success in his work was difficult for her to accept without latent jealousy. Her father had been a "cad" and walked out on her mother. In many ways unknown to herself she was still waging the battle of the sexes, had temporarily won, and was not a likely candidate for immediate "surrender" to her husband or any other man.

Within a short period of several months the parental families, community opinion, and the couple themselves had changed. Self-righteousness had changed into understanding and concern—concern about their own mental health, and the very difficult social and emotional adjustment of the children now groping for their own identity and security in a home. Eventually they remarried.

In their new relationship they took on roles much more

like those of young professional people, rather than the All-American Boy and Girl. They gave evidence of closeness, but not of any all-consuming romance. They became, again, active in community affairs, and returned to the circle of friends whom they first knew.

This case happened to turn out relatively well, whereas many do not. Their experience, however, is patently common as one general pattern of interaction in marriage. Their own different thoughts and feelings would match those of many other couples, with only the details altered—their backgrounds, their basic personalities, their best foot forward with a marital trap of potential hostility behind them, the battle of the sexes, their different reactions to an inadvertent way of spanking "mamma" while showing off and receiving personal response and recognition, the painful involvement of the children, the all-to-freely given advice of the community, relatives, and friends, the possible sustaining role of professional counsel who assisted them in working behind the symptoms to the substance of their difficulty, the will to make marriage a success, and even remarriage. These are all part of the actual experience of this very real and human family, and many others like them.

THE DECISION TO DIVORCE

There are some couples whose capacity for deeper intellectual and emotional involvement in another is so superficial that they can divorce without pain or personal dislocation. The more extreme narcissist might even take pride in the publicity of the newspaper account of the proceedings or the comment at a cocktail party, "My dear, I'm so sorry, I just heard." For many other sensitive and differentiated persons who entered marriage with serious, responsible intent, and with the expectation that their marriage would be permanent, divorce is at best painful. It involves crossing an intellectual and emotional no man's land. However painful, it does not necessarily have to be socially and psychologically traumatic. Divorce can mean for the couple, as well as their children, breaking painful and stifling emotional ties and clearing barriers to the growth of all concerned. The end results of divorce are determined largely by the steps leading up to it and by the maturity of the couple in: (1) testing, over a period of time and in a spirit of good will, their possible future compatibility; (2) understanding the deeper bases of their conflict; (3) considering the future welfare of one another; and (4) seeking professional assistance if necessary in considering the first three steps and continuing with professional help in building a new way of life following separation. The alternatives are to plunge into divorce with feelings of projected hostility at the presumed wrongs of the other, with overtones of guilt stemming from what one did or failed to do, and with anxiety in facing an undefined future without specific plans. Habits of attachment, even when positive emotion has gone, are not easily broken without leaving unfilled gaps in one's life.

Furthermore, when divorce is undertaken after prolonged consideration, there are fewer self-recriminations, less doubt, and less continuing preoccupation with the past. There is the feeling that, as in physical illness, every possible remedy had been considered, tried, and failed and that only the radical step of surgery can save the personal integrity and future growth of two people. It takes a great deal of maturity to reach this conclusion, and stands in contrast to the couple who, perhaps quite unconsciously, pose as "parting friends" but who undertook their divorce without understanding, real consideration, and genuine responsibility for the welfare of everyone concerned.

In this writer's counseling experience many couples who sought assistance in trying to assess their potential future compatibility, have come to conclude that one or both needed psychiatric treatment before they could determine whether it was their marriage that was at fault, or whether it was they as individuals who had to make personality changes before they could be happy with the present or any other spouse. In some cases they discovered that what they had supposed to be a faulty marriage was actually a rationalization of their personal inadequacies. In other cases, following treatment, they discovered that the marriage had served as a neurotic crutch and that they were truly incompatible beyond any reasonable expectation of getting back together.

THOSE WHO DO NOT DIVORCE

Divorce Dismissals

Statistics on dismissals are spotty and incomplete. Of those available, however, there is evidence that between 20 and 45 percent of all divorce cases filed are dismissed.[10] The major conclusions of one of the most complete studies of dismissals were:

1. The reason for nearly all dismissals is that the parties became reconciled and go back to living together.
2. In a large percentage of cases the reconciliation does not last and divorce eventually follows.
3. Dismissal is much more likely if there are minor children in the family, and the most common motive for dismissals given by plaintiffs is "the good of the children."

[10] Johnstone, *op. cit.*, p. 247.

4. Financial inability to proceed with the litigation and inability to prove a case as a matter of law rarely are factors of importance in dismissals.
5. Advice on the desirability of dismissing is frequently but not usually sought. Lawyers and judges seldom perform this counseling function.[11]

Details cited in this study indicate that a sizeable proportion of our married population are suffering some serious degree of marital dislocation, and not a single case in the study had seen a marriage counselor, clinical psychologist, psychiatrist, or social agency. Whether or not they were aware of such resources for professional help is not known. Many deceive themselves by believing that "things will be better," if they can only wait a little longer.

Psychological Divorce

Without knowing how many couples whose divorce petitions had been dismissed were emotionally divorced, it can be assumed that some of these and many others who would not consider divorce are couples whose marriages have deteriorated beyond the "normal" conflicts of marriage and critical stages of growth experienced by many if not most "successful" marriages. Their marriages are dead. Whether they invoke the burial ceremony of divorce or not, they have been severed from one another in the deepest social, psychological, physical, and spiritual sense of the term. To continue on together for whatever reason would seem senseless, even if children are involved and it were for the presumed sake of the children that they remained together.

Sometimes the reasons couples give for remaining together are rationalizations of their inability either to separate or to

[11] *Ibid.*, p. 5.

take constructive steps toward rehabilitation, for example, the mutually neurotic dependents cited in the chapter on faulty marriage. They may be leaning so hard on one another that if the support of one fell they would both collapse. If the parent's love, care, and responsibility toward one another are gone, the children in such a family are going to be seriously damaged. The argument that the marriage should be maintained at any cost in the interest of the children is a fallacious one. Underneath the self-sacrifical pose is virtually always an abundance of hostility, not too deeply suppressed, irrespective of the skill and sophistication of the parents' overt roles. Nothing is more devastating to the welfare of a child than a family atmosphere that is cold, and thus felt by the child to be rejecting. The child's feeling that *he* is somehow to blame gives rise to floating anxiety accompanied by feelings of guilt. Since he cannot understand what is going on, his relationships within the family remain undefined and he can only react according to his basic personality and become lonely, depressed, and compliant; hostile and aggressive; or lose contact with social reality and withdraw into his own world of fantasy.

DIVORCE CAN BE CONSTRUCTIVE

As painful and temporarily dislocating as divorce can be in its effects on a couple and the children, it need not be personally devastating and traumatic. Frequently, a couple who married at a time when they were quite immature and were attracted to one another because of mutual compensatory rather than complementary needs, can grow apart and find that they share nothing in common. Many people mature a great deal in the experience gained in a faulty marriage. As one woman said, "I sometimes believe that it takes the trials and tribulations of a poor marriage to learn how to choose and to live with someone more compatible. Though I did not know it, my marriage was in fact a trial marriage that did not work out. It was painful but I learned much and will not make the same mistakes again. I do not blame my former husband. We were equally at fault in our inexperience and immaturity."

Where both members of a couple have gained a requisite amount of personal autonomy and insight into the faulty bases of their marriage, they can face the painful facts honestly and free one another through divorce or legal separation. In such cases it is the marriage that has failed because of intrinsic incompatibility. This is quite a different matter from the marriage in which one or both members of a couple are so personally maladjusted that it is *they as persons* and not necessarily the relationship that is faulty.

Where children are involved they can be helped to face the unpleasant realities squarely and without evasion. Even very young children will sense the difficulties. When they are told the facts they will be less confused and disturbed by what they feel to be the uncertainties. However, they can be spared the burden of uncertainties that have not been resolved. This means that the many long and often emotionally loaded discussions leading to a decision can be held outside the child's presence, which often demands a great deal of forebearance on the part of parents who themselves may be under considerable tension.

Children of different ages react quite differently to the prospective divorce of their parents. Young children are assured not so much by verbal explanations as by the feeling of affection shown them. It is important that the child be affirmed by both parents. Older children may not only feel anxious and confused, but often have a sense of guilt and uncertainty about the future. Guilt can stem from the feeling of identification with one parent while blaming the other. The resulting ambivalence toward the presumed guilty parent may be so confusing that the child will react with marked deference, hostility, or withdrawal, according to his basic personality. Older children may also feel that they are somehow to blame for their parent's difficulties, especially when parents have disagreed about how to discipline the child, fix allowances, apportion household duties, or other such matters. The child does not know that these disagreements are symptoms not the causes of the marital difficulty. However, the child's guilt can be minimized by the assurance of parents that the child is not at all to blame, but is an innocent bystander witnessing the differences.

Younger adolescents are probably the most vulnerable to the consideration and effects of divorce than children of any other age. They are in the already confusing process of working toward their own psychosexual identity and gaining autonomy from the family. The conflict in the marriage may cast disparaging reflections on one or both parents with whom the child is trying to identify himself in the case of the same sex, or differentiate himself in the case of the parent of the opposite sex. In their insecurity they may cling unduly to the family at a time when they ought to be spending more time with and identifying themselves with their peer group. Parents who understand the child's deeper needs for affirmation and security at this time can do much to minimize and counteract the effects of the pending divorce.

Older adolescents who have had a reasonably good emotional development are freer to reason with parents and accept realities on an adult level and with more mature resignation. They are perhaps the least vulnerable to the effects of pending separation. The unstable older adolescent is vulnerable to continued emotional anxiety, confusion, guilt, and probably depression, and remains emotionally bound by his unresolved dilemmas. One possible effect is a pattern of faulty dating or courtship that he undertakes or avoids on a compensatory level. The socially affirming child will seek excessive personal affirmation, sometimes in sexual relations. The socially aggressive child will strike out in patterns of delinquency. The socially retiring child may become excessively withdrawn from members of the opposite sex into daydreaming and solitary activities.

The greatest single determinant of the effects of pending separation and divorce on children is the degree of maturity that parents express in the way they act during the trying period of effecting separation and building a new life. Deeper understanding of the child's need for assurance together with genuine concern and care of him will not eliminate the pain but it will minimize the damage almost to the vanishing point under optimal circumstances. Where parents inadvertently insist on spending this period in a prolonged, running battle fought in the presence of the child, he can be deeply hurt and even more permanently damaged.

ALTERNATIVES TO DIVORCE

Though divorces are necessary in order to maintain the integrity and permit greater growth and happiness of individual members of some couples, there are many others for whom divorce is the senseless pursuit of an illusion. The reader will recall the case of the girl who was rejected by her older brother, who later married the young doctor, then the golf professional, finding each, in turn, impossible to live with. She was the kind of person whose pattern of restless, unconscious striving could carry her through numerous romances to the brink of personal disorganization. What she needed from the beginning was a psychiatrist and not a lawyer. It was not her marriages that were at fault. It was her neuroticism. In an intensive study of eight different men who ordered their respective series of romantic pursuits much as the girl cited above, none was satisfied with his successive amours. Each ended up disillusioned and deeply unhappy. Divorce is not a panacea for all marital difficulties.

No solution to these deeper marital rifts is easy. Many couples have learned, however, through painful but growth promoting experience, that there was much potential promise in their marriage. Through honest examination of themselves and the relationship they have learned that their differences which seemed to provide the bases of their conflicts were really blessings in disguise when transformed into differences that complemented one another's needs. Take the couple who were initially attracted on a physical level then discovered that they shared a common interest in music. When people are "in love" they are often temporarily anesthetized against sensing anything divisive in their relationship. His interest was in contemporary jazz, which she had in the past tolerated but not really enjoyed. She had an intense appreciation of Bach, which to him was "too traditional and too predictable." But during courtship anything the other played sounded like an angelic choir. Catsup on ice cream would have tasted good to either. After they were married and the scaling-down process had taken its toll, they became increasingly annoyed with one another's playing. Bach, to him became more than ever a boring series of scales and arpeggios. His improvising on popular blues themes was to her superficial, dissonant, and utterly monotonous in rhythm.

After contriving in many ways to patch things up, but without an honest examination of the basis of their conflict, their relationship finally reached an impasse. Nearly everything that each did was judged by the other to be part of "the same (different) pattern." There seemed to be such a basic difference in tastes that separation was seriously considered. At this crucial time in their marriage a friend suggested that they undertake a study of the compositions and playing of Oscar Peterson who was known as one of the best contemporary jazz musicians and who practiced for his concerts by devoting several hours each day to playing Bach.

To make a long and more complicated story short, they became fascinated with their mutual discovery of a musical idiom that was truly a combination of what they had heretofore regarded as "impossibly different." Each had a great deal to contribute to the other. Each was in a position to complement the other. Surrounding themselves with friends who enjoyed their same interests was the final step in the movement of their marriage to a high plane that had all the prospects of growth and permanence.

Marriages of romance alone that do not have intrinsic common, creative interests and extended purpose often have little to discover and rekindle. Many marriages, however, have much potential lying hidden beneath petty irritations and gnawing boredom. The solution to many faulty marriages, though admittedly not all, is to achieve a creative orientation (see Chapter 4), to work together to discover the potential in one another as individuals and successive stages of growth in the relationship.

Chapter 18

TOWARD EMERGING FAMILISM

"THE MORAL regeneration of mankind will only really commence when the most fundamental of the social relations (marriage) is placed under the rule of equal justice, and when human beings learn to cultivate their strongest sympathy with an equal in rights and cultivation."[1]

In this strong denunciation of the Victorian deference of women to men written almost a century ago, John Stuart Mill defined the moral problem of his times. The unemancipated social and psychological status of woman epitomized the Victorian ethic in its larger cultural matrix of authoritarianism. In chorus with other like-minded writers of the nineteenth century in England like Samuel Butler and Havelock Ellis, Mill was not only protesting against such paternalism, but was prophetic in describing the great change

[1] John Stuart Mill, *Subjection of Women,* 1869.

that was to take place in our American version of this cultural pattern.

The American revolt was in its incipient stages of development during the latter part of the century, but broke out as a cultural rash quite suddenly at the turn of the century. Frederick Lewis Allen has been most articulate in describing what he calls "the revolt of the American conscience."

> The times were ripe for it . . . As the historians Hacker and Kendrick have pointed out, this revolt was not an organized movement, but incoherent. It had no overall program. Those who took part in it ranged all the way from the rich to the poor, and were in many cases fiercely at odds with one another. It was rather a general movement of very diverse people working for different specific ends . . . There were the proponents of measures to permit more direct popular government, unfettered by bosses, . . . the advocates of municipal housecleaning, the experimenters with commission government of cities, the budget experts. There were the battlers for workman's compensation laws, the people who were trying to get decent legislation on working conditions in factories. There were the conservationists, who wanted to stop the headlong destruction of the nation's natural resources . . . There were the suffragists, campaigning for votes for women; the crusaders for pure food and drug laws; the investigators and chastisers of "frenzied finance"; and the men who, after the Panic of 1907, labored to devise an adequate central banking system.[2]

This widespread protest against authoritarianism in our society had largely spent itself by the time we entered World War I. People were left quite free from the overt binding ties of the past. However, they were not free to find morale and morality within themselves. During the decade that followed the war American youths kicked up their heels to the ribald tones of the newly invented saxophone, and "It" girls danced

[2] Frederick Lewis Allen, *The Big Change, America Transforms Itself 1900–1950,* New York, Harper, 1952, chap. 6.

the Charleston to the tune of Barney Google. It was a new era heralded by a new but as yet inarticulate quest for "personalism" vs. the older "institutionalism." Political freedom had been largely won for American men and women by this time, and what now remained was to break the last remaining strands of the strong umbilical cord that bound people rigidly to the institutions of the past. American youths and many adults were pulling for all that they were worth.

Now, after an economic depression and another world war, we are facing new dilemmas. The dislocation occasioned by the political, economic, and intellectual emancipation of women, the freeing of children from the emotional austerity and rigidity of paternalism, and the emergence of more equalitarian roles on the part of both men and women has presented us with a new moral problem. We may become victims of forces outside ourselves other than authoritarianism. As Fromm writes, "If freedom, the ability to preserve one's integrity against power, is the basic condition for morality, has man in the Western world not solved his moral problem? It is not only a problem of people living under authoritarian dictatorships which deprive them of their personal and political freedom."[3] He goes on to say that it is not the power of the dictator or the political bureaucracy that now threatens us, "but the anonymous power of the market, of success, of public opinion, of 'common sense'—or rather, of common nonsense—and of the machine whose servants we have become."[4] In the words of Riesman a segment of our society has become excessively "other-directed."[5]

Another mode of reaction to the present situation is that

[3] Erich Fromm, *Man For Himself*, New York, Rinehart, 1947, pp. 247 ff.

[4] *Ibid.*, pp. 247–248.

[5] David Riesman, *The Lonely Crowd*, Garden City, Doubleday Anchor, 1953.

of the cult of sociopsychological "realists." These are people who have dissociated themselves from the "crowd," have become excessively self-centered (or clique centered), and are a kind of nonconformists. They hold that there is really no problem of ethics and argue on the basis of cultural relativity, i.e., when a variety of cultures are studied their values are found to be so different that they represent an ethical smörgasboard from which the "sophisticated" may choose the rules of the game by which they wish to live according to individual tastes.[6]

THE DILEMMA OF THE AMERICAN FAMILY

Some families have become victims of success seeking and slaves to conformity to the expectations of the crowd, while others have become "atomistic" with each of its members going his own way. As sociologists have recently asserted, there remains for those who care, the problem of trying to evaluate what has taken place and to assess future developments.

Recent trends in the American family are viewed by some contemporary scholars with grave apprehension for the continuation of the family as we now know it.[7]

These may be writers of gloom but not prophets of doom. There is an important "if" in their writings. "If we sense the nearness, the inescapability, or the seriousness of the impending crisis," then we shall as a society do something to stem the flood waters and change the course of the stream. As Fromm writes, "Prophecies of doom are heard today with in-

[6] Ben Hecht, "Sex in Hollywood," *Esquire,* May, 1954, pp. 35 ff.

[7] See Ruth N. Anshen, ed., *The Family, Its Function and Destiny,* New York, Harper, 1949, pp. 426 ff.; Carle C. Zimmerman, *Family and Civilization,* New York, Harper, 1947, pp. 798 ff.

creasing frequency. While they have the important function of drawing attention to the dangerous possibilities in our present situation they fail to take into account the promise which is implied in man's achievement in the natural sciences, in psychology, in medicine and in art. Indeed, these achievements portray the presence of strong productive forces which are not compatible with the picture of a decaying culture. Our period is one of transition."[8] He goes on to say that our moral problem has been man's indifference to himself, the fact that we have not yet found a sense of significance and uniqueness in ourselves, having been first victims of institutional authority and now of social conformity or of neurotic social isolation.

A consensus of professional opinion would seem to be that, "We can create stability by the very processes of freedom, if we know that freedom itself requires personal self-discipline for its fulfillment, and also that stability must be found in the balance of movement rather than in the fixity of any status quo."[9] The late anthropologist, Ralph Linton, said, "The ancient trinity of father, mother, and child has survived more vicissitudes than any other human relationship."[10] In a recent address Margaret Mead told of the change in the Manus culture that had taken place during the 25 years since she first visited them and her revisit of 1955. She described the orderly transition, during that time, of persons of all ages from their Stone Age culture to twentieth-century ways of living and thinking without social and psychological disruption and without family dislocation.[11]

[8] Fromm, *op. cit.*, p. 249.

[9] George Hedley, "The Changing Family in the Changing Scene," *Family Life*, July, 1948, pp. 3–4, quoted in Ray E. Baber, *Marriage and the Family*, rev. ed., New York, McGraw-Hill, 1953, p. 680.

[10] *Ibid.*, p. 681

[11] An Address given before the Human Relations Division of the University of Kansas, March, 1957.

During the latter part of the 1920's the pioneers of a new academic, educational, and clinical interest in the family emerged on the American scene. Living in different parts of the country their research and writing appeared almost simultaneously. The Groves, Burgess, Cottrell, the Stones, Terman, Poponoe, to mention a few, were pointing up the direction of the new family life movement. It was a movement that, like the reform movement of 1900, had no common source and was in no sense organized. The times were ready for these academicians and clinicians to focus their "intraceptive" spotlights on the family.[12] It was socially and culturally something like the frontiersman who had been so busy digging ditches and killing rattlesnakes that he had "just taken his woman (wife) for granted," and then suddenly discovered that she had thoughts, feelings, and deeper needs. Professors Burgess and Cottrell at the University of Chicago had turned from their research in the prediction of criminal recidivism to the study of the prediction of marital adjustment. Professor Terman at Stanford turned partially away from his study of gifted children to that of the psychological factors in marital adjustment. Dr. Popenoe and the Stones, in Los Angeles and New York respectively, had begun the practice of marriage counseling. Courses in marriage and the family were appearing in college curricula. A new era was born.

The economic depression that was to follow gave impetus and acceleration to the movement, but did not create it. The

[12] The word "intraception" has been used by H. A. Murray to describe the person who was capable of recognizing and evaluating his own deeper thoughts and feelings with "introspective insight" as compared with one who tends to recognize and deal only with "things outside himself."

men and women mentioned above had already begun their studies and activities before the onset of the depression.

Since these beginnings a quarter of a century ago, the "family field" has grown at an accelerated rate until now when over 40 million people are members of one or more of the existing family life organizations in the United States. In the following pages this writer has tried to sketch the extent and suggest the momentum of our contemporary interest in the family.

Family Life Movement in the Schools

About half of our American colleges and universities offer courses in marriage and family relations. This has developed during the short period of the past 25 years, and the number is increasing steadily. As teachers are being trained, more and more primary and secondary schools are adding family courses to their curricula, and there are isolated examples of highly developed programs.

In Highland Park High School, Michigan, all students of both sexes, start in the freshman year to receive training and experience in their nursery training school which is regarded as a human development laboratory. Then, as seniors, they have a continuation course in child development and an adult course in courtship, mate selection, and preparation for marriage and parenthood. When the program was started about 16 years ago, Mrs. Marjorie Cosgrove and her colleagues at Highland Park did not know whether the boys would enter these courses willingly or whether they would regard them as "sissy stuff." There is no question about it now. The boys report great interest in the child development laboratory as well as in the courses on preparation for marriage, and they regard the program as one of the most significant experiences in their entire high school career.

Another example of an extended high school program is an eight-section course in education for marriage, with boys and girls participating and sharing experience in the Wichita East High School, Kansas. This program has an adjunctive counseling program. These examples could be multiplied many times throughout the country.

Some colleges and universities offer advanced degrees in family life education and marriage counseling. As the field becomes more established and can offer the beginning teacher more personal and professional security in a still "touchy" subject, the number of teachers in this field will grow more rapidly. On the higher education level, family life study and training centers are emerging. The Family Study Center at the University of Chicago was one of the first to be instituted. There interdisciplinary research is undertaken and summer institutes have been established for teachers, counselors, and research workers.

Family life education is by no means exclusively professional in its organization and goals. The field has emerged as an area in the liberal arts. It offers an almost ideal educational vehicle for conveying general education objectives. Subjects in the behavioral arts and sciences and the humanities can be treated in a common context that has heightened motivational interest to students The respective academic fields cannot be treated thoroughly, but they are being more than introduced. The student may then pursue anything from biochemistry and genetics to literature and philosophy in larger contexts. Introduction to many subjects in this manner, can result in the feeling that the pursuit of the liberal arts and sciences can have tremendous personal relevance as well as intellectual stimulation for the less gifted and the more gifted alike. Furthermore the family field provides the context for a more general approach to the liberal arts as contrasted to much existing fragmentation of knowledge.

During 1957 an infancy study center was developed at the University of Kansas in the Department of Home Economics. Its threefold purpose is to provide a research laboratory for the study of the growth and development of infants from the ages of 9 to 24 months; to provide opportunities for mothers and fathers to observe their infants in relationships with other infants and to attend meetings where specialists lead discussion groups on problems of infant growth, health, and development; and, to provide a center where students of child development in the University can observe and study infant behavior. The project, made possible by a grant to the University, provided for the purchase of a home that was remodeled and furnished to meet the needs of infants as well as the students, with one-way vision observation booths, audio-visual recording equipment, and other facilities for study and observation. One of the unusual features of this child study center is the provision for adult education in addition to the more traditional study and student training functions.

One of the important innovations in family life education is the development of a College of Family Living at Brigham Young University in Provo, Utah. The new college includes the Departments of Home Economics, Sociology, Psychology, and Social Work. Two deans administer the multimillion dollar building and program, one a sociologist and the other a home economist. The purpose of the program is to provide liberal arts courses, applied courses, and professional training for persons majoring in family arts and sciences. In addition to meeting the more traditional educational functions, the Family Living Center was planned as an adult education center where married couples could study and work on projects together. Whether this center will be a prototype that other schools will follow remains to be seen. It is, however, a significant example of the growing importance of family life education.

The number and types of associations sponsoring family life courses on college and university campuses have grown phenomenally. The "base" of Lawrence, Kansas is not unlike some other small university cities. During one year a workshop was held at the University for teachers of family life education. Judge Paul W. Alexander of the Toledo, Ohio Family Court met with students of the Law School to discuss the family court. The State Health Education Work Shop had a section on the family. The American Home Economics Association held a workshop with a traveling team of family life education specialists, supplemented by the University of Kansas staff and representatives of the Marriage Counselor Training and Service Division of the Menninger Psychiatric Foundation. A conference was held with sections devoted to marital adjustment during the later years of life. The Lawrence Mental Hygiene Society met to discuss the new Infancy Study Center. Members of the University staff met with student professional fraternities (medicine, etc.) to discuss family aspects of professional orientation and practice. The University Executive Development Program, a five-week training program for industrial executives, devoted discussion sessions and luncheon meetings to "The Executive Wife" and marriage and the family. Two radio programs were broadcast to the Kansas City and Topeka areas over the University FM radio. One was broadcast from the classroom of a marriage and family relations class. The other consisted of reading a book, *The Happy Family*, by Drs. David Levy and Ruth Munroe, on the "Chapter a Day" program. The local Ministerial Alliance devoted sessions to the discussion of marriage and family relations. In addition, the University staff sent its members to all parts of the state and eastern Missouri to participate in family life programs. Discussions were held in Negro churches on marriage and the problems of interracial marriage. The Foreign Relations Club met to discuss the American family. The United Nations Tape Network serving radio stations in the Midwest recorded discussions between University staff members and foreign students comparing the American family and family life in different foreign countries. Young married couples met in groups at campus religious centers and devoted supper meetings to speakers and discussions of marriage and the family. The Jewish Community Center invited University staff members to discuss the family. The principal of the high school discussed with the University staff the extension of the home economics curriculum to include orientations in preparation for marriage. Several student religious centers offered courses on marriage. Local marriage counseling services were announced and sought by doctors, lawyers, clergymen, and laymen.

State, regional, and national organizations carrying on family life education are numerous and diversified.[13] The American Home Economics Association, the Parent Teacher Association, The Child Study Association of America, The National Council on Family Relations are but a few. It is estimated that 40 million persons are now members of these family life associations and participate in classes, institutes,

[13] Baber, *op. cit.*, pp. 567 ff.

and workshops, in addition to studying the literature and audio-visual aids made available. During one week the Kansas City Social Hygiene Society held a Family Life Institute with 34 sessions and over 7000 persons attending. The National Conference on Family Life held in Washington, D.C., is sponsored by 125 national organizations, with delegates from the 48 states and 25 foreign countries.

These figures give some idea of the phenomenal growth of interest in the conservation of American family life through education at all age levels from infancy through old age.

Family Life Movement in Religious Organizations

The growth of the family life movement in American religious organizations has paralleled that in secular organizations. For many years ministers, priests, and rabbis have given religious instruction to those about to be married and have counseled on family matters as a part of their pastoral roles. More recently, however, the family life educational and counseling services of the churches and synagogues have greatly expanded.

Serving the Protestants, the Federal Council of Churches has a fulltime staff of professional family specialists to serve the family life boards and committees in the member organization. For example, the Methodist churches have a national Committee on Family Life that stimulates and plans family life education, education for marriage, and counseling programs. It produces and distributes a great many books, pamphlets, and audio-visual aids. Each year a research program is conducted on a national scale with young people in communities throughout the country going into member homes with research questionnaires to get data for community, regional, and national tabulation and analysis. In addition to the research function served, this program helps young adults become conscious of the many problems and opportunities for growth and adjustment in marriage and family living.

The youth organizations of the Protestant churches are becoming very active in a broad educational program for marriage and family living, meeting on the local, regional, and national level. At the national YW-YMCA conference held in 1955 one section was devoted to the subject of sex and morality. They did not talk in traditional cliches but tackled the problems facing the youth of a rapidly changing culture. Summaries of these meetings were published and distributed nationally.[14]

Ministers, priests, and rabbis are receiving more training in diagnostic and supportive marriage counseling. They may help the more seriously disturbed marriages through crises themselves, or refer them to appropriate professional counseling services in the clinical fields. Other ministers are receiving extended training in marriage counseling in such centers as the Menninger Foundation's Marriage Counsel and Training Program. Here the trainees spend a year's study and internship as members of a psychiatric team. This training serves as an adjunct to their traditional pastoral duties. It enables them better to develop other family life educational services in their churches and synagogues. In the Midwest, ministerial alliances are sponsoring marriage counseling work-

[14] *Faith, Sex, and Love,* published by the National Student Council of the YMCA and YWCA, 1954.

shops. For example, the Kansas State College Extension Division holds an annual workshop for ministers of 4 countries, with a recent attendance of 35 Protestant ministers.

Catholic and Jewish religious organizations also have extensive family life programs of education for marriage, counseling, retreats, and extensive publications. The Catholic confessional has served to relieve guilt and anxiety, and to point up new solutions to marital and family problems. In 1943 a Catholic movement was started in New York that has become nationwide. It is an organization called Cana whose activities consist of retreats where couples retire from their day-by-day activities for a day, a weekend, or longer, to pursue the meaning of the good life through the fuller marriage. The Family Life Bureau of the National Catholic Welfare Conference sponsors Cana and other programs that include summer workshops and the extensive YMCA and YWCA activities in an extensive marriage education program.

The orientation that "a Jewish home is a miniature synagogue" reaches back into antiquity. Judaism is deeply rooted in familism. The Torah and the Code of the Jewish Law offer many detailed suggestions on marriage and family living for those of the faith. Jewish rabbis carry on premarital and marital counseling in their synagogues as do Protestant ministers and Catholic priests. Their education for marriage programs are extensive as are their official publications.

There is widespread coöperation between Jews and Protestants in their joint participation in family life education programs sponsored by community social welfare agencies and civic groups. For example, in Kansas City, Missouri, during the fall of 1957, an experimental education for marriage program was undertaken under the sponsorship of the

Junior League, the Greater Mental Health Foundation, and a special committee within the Recreation and Welfare Division of the Council of Social Agencies. Young adults ranging in age from 17 to 24, from private schools, public schools, and out of school, Protestant and Jewish in faith, white and colored, and representing different socioeconomic levels of living, met for 2 hours each week for 4 weeks. Each group of about 25 persons, kept small so that freer participation could obtain, was led by a team of 3 specialists—a minister or rabbi, a gynecologist-urologist, and a family sociologist or social worker. Community Studies of Kansas City, Missouri, made an intensive study of the effectiveness of the program. Their report was so favorable that a continuing committee was formed of social agency members, clergymen, and laymen to continue to sponsor education for marriage and family living in Kansas City's schools, churches, and synagogues.[15]

Many of the smaller churches do not have the staff to carry on more complete family life programs. Some of the larger churches do. Others have felt that the program was so important that members have dug deep into their pockets in order to finance permanent, extensive family life education, counseling, and training programs administered by professional personnel. In some instances this staff has been augmented by lay church members who work in the professional family and counseling fields. During World War II the Reverend Thomas Shannon of the First Christian Church in Portland, Oregon, instituted a nursery school that was no mere play pen for the children of parents attending church. He obtained the services of the director of the multimillion dollar Kaiser Nursery School to introduce the latest nursery

[15] *Choice Cuts,* News Sheet published by the Junior League of Kansas City, Missouri, XXIX (May, 1957), 34–35.

school methods and materials to the adolescent girls interested in working with children. Classes on education for marriage and family living were taught by a professor of sociology from Reed College who, together with Dr. Shannon, carried on marriage counseling with individual couples and groups of couples.

Family-Centered Medical Practice

Traditionally physicians have performed premarital examinations, given contraception instruction and service, gynecological-urological treatment, obstetrical instruction and service, veneral disease treatment, and public health and psychiatric services. From each of these fields of medical specialization have emerged extended programs of education, counseling, and medical service that have become increasingly family oriented, with the social and emotional life of the family as the focus of attention in research, diagnosis, prevention, and treatment programs.

The extension of these family-oriented medical programs stemmed from the reciprocal influence of lay "reform" groups and medical groups. The early crusading of Margaret Sanger was joined by other nurses, social workers, marriage counselors, and family life associations such as the social hygiene associations. Within the adult life of Margaret Sanger the Planned Parenthood Association with offices in all major cities throughout the United States was established. It offers educational programs in "planned parenthood" which deal with a broad subject matter ranging from involuntary sterility and consideration of the mental health of mothers and fathers in planning or planning not to have their families, to the consideration of world population problems. An example of their work is the Greater Kansas City Area teams of nurses, social workers, and gynecologists who have appeared on invitation in a number of schools and churches, with their "extension" program just beginning. The Planned Parenthood clinical program offers instruction in the physiology and anatomy of reproduction, fitting of the diaphragm and instruction in its proper application when this service is requested, instruction in the rhythm method of contraception when this is requested, diagnosis and treatment of involuntary sterility, and the dispensing of contraceptive materials on a continuing basis. Often, during consultation with the nurse, doctor or social worker, all members of the permanent staff, personal problems of orientation or adjustment in the marriage come up. Some marriage counseling on these problems is undertaken, where attitudes regarding sex and reproduction are involved. Other problems are referred to other professional consultants in private practice or in associations such as the Family Service Society.

This illustration of the extension of a medical service to a family-oriented service could be multiplied many times. For example, the program for the treatment, prevention, and control of venereal disease has become an extensive family life education endeavor now known as the American Social Hygiene Association.

The private practice of medicine is placing increasing emphasis on psychosomatic disorders, seeking the etiology, diagnosis, treatment, and prognosis of cases in the larger context of the patient's past social and emotional relationships. Doctors are being trained more and more to think about their patients as people meeting and reacting to prolonged stress. They are being trained to diagnose and treat causes as well as symptoms. Recent research has shown that significant biochemical changes take place in the body in accommodation to stress, and that these changes have somatic effects. While this recent trend in medical practice stems largely from psychiatrically oriented physicians, it is gradually becoming extended to all medical training and practice.

One of the recent trends in family-centered medical practice is the addition of family life specialists with professional training in marriage and family counseling, to medical staffs. Medical teams in Omaha, Topeka, and Wichita, have added men with doctor of philosophy degrees to their staffs. They work alone and with psychiatrists and handle cases referred by other specialists on the staff. Educational programs have been set up for expectant mothers and fathers that include natural child birth, child development, group marriage counseling, and the diagnosis and treatment of children's behavior problems, in addition to private marriage counseling. The purpose behind this endeavor is to encourage patients to come to the clinic to attend discussion groups on the particular medical problems they might be facing. This is a program in preventive medicine, with "medicine" defined to include treatment of both the physical and mental health of the family.

An increasing number of physicians are extending their private practice to include marriage counseling. This is evidenced in the membership roles of The National Council on Family Relations and The American Association of Marriage Counselors. Some of these men and women are attending the regional and national meetings of these organizations and participating in the general as well as the clinical sessions.

The Family Court

Judicial interest in the family was first evidenced in the United States at the turn of the century when Chicago and

Denver established juvenile courts. In 25 years they spread to every city of 100,000 or more and many smaller ones. By the 1930's there were well established relationships between the social workers of communities and the courts. What was an initial interest in the juvenile delinquent soon became an interest in the family of the delinquent. Probation officers and social workers worked together between the court and the home. Parents were enlisted to try to understand the causes of delinquency and to provide a better family milieu for the rehabilitation of the delinquent.[16]

The phenomenal growth of social-work services and trained personnel, incident to meeting the family problems arising out of the depression, served to change the general climate of opinion from regarding family problems as strictly personal problems to seeking and accepting professional help from social agencies. With the steady rise of the divorce rate and its attendant legal actions it became more apparent to many judges and lawyers that the court had more than a strictly legal obligation to families. The family court, or court of domestic relations, was the next logical step in the development of the philosophy of the juvenile court.[17]

Today, the courts of domestic relations are usually made up of a children's division and a family division. Five or more types of such courts are now to be found throughout the country, differing more according to jurisdiction (the kinds of cases they will handle) than to social philosophy. The family court is organized around the principle that the adjudication of family law must be humanized, that the treat-

[16] Baber, *op. cit.*, pp. 666 ff.

[17] See Paul W. Alexander, "The Follies of Divorce: A Therapeutic Approach to the Problem," *American Bar Association Journal*, XXXVI (February, 1949), 106; Paul W. Alexander, "The Family Court of the Future," *Journal of The American Judicature Society*, August, 1952, pp. 44–45.

ment of the case in an attempt to reconcile or rehabilitate should be attempted before any legal action is undertaken. As a result, such advanced courts as The Family Court under the direction of Judge Alexander in Toledo, cited in the chapter on divorce, are operating. It is staffed with legal aid, social caseworkers, probation officers, marriage and family counselors, clinicians, and physicians. Contenders in legal action are invited to receive the diagnostic and treatment services of the social service division. Instead of immediate legal action, each case is considered by a social worker who, with the help of the other specialists on the staff, seeks the causes of the difficulty and tries to effect a solution. If the case continues into court action a social service summary is made for the judge before he will hear either the plaintiff or the defendant. In many cases no lawyer, judge, or jury is involved, but a private settlement is reached through the efforts of the social worker. Other cases are heard in the private chambers of the judge. One court reported that during one year 90 percent of its children's cases were adjusted out of court. In another court 70 percent of all of its cases were settled this way.[18]

Not only has progress been made by some courts in humanizing the adjudication of the law, but concerted efforts are being made by members of the American Bar Association to humanize the law itself. Changing law that is based on precedent is a long, difficult, and often bitterly fought process. Nevertheless, the millstone is grinding slowly but decisively. The American Bar Association committee on divorce law presented a report in 1948 that was so well received by the Association that an interprofessional commission made up of lawyers, clergymen, sociologists, psychiatrists, and others was formed. In short, the Commission is attempt-

[18] Baber, *op. cit.*, pp. 669 ff.

ing to change the law that now holds that a divorce proceeding must be a legal contest, to the procedure outlined above with the intervention of the social service division. Rather than filing a petition for divorce, the couple would file a petition for state intervention in the marital difficulty, thus seeking the aid of the court in an attempt to resolve their problem—if not socially *then* legally.

Marriage Counseling and Family Service Agencies

With the onset of the depression in the 1930's, there arose a need for social workers to administer financial aid to families in distress. Public welfare agencies emerged to give relief to families in need. The professional field of social work was already established at the time but trained social workers were far too few to meet the demand. Public welfare agencies were equipped to give financial assistance but little social and psychological rehabilitation treatment. The case loads were too heavy and "public assistance" workers were not trained to handle the complex social and psychological problems of families in distress.

From these beginnings family agencies have multiplied in number and specialization of services. The Family Service Society, one of the oldest and best of our professional family service associations, offers the traditional social work services to dependent mothers, families temporarily dislocated through the sickness or death of the breadwinner, supervises adoptions, aids the aged, assists in disasters, and performs other similar services. In addition, they offer social and psychiatric services in the form of marriage counseling. Their services are available to anyone seeking them at a very nominal cost based on the client's ability to pay.

Developing concurrently with the "social work approach"

to family services have been other counseling agencies whose services have been aimed more directly and exclusively at marriage counseling. Within three years of one another three pioneer marriage counseling agencies emerged. Drs. Abraham and Hannah Stone founded the Marriage Consultation Center in New York City in 1929. A year later in Los Angeles, Paul Popenoe organized the American Institute of Family Relations. It is now the largest marriage counseling agency in the United States, and offers marriage education institutes, marriage counselor training, and personnel who participate on nationwide radio and television programs. In 1932 Emily H. Mudd organized the Marriage Council of Philadelphia which has now become a part of the Division of Psychiatry in the School of Medicine at the University of Pennsylvania. Such centers have multiplied during the past 25 years and are to be found throughout the country. One of the significant recent developments has taken place at the Menninger Psychiatric Foundation in Topeka, Kansas, where Robert G. Foster has developed the Division of Marriage Counselor Training and Marriage Counseling. Trainees are selected for their maturity, experience, and training in one of the behavioral sciences or the ministry. They spend a year in residence at the Foundation, training to become marriage counselors. During the seven years that the program has been in existence, a high proportion of the trainees have been from the ministry and the Armed Services personnel programs.

The number of professional marriage counselors is steadily growing. In 1948 the American Association of Marriage Counselors was organized, with high professional standards of training and experience exacted of its members. Its membership is made up of people who have been trained in the allied professions of medicine, university teaching and counseling, the ministry, social work, clinical psychology, and law. Some practice marriage counseling as a primary pursuit. Others practice it as an adjunct to their other professional work.

AN EMERGING PROSPECT

The phenomenal growth of interest and activities related to marriage and family living during the past 25 years, seems to mirror a significant change in American culture in general and in the American family in particular. We have moved at an accelerated pace away from "institutionalism" toward "personalism." The emotional austerity and neurotic dedication to duty which comprised much of the atmosphere of the early American home, is changing to companionship, informality, and self-expression symbolized by the "outdoor living area." This is a social and psychological atmosphere, achieved for the first time by any sizable proportion of our population, in which members of the family are now free to be themselves, to experience the spontaneous expression of love, appreciation, confidence, mutual affirmation, and profound sense of relatedness to one another. These are the "roots" that Eleanor Roosevelt speaks of. This is where "human beings learn to cultivate their strongest sympathy with an equal in rights and cultivation," of which Mill wrote. These are "men for themselves" and for one another, the foundation for the development of altruistic love that is a continuing theme in Fromm's writing. To use Riesman's terms, this is not the "lonely crowd" but a meaningful balance between the "inner-directed" and the "other-directed."

It is in this kind of a family that young men and women will develop the personal resources that will enable them to marry more wisely, and to choose out of their *own* conviction and volition to identify themselves with the institutions of the community. They will be able to forge for themselves meaningful philosophies of life that will serve to guide them toward increasing self-other transcendence. Is there anything more important?

INDEX